ASTROLOGY

ASTROLOGY

How to Create a Birth Chart &
Produce your own Horoscope

Christopher Lee

Published in 1990 by
The Self Publishing Association Ltd,
Lloyds Bank Chambers,
Upton-upon-Severn, Worcs

A MEMBER OF

in conjunction with
CHRISTOPHER LEE
130 Christine Avenue,
Rushwick, Worcester.

© CHRISTOPHER LEE 1990

British Library Cataloguing in Publication Data
Lee, Christopher
  Astrology: how to create a birth chart & produce your own
  horoscope.
  1. Astrological predictions. Horoscopes
  I. Title
  133.54

ISBN 1 85421 094 7

Designed and Produced by The Self Publishing Association Ltd
Printed and Bound in Great Britain by Billing & Sons Ltd, Worcester

CONTENTS

introduction

"what's your birth sign?"

That is the question most people ask when the subject of astrology is mentioned. Nearly everybody knows whether they are a Piscean or an Aries or whatever but that's where it stops for most people.

The first question many people ask when they find out that I'm an astrologer is, "Oh, you don't believe in that stuff, do you?" When they further discover that I used to be in business as an accountant they start to get worried. What makes someone turn in a boring, respectable reasonably well-paid job and apparently metamorphose into some sort of modern-day quack, taking his chance in a rather disreputable line that one hesitates to call a profession? "Oh all that stuff in the daily papers, the stars, it's rubbish isn't it?"

Well, that sort of astrology may for the most part be a waste of time, and yes, it does give astrology a bad reputation. After all, if you take the number of zodiac signs and divide 12 into, for example, the 55 million population of the U.K., that gives you over four-and-a-half million people per sign. Clearly a daily horoscope in a newspaper can't apply to all of them. Obviously, the four-and-a-half million Aquarians in the country – the N Million Aquarians in the world – can't have the same things happening to them on any one day.

I suppose that most of us are inclined to hold forth about subjects of which we have an inkling but no real knowledge. Nuclear power, the legal system, medical diagnosis, and so on are all subjects people find easy to generate unconsidered opinions on. Astrology suffers a lot from this. Like most subjects, when you actually investigate it, you begin to discover that its projected image isn't the truth. Astrology isn't just about your 'birth sign'. Astrologers do not just talk about whether you're a stubborn Taurean or a changeable Cancerian. They go on from there and start telling you your Moon is in Scorpio or Leo or wherever. They will talk about your Mars position and Jupiter position and Neptune and Pluto. They may say something like "You've got a sixth-house Venus and an afflicted fourth-house Sun."

Let your friendly astrologer go and he'll tell you about conjunctions and oppositions and squares. With a glint in his eye he may tell you Venus is trined with Mars and "Oh dear, you've only got one planet in air and THAT's retrograde."

Some of us even start talking about asteroids, and the north node of the moon, the part of impersonal consciousness, the vertex and even hypothetical planets! (Well, mathematicians invented imaginary numbers – why should they have all the fun?)

Don't worry. Getting to grips with astrology is not difficult. Learning the basics is easy. But it has to be said that astrology has such a vast subject matter – one that is being added to all the time – and dealing as it does with human character and potential, one can go on learning almost ad infinitum.

This book introduces, stage by stage, the methods that will enable you to draw up your horoscope yourself, and begin to interpret it. Of course, you can still learn about the fundamentals of astrology without actually going through the process of drawing up a horoscope.

If you have already had a horoscope drawn up by an astrologer, this book shows you the principles from which it was derived. You should be able to go on from there and develop your understanding of your own horoscope and be able to look at the horoscopes of others. The most useful tool when you start learning the subject is your own horoscope. After all, it's always there for you to refer to and gives you immediate examples.

what do astrologers do?

It took me a long time to realise that most people don't really have much idea of what astrology is really about. Most people who come to an astrologer seem to want to know if they're going to be rich and famous or meet a future partner next year or when they're going to get sick. Some astrologers do work like that and there's a lot of money to be made out of it. With most of us feeling perpetually insecure there are plenty of people who would like to know what is going to happen next.

You can forecast the future with astrology and at times it can be astonishingly accurate – particularly with hindsight. It is easy, when someone's just been hit by a bus to look up their planetary data and say "Oh well, they had Saturn conjunct Mars by transit today, squared to Mercury, so what do you expect?" It's another altogether to predict it in advance, because, whilst the energy inherent in that planetary set-up would be affecting that person in some way, it could actually manifest in a hundred-and-one ways, given the complex and varied lives we lead. Some astrologers can and do predict things like that but it has always seemed to me that we're talking a lot about clairvoyance here, with the astrology only being a peg to hang it on, a way of tuning in.

It is a source of annoyance to many of us that when your neighbourhood astrologer sticks his or her neck out and predicts something, and it doesn't happen, then scorn is usually heaped upon them. People use the event to re-assure themselves that astrology is bunk. The fact is that weather forecasters get prime-time t.v. slots (at least in the U.K.) every day and yet it's well-known that their success rate leaves much to be desired. If you start looking at the performance of economic forecasts it becomes even more laughable. Scientists in many fields are always making apparently reasoned predictions which turn out to be wrong. Yet these are on our screens and in our newspapers and used by everyone from politicians to the pub bore every day with total respectability. Yet woe betide the astrologer who gets a forecast wrong.

An experienced astrologer knows that astrology is just as valid, if not more so, than any other form of forecasting, but that human beings are so complex that being precise is not at all easy.

To give an example: in the 1988 U.S. Presidential election, a number of astrologers did stick out their necks and predicted Michael Dukakis would defeat George Bush, and continued to say so even when the opinion polls showed a landslide against him (Opinion polls are wrong almost as much as astrologers.) Certainly, the astrological data related to the charts of both men round about the election date showed very important positive factors for Dukakis' chart. It was very easy for an astrologer to say that round about the day of the election something was going to happen that would be the best thing that ever happened to him. Perhaps losing the election was.

If you think politicians don't bother about astrology then look up the time for Ronald Reagan's inauguration as Governor of California. It was planned to take place at 16 minutes past midnight on 1.1.67. 16 minutes past midnight? Usually these public events are at mid-day or coincide with prime-time television. The rumour was that this time was chosen not by P.R. men or political advisers but by an astrologer. It has been said that Reagan's whole political career was mapped out like this. And certainly during Reagan's presidency it was revealed that this world leader WAS consulting astrologers.

When you first start to learn about astrology, like when you begin most subjects, there are a few important points that need to be emphasised, because conventional wisdom has got the wrong idea. It seems to me that the first misconception is that astrology's main use is as a forecasting tool. In actuality it is not. The most important work that most astrologers do is the preparation of charts based on the birth data of individuals (time, date, place) and the interpretation of character, personality and potential strengths and weaknesses from them. An astrologer will prepare a written report for you or, at a personal consultation, will discuss your chart with you and (I hope) explain it as far as is practicable. Knowledge about your astrological characteristics is far more useful than predictions.

If you can't get the planetary energies revealed in your birth chart working for you then you might as well forget about forecasts.

It seems to me that what is important for anyone is the ability to deal with the present. If you cannot deal with the present effectively, how can you expect to deal with the future? With an understanding of your birth chart, coupled with knowledge of the basics of astrology, you are well on the way. Having said that, the astrological techniques used in forecasting need not be applied to, say, the next six months or year —

12

they can be applied to the present only. The planetary influences in your life at present are important. But what this book looks at is the influences always at work in you as expressed by planetary positions at your time of birth.

sun, moon, planets, stars

At this stage, it is probably a good idea to give a brief description of the bodies found in the sky.

Most obvious is the Sun. It is a star and is at the centre of what we call the solar system. Around the Sun, at varying distances, the planets are in orbit. The Earth is a planet, on average about 93 million miles from the Sun, a distance astronomers use to define a unit of measurement – the 'astronomical unit' or 'au'. So the Earth is 1 au from the Sun. Mercury and Venus have orbits closer to the Sun than the Earth's, at about .38 au and .72 au respectively. Moving further away from the Sun, beyond Earth's orbit, we come, with increasing distances, to Mars, Jupiter, Saturn, Uranus, Neptune and Pluto. The last of these planets is so far away it has an average distance from the Sun of about 39 au, so it is 39 times as far from the Sun as the Earth is.

One feature that we should be aware of is that the orbits of the planets are all in a very similar plane. If we drew a diagram of the solar system on a piece of paper, and turned the paper to view it edge on, all the planets would appear on the same level. This is approximately how the planets are found in space. This plane is often referred to as the 'ecliptic', defined as the path the Sun takes around the sky, as viewed from Earth.

Many of the planets themselves have further bodies orbiting around them, which we call satellites, or moons. Saturn, for example, has at least 20 moons, but the Earth has just one – which we call THE Moon.

The Sun and Moon are of course visible to us, but it is also possible to easily see the planets out as far as Saturn with the unaided eye. Indeed, Venus and Jupiter can at times be the brightest objects visible in the night sky. Also visible in the night sky are the stars. When we look up at night, we see that the sky is covered with stars, and if we look through binoculars or a telescope, we will be able to see thousands more than we can with the unaided eye. Though there are a number of different types of stars, they are inherently similar, and the Sun itself is a star. It is safe to say that many of the stars will also have planets in orbit around them. The stars, however are very great distances away. The star nearest to our solar system is Proxima Centauri, which is about 4.3 light years away i.e. light, travelling at 186,000 miles per second, still takes over four years to reach us. 4.3 light years is about 270,000 au, so we can see that even this star, close by interstellar standards, is a long way away compared to the distance between the Sun and the farthest planet of the solar system. Most stars are much further away than this. For example, the easily visible constellation of stars we call Orion, has stars ranging in distance from 470 to 2,100 light years away.

All the stars we can see are grouped together into what we call a galaxy. Our galaxy contains something like 100,000 million stars and its distance across may be as much as 100,000 light years. To put even these distances into perspective, we can look outside our own galaxy to see further galaxies, which themselves contain thousands of millions of stars. The nearest galaxy is about 170,000 light years from us, and there are about 1,000 million galaxies, most of which are much further away again.

To come back a bit closer to Earth, astrology is concerned with measuring the movements of the Sun, Moon and planets. It is concerned with their position in the sky, relative to us and to each other. Since the stars are so far away, their positions will not significantly change from one year to the next, but the planets are close enough that we can plot their movement; they will appear to move against the star background. If you look out at the same time on successive nights, you will see that the Moon will be close to a different set of stars on different nights.

Astrology's basic premise is that the positions of these bodies can be related to the characteristics of people born on Earth.

It is worth pointing out that we will be looking at what we can broadly call 'Western' astrology. There are other systems of astrology, such as Chinese, Indian and Arabic ones, and whilst all systems are derived from this basic premise, the methods used from thereon differ. Whilst these astrologies provide valid interpretations and have been increasingly used in the West in recent years, it seems to me best to stick with the system that has developed within our own culture. Astrology is not a recent phenomenon – its practices have developed over thousands of years of history.

what is a 'horoscope'?

It is not that paragraph in the news paper, of the "today is a good day for meeting friends" or "tomorrow you will meet a tall, dark stranger" variety – they are forecasts or predictions. Correctly, a horoscope is fundamentally a two-dimensional map of the heavens, showing the positions of the Sun, Moon and planets at the moment of a person's birth. It will, amongst other things, show in what zodiac sign each planet was when you were born. More generally 'horoscope' can be taken as referring to a description of the characteristics this map indicates.

Unfortunately, the word 'horoscope' is linked in people's minds to newspaper predictions. To avoid confusion it now seems favourite to refer to them as 'birth charts'. The old fogey school of astrology still talk about 'natal charts' or 'the natus'. You are not the client, but 'the native'. New fogeys sometimes use the even more arcane 'radix' – surely what we want is to make astrology available to all, not try and baffle everyone with obscure terminology. It is bad enough with some of the stuff we do have to use – words such as 'quincunx' and 'sesquiquadrate.'

On the opposite page is a full birth chart. It seems a little complicated, but by the end of this book, you should be able to understand what it all means – and perhaps be able to draw up a chart yourself.

Your birth chart can reveal your weaknesses and strengths. What you're afraid of, what sort of things you shine at doing. If you are easy to get on with or whether you try and push people around. It can say if you would use your energy more effectively being a lawyer or a photographer. You can't tell someone's gender from a birth chart. You cannot tell their marital/ partnership status either – though you can say whether someone is likely to have fruitful partnership relationships or if there's a likelihood of marital strife. And although in interpretations we tend to lapse into making value judgements about what's good and what's bad, when you really get down to it, astrology does not make such defined statements. It is all about energy potential. People with difficult charts often end up feeling more fulfilled then their friends who have easy ones.

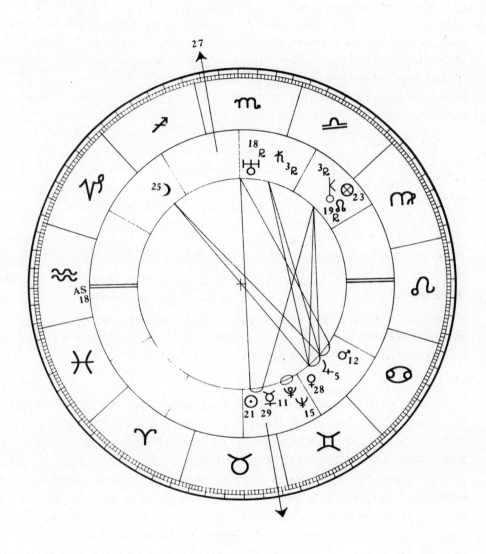

17

While we are talking about predictions in newspapers, let's get something else out of the way. Let's get rid of the common parlance that refers to astrology as being about your 'stars'. It's a misleading term. Basic Western astrology deals with the planets of the solar system. Incidentally, for convenience sake, we usually refer to just "the planets" rather than "the Sun, Moon and planets", even though the Sun and Moon are not actually planets. Although the Ancients did use many actual stars in their astrology, much of the knowledge has been lost and very few people today use them – although they are beginning to come back into fashion, now that we can use computers for all the number-crunching.

There are in the sky the twelve constellations of stars that bear the names of the zodiac signs – Aries, Taurus, Gemini and the rest. We will not right now make things complicated by going into the astronomical details, because it may not be important. What we will do is take a look at these twelve zodiac signs and how they form the basis of a birth chart.

A key symbol is shown in the margin to *symbolise* certain key points. Wherever you see the key symbol, you will find a useful hint that will give practical assistance and aid your understanding.

part one

the sun sign

Remember what we said about dividing the population by twelve so that we can allocate a zodiac sign to everybody. We decided that it was too simplistic to be of use in forecasting. But what about character analysis? This is often the point where people begin an interest in astrology. Look at the people around you and you *can* see similarities between many of the Aries people you meet. Most of them are impulsive, go-ahead, egocentric. Most Leos *do* tend to think they are the best of the bunch. Most Virgoans *are* a bit pernickety. What you have to remember is that it is not the be-all-and-end-all. Remember that we look at the positions of the Sun, Moon and planets and the relationships between them when we interpret a birth chart. The 'birth sign' is nowhere near everything.

I have a Geminian friend. He has the Moon and Mercury in Gemini as well, so he's pretty Geminian. Somebody else told me they thought he was confused, because he didn't know if he was a Taurean or a Gemini. "He *acts* like a Taurean," I was told. Look up his planets and you find Mars was in Taurus when he was born. A good description of Mars is that it represents how we take action – someone with Mars in Taurus will tend to *act* like a Taurean.

And every astrologer has heard this sort of thing no end of times: "I'm a Leo, but I don't behave like a Leo at all." Usually you can put them right. "Well what do you expect with three planets in Virgo and Pisces rising?"

The most important basic information that you need to learn is what each sign represents. Think of each sign of the zodiac as representing a different type of energy. An easy way to begin learning about each type is to examine the characteristics of each one and relate it to someone you know. This is a little game we can all play, because the information we need is easily accessible – all we need is the person's date of birth – for the moment we don't even need the year. We can look at our loved ones, friends, colleagues, find out what sign of the zodiac they were born into and relate the characteristics attributed to the sign to them. There is so much more to the subject than just this, but there's no doubt that we *can* say things about people from their 'birth sign'. Starting to learn how the energy of each sign manifests itself through is a good way to remember sign characteristics.

The first thing we can learn here is to stop calling it the 'birth sign'. When someone says "I'm a Sagittarian", for example, what they mean is that the *Sun* was in the zodiac sign Sagittarius at the time of their birth — correctly, that Sagittarius is their 'Sun sign'. The 'horoscopes' given in newspapers and magazines are based on Sun signs, and as we have seen, are far too generalised to be of serious use.

The dates given in such forecasts have perpetuated a further misconception — they have misled people into thinking that precise dates can be given for Sun signs and that for example, anyone born from March 21 to April 20 is an Aries. The Universe does not run at the beck and call of the human calendar however. In fact, the Sun moves into Aries at a specific time, which during this century has varied from as early as 07:36 on March 20 to as late as 19:15 on March 21. Similarly it has moved on into Taurus at varying times on April, 19, 20 or 21. So if you are born round about these dates, you cannot say what your Sun sign is — you need the time of birth as well.

When we say that the Sun "moves into" a particular sign, what do we mean? To understand this, we need to be familiar with the concept of longitude. A line of longitude is an imaginary line going north-south on the surface of the globe, linking the north and south poles. We divide the surface of the Earth into degrees of longitude, and just as we put 360 degrees in a circle, so we put 360 degrees of longitude around the globe of the Earth.

Similarly, we can divide the sky into 360 degrees of longitude. More specifically, we can divide the ecliptic — the circular plane in which the Sun, Moon and planets are always found — into 360 degrees of longitude. Astrologers divide this into twelve zones and to each one they allot a zodiac sign, so that each sign represents thirty degrees of longitude. At one time, these areas of the sky contained the constellations with which the signs are associated, although, for astronomical reasons, the constellations have now shifted in relation to the zodiac zones. What does change as the Earth orbits the Sun is the Sun's position relative to the star background as viewed from the Earth.

We cannot see the stars during daytime, because the light from the

Sun outshines them. Nevertheless, the stars are still there, behind the Sun.

Let's divide the sky into the twelve zodiac signs. We can draw a two dimensional diagram and include the Sun and the Earth as it orbits round it. If we look at figure (i) we can see that around February 1, as viewed from the Earth the Sun appears to be in the part of the sky allocated to Aquarius.

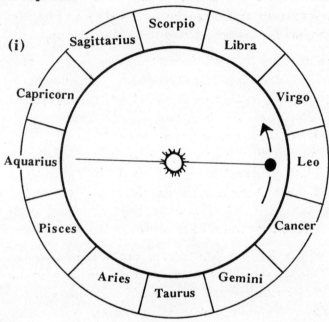

(i)

One month later (figure ii), the Earth has moved on one-twelfth of its orbit and the star background behind the Sun is now that associated with Pisces. To the ancients it appeared that when the Sun was in a particular sign, it gave particular characteristics to those born at that time. We will not digress into discussing theories of how astrology works here, but we should be aware that the factors involved are probably not physically caused by the star background. The constellations were merely a way of providing a symbology for astrologers to work with.

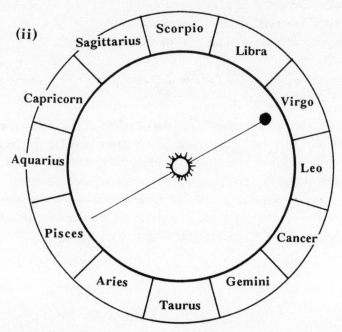

(ii)

Through the year, as the Earth moves around its orbit, the Sun will appear to track through all the signs and we can calculate the exact time when the Sun changes from one sign to another. We can also calculate how far the Sun has passed through a sign at any given time. We will see later how the exact position of a planet is important, not just its sign. We express a planet's position in degrees and minutes of longitude (a minute is 1/60 of a degree). Since there are 30 degrees to each sign, this will always be a figure between 0 degrees 0 minutes and 29 degrees 59 minutes.

The time someone was born is useful as well as the date. If we know someone's time and date of birth, we can calculate not just their Sun sign but the position of the Sun in the sign at that moment. For example we would find that someone born at midday on 30.10.56 has their Sun at 7 degrees 3 minutes of Scorpio. Later on we will see how you go about finding this information.

We are assuming that we are correct in allocating to each sign an exact one-twelfth portion of the sky. Things in Nature don't often work out so regularly, but it's probably the best we can do at present.

We must remember then, that when we start playing the Sun-sign game, we have to be careful. Many people born near the beginning or the end of a sign are confused as to what their Sun sign is, or even think they were born in a different one to which they actually were. The Sun is so strong an influence in most people's birth charts however, that on meeting someone born near a change of sign, it is often very quickly apparent which a person's Sun sign is. You cannot mix-up a passionate Scorpio with a procrastinating Libran.

I had the most first-hand experience possible of Sun-sign confusion. If you go by my date of birth, most newspapers say I'm an Aquarian. Somehow, I always felt uneasy about this. Even though I didn't have any real knowledge of astrology I always felt at heart I was a wishy-washy, emotional Piscean not an inventive, eccentric Aquarian. When I became interested enough to actually have my chart precisely drawn up, it turned out I was half a day into Pisces.

Here are the APPROXIMATE dates for the Sun Signs :

ARIES	MAR 20 TO APR 20
TAURUS	APR 20 TO MAY 21
GEMINI	MAY 21 TO JUN 21
CANCER	JUN 21 TO JUL 22
LEO	JUL 22 TO AUG 23
VIRGO	AUG 23 TO SEP 23
LIBRA	SEP 23 TO OCT 23
SCORPIO	OCT 23 TO NOV 22
SAGITTARIUS	NOV 22 TO DEC 21
CAPRICORN	DEC 21 TO JAN 20
AQUARIUS	JAN 20 TO FEB 18
PISCES	FEB 18 TO MAR 20

This is a good place to dispel another myth of lay astrology. If you are born near the change from one Sun sign to another (near a 'cusp') you might think you're a bit of this and a bit of that, half Libra and half Scorpio perhaps. Not so. Each sign has very different characteristics from the ones either side of it and if you're born near a cusp, you don't get confused and struggle to know which one you are. However, other astrological factors may mean you are not particularly like your Sun sign. You have to face up to the fact you are one or the other. Experience does however tell me that if your Sun is near the beginning of a sign it seems to make it express with a much stronger influence.

Next to the symbol for each planet and zodiac sign, is a list of five 'keywords' describing its major characteristics. These can be noted down and remembered – others can be added from the main description. Remembering these keywords is an easy way to recall just what each planet and sign is like.

Here is the symbol for the Sun. Try drawing it now to help you remember. It always seems to me the circle is the big wide Universe, the whole of creation, and that little dot is you. The Sun represents the most fundamental energy type within you, your basic mode of self-expression, your spirit. In the sky, the Moon and planets only shine by the reflected light of the Sun, and of

SUN

personality
the self
will
energy
egotism

course life on our planet wouldn't exist without the Sun. The Sun can light up the rest of your chart.

If I was to give one piece of astrological advice to someone, I would say, "Develop the positive characteristics of your Sun sign". The Sun's energy can then be used to light up the qualities of all the other planets in your chart.

Sun in ARIES

The traditional emblem of Aries is the ram, headstrong and competitive, energetic and somewhat aggressive. Look at the symbol. It's a representation of a ram's head. Also think of it as a fountain, or a seedling springing to life. Aries is traditionally the first sign of the zodiac because it is the instigator of all that follows.

*egocentric
courageous
impulsive
assertive
energetic*

ARIES

Being first pleases the Aries person. Arians have a drive to prove themselves to the world and want to be first and best at everything they turn their hands too. They are the great instigators in life and often show leadership qualities. Arians get things moving. Born in a fiery sign, they have a fundamental link to creative and enthusiastic energy and if they can only learn to control impulsiveness and listen to advice, can be a driving force in the world.

The guiding principle for Aries is "I am". They want to be bigger, bolder, better than the rest. There is a tendency to be self-centred and selfish, but at least they're usually open and prepared to discuss themselves with you. On the other hand they can be so self-centred they'll wittingly or unwittingly, trample over everyone else. And yet no sign is probably more capable of actively giving its time, possessions or even its life for those it loves. The ram can become the sacrificial lamb.

Not usually good judges of character, they can be easily taken in by superficiality and confidence trickery, and yet dismiss someone of worth if they cannot immediately see anything of value in this person. They want to see the best in everybody – so long as they see it straight away. It is a sign for *now*. If they can't do something, see someone, go somewhere straight away, they usually want to forget about it. This can lead them to be irritatingly unreliable. They will start off a hundred projects and not finish any. The shine of anything new soon wears off.

They will start the ball rolling, and before they know where they are the ball will be rolling out of control. They will not usually admit they cannot cope, though; they just keep plugging away. The "I am better" principle keeps them from asking for help. They want to do everything, and if they cannot learn to concentrate their energies, they will probably not do anything justice. Arians need to learn that asking for the help of others is not self-demeaning, but part of learning to live.

When their energies are concentrated, or they can find the right people to back them up, Arians can achieve great things. They can make good leaders and have strong creative abilities and will power. It is a question of using their dynamic energy responsibly, and not letting it spill over into aggressive, self-centred competitiveness, or even physical violence. Many Aries direct their energies in sports or other physical pursuits.

They must watch their heads. Their metaphorical butting into everything can actually lead to head injuries. The deep concern for the self, often leading to deep self-analysis, actually learning to face up to the fact that they are no better (or worse) than anyone else is said to lead to a much higher than average incidence of mental illness.

The secret desire that drives all Arians deep down is that they want to be loved. This is why they want to be the best at everything; they think it will make you like them. The easiest way to upset them is to make out you *do not like* them.

Sun in TAURUS

persistent
stewarding
sensual
stubborn
dependable

TAURUS

Mention Taurus to the lay astrologer and the usual reaction is a yawn. This placid, earthy, practical sign has the reputation of being the most boring in the zodiac. Adolf Hitler, Bertrand Russell, Jiddu Krishnamurti, Karl Marx, Salvador Dali were all Taureans. Were these people boring? So what's the truth about Taurus?

Look at the symbol – it's a bull's head (See how easy it is learning the symbols? Everybody knows about Taurus the bull) Think of a herd of cows peacefully, placidly grazing. Try and get them moving, try and get a response. Taurus just sits there. Of course you can keep prodding and poking and eventually old Taurus does move. Then what do you get? A stampede!

Taureans can be slow to make up their minds, but that doesn't mean they are stupid; they like to work things out practically, not rush off into pie-in-the-sky schemes like some signs that could be mentioned! Once their mind is made up, they persevere; this makes them good at overcoming obstacles and getting things done, or may make them obstinate and unchanging. You might say they take over where the Aries people started off.

Taureans have a good sense of beauty and art, but may place too much value on appearances; Taurus is the sign most impressed with smart clothing and many Taureans end up with vast wardrobes. There is usually only one thing more attractive to a Taurean than a new set of clothes – a big meal! Food is central to most Taurean lives, and even the ones who don't place great importance on their food intake usually end up trying to make sure everyone around them is well fed – force-fed even!

Taurus also has great affinity with the land and many Taureans are interested in gardening, farming and environmental matters. They usually feel at home in the countryside and secure and comfortable in a garden they can mould with their own efforts.

They must have comfort and security and this is often found in material possessions as they surround themselves with things that can be touched and made use of. If you really want to annoy a Taurean, when you go to their home move some of the ornaments about when they're not looking – even a fraction and it drives them wild. This possessiveness can lead to excessive materialism, but in the more spiritually developed types, Taurean practicality means they can put spiritual ideas into practice and can be steadfast in following them. Taureans place great importance on values and ultimately won't trade in their moral standards in exchange for material reward – unless their moral standards *are* to be grasping and materialistic.

Concerned mainly with what they have and hold, Taureans can be extremely possessive in relationships and manifest extreme jealousy;

their fixity however means they can be unswervingly loyal. This possessiveness also extends into circumstances – there can be a tendency to inaction (often seen as laziness) because they do not wish to risk changing what already exists. Taurus, more than any other sign, represents stability and they can represent rocks of friendship although their fixed ways can make them appear boring to more changeable, less reliable people.

Taureans have their own way of doing things and do not like interference. Often they can be blind to the other person's point of view. Few signs, however, can be more gentle and caring, and the Taurean bonus is that they offer practical help. They are always keen to offer practical suggestions to help you with your problems, but often oversimplify, failing to understand the complexity of your situation and why you will not take their advice.

Sun in GEMINI

intellectual
flighty
dualistic
communicative
undependable

GEMINI

It is often observed that children tend to scatter their energies, finding it difficult to concentrate on any one area for a long enough time to produce results. Gemini's trouble is that he is like this when he grows up.

Born into an airy, intellectual sign, Geminians are full of ideas and adaptable with it. They spend all their lives thinking, their active minds flitting from one subject to the next. This can make them brilliant communicators, or idle gossips. They may run their whole lives like this flitting from one job, relationship, home to the next. Their potentially brilliant minds seek constant stimulation.

Gemini is represented by the Twins (originally the twin goat-children) and this is indicative of their dualistic nature. The symbol is two vertical lines and two horizontal ones. This can mean they are able to do two completely different things at the same time, or may make them two-faced. Geminians want knowledge, they want truth. But if it is unpalatable, they do not want to face it. Geminians have a simple solution for coping with stressful problems: they ignore them.

They shut themselves off from them and hope they'll go away, using their silver-tongues to persuade others to do their dirty work, while they go out and have a good time. Surprisingly enough, the problems often do go away by this method. Perhaps everyone else becomes so exasperated trying to keep up with them, they give up. If the problems do actually come home to roost, nervy Gemini can often crack-up. Facing up to themselves, finding out what they are really like, is one of their biggest tests.

They are usually popular, the sort who get invited to parties. They are usually charming, persuasive, good public-relations types — although it is often so superficial it upsets people when they find out what is going on underneath.

Male Geminians tend to think they're cute kids even when they're eighty. Females tend to just flit about in a sort of hopeless restlessness, worrying what they should do next. Both hate you to ignore them. Both must learn that truth is only found in the stillness of the mind. This is perhaps more difficult for them than any other sign. Unfortunately, the spiritual side of their nature can be difficult to bring out. Whilst not overtly materialistic, they are very easily distracted by the temptations offered by today's world.

Geminians flit and fidget. They make words work for them and have a habit of turning everything round to their own advantage. They get their way by persuading you against your better judgement. They are usually good talkers, but often talk too much, and there may be so much energy that the talk comes out in an unstructured way. Gemini rules broadcasting and communications — these can be used to spread knowledge, or malicious, embroidered gossip. Geminians often have difficulty pinning down the truth and can seem notoriously unreliable to others — what they said yesterday doesn't matter to them any more, now their mind is working on something else.

Geminians must learn to use all that intellectual energy wisely. They must learn to concentrate it to further their own knowledge and spread it to others, rather than rushing around dissipating their energies in worthless pursuits.

*protective
moody
domestic
loving
oversensitive*

CANCER

This is the most emotional of the signs we have discussed so far. Above all, Cancerians *feel*. But do they show it? Well, not often, no. Their creature is the Crab and this is typified by the soft, vulnerable body inside – and the tough, protective shell on the outside. Cancerians need this protection to stop themselves getting hurt. The trouble is they can become so adept at shutting off their feelings they can forget they ever had any.

Moodiness is another problem. When we discuss planetary rulerships we will see that Cancer is ruled by the Moon. Since this orbits the Earth – and thus goes through all the signs of the zodiac – about every four weeks, Cancerians are readily exposed to the changing energy of all the signs.

The Cancerian never seems to realise just how changeable he or she is. They start things off and don't finish them. They will deny that they said what they did yesterday, or behaved in the way they did – they're not lying, they actually believe it.

Another advantage of a shell is that you can withdraw into it. Try getting a Cancer out of his or her home in time for an appointment. Upset them, try and make out they're wrong or criticise their mother or home and watch them retreat. Try and get them to come round to your way of thinking. You can prod and poke them all you like, but this will make them retreat even further behind the protective facade. They can be impossible to deal with and somehow they nearly always seem to end up getting their own way. Better make sure you get to the bathroom first in the mornings too. Cancerians hate dirt. Cleanliness and respectability is everything.

Crabs have claws. Once a Cancerian gets his pincers around a relationship, a job, a house, try getting them to let go. What they will hang on to most of all is the past, and letting go of it is perhaps their biggest test. They need to learn to live in the present and stop regaling everyone with tales of the past all the time. They can be as fickle as anything (as the Moon, actually), but they expect everyone else to stay the same.

Like all the emotional signs, they suffer from the restrictions we place on them. The males in particular have a hard time of it. We think it's wrong for men to emote and everyone suffers because of this emotional blockage we instil or are instilled with. Of course Cancerians have good points. Look at the symbol. They're curving round in on themselves, protecting, caring, and they can be like that to you.

As long as they can learn not to be overprotective, Cancerians can be the most caring of people. Cancer is a powerful sign. In it there is a deep well of energy that can provide nourishment, sustenance and love to the world. Cancerians see everyone as babies to be looked after and fussed over and cared for. Not just people, but jobs, homes, organisations, everything in which they get involved. Given the opportunity to open up, their strong feelings can move mountains.

Sun in LEO

After the changeability of the previous two signs, we are back to fixity with a vengeance. There are three other 'fixed' signs, but it seems to me that Leo is often the most fixed of all.

genial
haughty
creative
domineering
fun-seeking

LEO

No other sign seems to find it so easy to get into a rut and stick with the same job or marriage or home for years, even if they are patently wrong for them. Very often the Leonian propensity for good nature seems to keep them smiling through their problems so that they never get dissatisfied enough to change things for the better.

Often they find it hard to see that everyone else does not possess the same level of integrity and idealism as they do. Their outspokenness and tendency to take action without consulting those around them gets them into difficulties. When they cannot avoid public disapproval they resort to self-approval. Often there is a belief that means are justified by ends, although fairness is always a major consideration for them.

The planetary body most closely associated with Leo is the Sun itself, and just as the Sun is the centre of the solar system, so do Leos think themselves to be the centre of everything. Their enormous egos get hurt when people don't treat them with the respect and attention they feel they deserve.

Everyone knows Leo's animal is the lion. Leo is also traditionally king of the animals, and that is how they see themselves. They want to lord it over the rest of us, and a lot of them have the dignity, courage and benevolence to be very good at it.

Leos will walk into a situation and take over. With the more benevolent ones you do not even notice, but some of them get into all sorts of problems when people resent their interference. Very often they are so sure of themselves, they do not notice the trouble they are causing. They just go on strutting around the place, displaying themselves and thinking how wonderful they are. It can be hard for them to change their ways.

Leo is a very playful sign, and Leo children can be very bombastic. As they grow up the playfulness remains, but everything has to be done with dignity. They don't like to be laughed at, or put down. They demand respect and don't wish to be reminded of their faults.

The link with the Sun can give them a tremendous persistent creative energy. Often they never really grow up and there is usually a strong urge to turn the creative drive into a procreative one by having their own children. Leos seek to express their ego by creating in their own image.

The symbol reminds me of the lions tail. You can pull the tail if it is all in fun. Children can get away with murder with the more benevolent Leos and if you want to see one get wrathful then try and criticise their kids. Even their projects, their creative work, they subconsciously see as their offspring. Perhaps that's why criticising their noble and courageous efforts hurts them so deeply.

Leo is associated with the teaching profession, but try and tell *them* something they do not know, and they hate it. Sometimes they will clam up when you try and teach them something and refuse to let the knowledge filter into their heads as if subconsciously they feel it is below them to have someone else telling them what to do.

If you want to get your way with one, put them in a position where they can organise, be in charge of something. It does not matter if it is not important at all so long as they think it is. But try and give them a task that they think is menial and you will heartily offend them.

Accusations of laziness are sometimes made at them, but given the right encouragement few signs are prepared to work as hard, energetically, generously and benevolently in positions of authority. King and Queen Leos can be the epitome of benevolent leadership – or truculent despotism.

Sun in VIRGO

Virgoans tend to judge things by their practicality. They are happy dealing with boring, mundane, repetitive tasks if they can see a practical result. Highly adaptable, they are good at coming up with practical solutions to problems, but this inherent versatility can lead to them being easily swayed by others as the end up rushing around finishing off the things that others really should have completed.

meticulous
pernickety
practical
aloof
worrying

Their concern with details can make them good at any work that requires precision or intricacy. Perhaps more than any other sign, they are great at sorting out the fine details, but this also has its drawbacks; in paying attention to minutiae they can easily overlook the larger issues. They might waste time fussing over the inconsequential whilst the important is forgotten. It also leads to a certain narrowness of outlook. They are not necessarily narrow-minded, but just fail to take opportunities that are presented to them so that their horizons are never broadened. Often they will reach middle age and suddenly wake up, beginning to try out all sorts of new avenues and realising what they have been missing all along. Because they start from such a small viewpoint, no other sign has a greater potential for spiritual awakening.

Virgoans often make good talkers and have an eye for language — unfortunately it is usually the Virgoan who is boring you to tears with endless talk about matters which are important to them but trivial to you. Trust the Virgoan to chatter on and on about their work.

Virgoan meticulousness would be very useful for dealing with the mathematical side of astrology, but they are just the ones who will seize on the inaccuracies in the interpretation, ignoring all the stuff that *does* apply to them. Harping on and on about detail can turn them into awful nags. Perhaps above all, the Virgoan seeks after perfection and may waste a lifetime trying to achieve the impossible.

Virgo is said to be the sign of service. They are at their best when doing things to help other people. Usually they are very hard workers and have a greater than average potential for good health. Unfortunately, the innate tendency to whine and moan and look on the black side can turn inward. Couple this with the innate Virgoan concern about matters of health and hypochondria can very readily result. What starts out in a desire for good health and fitness can develop into obscure dietary practices and worries that they're mortally ill. Often there is nothing wrong at all. The symbol seems to represent coils of energy, and indeed Virgos often possess great fortitude and forbearance, but the last stroke of the symbol is turned demurely inward. And so is the energy often turned inward. Virgo is a passive, worrying sign, for all the outward show of practicality. Sometimes Virgos suffer because people get the impression they can cope, even when they are inwardly screaming for help.

Their analytical ability is often turned to relationships, where it does not always work to good effect. The traditional emblem for Virgo is the virgin — often their search for perfection can mean that no partner satisfies the ideals they seek. The purity comes through in a desire for tidiness and cleanliness. It can be particularly irritating for others who find themselves constantly under Virgo's scrutiny, especially when the Virgoan is so often oblivious to his or her own faults. This is no stumbling-block to them criticising others. Then there is the Virgo capacity for guilt, with a certain amount of lack of realism about the self. If you want to really annoy a Virgo, try criticising them and see what happens.

34

Virgo is a sign of the zodiac that has come in for a lot of criticism. They can be pernickety and short-sighted and whinging – but if you're in a spot and need some help there are few better than old Virgo to come up with the solution and put the work in to help you out. Perhaps the rest of us get so fed up with them because they do actually try and put their ideals into practice.

Sun in LIBRA

Libra, the scales. The symbol is a stylised balance. When I had been studying astrology for some time, the truth about Libra dawned on me – it is the only sign in the zodiac depicted by a machine. The scales represent balance and fair play, but it is a fault of Librans that they tend to be machine-like, too cold and restrained in emotional response and lacking depth of feeling.

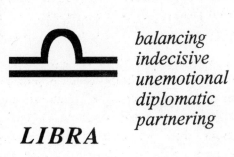

balancing
indecisive
unemotional
diplomatic
partnering

LIBRA

It usually takes a lot to make a Libran lose their temper. They get annoyed certainly but not really angry – if they finally do, it is often like a hurricane – nothing is left unsaid and every little detail of what you said years ago is recalled. Then afterwards they usually feel ill.

Because they are always seeking balance and justice, they try and avoid extremes. They also exhibit what is to others an exasperating indecision. What does a Libran do best? Procrastinate. They will dither about trying to make up their mind, considering all the pros and cons and then at the end of the day probably make what is an impulsive decision anyway. Despite the need for balance, it can be one of the signs most stubborn in opinion. Once a decision is made, they will very often stick obstinately to it, come what may, subconsciously choosing not to go through agonies of indecision again. The need to present different points of view can make them argumentative or turn them into 'devil's advocates', though they will often back off if they think they're upsetting you.

An airy, intellectual sign, Libra seeks knowledge and mental stimulation and is good at coming up with the ideas. However it is not always easy for them to put the ideas into practice, because even if they have managed to make up their mind to do something, by then a new and different idea has probably presented itself and caught their attention.

Ruled by Venus, Librans seek harmony and friendship and can be charming and graceful in expression. They are generally sociable and usually work best in partnership – particularly if their partner can make their mind up for them! This is another perfection-seeking sign, particularly in relationships, and their scrutiny of their associates may lead to disillusionment. They must learn that the balance of harmony which they seek can very rarely be perfectly achieved.

Striving for harmony, they can be too easily influenced by others for they will often give in rather than cause an upset. Very often they will not speak up for themselves. Sometimes they will go to great lengths to secure the approval of others and will compromise their principles, fickly changing to suit the latest environment. They have to learn that whilst this may lead people to like them, ultimately respect and deeper attraction is only obtained when they stand up for their principles.

Librans usually have a good appreciation of the arts and, disliking to have to do the same thing twice, they show good attention to detail as they try and achieve perfection. However, their sense of beauty and muted emotional response makes them easily offended by vulgarity, exaggeration and ugliness. They believe that appearances count and like to dress to impress. Their lack of feeling and inherent mental stability can also make them lack compassion for those who are under stress, ill or depressed.

At their best, Librans can bring harmony and diplomacy to situations in which they are involved. At their worst they can be unreliable ditherers, not necessarily lazy, but just not able to do anything much with their lives.

Be careful with this symbol, particularly when reading planetary positions in charts, because of the similarity to the Virgo symbol. Scorpio has the coils of energy too, but they end up with that arrow, projected out into the world in a no nonsense way. The traditional animal of this sign is the scorpion, a creature that lives in dark places and with the infamous sting in the tail.

passionate
obsessive
controlling
forceful
transforming

SCORPIO

Scorpios are usually very private people. They are the sort who grow tall hedges round their gardens and they hate to have their innermost desires exposed to the world. They are attracted to life's hidden mysteries, and may be particularly fascinated by the transformational experiences inherent in sex and death. Scorpio is raw power at its most fundamental level. They believe that desire is the fundamental human drive, and those for reproduction and survival most fundamental of all. They can have very strong occult capabilities, for they have access to the deeper spiritual energies, but often they fearfully withdraw from these and may not give anything credence other than what they see as hard fact.

Although they make loyal friends, once crossed, they can be fearful enemies. It is not that they do not forgive easily, rather that they usually don't forgive at all. Their moral viewpoint tends to be of the 'eye-for-an-eye' variety. They may not react immediately, but they will bear a grudge for years and strike when the moment is right. Even the less revengeful ones do not forget the wrong you did them.

Scorpios like things to be black or white – not grey. They can shut things off, let go, just like that. They hate haziness and once moved, they want to get on with things. Scorpio has perhaps more power to get things done than any other sign, but of course that power can be used for good or evil. The key words are transformation and regeneration.

Scorpios like to impose themselves on the environment and the people around them. They don't say you *should* do something, rather that you *must*. It is a fixed sign and their power of will can move mountains; it can also make them extremely wilful, stubborn and resistant to change. When change does come, it usually comes suddenly and explosively.

Being a watery sign, Scorpio is very emotional. So strong is their passion that they very often shut off from it for fear it cannot be handled. They hate to show their feelings – or their faults – in public and woe betide anyone who gives away their secrets. Power is what concerns Scorpios. They think there is no strength in weakness. They can feel constantly threatened by the world and thus seek to control it. These desires may make it difficult for them to delegate responsibilities; they can be seekers after perfection in others ("perfection" is you doing everything the same way they do – except they always think they're better at it than you), not trusting anyone else to do things properly. Extremely loyal to their loved ones, they can be possessive and jealous.

Although they often keep their views to themselves, once asked they may appear very undiplomatic, expressing the unvarnished truth and not sparing anyone's feelings. They would rather remain silent than deal in half-truths. It is not advisable to annoy a Scorpio, but if you really want to, then pester them trying to get their secrets and when you do, tell everybody.

It has been said that Scorpios come in three varieties. The Scorpion-types are revengeful and ambitious. They have little truck with fair play, rationalising their actions as being morally correct whatever they are, and then like to get you down to their level. The Eagle-type does not go out of the way to be nasty, but when threatened will fight for what he or she believes to be right. He flies over situations, only becoming involved when it suits his purposes. Always watch for the hidden motive with a Scorpio. The Dove variety's search for power is that over her own desires. Scorpio-doves seek the state of harmlessness where others' sorrows are absorbed and given back as love and healing. Of course, most Scorpios are a mixture of all three types – though just what blend, the individual Scorpio decides.

The higher types will go out of their way to help you, but always with the idea that with a little assistance you will be able to stand on your feet unaided. They will invigorate you with their passion. The lower types will do anything for the satisfaction of their own desires.

The symbol of Sagittarius is an arrow as fired up into the air by the Centaur (half-man/half-horse), Sagittarius' animal (that little line across the shaft represents the bow string).

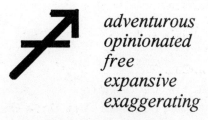

adventurous
opinionated
free
expansive
exaggerating

SAGITTARIUS

The symbol is indicative of the Sagittarian's need for a target. However, actually achieving that target is generally unimportant as it is the actual doing which counts. For this reason, many Sagittarians set higher and higher goals which ultimately prove impossible to attain, and they need to learn that, whilst lack of competitiveness is a commendable trait, achievement can be rewarding and useful. Indeed, in today's society, achievement can be a way of attaining the approval that they often desire.

Without a target Sagittarians can become depressed or physically ill. To fulfil their potential, they need to have goals – and freedom to aim for them. It is also important for them to have some form of support and encouragement. Underneath the outward show of bravado there is often a lot of worry.

A fundamental Sagittarian tendency is to promise more than they can deliver. This does not arise from any sense of deception – Sagittarians are usually generally honest – but because they are so aware that there is so much to be learnt from and given to the world that they just try and do too much, setting too many targets at once. They make proficient sales people, being usually outgoing and likeable and with an honest belief in their product. And yet one should always be wary of them – they are always likely to promise you more than they can provide.

Sagittarians often have more than one job going at once, or a hobby or voluntary work interest that is very important to them. Even so they often find it difficult to change course tending to just carry on firing at the same old target beyond the time they should be considering new and more useful options.

Sagittarius is the sign of higher thinking, ruling philosophy, religion, law and the spiritual world in general. Sagittarians are seekers after this higher knowledge and are often at the forefront of the spirituality of their generation. They are usually intuitive, possessing natural insight and even prophecy and put the good of the whole before self. At its highest expression, Sagittarian idealism can lead to involvement in caring professions and tend towards an interest in holistic medicines. They can be jovial and beneficent – and often lucky too. The beastly side of the Centaur can take this luck and turn into a devil-may-care adventurer with its head in the clouds, always promising to help you along but never there when you really want them. Too busy off enjoying themselves probably. Most Sagittarians get upset if they think you're having more fun than they are.

Always seeking after knowledge, Sagittarians can typify the eternal student and yet often they do poorly at school. Because they are generally straightforward, it is as if the basic tuition given at most schools is an irrelevance to them. It is when they grow older that their intellectual capabilities can become realised, when they become interested in learning about more worthwhile subjects – and when they may regret having not paid attention at school earlier in their lives. Their inherent mutability makes them adaptable, though not always practical, and easily swayed by a new and potentially exciting interest that presents itself. They seek freedom and excitement when young and can be completely reckless with little regard for convention or authority. Yet later in life, whilst the love of freedom usually remains, they can become very conventional and opinionated.

The need for freedom can take Sagittarians on long and frequent journeys, usually more spiritual than actual physical travel, although they do usually have a love of the countryside and like to explore new places. Outdoor exercise is very beneficial.

Perhaps the most typical Sagittarian trait is their straightforwardness, as their arrow flies straight to its target. They will state the unvarnished truth, but must take care that this does not develop into a lack of tact or hurtful bluntness. Because they see to the heart of the matter much better than most, it is easy for them to jump to unwarranted conclusions and be blunt to the point of unmerciful criticism. They must also beware that their sure-footedness does not make them narrow-minded later in life, as they become so sure of their beliefs that they dismiss all other views and become completely bigoted. They have a poor grasp of detail (contrast Gemini, the opposite sign in the zodiac circle). There can be a terrific grasp of the overall view, but too often they let themselves and others down by overlooking or not wanting to know about the practical minutiae. It is not the most responsible of signs.

Sun in CAPRICORN

Most people find this the most difficult symbol to draw. It depicts the horned head and fishy tail of the sea-goat, climbing up from the ocean and sure-footedly scaling the highest peak. Mount-aineering involves a great emphasis on safety, and an important Capricorn trait is the need to exercise caution above all else. Before taking action, they always want to be sure of where

*cautious
authoritarian
serious
ambitious
structuring*

CAPRICORN

the next step will lead them and they just hate being embarrassed.

They may be slow to express their deeper feelings and even become emotionally repressed. The caution often leads to them being extremely reserved and unsure of themselves, but they do find security in work, often working long hours in mundane jobs. They will plan things slowly and carefully and always have high regard to the practicality of the proposed action. And yet they do not necessarily appear indecisive – once something is decided they will strive to put the decision into practice.

Their caution can extend to money, for they can be so careful they appear miserly, and their practicality means they always try to make do and mend, rather than extravagantly (as they see it) lash out on something new. They can be very materialistic, but their possessions are normally a badge of achievement, to show the world how clever or hard-working or long-suffering they think they have been – the possessions are status symbols. They may be proving great help to others, but they require a reward, the effort in itself not being reward enough. They know the world doesn't owe them a living, but expect a return for what they put into it.

Having said all that about caution, Capricorn is also the sign of ambition. The sea-goat may be careful, but it desperately wants to get to the top of the mountain. Even the ones without blind desire to achieve status will put this energy into getting things right. They expect to do a precision job correctly to the last detail, and may be slave-drivers to their underlings and nags to their families. And yet the energy can come out in intense loyalty, the sort of person who will stop at nothing to please you and fulfil your every whim to the last degree.

Capricorns have a fine sense of the structure of things, be it buildings, machinery, the human body – or the structure of society as expressed in politics and the rule of law and order. They think they know what's best for us and will make sure we do it, if necessary. Often great troubleshooters, they are concerned with how things are organised and the more aggressive ones will be those who get practical projects off the ground – with them in charge. It upsets them if *you* organise everything – they feel they have no purpose.

Once in a position of power, they get nervous about the security of their position and may take steps to put down anyone they see as a threat. They can be cold opportunists, using others for their own ends and being so concerned with and introspective about their own interests they do not worry if others get hurt.

They do take things seriously and may be melancholic; even the cheerful, outgoing ones with the dry sense of humour still feel that underneath life's a serious dog-eat-dog affair. Very often they have an old head on a young shoulders, yet seem as they get older and feel more secure to become younger at heart – you can almost see the worries slip away. Their confidence grows as they surmount life's problems, moving mountains where others fail.

Sun in AQUARIUS

The traditional emblem is the water-bearer, pouring out to humankind the gift of spiritual energy and life-force. It is the sign of humanitarianism and equality, magnetism and electricity. Aquarius' symbol can be confusing. Perhaps it is typical of the unexpected quality attached to many Aquarians – it looks like water, but it isn't a watery sign. Another idea is that it depicts the furrows of a

42

ploughed field, but that suggests earth, and it is not that. Actually Aquarius has an airy quality about it. Perhaps remember the symbol by thinking about light-waves, or electricity. Aquarius is a sign closely associated with scientific knowledge and technology.

inventive
eccentric
rebellious
innovative
detached

AQUARIUS

This sign is concerned with knowledge. Aquarians usually just don't want to know *some* things, they want to know *everything*. The sort whose favourite reading matter is an encyclopaedia. They will ask you question after question, with scant regard for any feelings of privacy you may have, and will delight in telling you what they know, particularly if it is something they have found out about you. Try asking them a personal question or two though, and they clam up. It annoys them if you keep asking them what they've been up to. They are usually aware of their faults and foibles, but do not want them dragged out before the public. Do not tell them your secrets – unless you want everyone in the world to know.

Many people who the world regards as eccentric have Aquarius strong in their chart. They may have explosive temperaments and they may be geniuses. Inventors are ruled by Aquarius. You never quite know what Aquarians might come up with next. They usually have high ideals, but this causes them problems because society is not ready for them. And so they turn into rebels.

There is another side to Aquarius. They can be cautious and conventional, fixed in their traditional ideas. The trick is to balance the rebellious and conservative energies. The staid ones should loosen up a little. The ones who are already eccentric enough have to realise that there are times when the line has to be drawn. Fighting all the authority figures in your life all the time, you may achieve something, but you may wreck yourself.

There can be a tendency to exaggerate their own problems. The scintillating charm can only make up for it so much. Eventually it turns people off.

Aquarius is a fixed sign, and stubbornness is a great failing. Hanging on to their ideas past their time can be a problem. If they have got an idea, however weird and wonderful, they will keep plugging away with it come what may. The whole world may be against them, but they will carry on, and sometimes they are proved right. They're here to bring forth these new ideas and make people sit up and think. One of the biggest lessons for Aquarians to learn is that not everyone else feels the same way about something as they do. Even when they accept this, it is very difficult for them to understand it.

Sometimes is can go the other way, dropping the previous idea when they think up a new and more inventive one. Aquarius will not be tied down. They like their freedom. They like to have friends around them and this can cause jealousy in their spouses by retaining these friendships after marriage. They relate to people on an intellectual level.

Aquarians can walk into a room and join a group of people, chipping into the conversation as if they had been there all along. Some may find this attitude aggressive, but they can often contribute the seed of an original idea that will blossom later. This habit of putting their spoke in leads them into being big 'foot-in-mouth' perpetrators.

They will appear superficially cool and calm, and yet underneath they can be great worriers, anxiety making them ill. They do not like you asking questions of them because it rouses their greatest fear – that you might be trying to get *intimate* with them. They like impersonality. They need to feel part of a greater whole and work best in groups or organisations which have some humanitarian purpose. They may be impersonal and intellectual but once they get going can be formidable achievers.

Sun in PISCES

This sign is traditionally represented by two fishes – one swimming upwards towards spirituality and enlightenment – the other downwards towards materialism. The two curves of the symbol stylise this, the horizontal line showing how the two are intimately joined.

It is perhaps the most dualistic of the signs, with Pisceans often a having a dual personality; they can be exceedingly generous or mean, optimistic or pessimistic, spiritual or materialistic, other-wordly or rooted in hard factuality. Very often, they change from one to the other – first the fish is swimming up, next minute it's going down.

It is also traditionally thought of as the last sign of the zodiac and in it is found something of all the other signs. It is where the individual merges with the whole Universe.

intuitive
impressionable
spiritual
dreamy
deceptive

PISCES

It is said that Pisces is perhaps the most difficult sign to understand, with only another Piscean truly understanding the depth of feeling being experienced by a fellow Piscean. Above all Pisces is the sign that feels, absorbing the energy in its environment and perhaps merging with it. They feel things so much that they usually have a need for time on their own so that they can deal with the negative energies they have absorbed, and this can make them very reclusive. However, the more time they spend on their own, the more likely it is that they will find themselves thrown into situations where they are forced to deal with other people.

They can reach the highest expressions of spiritual love and their grasp of the oneness of all things can make them visionary – or impractical dreamers. They are not renowned for earthy practicality and can have what to others seems an exasperating tendency to let things drift. Better not make a decision in case I hurt someone else – or myself – says the Piscean. Why bother with minutiae, personal appearance, sorting out finances, when the Universe is so big and awe-inspiring? Why bother accumulating wealth when there is so much out there to feel?

They feel things so strongly that a sort of inward terror of any experience can develop. Their fear of getting hurt can make them aloof and superficially cold, and yet their natural compassion can make them the most loyal and sensitive friends, willing to sacrifice their all for others. Pisces is the sign of the martyr.

Of course, not all Pisceans are so other-wordly. For many Pisceans all this feeling, and their openness to the suffering of the world is too much. Some retreat into seclusion, but usually the retreat is from the spiritual to the material. As a form of protection, they become extremely materialistic, watching every penny. Nothing is believed unless it is hard fact. For most Pisceans to achieve fulfilment, they have to do a perpetual balancing act between the two extremes. Many spend their early years with materialistic aims, but fulfilment for most only comes when they find expression for their natural compassion and creativity. If they can't do something to help others' suffering in some way, they suffer themselves.

More than any sign it is the one that reaches extremes. More than any other, they seem to be immediately sensitive to universal laws that produce equal and opposite reactions to what they do and feel. Pisceans can plumb the depths of despair, suffering, mental illness, drug-abuse or sheer ruthless materialism. They can reach the heights of spiritual awareness, love, creative expression and ecstasy. A lot of them swing from one extreme to the other. They are aware that the two extremes are actually very close together. The chance to achieve a sense of happiness that others cannot is balanced by the depth of suffering that can also be experienced.

The ability to absorb the personality of others can make them great confidence tricksters. Their vague dreaminess can often lead them to drift into all sorts of deception and they must be careful here for it is as if they have a subconscious urge to obscure and deceive. Their adaptability can be an asset, but it makes it very difficult to pin the slippery fish down. Count on a Piscean to make a clear issue vague. They can see how minor issues, the details, fade into insignificance in the vastness of it all. Planning their lives logically does not seem to work for them – it is intuition which counts. The more helpless ones live in a constant state of confusion, losing themselves in self-pity or escapist fantasy, never getting organised and perhaps in perpetual financial difficulties. The more sensible ones realise that if they do not get the material things around them organised, their world will just fall apart.

learn the symbols

This is perhaps the most important basic instruction one can give to someone learning astrology.

Here are some reminders of what the signs represent, to help you remember them:

Aries	♈	a ram's head
Taurus	♉	a bull's head
Gemini	♊	two lines x two lines i.e. duality
Cancer	♋	the two parts of the symbol curl around each other protectively
Leo	♌	the lion's tail
Virgo	♍	coils of energy, with the last curled demurely inwards
Libra	♎	a stylised balance
Scorpio	♏	coils of energy, with the last projecting; a scorpion's tail
Sagittarius	♐	an arrow
Capricorn	♑	the head and tail of a sea-goat
Aquarius	♒	waves of energy
Pisces	♓	two fishes, one swimming up, the other down

For one thing they work as an astrological shorthand. It's much easier to write

⊙7♏3

than

"The Sun was at seven degrees and three minutes of Scorpio"

When you want to write down a planetary aspect, you don't want to have to write "Mars is squared to Uranus", when you can jot down

♂ □ ♅

Secondly, there is the advantage that the symbols are understood by astrologers the world over, regardless of the language they use.

Finally, there are esoteric meanings to the symbols. We have seen how the zodiac symbols are descriptive in capacity, for example, the symbol for Aries is like a ram's head, but the symbols are in many cases so ancient, going back to the earliest recorded astrology some 6,000 years ago, that they seem to have picked up an underlying force. The planetary symbols are largely made up of ancient representations such as the cross of matter, the circle of spirit, the semi-circle of soul.

When I use the symbols, I feel I am tapping in to an energy that goes back to the dawn of time and which has much more depth of meaning than the actual words. Somehow, using the symbols seems subconsciously to contribute to an easier understanding of the subject. Perhaps it is the way the brain works. It is easier to take in the principal of a planet in one symbol, than translating a string of symbols – a word – into that principal.

finding the sun's position

If you've had your chart drawn up by an astrologer, you should find the Sun's position shown on your birth chart, either to the nearest degree or in degrees and minutes. Or you may have a computer chart which has a table of planetary positions, something like this:

☉	14 ≈ 18 12	
☽	23 ♌ 07	
☿	03 ≈ 34 ℞	
♀	01 ♈ 04	
♂	19 ♏ 19	
♃	05 ♎ 45 ℞	
♄	20 ♈ 24	
♅	03 ♎ 41 ℞	
♆	28 ♏ 31	
♇	24 ♍ 44 ℞	

Computer programs give positions in degrees and minutes and sometimes seconds as well. It really is a bit pernickety giving the seconds. Firstly, most people do not know an accurate enough birth time for the seconds of longitude figure to be exactly correct, and secondly, the figure has little application anyway. In the above example, the Sun is at 14 degrees, 18 minutes and 12 seconds of Aquarius. In practice, the position to the nearest degree is sufficient for most purposes, certainly for beginners.

In this chapter, we will look at how we use a planetary ephemeris to find the Sun's degree position. An ephemeris is a set of tables which gives the zodiac positions for the Sun, Moon and planets at specific times. We will use as an example the chart for someone born in Birmingham, UK, on 3.2.69 at 8.30 in the morning. Before we can turn to this, we need to look at time.

TIME ZONES

The data in planetary ephemerides is based on Greenwich Mean Time. So before we can use the ephemeris, we have to make sure our birth time is expressed in GMT. One thing we therefore require is information about time zones. For people born in the UK no time zone adjustment is required, but, to give an example, the clock time in Washington, USA, is five hours behind GMT. So for someone born at 08:30 in Washington we would have to *add* five hours to get the birth time in GMT – 13:30. When it's 8:30 in Washington it's 13:30 in London.[i]

If the person was born on 3.2.69 at 08:30 in Melbourne, Australia, where the clock time is 10 hours ahead of GMT, we would have to *deduct* 10 hours. This would give us a GMT of 22:30 *the previous day* – 2.2.69.

The thing to remember here is that for different time zones in latitudes west of Greenwich, you add the difference, and for those to the east you deduct it.

This does at times cause problems for astrologers. It is usually possible to find the time zone in operation in a country today, but remember that with births we may be going back many, many years and sometimes time zone information is not readily available. It may not be possible to find the time zone in operation in Kuala Lumpur in June, 1923. Different sources may also give conflicting information.

SUMMER TIME

The next thing to watch for is 'daylight saving' or 'summer' time. Many countries advance their clocks by one hour during the Summer months, so here you would have to deduct one hour to get to GMT.

Again a knowledge of the clocks in operation in various countries is required. It is not always easy to get information about when daylight saving time was in force in different countries. Sometimes there is 'double Summer time', such as during some of the World War II years

---

[i] *Actually, the time in ephemeris is expressed in either 'Universal Time', or 'Ephemeris Time'. We won't go into a detailed astronomical explanation here for the differences are only matters of seconds and for all practical purposes we can refer to GMT. We will use the 24 hour clock from here onwards. Strictly speaking, GMT is always used with AM and PM, but it is easier to use the 24 hour clock when making astrological calculations.*

in the UK, when the clock was two hours ahead of GMT.[ii] There is a table of the UK Summer Time in the back of the book.

There is something of a catch in the date of 3.2.69 we are using as an illustration. As an experiment, the UK government operated daylight savings time throughout the whole period from 18.2.68 to 31.12.71, so in our example we do have to deduct an hour, even though it is not Summer.

Remember that the daylight savings time is always deducted, because clocks are always put forward in Summer.

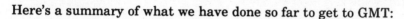

Here's a summary of what we have done so far to get to GMT:

	TIME	DATE
TIME OF BIRTH GIVEN	08:30	3.2.69
TIME ZONE ADJUSTMENT	-	
(w+/e-)		
DAYLIGHT SAVINGS TIME		
ADJUSTMENT	(01:00)	
(always deducted)	-----	
GMT TIME	07:30	3.2.69

We have to put the date in again because, as we saw above, sometimes deducting (or adding) time will change the date, though in our example, it has not altered.

Now we can turn to the ephemeris. Later in this book there is a an ephemeris covering the years 1936 to 1999.

Zodiac positions are given for midnight on the 1st, 11th and 21st of each month, in degrees and minutes of longitude for the Sun and Moon and to the nearest degree for the planets.

To find the Sun's position for our sample date of 3.2.69, first of all look up the Sun's positions on 1.2.69 and and 11.2.69. The dates are the first column, and the Sun's positions are in the third column, as

---

indicated by the Sun symbol at the top. The pertinent figures here are:

| 1.2.69 | 11 57 |
| 11.2.69 | 22 5 |

It's not easy on the eye to print the zodiac symbol in every column, so they are only included at the beginning of the year and when a planet changes sign. So going up to the previous row in the Sun column shows the symbol for Aquarius. On 1.2.69 at midnight, the Sun was at 11 degrees and 57 minutes of Aquarius, and at midnight on 11.2.69 it was at 22 degrees and 5 minutes.

Since there are ten days between these two positions, at midnight on 3.2.69 (two days on from 1.2.69), the Sun will have moved two-tenths of the distance between the two (remember there are 60 minutes to a degree):

11.2.69	22 5 ≈≈
1.2.69	11 57 ≈≈

Movement in 10 days	10 8
	=====
x 2/10 =	2 2
1.2.69	11 57 ≈≈

3.2.69 (midnight)	13 59 ≈≈

This can be rounded off to 14 degrees.

The distance moved by the Sun in one day is always very close to 1 degree.

If we did not have a time of birth, this is far as we could go. But since we have a GMT of 07:30, we can improve the accuracy by adding the movement in the 7½ hours from midnight to the time of birth:

3.2.69 (midnight)	13 59	≈
movement in 7½ hours :		
60 minutes x 7½ / 24	19	

3.2.69 (7.30 GMT)	14 18	≈

So the position of the Sun at the moment of birth was 14 degrees 18 minutes of Aquarius, or 14 degrees to the nearest degree.

Remember that since the twelve zodiac signs divide the 360 degrees of a circle into 30 degree sections, the degrees figure cannot be more than 29; also, the minutes figure can be no greater than 59. If your calculation takes you over 29 degrees and 59 minutes, you are therefore into the next zodiac sign.

As we work through the book, we can look up the positions of all the planets to the nearest degree. As we said, this is sufficient for most purposes.

THE SUN'S EXACT POSITION

If you want to go into astrology really seriously and draw up charts that are more accurate than just to the nearest degree, you will at some stage require a more detailed ephemeris, or an astrological computer program. In this section we will look at how this more detailed information is used. You can skip this if you are satisfied with positions to the nearest degree. Some suggested ephemerides are given in the section on 'Further Reading'. These give daily positions for all the planets in degrees and minutes of longitude (and sometimes seconds of longitude for Sun and Moon).

They are used in the same way as the ephemeris in this book is used. The date required is found and the figure extracted for the planet whose position is required.

So, if we want to find the Sun's position at midnight on 3.2.69, we look at the entries for February 1969.

Be careful when using an ephemeris – it's easy to pick the wrong month, or the right month but the wrong year.

Then we go across to the column with the Sun's symbol at the top. The figures will be 13 59 13, give or take a second. These are degrees, minutes and seconds of longitude. Go up the column and for the first of the month, and we see the symbol for Aquarius. So at midnight on 3.2.69, the Sun was at 13 degrees, 59 minutes and 13 seconds of Aquarius.

In our example we have a time adjusted to GMT of 07:30, so what we want is the position of the Sun at 07:30, not midnight. To find this, we need to know how far the Sun has travelled between midnight – for which we have a position in the ephemeris – and 07:30. What we can do first of all is find out how far the Sun travelled during the whole 24 hours of 3.2.69. Looking at the Sun's position at midnight on 4.2.69, the next day, we see it was at 15 degrees 0 minutes and 3 seconds of Aquarius. What we do is subtract the 3.2.69 midnight position from this. We'll make things a little easier by ignoring the seconds:

Position at midnight 4.2.69	15 00
Subtract : position at midnight 3.2.69	13 59
	------
	01 01

So during the 24 hours of the day, the Sun moved 1 degree and 1 minute. Remember that there are 60 minutes in a degree, so 1 degree and 1 minute is 61 minutes. So during the 7½ hours from midnight to the time of birth the Sun would have moved (worked out on a calculator):

7 ½ / 24 x 61 minutes = 19 minutes

All we then have to do is add this to the position at midnight on 3.2.89

Position at midnight 3.2.69	13 59
Movement from midnight to 07:30	19

Position at 07:30	14 18

We have to get used to the fact that when we get to 60 minutes, the next minute takes us into the next degree.

If the sign has changed from one midnight to the next, the easiest way to do the calculation is to add 30 degrees to the second time.

For an example we could take someone born in the UK at 10:30 on

20.1.69; deducting the hour for daylight savings time gives us 09:30 GMT. The calculations then are:

Position at midnight 21.1.69	00 47 ♒
Add 30 degrees	30 00
	------
	30 47
Subtract: position at midnight 20.1.69	29 46
	------
	01 01

9½ / 24 x 61 minutes = 24 minutes

Position at midnight 20.1.69	29 46 ♑
Movement from midnight to 09:30	24

Position at 09:30	00 10 ♒

One thing to be careful of is that some ephemerides give the daily positions of the planets at NOON, in which case you have to adapt your calculations accordingly.

It should be pointed out here that the movement of the Sun or any planet may not strictly be exactly proportional throughout a day. For all practical purposes, we need not worry about this.

part two

the moon

Astrologers do not just use the Sun. They use other heavenly bodies as well. The most obvious one after the Sun is the Moon. All cultures know about the Moon, even if they are not aware of the planets. The Sun and Moon have been worshipped as deities by most cultures. Even today there is an American Indian tribe whose culture states that it is their purpose on Earth to engage in rituals that will make the Sun rise every day. When their beliefs are lost, it is said, when they stop performing the religious ceremonies, within a few years the planet will fall into chaos. The Sun and Moon are seen as representing primal forces in our experience.

The Moon is not that large – about 2,160 miles in diameter – but its proximity to the Earth makes it appear larger in the sky than any other body except the Sun, and in relation to the Earth – at about 1/80 of the Earth's mass – it is actually proportionately larger in relation to its planet than any other planetary satellite in the solar system (excepting perhaps Pluto's satellite Charon, which is proportionately large, but is so far away we can't be sure of it's exact size).

*receptivity
emotions
security
conditioning
changeability*

MOON

Here's the symbol for the Moon. It's an easy one. It's always, as far as I know, drawn this way around, in the waxing phase. Think of it as the shape made by a pair of cupped hands, there to receive what life has to offer and react to it. The Sun goes out and gets things, the Moon receives; the Sun expresses, the Moon reacts.

We have seen how the Sun, by its changing position against the star background effectively travels through all the signs in the zodiac. Now let us consider the Moon. Since it orbits the Earth about every 27⅓days, it must pass through all the zodiac signs during that period. During one complete revolution, it will stay in each sign for, on average, 2¼ days (the period in each sign will vary slightly because the Moon's orbit of the Earth is elliptical rather than exactly circular). So we can see that during the thirty or so days that the Sun stays in one sign, the Moon will have passed through all of them. For example, at 5:38 GMT on 20.1.69, the Sun moved into Aquarius, the Moon at this time being in Aquarius as well. Later that day, at 09:20 GMT, the Moon moved into Pisces, and at 13:43 on 22.1.69 it moved on into Aries. By 15.2.69, the Moon was in Aquarius again – having in the mean time passed though all the intervening signs of the zodiac. On 18.2.69, when the Sun passed into Pisces, the Moon was in Pisces.

FINDING THE MOON'S POSITION

We can work out someone's Moon position in the same way that we did for the Sun. Let's take our birth details of 3.2.69, 08:30, (07:30 GMT) Birmingham again.

As before, look up the positions for 1.2.69 and 11.2.69, but this time for the Moon column :

1.2.69	24 ⊙ 42
11.2.69	5 ↗ 5

We can see that the Moon has moved a long way in the ten days, from 25 degrees of Cancer, through Leo, Virgo, Libra and Scorpio to 5 degrees of Sagittarius. At 30 degrees a sign, it works out at approximately 130 degrees in the ten days, or on average 13 degrees a day.

At midnight on 3.2.69, therefore, the Moon's position was approximately:

1.2.69	24 ⊙
add 2 x 13	26

3.2.69 (midnight)	20 ♌
add 7 1/2/24 x 13	4

3.2.69 (07:30 GMT)	24 ♌

Note that, because the Moon's orbit is elliptical, it does not move proportionally through the signs from day to day. Therefore, its position calculated using this method may be slightly inaccurate (for example, here the exact Moon position works out nearer 23 degrees than 24). For most purposes, it will not be significant, but you should be aware that this could be important if the position works out to be near a change of sign. An inaccurate birth time will in any case add to the possible discrepancy even if more accurate methods are used.

A MORE ACCURATE MOON POSITION

Again, it is possible to use a full ephemeris to get a Moon position in degrees and minutes. These more accurate figures work out as follows:

Position at midnight 4.2.69	01 ♍ 44	
Add 30 degrees (because sign has changed)	30	00

	31	44
Subtract: position at midnight 3.2.69	19 ♌ 14	

	12	30

During the 24 hours, the Moon moved 12 degrees and 30 minutes, which equals 750 minutes ((12 x 60) + 30). So during the 7½ hours from midnight to the time of birth the Moon would have moved:

7½ / 24 x 750 minutes = 234 minutes

= 3 degrees 54 minutes

This we add this to the position at midnight on 3.2.89

Position at midnight 3.2.69	19 ♌ 14	
Movement from midnight to 07:30	03	54

Position at 07:30	23 ♌ 08	

THE NEED FOR AN ACCURATE BIRTH TIME

Computing the Moon's position is an area where having a birth time is important. It does not usually matter too much with the Sun, because it only moves a degree per day, so unless the Sun changed sign on the day in question, you cannot be far out. But because the Moon moves so fast (between 11½ and 15 degrees in a day), quite often you will not even know the Moon's sign, let alone its position to the nearest degree, when the birth time is not known.

As we will see later, it's not just the Moon's position that is affected here. An accurate time also enables us to work out the sign on the horizon and plot the positions of the astrological 'houses', and so establish in which part of the birth chart each planet is placed. So it is important to find it out if you can.

Unfortunately, many people do not know their time of birth. Today, in many countries the times of hospital births are noted in the medical papers and on baby's identity tag. In practice, even this time is not exact because the staff are usually too busy with the birth to bother with something as apparently trivial as a birth time. I understand in France it has been noted on the birth certificate for many years.

If you cannot find the exact birth time an approximate time of birth will often suffice. For other people, a few minutes might make all the difference. In either case, the more inaccurate the time, the more chance that errors in the chart will creep in and thus interpretation will be affected.

Some people find that if the information is really necessary it unexpectedly turns up. A relative may suddenly appear on the scene and just happens to mention she was there when you were born. Or you may come across some old correspondence. Don't go deliberately hunting for such obscure sources, though. Let the unexpected happen. Uranus, the planet whose energy is most connected with astrology, is the planet of the unexpected. If you are familiar with dowsing techniques, you could try using a pendulum to find a time, or refine an approximate one.

When someone really doesn't know their time of birth, we can draw up a chart based on a birth time of midday. However, as with the Sun signs, one Moon sign varies considerably from the next. So if the Moon has changed sign that day, it may be possible to start narrowing down the time of birth by examining the characteristics of the two possible Moon signs and seeing which fits. Since the astrologer will know the exact time the change of sign took place, one can at least reduce the likely time period during which the birth took place.

It is possible to do this because the Moon is such an important factor in astrology. With experience, one can start to guess at people's Moon, let alone Sun, signs. As the treadmill continues to churn out more and more popularised astrology books, perhaps we will get away from Sun sign books and start seeing more paperbacks on Moon signs. Before we look at what the Moon means when it is found in each of the zodiac signs, we must look at what the meanings associated with the Moon are in general.

The Moon has traditionally been considered as fickle – consider the way her apparent shape changes as she goes through the various phases from new to full and back again. *Why she*? The Moon has inevitably been considered as female in all cultures as opposed the Sun's perceived masculinity. Sun as father, Moon as mother.

The Moon energy is concerned with many aspects of life. Its energy manifests very easily on an everyday level. Perhaps, because of its receptive nature, it's the energy that often comes out when we're about our everyday business, not really thinking about what we are doing.

HABITS and CONDITIONING

As we have said, the Moon is held to be a female planetary body. The Moon shows the sort of energy we pick up from our mother, or mother-figures early in life. Above all the Moon is about the sort of conditioning we are subjected to during the first few years. The person the majority of people have most contact with during the first two or three years of life is the mother. If mother isn't there, for whatever reason, we will look to whoever is around for our information. The infant often has no other guide for how it should behave than what mother is doing. Babies are generally very passive and receptive and are very open to what is going on around them. Parents just do not seem to realise that how they behave, not just to baby but to everyone around them, during early childhood, right from birth (or even before) are picked up by the child. Right from the time baby comes into the world it will be seeking information and will be soaking up what is going on around them.

SECURITY

We often think of mothers as providing security. The Moon becomes synonymous with security. You need to get your Moon position working smoothly to provide the stable base from which to launch out into other things. We saw that Taurus is a sign concerned very much with material things, comforts and beliefs. People born with the Moon in Taurus seem to need a strong material base before they feel secure. They must have things to touch, some material possessions, which sometimes may be valueless to everyone else but mean the world to them. Often they feel they must have definite beliefs to fall back on. Without these things they feel insecure and cannot get the rest of their life together. Moon-in-Aquarius people get insecure if they haven't got lots of friends. They feel insecure if the friends get too close, through the Aquarian sense of detachment and individualism.

FEELINGS

The Moon is concerned with our feelings, how we respond emotionally to day-to-day problems. Moon-in-Scorpio people get all worked up and paranoid about little daily problems that everyone else copes with without thinking. Moon-in-Aries try and resolve problems before they have even cropped up; in fact they can be so impulsively ahead of everyone they can end up causing the problems in the first place. Because for most of us our feelings are expressed most easily through speech, the Moon says a lot about the way we talk.

Looking at the Moon signs of people around you and seeing how they talk about what they feel, is a good way to begin exploring Moon signs.

WOMEN

Its very easy to grow up subconsciously thinking that all women are like our mothers. A woman may try and behave like her Moon sign because she thinks that is the correct way for her to behave in her female role. In a man's chart, the Moon marks the feminine side of his nature, and what he tends to look for in a woman. For smooth relationships, ones where you are actually living with someone, compatible Moon signs are a great help.

FOOD

Perhaps nowhere is our daily routine more enshrined than in our

61

eating habits. We have to eat to survive, and most of us do it several times a day, often at regular times. People with Moon in Cancer, cling on to the past, and do not like to risk anything new. They're quite happy with the food they have had for years, even if it is bland, boring or unhealthy. People with the Moon in Virgo behave in typical Virgoan style towards food. They pick at it and worry what is in it, go on food fads and hope you sterilised the plates you served their meal on. Moon in Sagittarius ones tend to eat all you give them in true expansive, Sagittarian manner.

DOMESTICITY

When discussing the Moon's effect, domestic affairs always seem to come up. Most of us organise our daily lives around a routine and that is centred on the home. The exceptions are the Moon in Pisces people, where the wishy-washy Piscean energy tends to make things very disorganised. When we discover planetary aspects, we will see that difficult aspects involving the Moon tend to make for domestic disharmony, and that home-life goes smoother with the softer aspects.

FICKLENESS

Of course, with some Moons, fickly changing all the time may be a habit in itself. Where the Moon is in your chart shows the area of your life that your feelings are likely to change about, where you are likely to go through phases. Because of the Virgo connection with food, Virgoan Moons tend to be food faddists. Moon-in-Scorpios can go on and off sex. Moon-in-Geminis get fickle about everything.

The connection with the Moon and security means that it is very easy to persist with bad Moon-sign habits. They come out just when you are not expecting it, when you're about your everyday business. It's easy to act without thinking in habitual, Moon-sign ways, rather than reacting spontaneously to the present.

Here are some comments on the how the Moon energy manifests itself through each of the zodiac signs.

moon signs

Moon in ARIES

When they want something, people with this Moon want it straight away. If they have to wait for something, they lose interest and this can make they seem infuriatingly unreliable to other people, as they mess people around, breaking appointments or as they realise that what they thought was wonderful yesterday, they've given up on today. They make impulsive changes to their daily routine and then regret it.

They want to be in charge in the home. That is true particularly of women. The men may seek a woman who will take charge domestically.

When it comes to food, Moon in Aries has "eyes bigger than its belly".

The receptive quality of the Moon does not go well with Aries' assertiveness, so they are usually not very good listeners and they always want to have their say first.

Moon in TAURUS

People with the Moon in sensuous, materialistic Taurus seem to attract the good things in life. It's easy to become attracted to particular possessions, which may often have no value other than a sentimental one. If they are depressed, they like to have their 'things' around them. They are good at running a home, but this aspect of their life may have too much emphasis. They need the security of domestic and financial well-being before they can really be happy with their life.

Common sense solutions to problems are the ones that appeal, and being reliable is important. Thus they may find people come to trust them, seeing them as a shoulder to cry on. They make good listeners, staying unflappable as people pour out their problems. They are not quick to commit themselves emotionally, so often romantic partnerships do not crystallise until later in life. Once involved in a relationship they are loyal and supportive.

It is a good game to play, trying to find something that will shock the Taurean Moon. Very little does, and even when something does finally offend, they still do not provoke any reaction.

Sometimes security is sought in attachments to beliefs rather than material things. It is easy for them to have an rigid outlook on life, and their conditioning is to react to obstacles by being stubborn and unresponsive.

Moon in GEMINI

Moon-in-Gemini's talk about anything. They chatter about their own feelings, but it may not occur to them that people do not always want to hear about them. Those feelings can change from day to day as well. They try and rationalise their feelings, but emotions are not like that and if there's no-one to talk to, they get fed up.

This Moon is quick-witted and can always think of something to say, always coming up with ideas to solve day-to-day problems, but it lacks the concentration to follow through on those ideas, and others might get tired of hearing all their suggestions, however helpful they're trying to be. It's a fidgety Moon, that doesn't like sitting still for a minute.

Moon in CANCER

This is the most habitual Moon of all. The Moon's at home in Cancer. The Moon-in-Cancer person is at home doing the same old routine, day after day, year after year. People with this Moon need to be careful that when they are continuing to do something they are doing it because it's useful or satisfactory, not just out of habit, it is easy to carry on doing things habitually after they cease to become necessary.

A secure and stable domestic situation is of paramount importance to their emotional health. Because of the link with the past inherent with both the Moon and the Cancerian energy, it is also very easy to become trapped in the past. The biggest thing for this Moon position is letting go of unfruitful situations and relationships.

It is a very caring, protective Moon, but these people are so tied to the Moon energy that every time the Moon changes sign (every 2¼ days) they change too. Thus they get a deserved reputation for moodiness.

64

Moon in LEO

This Moon demands respect in everyday situations and gets self-important and stubborn when it does not get it.

People who live with a Moon-in-Leo person can end up rushing around doing everything for them, catering to their every whim and fancy. Moon-in-Leo's think they are the king and queen of their home and everyone else is their minion.

This Moon can make someone a good organiser, but they expect too much from those they are ordering about, who get mad at how Moon-in-Leo is not doing any *real* work. They are happy when they are centre stage and can take charge in dramatic situations. Sometimes the drama occurred because they overreacted.

The urge for self-dramatisation can be made up for by their sincere attempts at self-improvement and their sunny disposition.

Moon in VIRGO

They tend to be over-critical of others and this can lead to them being thought of as a nag, particularly in the domestic situation. They also tend to look on the black side when opportunities are presented to them, looking for the detail that spoils the overall plan and then rejecting it. Fussiness can particularly extend to food. They are usually interested in a healthy diet, but they can be too particular about what they should or should not eat.

They like to have little routines, but then are surprised that, when they fail to stick to them, their oversight is immediately pointed out. After all, that is what they do to others. This Moon likes things clean and tidy. It will help you get on and do the housework. They like things to be in their proper place. But they too have a few nasty little habits themselves.

Because they will work out things in detail, they can be practical at finding solutions to everyday problems. They feel insecure if they are not actually doing something that they think is of use.

Moon in LIBRA

Moon-in-Libra's hate to do anything unharmonious so they will agree with everything you say. Usually their feelings are impulsive so they blurt things out and then spend all their time backtracking in case they have upset you.

This Moon positions seeks security in friendship and harmony, so, with typical Libran superficiality, they'll present a friendly, placid face to the world, whilst inside they might be a bag of nerves. They only feel secure if they have partner.

People with this Moon like to be fair. They will give credit where it's due and expect the same in return. This Moon can cause problems in a domestic situation by being too nice. They will always agree with what their partner wants to do. They mean it, but they do not get a proper feedback from them. They end up with other people's feelings inside them instead of their own.

Moon in SCORPIO

This is perhaps the most difficult Moon of all. It feels things with the depth of Scorpio intensity and learns from an early age that it gets easily hurt – and so responds by shutting off its feelings.

People with this Moon just hate showing emotion. They feel vulnerable and tend to see everything as a threat. Little day to day events are seen as challenges to their authority. Little hiccoughs that most people sort out with barely a thought seem enormous obstacles. They get blown up out of all proportion and can end up being *real* problems.

As with all the difficult astrological configurations, there's another side to the coin. The worst ones also have the biggest potential for improvement.

They'll tell you it's best to have the Moon in Cancer or Taurus. They are perhaps the easiest Moons, but what good does it do living in the past all the time, or losing yourself in possessions and beliefs? With this Moon you have power. The Scorpio connection means that no other Moon has as much potential for breaking with the past. The conditioning of many years can be thrown over and a totally new productive lifestyle initiated. This deepest of feeling Moons can really reach an understanding of the nature of desires and eliminate all those that do not arise from genuine needs.

Moon in SAGITTARIUS

Those with this Moon have lofty aspirations. They aspire to high goals in their day-to-day life, but realism is not this Moon's forté. Realism is not fun. They can appear unreliable through expressing their aspirations, saying they are going to do this and that, but then failing to take practical steps to achieve them. There is a desire to travel and see the world, but whether this becomes a reality or remains fantasy is up to them.

Religious and philosophical beliefs are picked up in early childhood by this Moon. They are strongly influenced by their parents and their sense of morality is based upon what they learnt from them. They can lack objectivity about the wider social issues of life, basing judgements on the moral viewpoint instilled in childhood. Opinionation becomes a problem.

There is a tendency to exaggerate at times, and they place too much importance on their home and family, particularly the influence of their parents. They would like to live in a palace. All Moon-related areas may be subject to some form of exaggeration. That is why so many with this Moon have huge appetites, if not for food, for fun.

They need to feel they are on their way somewhere and do not like being tied down to a routine job. They may refuse to acknowledge the truth about themselves, to grow up and accept responsibilities. They try to ignore things which spoil their fun, and so everything can end up in their eyes as someone else's problem, not theirs.

Moon in CAPRICORN

This is a bit sobering after the previous Moon. It brings a restrictive early home environment so that they look back on childhood with a serious view. Their parents, or circumstances, probably forced them to 'stand on their own feet' at too early an age.

When they feel that someone has become of no use to them, they leave that person. Somewhere along the line, it was instilled in them by their parents that they can only be loved if they are successful in terms of power, career or money. They strive to be better than everyone else and to compete rather than co-operate. They feel that emotions must have a practical purpose, so they only get friendly when they want something.

They overreact to criticism or imagined slights and seek security by withdrawing into themselves and their desires.

They can make hard workers, and it is important that they get their career sorted out before anything else really works. There is also a tendency to form relationships for reasons of security.

Sometimes these Moons find mealtimes an annoyance and wish it all came in pills and plastic tubes.

Moon in AQUARIUS

Above all this Moon seeks security in friends and social groups. People can get a strange sense of detachment emanating from a Moon-in-Aquarius when they first meet him, which may be off-putting, but if they take the time to get to know him, and give him enough freedom, they can have a very supportive companion.

Someone with this Moon does not like to become emotionally tied to anyone and probably dislikes to see displays of emotion. They may not like, or be prepared to admit the fact that we are all influenced by our emotional states. If they are able to remember their early childhood, they may find that there was much encouragement given to them to find their own way and express themselves individualistically. It may also be, however, that mother was somewhat emotionally cold towards them and so they never learned the accepted emotional responses. In a family, it is always the Moon-in-Aquarius kid that gets left out while his brothers and sisters are feted.

Housework is not their strong point. So they may get lots of gadgets to try and deal with this problem, get friends in to do household jobs, or 'provide work' for a cleaner or a cook – particularly if they will prepare exotic and unusual meals for them. They try and work out solutions to day-to-day problems intellectually, rationalising emotions. Anything which makes a change from routine is welcomed.

Moon in PISCES

As with all things Piscean, there is a sense of understanding and a sense of deception. All areas affected by the Moon can be subject to this. They have the possibility of an excellent home life, with very understanding familial relationships – but it could so easily be an illusion. Day-to-day routine is something of a drag and it is difficult to actually plan things.

Very sensitive to their surroundings, the Moon-in-Pisces person picks up the thoughts and emotions of those around them. With this Moon they can be psychically aware of what the people around them are thinking and feeling. Because they so easily pick up these energies it may be necessary to spend time on their own, or engage in some form of cleansing practices, to rid themselves of the negative energies they have absorbed.

They have a vivid imagination and can be artistically inspired. They are kind and compassionate but easily hurt and can tend towards mild paranoia. Their intuition is not always correct and they may ascribe hurtful thoughts or feelings to others, or think they are silently blaming them for things, when they are not.

We have just applied some of the basic characteristics of each zodiac sign, such as we explored when we looked at each of the Sun signs in turn, to the areas of life that we said the Moon related to, feelings, habits, going-through-phases etc.

> **If you know the underlying principles, you do not need a text book to learn parrot-fashion from, because you can start to work things out for yourself. For example :**
>
> **Gemini = communicating a lot**
>
> **Moon = feelings**
>
> **Moon + Gemini = talk about their feelings a lot**

Of course, that simplification is not everything. One can go on and blend all the various characteristics of Gemini and the Moon. And, there are characteristics which are not always readily ascertained from such basic principles. They have arisen from the experience of astrologers over the centuries, which has continued to be refined. It seems with modern methods we may be about to experience a vast increase in the information which astrologers are able to provide. If you start looking at other people's birth charts, your experience will enable you to add your own interpretations.

One thing of which we must beware is that not all the possible characteristics that can be attributed to one Moon sign, say, will apply to every individual with the Moon in that sign. There will be the occasional Moon-in-Gemini who is not a good talker. When you do find instances like that, often there is an explanation, as we will see later, such as another planet affecting the Moon's influence. Even so, some things just cannot be explained by astrology.

 Little things you can look out for with the MOON signs of people you know:

ARIES	late for (or cancel) appointments; order too much food in restaurants.
TAURUS	totally unshockable; marry late.
GEMINI	talk, talk, talk ...
CANCER	always stick to the same old routine; moody.
LEO	need to be the centre of attention; think that they are still children.
VIRGO	point out your nasty habits – and ignore their own.
LIBRA	agree with whatever you say.
SCORPIO	feel they are persecuted; want you to make all the decisions.
SAGITTARIUS	opinionated; think it's always someone else's problem.
CAPRICORN	they can be very nice – when they want something.
AQUARIUS	hate to get intimate; aloof from parents.
PISCES	always think it's *their* fault.

part three

elements and qualities

Here are the symbols for the other planets:

☿	Mercury	♀	Venus	♂	Mars
♃	Jupiter	♄	Saturn	♅	Uranus
♆	Neptune	♇	Pluto		

We can use the ephemeris to look up positions for all of the planets. We can refer to the planetary symbols above, and the symbols for the zodiac signs to see at a glance which sign each planet is in for a given date. For our date of 3.2.69 these are:

Sun	Aquarius
Moon	Leo
Mercury	Aquarius
Venus	Aries
Mars	Scorpio
Jupiter	Libra
Saturn	Aries
Uranus	Libra
Neptune	Scorpio
Pluto	Virgo

We have seen the sort of characteristics associated with a Leo Moon – seeking security through being respected, a need to feel centre-stage, naturally sunny emotions. We can go on say things about the other planets in this birth date. Mercury in Aquarius is intellectually inventive, Venus in Aries has impulsive desires, a Scorpio Mars tends to act secretively, and so on.

With experience you learn the characteristics of all the planets and all the signs, so, at a glance, will be able to give some quite detailed information without actually drawing

up a chart, just from the sign each planet is in.

Another thing that we can do at this stage is to consider the distribution of the planets by sign according to the astrological 'elements' and 'qualities'. This should also help us to learn more about the nature of each sign.

ELEMENTS

Western astrologers use four elements: fire, earth, air and water. Each sign is particularly associated with one element, which means three signs to each element. The old fogey school sometimes refers to them as the 'triplicities'.

FIRE signs are the ones concerned with action and idealism.

EARTH signs are the practical, pragmatic ones.

AIR signs represent the intellectual part of us, the ideas.

WATER signs concern themselves with feelings and intuition.

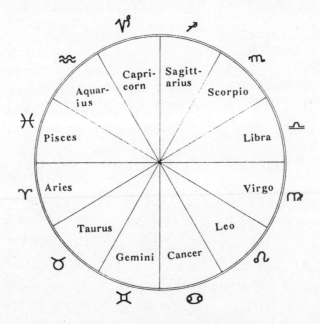

Here is a zodiac wheel with all the signs marked in. Let's start with Aries first. It is a fire sign. People with this Sun are often described as fiery. Aries wants to go out and do things, get things started — take action. Often their idealism involves seeing the best in everybody and really believing that they will finish all the things they set out to do.

Next comes Taurus, an earth sign. Here's a most reliable, down-to-earth sign. Taurus can come up with practical solutions. There is also the sensuality and materialism associated with the earthy nature.

Gemini is next, an air sign, full of ideas and communication. Ephemeral, difficult to pin down.

Water is the element associated with Cancer. This emotional sign has very deep feelings. It operates on what it feels, not upon ideals, practicality or ideas.

Next there's Leo, and we're back with the fire. Leos are idealistic too. They like to take action so that they can be seen to be in command and their idealism often leads to a geniality and faith in others that can turn out to be very unproductive. They get stuck in ruts because they idealistically think something will turn up to help them out. Usually it does not, but they still go on believing.

Virgo is an earth sign. Highly practical and concerned only with the nitty-gritty and what will produce material results.

We started at Aries and allocated Fire, Earth, Air, Water, Fire, Earth and so on. If we carry on around the zodiac wheel, we go all the way round and end up with watery Pisces. Note that Aquarius is not a water sign, but airy. The water-bearer is merely symbolic of the knowledge (an air characteristic) Aquarius pours out to nourish the world.

QUALITIES

This is perhaps a confusing word, because it does not have the modern sense of something which is of good value, but the less usual (and original meaning) of that characteristic which distinguishes one thing from something else. Originally, if a haberdasher was described as selling "materials of different qualities", it merely meant a variety of materials with different characteristics. Nowadays, the phrase has obtained a pejorative sense that some of the materials are intrinsically better than others, when all it meant was that some of those for sale are better suited for different purposes than others.

So when we refer to the astrological qualities we do not mean that some are better than others, nor are we talking about your good points.

It can get confusing when we start to use the word in its modern sense and say things like "your horoscope will reveal both your failings and qualities". To get round this, some people use the word 'modes' instead of qualities. 'Mode' is perhaps easier than the old term 'quadruplicities' – that might lead you to believe that there are four of them – in fact there are four signs of each of the three qualities:

CARDINAL signs are the instigators, the impulsive ones that get things off the ground.

FIXED ones are the steady, reliable, stick-in-the-mud signs that persevere with things.

MUTABLE signs finish things off. They are adaptable, changing to suit their surroundings – or evade responsibility.

As we did with the elements, we can go back to the zodiac wheel and find which sign has which quality.

Let's start with Libra this time. Definitely impulsive, always coming up with ideas to start things off but not so good at persevering; they lose interest as a new idea presents itself and for all their sense of balance end up making impulsive decisions. This is a cardinal sign.

Then there is Scorpio. Once moving, it can be difficult to deter a Scorpio from what he has set out to achieve. It is the sign of obsession and a memory that never forgives or forgets and will not change for anyone. Definitely fixed.

As you should by now expect, the following sign, Sagittarius, is mutable. It is a highly adaptable one, able to change when faced with different situations and which would rather change to evade responsibilities than face up to the current problem.

Then we are back to cardinality again, with Capricorn. This is the sign of order. And one meaning of the word is to order you around. Capricorn's cardinality comes up with the practical solutions, but would rather get you to actually put them into practice. They start organising before you have realised there was anything to be organised. They are not the best concentrators either, and would rather delegate than have to slug away at the same old thing.

And so on around the wheel, cardinal, fixed, mutable, cardinal, fixed and so on.

With four elements and three qualities, we can describe each of the signs uniquely by combining the two. As follows:

	QUALITY	ELEMENT
ARIES	Cardinal	Fire
TAURUS	Fixed	Earth
GEMINI	Mutable	Air
CANCER	Cardinal	Water
LEO	Fixed	Fire
VIRGO	Mutable	Earth
LIBRA	Cardinal	Air
SCORPIO	Fixed	Water
SAGITTARIUS	Mutable	Fire
CAPRICORN	Cardinal	Earth
AQUARIUS	Fixed	Air
PISCES	Mutable	Water

The qualities and elements can be used to help you remember what each sign is like.

Aries is impulsive in action, Taurus steady and practical and so on. We can also play a little game and invent some analogies to describe the signs in the above table.

If we take the fire signs, we could think of Aries as brushwood. You set fire to it and it blazes up and provides tremendous heat for a while – but it soon goes out without constant re-stoking. Leo is more like a log fire, difficult to start, but it will burn all night. Sagittarius is more like a finely tunable stove. You can turn it down at night so that very little fuel is used, and then first thing next morning, open it up again and away she goes, but it is somewhat unreliable.

What about air? I suppose we could use an air balloon. Libra is the gusts of air used to inflate it and get it off the ground. Aquarius is the steady air inside the balloon that keep it in the air. Gemini is the hot air burner used to adjust the altitude.

I expect you could think up some better ones. How about thinking up some for Earth and Water? For Earth, you could think of a building rather than the land itself.

What about that last suggestion? The cardinal ones among you will start off with good intentions about thinking of analogies but soon lose interest and give up. The fixed ones will persevere, if they can manage to summon up the energy to start. The mutable ones could come up with good solutions, but might try and avoid doing it altogether – after all, an answer will be given in a few lines time. Notice how with astrology, there are nearly always two sides to things.

Here are some suggestions for Earth and Water:

Earth: Capricorn, the architect/designer; Taurus the bricklayer/roofer; Virgo, attends to the details, the doorknobs, kitchenware, goes around making sure everything was done right by the first two.

Water: Cancer, a spring; Scorpio, a river (or an iceberg?); Pisces, the ocean.

If you know what sign each planet is in, you can say how many planets there are in each element in quality. For our sample date, they work out like this:

PLANETS BY SIGN

Elements		Qualities	
Fire	3	Cardinal	4
Earth	1	Fixed	5
Air	4	Mutable	1
Water	2		

 The distribution of elements and qualities alone is enough to say a lot about someone.

The pertinent factors in the above tables are a shortage of planets in Earth and in mutable signs. It is perhaps best for you if there is a fairly balanced split, like 3-3-2-2 for elements and 4-3-3 for qualities, because this balance of energies helps give you a good all round approach. The distribution for most people does not usually turn out as balanced as that. And it has to be said that, like most things in astrology, whilst harmonious, balancing factors make your life easier, imbalances and disharmonies tend to prompt you to actually do something with your life. Here are some things we can say about the distribution of elements and qualities in a chart.

DISTRIBUTION OF ELEMENTS

The main point to remember with elements is that we tend to seek the element we are short of, as if we are trying to rectify an imbalance. Having a lot of fire doesn't make you 'fiery' – if anything it tends to have the opposite effect.

ABUNDANCE – say, five or more planets in one element:

FIRE – makes you inspired but super idealistic. The fiery stuff tends to only come out with people they know – with strangers these people can be quite shy. They expect everyone to be mind readers – problems can be caused because they idealistically expect everyone to know just what they want without them having to ask for it. So they stay quiet and then wonder why they do not get it.

EARTH – inherently practical, but may not see it as particularly important to be so. They may not regard security and stability as important so have little regard for doing or saying things that might backfire. They may tend to rigidly do things just how they want to do them without thinking of anyone else.

AIR – because there's already potentially a lot of it, intellectual development may be ignored. Lots-of-air people are mainly interested in a changing environment, particularly if they can do lots of communicating. Abundance of air brings a good sense of detachment which can be useful but may make others regard them as cool or unemotional.

WATER – if you have got lots of water, you're so sensitive, so emotional that you actually shut off your feelings and can appear exactly the opposite. Water is reluctant to get involved in relationships just in case it gets hurt. Often these people may run their lives along a rigid routine to avoid any possible upsets change might bring.

LACK – say, nought or one in an element:

FIRE – with no fire there is a lack of inspiration. These people may therefore learn to seek it and have a desire for action that makes actually doing something seem all important, even when considered non-action might be more prudent. No-fire people need lots of attention, constant re-assurance that they are nice people. This can upset others as they try to prove themselves by imposing their own needs on others. Often there is strong career-orientation in the desire to prove their worth.

EARTH – here practical considerations become all important, because no-Earth people sense their inherent lack of practicality. Everything stands or falls by its practical worth – this can be very valuable so long as they do not take it to extremes. There is a lack self-assurance and maybe a willingness to go to great lengths to acquire money or possessions or position in an attempt to gain security. There is a tendency to hang on to relationships that have outlived their productive life.

AIR – you seek intellectual improvement. Some no-air people are head-stuck-in-a-book types, or go on further education courses. They want to find things out, and their willingness to take in new ideas means they are not usually boring. The no-air mind stays fresh and does not easily get in a rut, but the way it is always swanning off after some new idea can irritate people, and it may lack a sense of detachment.

WATER – with a lack of water, you need to be very aware of people's feelings. It is easy to tread on their toes because you do not have the inherent understanding of just how deep the other person's feelings might be. These people may overreact because they seek emotional experiences to make up for the shortage of the element and will try to wring every last drop of feeling from any experience.

DISTRIBUTION OF QUALITIES

With these, there does not seem to be the opposite effect that often occurs when there is an abundance or lack of an element.

ABUNDANCE – say five or more planets in one quality:

CARDINAL – tends to make people leap into new situations without the necessary forethought. Though there is an abundance of energy, much of it is wasted in extricating themselves from situations they have jumped into without care. There may be a lot of tension if they cannot channel the energy productively, but bottle it up instead.

FIXED – here there is likely to be excessive stubbornness and rigidity in outlook. Though fixed people have the energy to persevere, they become easily stuck in a rut and may be blind to the views of others. On the other hand, they will weather storms when less fixed people fail.

MUTABLE – the problem here seems to be that, whilst they can put the finishing touches to things and be very open to the new, these people can rush around without ever settling for long enough on anything to do it justice. Mutables are highly adaptable, but can be easily persuaded – everyone sounds so convincing. They might end up rushing around doing things for other people and forgetting what is really best for them.

LACK – say nought or one in a quality:

CARDINAL – there is often a problem with a lack of actual physical energy. It can seem so difficult to actually get motivated and moving. It is easy to get into trouble through taking on things they don't have the resources to complete.

FIXED – usually there is a sense of instability that means these people do not fix around a set of values. Whilst this is probably commendable, it can cause problems because there is no place of security to retreat to in times of crisis.

MUTABLE – these people are not that bothered about what others say or do, but those with a low mutable count can be unresponsive to new ideas. They may be too interested in their own affairs and unconcerned with those of others – this can particularly cause difficulties in relationships if they are not interested in the other person's needs.

We could combine the effects of the above. Someone with lots of cardinal planets but no fire will feel the need to rush around and get involved in all sorts of things, but will lack the underlying energy to be successful and probably get very physically tired. Someone with lots of fire and no air, will always be idealistically reading up about new things but likely to remain a perpetual student with no concrete results.

All the above are obviously interactive – a shortage of one element may also mean an abundance of another. We could go on to list all sorts of combinations of the above. You could look at the planets of the people you know and work it out for yourself.

With these distributions, you should also remember that some planets are probably having a greater effect than others. For example, the Sun and Moon are so important that they may have a disproportionate effect. If you have seven fixed planets, but the Sun is mutable, the easily accessible solar energy means you will not be as rigid as someone with six fixed planets which include the Sun. If your lone fiery planet is the Sun, it is much more useful than it being Saturn, which does not particularly work well in fire signs.

Perhaps in time, we may be able to develop a system of weighting of the planetary energies that will produce even more useful distribution figures. As well as the Sun and Moon, we will see later that the inner planets Mercury, Venus and Mars tend to carry more weight that the outer ones. Together these five are know as the 'personal' planets, because they act more internally, rather than the more external factors brought to bear by the outer planets.

part four

planetary positions

We can use the ephemeris to find the positions of Mercury, Venus and Mars. For our sample chart, these are, respectively, 4 degrees of Aquarius, 1 degree of Aries and 19 degrees of Scorpio.

If we look at the positions for the Sun and Moon over several months, we will see that they move through the zodiac at a fairly regular rate, the Sun by about one degree per day, for example. But if we look at Mercury's position we see on 1.2.69 it is at 6≈, but by 11.2.69 it has moved lower to 0≈. By 21.2.69 it is back at 6≈. If you follow Mercury's movement over the next few months, you will see that it then continues to move forwards, usually by one or two degrees a day. Starting in the middle of May, however, it again goes through a period where its movement seems to be backwards.

RETROGRADES

The word given to describe this motion is 'retrogradation' – Mercury here is said to be 'retrograde', which translates literally as 'moving backwards'. The planet is not actually moving backwards in space – it is carrying on along its orbit around the Sun as usual. The phenomenon is brought about because of the combined movements of Mercury and the Earth taken together. Relative to an observer on Earth, it appears that Mercury is moving backwards.

Here are some examples to help explain how planets have retrograde movement. In (i), a cat is sedately walking along a path, past a dog who is tied to a post. The box in the right hand corner shows how the dog sees the cat in front of the trees and people beyond the path. In (ii), the cat has moved on a little and the dog has run round, straining on his leash; to the dog, the cat now appears to be in front of the people. By (iii) the cat has walked on some more and the dog has run round more too – but it appears to the dog that the cat is still in front of the people.

When, as in (iv), both animals have moved on further, it appears to the dog that the cat is now in front of the bush, having moved backwards, whereas actually the cat has moved further along the path as before. Finally in (v), the dog is pulling his leash back round behind

the post again and the cat now appears to him to be moving forwards
again.

(i)

(ii)

(iii)

(iv)

(v)

Relating this example to astronomy, the post is the Sun, the dog the Earth, the cat an outer planet, and the trees and people are the star background! A similar process operates in respect of planets orbiting closer to the Sun than the Earth.

In a full ephemeris, the letter "R" is included to denote the day on which a planet goes retrograde. When it begins to move forwards again, the letter "D" for "direct" is shown. The symbol "Rx" is often used in birth charts to indicate planets which were retrograde at birth.

The word 'planet' derives from the Greek 'planetes', which means 'wanderer'. The ancients were well aware that the planets did not stay in fixed relationships as the stars do – the patterns of stars in the sky are the same as they were thousands of years ago – but change their positions against the star background. And also, sometimes they would stop and appear to go into reverse for a while, before stopping again and returning to their forward motion. Explaining this retrograde movement was a major problem whilst it was believed that the planets orbited the Earth, rather than the Sun.

All the planets except the Sun and Moon exhibit this retrograde motion. Mercury goes retrograde for about three weeks, three times a year. Some of the outer planets spend more than 40% of the time retrograde.

If you are using a full ephemeris to calculate planetary positions to the nearest minute of longitude, you have to remember to adjust your calculations accordingly.

POSITIONS OF THE OUTER PLANETS

As we go on to deal with Jupiter, Saturn and planets beyond, we are looking further and further out into space, and the planetary orbits are larger. Whilst Mercury goes around the zodiac in about a year, Pluto, the outermost planet, takes about 248 years, so its daily movement through the signs will be tiny. [*]

---

[*] *The farther a planet is from the sun, the larger an orbit it has. If all the planets were travelling at similar speeds, it would take an outer one longer to complete its orbit, just like the runners in the outer tracks of an athletics race have farther to go. Planetary motion is such that in fact the farther a planet is from the Sun, the slower it moves, or more correctly, the slower the speed it needs to stay in orbit, rather than fly off into space, escaping the Sun's gravity which gets weaker with distance. It should be remembered that the outer planets are still travelling at thousands of miles per hour. They only appear to move slowly because of their distance from Earth, just as a plane high in the sky will appear to an observer on the ground to be moving slowly, even though it may be travelling at several hundred miles per hour.*

For our sample chart, the positions for all the planets, to the nearest degree, are as follows:

☉	14	≈
☽	23	♌
☿	4	≈
♀	1	♈
♂	19	♏
♃	6	♎
♄	20	♈
♅	4	♎
♆	29	♏
♇	25	♑

It should be possible for you to list the planetary positions for your own birth chart.

If your time of birth is not known, the best you can do is use noon as your birth time – unless the Moon changed sign that day, in which case you might be able to narrow the time period down by deciding which Moon-sign characteristics apply to you.

In the next few chapters, we will look at each planet in turn. Each planet can be thought of as representing a different kind of energy that will accordingly relate to different parts of a person's life and psychological make-up. We will look at the basic meanings of each planet and how the energy of each is modified as it passes through each sign of the zodiac.

 For each planet you can look up its zodiac sign for your own birth date and then see if the brief description of the planet when it is in this sign applies to you. Look up positions for friends and relatives too and use this as a way to begin to learn the characteristic of the planets.

the planets

mercury

The word 'mercurial' means active, rapidly changing, talkative. In mythology, Mercury was the fleet-of-foot messenger of the Roman gods.

The sign Mercury is in shows the way we communicate, the way we take in information and give it out. It is involved with teaching, the accumulation of knowledge, the spoken and written word. Mercury in Aries means you have a good way with words, but tend to blurt things out too soon. Mercury-in-Leos can make good teachers because they do not mind going over the same old

intellect
communication
local travel
education
detail

MERCURY

stuff all the time, but get stuck in a rut when it comes to learning new things.

Because the energy of Mercury cannot keep still for a minute, it's involved with travel, particularly of the local variety. In Virgo, every trip has to have a practical purpose; in Capricorn you worry and make contingency plans in case you miss the train home. Fidgety Mercury is highly adaptable, changing very easily. It is a small planet and shows how we deal with all the details, the nuts and bolts and trivia. In Pisces, pernickety Mercury cannot get to grips with the details as feelings get in the way of logical thinking. In airy Libra, Mercury is at home using its rational quality to make balanced judgements.

Other areas which Mercury affects are relationships with brothers and sisters, neighbours, news, technology of communication, hands, the nervous system, duality. We attributed polarities to the signs, and we spoke of father Sun and mother Moon. We can attribute such characteristics to all the planetary energies, but Mercury is neither male or female but both. The word is 'hermaphroditic'. Mercury is about finding the exact word to describe something. It can deal with detail efficiently – or with pernickety criticism.

Mercury rules the senses of speech and hearing. Its position in your chart can show how easily you communicate with others. Here is the symbol. Esoterically, it is made from the cross of the matter supporting the circle of spirit and a semi-circle of soul, but it might be more helpful to think of the two little 'horns' as antennae.

Above all, this is the planet of INTELLECT. The sign Mercury is in shows the way your mind works. In Taurus, Mercury gets slowed down a bit, does not pick up things very quickly but at least will try and stick at learning something. In Sagittarius, it is not too good because it cannot be bothered with the details. See again how we are relating basic zodiac characteristics to the meaning of the planet. In Gemini, it is much better because the detailed, fidgety energy of the sign goes very well with the energy of the planet – perhaps too well, overemphasising it. Perhaps it is best of all in Aquarius. Here it can be highly inventive and intellectual and have some persistence as well. It is associated with the air element and so works most comfortably in airy signs.

Look at the position of Mercury in your chart. You will find that it is in one sign either side of your Sun, or in the same sign.

If we ignore Vulcan, which scientists say cannot possibly exist that close to the Sun, but which occultists say has now "materialised on this plane", Mercury is the planet closest to the Sun. It is so close that, seen from the Earth, it is never more than 28 degrees of longitude from the Sun. So with 30 degrees in a sign, the farthest it can be, if it is not in the Sun sign, it is one sign away.

It is perhaps more helpful to have Mercury in a sign different from your Sun. If it is in the same one, it can be a bit limiting, because it's more difficult to get a different, objective intellectual perspective on matters.

Here are some more of the characteristics of Mercury in the various signs.

For Mercury and all the planets, you can develop interpretations by using keywords for the planet and sign involved, e.g. Mercury in Aries implies impulsiveness in communication.

Mercury in ARIES

This Mercury position has a way with words, being instinctively able to come up with the right ones. These people have voices that are warm and friendly and they get straight to the point, seeing the nature of their environment with alacrity. They think quickly but there is a tendency to make snap judgements and then take immediate action based on them.

When Mercury is in self-centred Aries, it can be difficult to see the other person's intellectual viewpoint. There may also be problems in concentrating owing to the cardinal nature of the sign.

Mercury in TAURUS

They do not always learn quickly, but once they have learnt it, they remember it for good and there can be great depth of thought. Their thought processes are based on sound, practical sense; they always seek out ways of putting their ideas into practice.

The Taurean steadfastness gives excellent powers of concentration enabling they to stick at intellectual tasks and ignore extraneous circumstances. There is a tendency not to perceive that which they do not regard as important.

Mercury in GEMINI

Mercury is naturally at home in Gemini. It enables people with this Mercury to find out just what is going on. They find out the facts – though they may not face them. They have an inordinate intellectual curiosity, although it is hard to maintain sustained interest and concentration in a particular area, as Gemini always tends to scatter the energies of planets. Thus they become knowledgeable on many subjects, but that knowledge is likely to lack depth unless they can learn the discipline to channel it.

This position gives an agile mind, admirably able to grasp opposing viewpoints, and there is the potential to be an impartial arbiter – but this also makes it difficult for them to make up their own minds.

Mercury in CANCER

With intellectual Mercury in emotional Cancer, decisions which appear to be based on reason are often based on feelings. It is easy for them to appear biased for they will tend to pick only factors that support their current feelings rather than look at all sides of an argument.

There is usually a retentive memory although sometimes this continues into a tendency to hang on to ideas when they have ceased to be useful. Intellectually sensitive, learning is often accomplished through absorption rather than logical persistence.

They may see their home as a place of intellectual retreat. Their thoughts may indeed be centred on running a home and dealing with family matters.

Mercury in LEO

This is not an easy position for Mercury, for the fixed nature of the sign is not in keeping with the ephemeral nature of the planet. It can be very difficult for people to get through to them on an intellectual level.

Once they have taken something in, they can be very memory-retentive, but the problem of inflexibility very quickly occurs. It can seem to take so much effort to learn something in the first place that they do not want to have to go through the whole process again and learn something new.

This position can favour teaching, because they do not mind having to go over the same lessons, lectures etc. every year. They'd much rather teach than be taught.

Mercury in VIRGO

This is generally regarded as a good position for Mercury because it is a planet concerned with attention to detail as is the energy of the sign Virgo. Thus the ability to deal with all things small will be enhanced and there can be tremendous analytical ability. A person with Mercury here can think out the logical details of things, find out all about the constituent parts, and express themselves with clarity and precision.

Perhaps the main problems here are that too much attention to detailed intellectual thinking can close their eyes to the wider issues. They can be nit-picking and overcritical, noticing others' faults whilst being blind to their own.

Mercury in LIBRA

The Libran sense of balance means that from an intellectual point of view, they are able to see all sides of a situation. Before making a decision, they try and explore all possible avenues, but this can lead to indecisiveness so that opportunities are missed, or they end up deciding impulsively because they cannot make up their mind.

People usually find it easy to communicate with Mercury-in-Libra people because they seem interested in what they say, but this might be pure Libran superficiality. Their natural sense of justice and harmony, and their desire to be honest makes them well thought of.

Mercury in SCORPIO

Be careful when the planet of communication is here. People with this Mercury believe in expressing the truth – they say what they think or remain silent. But often they shut up for so long and then blurt out what they think just at the wrong moment. They have a determined mind and can get to the bottom of things – this energy would be good in any kind of investigative or research work, but their secrecy can lead to scheming for ulterior motives.

With Mercury here they are able to blend the intuitive with the intellectual. Rather than having ideas, they deal in instincts and beliefs. Although persistent in following their ideas through, this can lead to obstinacy in opinion.

Mercury in SAGITTARIUS

We said that Gemini was a good Mercury position. Sagittarius is not so helpful. We will find that this always holds true – when a planet works well in a sign, it does not express at all well in the opposite one. Here Sagittarian expansiveness and ability to deal with the overall view does not go well with the Mercurial ability to deal with detail.

People with this position can struggle at school. They'd rather be outside playing in the sunshine. They are intellectually concerned with philosophical and religious matters, finding out about spiritual things.

Whilst they absorb overall intellectual pictures well, often subconsciously, they have to be careful that they do learn enough of the basic details about any subject they want to advance in. Sagittarian bluntness comes out very easily with Mercury here.

Mercury in CAPRICORN

Those with Mercury here are mentally ambitious, and like to work things out in a logical, structured way. They are prepared to sit down and deal with statistics and mathematical formulae if they can see a concrete purpose in them.

When it comes to beliefs, they tend to support those which have stood the test of time and which are above all of practical use. They are prepared to seek professional education to further their aims and will go on learning if they can see a concrete result. Mercury here brings good business ability, although it may mean they are not prepared to take the risks necessary for really big success.

Mercury is something of a worrying planet, finically picking over the details. In cautious Capricorn, pessimistic thinking and concern about every possible eventuality can hold someone back.

Mercury in AQUARIUS

This Mercury is always full of ideas; half the time they may be totally potty, but some are spot on. They are here to experiment with ideas, and let other people worry about the practicalities.

They do not have much regard for conventional ideas as the wildly different and unconventional is perfectly acceptable if their own experience or the facts, as they appear to them, show the unorthodox view to be more valid. There is much creative potential within them, for they can come up with original ideas.

This is a brainy, highly intellectual, impersonally objective Mercury, that likes to spend time communicating with its intellectual equals.

Mercury in PISCES

Here is another example of the effect of opposite signs. In Virgo, Mercury worked well, being clear-headed, rational, precise. Now those are not very Piscean characteristics. At its worst Mercury here is muddle-headed, irrational and obscure. On the face of it, its only good point is a photographic memory.

It is a worrying Mercury, unable to make up its mind and finding it difficult to think logically. The problem for many planets in this sign is that the more they concentrate on following logic the more poorly they express. Mercury is the most logical planet of all so the more these people try and actually rationalise, the more off-centre their thinking becomes.

When they learn to blend their feelings with their intellectual capacities, this can be a most rewarding position to have – creative, psychic, imaginative, capable of merging the detailed with the Universal.

Venus is another planet whose orbit is nearer to the Sun than the Earth, so again, it is always found in signs nearer to the Sun, this time either in the same one, or up to two either side.

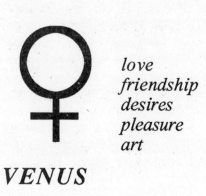

*love
friendship
desires
pleasure
art*

VENUS

Venus was traditionally the goddess of love, and that's one of the areas the energy of the planet is concerned with. Venus is traditionally a feminine planet and the symbol may be familiar from biology as that used to denote females of species. Venus shows the sort of people you find attractive – compatible Venus signs are helpful in partnerships.

This is the planet of both friendship and deeper attraction. Venus-in-Aquarius people can be dreadful flirts (the Aquarian desire for freedom) – it can be a problem if they are in a relationship with a Venus-in-Scorpio person who may be obsessively watching their partner's every move. A playful, idealistic Sagittarian Venus would fit in more harmoniously with the Aquarian one, though it might not be as exciting.

The way Venus is placed in your chart can show your attitude towards the seeking of harmony and beauty, but this often means that it is implicated in laziness. Venus represents desires, certainly, but if there's hard work involved in attaining them, other things being equal, Venus may not want to know. And the desires expressed by the planet can very often be exaggerated into pure pleasure-seeking and lust. Venus-in-Taurus is traditionally regarded as a good position. The planet's energy is well-suited to the Taurean love of material things, especially clothes, but overindulgence easily sets in, the pursuit of pleasure purely for its own sake. A Venus-in-Capricorn, though harsher in essence, may take a more practical approach to getting what it wants.

Venus is usually involved in any creative and artistic abilities shown by the birth chart, when the influence of other planets is also taken into account. Venus-related feelings run deep and art is usually the product of emotion, not reason.

Perhaps the key word for Venus is DESIRE. Venus shows what sort of things you really like, and which often cannot be explained intellectually. Venus-in-Aries people think they know what they like or dislike about something the moment they see it, but may change later. Venus in a fixed sign would be much more persistent. Those with Venus-in-Aquarius do not really like to admit they cannot intellectually explain their desires.

We must remember that Venus represents a somewhat passive energy. Its influence often seems connected to our mother's psychological state when we were young. It will also show how, male or female, we will or will not express characteristics traditionally described as feminine. Venus is involved with the receptive, passive side of sexual activity and romance.

We saw that the Moon was about feelings. So is Venus. But whereas the Moon is about instinctive or conditioned emotional responses, Venus relates to deeper emotions. The Moon sign may show how we relate to family members, what feelings about day-to-day matters are and how we become attached to people through habit, but Venus is concerned about the expression of love, passion and desire. The Moon may make us respond to someone out of a need for security, but passion generated by Venus may be beyond mundane explanation and find security an irrelevance.

Venus in ARIES

These people are inclined to be self-centred in close personal relationships. Once they set their sights on something they desire they will immediately set out to get it. Venus is not easily placed here, because the harmony-seeking energy of the planet does not blend well with the aggressive characteristics of Aries.

Competitive when seeking the affections of others, they make passionate lovers, though they may find their initial enthusiasm for someone soon wears off. Pleasures are most enjoyed when they can be experienced immediately.

Venus in TAURUS

These people are capable of giving constant, lasting affection. They are loyal to those they love, but can be possessive and jealous if they see relationships threatened. There is in them an innate sense of beauty. They like to surround themselves with beautiful objects and seek to make their home attractive. It can lead on to an excessive love of luxury and comfort.

They feel a close attraction to the earth and natural things and are often interested in gardening. A very sensuous, tactile position.

Venus in GEMINI

It's easy for this Venus to become some sort of social butterfly. Their natural wit and conversational ability do not leave them short of admirers. They can flit from one intimate relationship to the next, or even have several going at once and they will travel in search of pleasurable experiences. Long-term relationships are not easy for them – the trick is to find someone who is at least their intellectual equal.

They often distinctly love light, roomy, airy places. Dark, stuffy rooms depress them and they disapprove of anything vulgar.

Venus in CANCER

These people are just soppy and sentimental at heart. They can become very attached to others, which can make them caring and sympathetic to loved ones, but can be a curse as they struggle to hold on to relationships for too long. Their feelings for others fluctuate. They can be extremely strong in emotion and difficult to handle.

Extremely sensitive, they are easily hurt but they hide their feelings behind a dignified facade. They are afraid of being rejected, yet they often behave coldly to others. To boost their sense of security, they need the little demonstrations of affection that will make them feel wanted.

Venus in LEO

Leo gives Venus the power to be loyal in relationships. It also instils a romantic spirit – the trappings of romance may be more important than love itself. They do tend to be too involved in their own ego-centred desires, not caring about what others want.

This is a theatrical Venus. People with it like to put on a show about what they are doing and will show off and idealise their partners. Woe betide their partner if he or she does not give them the respect they think they deserve.

Venus in VIRGO

People with Venus here have excessive ideals about their romantic partner – they want in them Virgoan perfection. We saw that Mercury was well-placed in Virgo – Venus is not. When these people see something beautiful, the tendency is for them to try and take it to pieces, the Virgoan energy causing them to analyse the parts in an attempt to discover how the whole is made up. Feelings cannot readily be subject to such scrutiny.

It is easy for a Venus-Virgo person to be endlessly critical about their partner. Sometimes it works the other way round – with them the butt end of their partner's criticism. Trying to analyse relationships to the nth degree, they forget that they are based on emotions, not rationality.

Venus in LIBRA

Libra and Venus work together to bring charm and a good artistic appreciation, fine sense of form and structure and a desire for all that brings harmony. They need to be liked, so appearances, clothing and hairstyle may have excessive value for them.

This can sometimes appear to be a lazy position, for actually doing something might risk causing disharmony or upsetting someone. Attractions for others arise impulsively and may wear off quickly. Desires tend to be superficial.

Venus in SCORPIO

This Venus needs to develop a sense of balance for it is easy to obsessively hang on to a relationship sometimes, and at other times suddenly drop friends or lovers without warning.

They appear reserved and perhaps superficial, but inside they are deeply emotional. Their strong sexual feelings tend to be suppressed as the need is felt to be in control of these feelings — and perhaps other people as well. Desires are strong and Venus-Scopio people can become passionately involved in following them, leading them to disregard another's point of view when they get worked up about something.

Venus in SAGITTARIUS

This friendly Venus position will let its owners get to know many people round and about, but will make them reluctant to commit themselves to deep relationships. They feel secure when they follow traditional moral principles, although they are not afraid to embark on unusual relationships — this brings them the emotional excitement they desire, since they regard romance as an adventure.

Relationships do not really work unless they and their partner share similar philosophical views. This can be a source of disharmony for they may start seeking to convert their loved ones to their own moral, religious and political viewpoints.

Venus in CAPRICORN

People with this Venus try to apply common sense when dealing with relationships. They become involved with people who they respect or who have status. They are attracted to practical people, those they feel can be of use to them. Partners must be able to contribute to relationships in a material way.

Romantic involvements can be nipped in the bud because they can appear superficially uninterested, not readily expressing deep feelings. Public displays of affection are frowned upon but in private they can be very sensual. They can be loyal in love because they have a sense of responsibility when it comes to relationships.

Artistically they have a fine sense of structure and composition, but there is a feeling that art must be allied with usefulness. Often there is business ability when it comes to dealing with artistic matters.

Venus in AQUARIUS

The rebellious Aquarian energy means that these people do not like being tied down to others, but are adventurous in their choice of friends. There can be problems in romantic relationships, for whilst they can strike up quick friendships, they do not usually want to get too involved – the other party might think they are more serious about the relationship than they actually are. They are often inveterate flirts.

When romantic attachments develop, they are sincere in their loyalty – but their sense of freedom can always lead to temptation elsewhere. It can also be difficult to express really deep feelings to a chosen partner, who is first and foremost seen as a friend, someone to relate to intellectually, rather than a lover.

Venus in PISCES

The planet of love is at home in compassionate Pisces, for the Venus-based desires can be elevated by the addition of Piscean compassion and selflessness. They can tap into an endless well of love. They are sensitive and get easily hurt if partners do not show them open affection.

They do have problems in getting involved with people merely because they feel sorry for them. And they can become unsure of what they really want, though happy just to drift along with whatever is going on around them. They cannot readily express what they like in reasoned terms – it is all about pure feeling.

If you are having difficulty choosing a present for someone, choose something that fits with their Venus sign. Hints . . .

ARIES	anything if the wrapping is expensive; don't give them presents in advance.
TAURUS	something they can finger and feel; food; clothes; avoid anything used or artificial.
GEMINI	give several small gifts rather than one big one; puzzles, books, tickets, jokes.
CANCER	posh chocolates; take them for a meal but not 'foreign' food; something sentimental; antiques; give a romantic card.
LEO	something big; give them your time and attention; throw a party; personalised gifts.
VIRGO	something they can take to bits or build; games, puzzles, health foods; avoid very expensive presents.
LIBRA	romantic gifts; don't leave them on their own; don't forget an expensive card.
SCORPIO	difficult! Don't waste money on expensive wrapping; be consistent; things to grow; be practical; find out what they collect.
SAGITTARIUS	jumpers; fun things rather than practical; a party; anything big; foreign things.
CAPRICORN	practical gifts; anything with a top brand name; the latest fashion; things they can use at work, or show off.
AQUARIUS	something for today's hobby; factual books; clothes in modern materials; ask what they want; avoid run-of-the-mill stuff.
PISCES	something mystical; books; art; experiences – but not wild parties; be impractical and romantic.

If you don't know the Venus sign - give to their Sun sign instead. And remember, give according to *their* sign, not yours.

A key word for Mars is ACTION. Mars is about desire as well as Venus, but there is nothing passive, dreamy or romantic about it.

The symbol for Mars can be thought of as a circle of self-centred desire, with the arrow forcefully projecting out into the world, taking action to get what it wants. The symbol is used in biology to mean 'male' and its position can show how we express characteristics traditionally considered to be masculine.

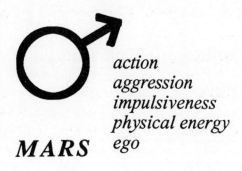

action
aggression
impulsiveness
physical energy
ego

MARS

The Mars position shows how an individual will go about getting desires satisfied. It's an ego-centred planet that says "give it to me, and give it to me now". The sign position of course modifies the way action is taken. If Mars is in Cancer in a person's chart they are likely to take action to protect themselves and those others they feel they have to protect. It is not above going into a sulk to get its way. Mars in Capricorn will often be ruthless in its drive to achieve and seems to be related to people with strong drives to succeed in their careers.

Mythological Mars was the god of war and it is certainly the planet of aggression. One of its effects is to show the sort of things we get angry about. Mars-in-Taurus people get angry when they feel territorially threatened. Mars-in-Leos get upset when they feel they are not being given the respect they deserve. And it shows in the way anger is manifested. Mars-in-Aries and there is a tendency to fly off the handle but for anger to quickly burn out. Mars-in-Scorpio and the anger may be suppressed, but a grudge held until a suitable moment is found to effect retribution. Some Mars-in-Libra people very rarely get angry at all. The refined sensibilities of Libra do not fit in with the aggressive, ego-centred Mars energy.

Mars is also involved in the sexual drive. Whereas Venus is more interested in the courtship and romantic side of matters, Mars is more directly concerned with sexual experience and enjoyment. Expanding beyond the sexual, Venus' position can show what sort of things we like to experience at the hands of others, whereas Mars shows the way we like to impose ourselves upon the world.

So Venus does emphasise how broadly feminine qualities are emphasised in a chart, and Mars masculine ones.

The orbit of Mars is outside the Earth, so its position in the chart will not be related to that of the Sun. It can be in any sign and takes about two years to go around the whole zodiac.

Mars in ARIES

This Mars position brings energy, initiative and courage. There is no stopping people with this Mars, for once they get an idea into their head, they like to act on it at once.

They set out on projects without enough thought. The Mars energy in this sign is so difficult to contain that it is not easy to channel, but tends to be expended on new projects that soon lose their shine. Mars is the planet of ego and Aries is also an ego-centred sign — 'headstrong' is often a good word for these people. They are inherently competitive and this is often channelled via physical activity.

Mars in TAURUS

Mars' energy (like that of most planets) is slowed-down in Taurus. These people do not like to act unless they can see a practical purpose, but once they do move they are persistent. There may be an attraction to farming and gardening, or to such things as sculpture or building work. They get angry about environmental issues.

It is an inherently territorial position, with them getting angry when they feel their space is being challenged. Often, when the Mars energy bursts out of its Taurean-enforced placidity, they pick fights, which belies their outwardly placid appearance. They can be slow to physically react and, whilst they are not unduly aggressive, they can be a fearsome and unforgiving opponent if forced into a corner.

Mars in GEMINI

This is an active Mars, much inclined to travel intellectually and physically — just so long as the journey is not too long. Usually there are sudden desires to make local trips and an interest in acquiring information.

This Mars likes to take action on its ideas — and gets aggressive when those ideas are challenged. Thus there is usually a love of debate and argument for its own sake and the tongue is sometimes too sharp. The nature of Gemini is such that although this position gives a lot of intellectual energy, the ideas tend to be very changeable. There is always a risk of acting with a duality of purpose.

Sometimes this position is the mark of the perpetual student, for the Mars energy is easily directed into the pursuit of knowledge.

Mars in CANCER

These people have intense emotions, and emotional frustrations can lead to outbursts of temper, often directed at whoever happens to be nearest, not even the perceived cause of the frustration. They have difficulty in asking directly for what they want, sidling up to people and insidiously trying to get their way. Sometimes anger is sulkily repressed.

The Cancer influence means they like to run their own home, be king or queen of their own castle. This is O.K. as long as the people who share their home accept it, but it is likely to lead to domestic discord. This sort of energy is often worked out by working at home improvements, D.I.Y. etc.

Mars in LEO

With Mars here aggression is a likely result when people feel they are not getting the respect that they deserve. A lot of energy will be easily channelled into Leonine pursuits – having fun, being romantic, engaging in creative activity and making sure they are in charge!

This Mars is particularly good at pursuing causes, but can be too idealistic in doing so. They are able to act passionately for what they believe in, though their stubborn opinions and the way they may keep going over the same ground when dealing with problems can annoy others and lead to arguments.

Mars in VIRGO

Planning their actions carefully, these people try not to act without good reason; they have to see it leading to a practical result if they are to do so. Their excellent attention to detail can make a someone with Mars-in-Virgo into a skilled craftsperson; work in any field where physical precision is required will benefit. They can bring a meticulous, analytical approach to that with which they are involved.

The problem is, it is so easy for this energy to be frittered away in unimportant projects, paying excessive attention to triviality and trying to plan the future to the last detail. They worry unnecessarily about their health and diet. Whilst they are fiddling about, and nagging others to get things done, the world passes them by and nothing really is effected.

Mars in LIBRA

The ego-centred, competitiveness of Mars does not blend well with Libra's inherent desire for harmony. These people are inherently implacable – it usually takes a great deal for them to lose their temper, but if they do all hell breaks loose or sometimes the cardinality of the sign and planet mean that temper will be lost very readily. People just do not get the expected emotional response from this Mars. Their energy is well expressed in reconciling people for they hate to see discord in relationships. Their sense of harmony can also be used in artistic expression.

They are most easily angered when they believe the principles of justice are being violated, even when it is not them being done down – they know it could be them next. They usually support the letter of the law. With this Mars it can be difficult to know when to act. It's easy for someone to spend a lot of time *thinking* about what they could be doing, but not so easy to get round to actually *doing* it!

Mars in SCORPIO

Here Mars will be blended with all the faces of Scorpio. There can be a crusading spirit, the ability to take persevering action where others will give up. They commit themselves emotionally and passionately, though this may not be apparent. This of course can be used for good or evil. Action may be taken obsessively or secretively – it can be difficult to know what a Mars-Scorpio person is really up to. Inside, they know what they want and what they do not want.

They act for emotional rather than rational reasons, and very often this Mars gets on by learning from the mistakes of others, letting people make the mistakes and only then stepping in to right matters.

Mars in SAGITTARIUS

People with this Mars believe that there are certain moral rules to life and get angry when these are flouted. They will not be slow to express an opinion when they see these laws being broken. The problem is that it is usually them who made the rules in the first place

As they act candidly and openly, you usually know where you stand with Mars-in-Sagittarius. They can use this energy to work forcefully though idealistically in organisations involved in fighting for social justice. But because they will try and convert everyone to their beliefs, they have to be careful they do not get completely dogmatic and opinionated.

There is in them a desire for adventure, but their search for excitement can lead them to overlook mundane details and take physical risks.

Mars in CAPRICORN

In today's society, Mars is well placed in Capricorn, for we tend to respect the person who is able to put a lot of energy into seeking status and a material wealth. They have a high degree of self-control and this energy can be easily channelled into achieving professional ambitions; but their desire to succeed within their career can lead to ruthless competition.

Liking to see a job well-done, they hate sloppiness in work and do not respect the unambitious. They must be able to see a practical result to all their actions, otherwise they will not act. They are likely to sacrifice emotional and spiritual satisfaction for the sake of material gain.

Mars in AQUARIUS

If these people so desire they are easily able to channel their personal energy into humanitarian work, the occult, or scientific and technical channels. Problems may arise, though, from desires to reform existing systems which put them in positions of challenging authority. There can be a wilfulness to act just for the sake of being different, and they may get very aggressive when they feel tied down by existing traditions.

The things which most easily anger these individuals are bureaucracy, any part of the establishment doing people down, inequality of all sorts, and being ordered about.

Mars in PISCES

This is not an easy position for Mars, for it is subject to the ego-dissolving power of Pisces. These people tend to act in a confused way, so that others are not sure what they are really up to and give them a wide berth. Physically, they may be subject to illness that is difficult to diagnose, or may have bad co-ordination. They may brood, rather than take action, or act in a scheming fashion behind the scenes.

They do have a lot of energy for compassionate pursuits. Mars here can help artistically, or in psychological or caring professions.

MARS signs show what people get angry about – here are some Mars-sign characteristics that will annoy _you_ :

ARIES	how they are always so full of energy.
TAURUS	how they stay placid when others panic.
GEMINI	the endless quest for knowledge and their sharp tongues.
CANCER	how they don't ask directly for what they want, then sulk when they don't get it.
LEO	how they get annoyed when you ignore them.
VIRGO	their taking ages to do things through picking over every detail; and how they nag.
LIBRA	how they never give you the expected emotional response.
SCORPIO	they have fun watching you make mistakes.
SAGITTARIUS	they insist on everyone doing things by the rules – the ones they made.
CAPRICORN	their career-orientation and how they must be in charge.
AQUARIUS	how they have to do things their own way.
PISCES	their disorganisation; the way they do things that trip themselves up.

jupiter

The symbol for Jupiter is a little like the number four. Esoterically it is the semi-circle of soul rising above the cross of matter.

relation
expansion
exaggeration
benevolence
opportunity

JUPITER

You can't miss Jupiter. On a clear night when Jupiter is above the horizon, it is the brightest object in the sky. Even though it is on average 483 million miles from the Sun (the Earth is 93 million), it is so large – nearly twelve times the diameter of Earth and over 300 times the mass – that it is clearly visible by the Sun's reflected light. It is the biggest planet in our solar system and that is a good starting off point for its astrological meaning.

Jupiter is concerned with all that is large. In a birth chart it shows how we reach out to the wider Universe. We have left the realms of our personal affairs and are expanding our knowledge of wider issues. Jupiter was the ruler of the mythological gods. His other name was Jove, and from this we derive the word jovial, which is a good keyword to use in understanding Jupiter. It is a fun planet.

Jove was only concerned with wider, important issues. He would not stoop so low as to get involved in trivia, though he was not an aloof god, being quite prepared to come down into the realm of mortals and have a good time. There are many myths about Jupiter's liking for sex with mortal women. He just had fun and left the women with the problem of bringing up the demi-gods.

Jupiter's position shows how we can take a broader view of things. So Jupiter is involved with religious, philosophical and moral beliefs, for these are ways we attempt to give meaning to our place in the scheme of the Universe. Of course, it is easy to take too wide a view and ignore details to our cost. And a Jupiterian characteristic is exaggeration. Jupiter in a fire sign is likely to lead to excessive idealism and religious or moral opinionation and crusading. Jupiter in air and you

108

may have a good grasp of overall intellectual theories – but may prefer to leave others to work out the practical details.

Astrologers have often referred to Jupiter as 'the great benefic', for its action in a chart can seem to represent where we have unlooked-for good luck. It is very easy for astrologers to become carried away by this influence of Jupiter in someone's chart, overemphasising its effect. Because of the apparent connection with good fortune, we must be careful not to mislead people. For example, people with Jupiter in Taurus do seem to attract money and possessions more easily – but as well, Jupiterian extravagance can lead them to waste resources; the money may go as quickly as it comes.

A better way to think of Jupiter, rather than to get involved with the idea of fortune, is to think of it as bringing opportunity. The chance to reach out and relate to others, to expand. Jupiter's sign position will show the way someone does this: Jupiter in Libra people will attempt to form relationships by expressing fairness and harmonious ideas, but their willingness to go along with others may cause them to neglect their own ego-centred wants; in Capricorn, Jupiter will cause someone to be cautious about forming relationships. Laziness is a characteristic sometimes associated with this planet. People with Jupiter helpfully placed may feel a sense of good luck and do nothing with their opportunities, while those with a harder birth chart may fight to achieve.

It is also involved with the principles of government and law, but in the sense of beneficent advice given from those who know better. There is not authoritarianism in Jupiter, but there can certainly be opinionation.

The bodies we have looked at before are sometimes referred to as the *personal* planets. This is because their effects are seen in terms very personal to the individual. Jupiter and Saturn are known as *impersonal* as their effect is much more externalised and relates more to issues of ethics and morality.

Mars is about half as far again from the Sun as the Earth. Jupiter, the next planet out from the Sun, is five times' the Earth's distance. It therefore takes a lot longer to go around the whole zodiac – just under twelve years. It means that Jupiter will be in one sign for about a year at a time, and everyone born in that time will share a Jupiter sign, though many combinations of the personal planets will occur. So we must be careful not to ascribe too much influence to Jupiter's sign position, rather thinking of it as having a background, impersonal effect.

Jupiter in ARIES

There can be a tendency for areas of enjoyment and expansion to get out of control. These people have faith in their ability to achieve what they set out to do, but too often they can set out on endeavours that are beyond their ability. When stumbling-blocks appear, they usually have the vitality and stamina to surmount them, but sometimes they fail through over-expansion or over-optimism.

They can be too idealistic and whilst there may be leadership ability and innovative energy, they can easily become involved in crusading for what they currently believe in, without enough concern for other's beliefs.

Jupiter in TAURUS

These people seem to attract material wealth and possessions more readily than others, but they like to spend that money too, and this can be seen by others as extravagance. What others regard as luxuries, they think are necessities.

In religious matters they accept the social and moral standards of the social class in which they live. They do not appreciate spiritual values unless they can see their practical application. There is a tendency to exaggerate the importance of belief as a basis to life.

Jupiter in GEMINI

These people have expansive minds that can take in lots of facts through which they broaden their knowledge. Travel also brings new and interesting experience. The problem is that they can end up being a mere repository of facts, but have no integration of them into an overall outlook on life.

They are mentally restless and whilst they are always on the lookout for items of interest, their mental restlessness makes it difficult for them to gain enough knowledge of one subject for it to be of use. Jupiter-in-Gemini people can turn into 'armchair philosophers'.

111

Jupiter in CANCER

With this Jupiter, people are able to make others feel at home, because they are soft and kind at heart when relating. It makes them feel secure when they reach out to people by mothering them. They seek to establish a secure home environment and attract material possessions for their home. They pick up the morality of their parents, who often provide financial assistance.

They may need to watch their weight. There is a tendency to overeat and to pay little attention to their diet. There is a love of home comforts; they feel most at home in their own home – it gives them security and it is easy to stop at home rather than going out and actually doing something.

Jupiter in LEO

People with this Jupiter can be a guiding light in whatever activities they choose to express themselves. They can inspire confidence in others, encouraging their creative abilities to develop. Setting about things with enthusiasm, they get on well with people when they let their playful side come out.

With these qualities, they do however need to be careful that pride and conceit do not creep in. They may be generous but expect generosity in return. Leadership abilities may make them self-important and their generally robust constitution and wealth of personal energy can lead to lavishness, over-optimism and exaggeration.

Jupiter in VIRGO

The broad-viewing Jupiterian energy does not sit easily in narrow-viewed Virgo. There is a conflict between the way they try to expand their horizons, general happiness and pleasurable pursuits and a tendency to have too much concern with detail. They have a tendency to be over-critical regarding philosophical and religious concepts. Sometimes exaggeration is placed upon personal hygiene and diet.

They are capable of processing large amounts of data accurately, but will make mountains out of molehills when they detect errors. Following on from this, they may take on too much, unsatisfied with the standard of others' work, and must learn to delegate.

Jupiter in LIBRA

These people reach out to others in a spirit of co-operation and are prepared to share their knowledge so that it can be used for the greater benefit of the many. They gain satisfaction in encouraging others to learn and express themselves creatively; they are discouraged when they see people making so little of their potential. They become very aware of the needs of others, but this may lead them to promise more than they can deliver as they try and please everyone.

They try and be fair to their partner – and expect the same brand of justice in return. Close relationships will work best where they can share a common goal related to furthering social justice, religious or philosophical thought.

Jupiter in SCORPIO

Jupiter here implies the expansion of knowledge through investigation and research of life's mysteries. Often they will be attracted to research work, or the occult. They make good psychologists – but often of the armchair variety. When they reach out to others, sometimes there are hidden motivations involved.

Friends are often made through occult or philosophical endeavours and they will reach out to others with intensity and commitment, though relationships may be abruptly broken off when disagreements occur. There is a strong sexual drive but a tendency to exaggerate the sexual side of relationships.

Jupiter in SAGITTARIUS

These people have an underlying attitude of optimism and youthfulness in the way they relate to life. They are attracted to philosophy or religion in an effort to develop a system of thought whereby they can order their life. They are prepared to spread their knowledge of such matters to others, but this may lead to dogmatism and attempts to convert people to their beliefs.

Interested in the way people relate to society as a whole, they work well in the fields of sociology and social work. They are able to see the whole picture, but may have to work at the attention to detail. They can be a touch too idealistic when it comes to philosophical or religious matters.

Jupiter in CAPRICORN

Often Jupiter-Capricorn people reach a state of maturity earlier than most people, but because the fun-loving and adventurous side of their nature has been suppressed, they may be scared to take what they see as risks. They can express good common-sense in decision-making, but too easily come down on the side of the status quo and lack imagination to come up with new ideas.

They do not mind making sacrifices in the pursuit of what they want, hating to see waste or extravagance. They will scrimp and save and their ambition to achieve can mean long-term material success and status. They see themselves as morally upright and attempts will be made to force their morality on others.

Jupiter in AQUARIUS

They are usually open-minded when it comes to experimenting with new ideas, particularly when it comes to religion and philosophy, but because they will be attracted to unusual beliefs, sometimes opinionation will occur as they feel a need to crusade in promoting their views.

Generally fortunate in their choice of friends, they are able to maintain long-term friendships, working out the problems that would break up those between others.

Jupiter in PISCES

Essentially compassionate in nature, these people feel at their best when doing something to help others. They are naturally empathetic to the needs of others and will attract people who need help. Often they are involved in charitable work or counselling.

They may be attracted to the more mystical religions, for their spiritual awareness involves being in touch with the whole Universe. They feel it is important to have a faith and sometimes blind, opinionated attachment to a religion or guru occurs. Extravagance with money and resources is sometimes a problem.

The energy of Saturn in many ways represents the opposite of that of Jupiter. Far from being benificent, Saturn has traditionally been seen as a bringer of misfortune and was termed the great 'malefic', an old word meaning a bringer of bad luck. It's symbol is a reversal of Jupiter's, for here the cross of material practicality is above the semi-circle of soul.

contraction
caution
structure
authority
fear

Today we may be less tied to the idea of fortune, and we are probably wise to avoid talking in terms of good and bad luck, but Saturn's effect in a chart certainly works to suppress and constrict. Planets it is related to in an individual birth chart often have their energies restricted so that they fail to manifest fully. Often its effect will manifest as a propensity to certain illnesses

SATURN

implied by how it is placed in a chart.

The restrictive effect of Saturn in a chart often appears to come from people or organisations in positions of authority, telling us what to do and forcing us to do it if we resist. It is involved in the authoritarian side of political and moral thinking. It may also show the sorts of things we are afraid of. Saturn-in-Cancer people may feel uncomfortable about emotions and be cautious in expressing their feelings. Saturn in Virgo and the individual will worry about losing control of the details.

The Greek equivalent of the Roman Saturn was Kronos, from which we derive the word chronology. Saturn is often viewed as the personification of the effects of time and is connected to the idea of the grim reaper who ultimately harvests us all unto death.

But Saturn is not all gloom and doom. Saturn is the voice of authoritarianism which may take away our freedom and yet may contain the voice of reason. Really, its effect is that of a teacher. Through struggling to cope with the inadequacies and problems Saturn produces, we can learn much about ourselves and the order of the Universe.

Whilst not inherently concerned with detail, Saturn is certainly a planet of structure and physical reality. When we are able to incorporate Saturn's energy into our chart, it stops us from being unrealistically optimistic and helps us to put our affairs in order. Certainly it tones down and represses that with which it is in contact, but the positive side is that, in bringing us down to earth, we are made aware of practical reality. It is perhaps most helpfully placed in earth signs, for whilst here practical affairs may face obstacles and delay, Saturn's inherent common sense will be most readily expressed. Ultimately, one of the principles of Saturn is that through the lessons of time, we achieve wisdom.

Just as we said that we must not overemphasise the benefic effects of Jupiter, so we should try to avoid concentrating too much on Saturn as a bringer of bad luck. So often, when things go wrong, the cause and solution of our problems are to be found within us, whereas we usually insist on blaming outside influences. That way, we avoid the perceived unpleasantness of dealing with the problems, but as a result must continue to undergo Saturn's harsh lessons.

Saturn is even further from the Sun than the planets we have discussed so far, taking about 29 years to progress through the zodiac. As it therefore stays about 2¼ years in each sign, its sign position will have more of a general significance than the personal planets. Later we will see how the Jupiter and Saturn can be integrated into our birth chart by reference to the astrological houses and planetary aspects.

Saturn in ARIES

Saturn's energy, which represents caution and practicality is not easily placed in this impulsive, idealistic sign. Often it leads to a lack of confidence as acting in the fashion of Aries leads to disappointment. Circumstances force them to be patient because when they act impulsively, practicalities catch up on them and nip their idealism in the bud.

They may find it difficult to give structure to the consequences of their own actions, but do learn to be resourceful. They want to be number one, to be a leader, but they lack confidence and are scared about having such feelings – and they are above all scared that people will not like them.

Saturn in TAURUS

Great strength and determination of purpose is available for Saturn-Taurus people when they decide to work towards specific goals. They are able to plan over long periods of time towards achieving their ends, being prepared to work hard to acquire material possessions – and they usually have to. They worry about money, always thinking they are careful with it, even when they are not, and they are scared about losing their possessions .

They are concerned about their moral standards – they want to have them, but they are unsure of them. They have a need to re-examine them as they go through life and thus they learn new values. This also makes them tolerant of the morals of others.

Saturn in GEMINI

Here, mental processes will be restricted, producing a struggle to learn, particularly where the absorption of detailed information is necessary. If these people are prepared to work hard to learn, Saturn's structure can be applied to bring deep intellectual understanding. Communication can be structured so that precise ideas are communicated and there is adaptability of purpose.

Ideas are judged on their practical usefulness. New ideas may be criticised and there may be attempts to impose rigid thinking on

118

others. Sometimes relations with brothers and sisters are cool or problematical.

Saturn in CANCER

These people hide their inner emotions from public view and hate to be criticised in public situations. Often they fear bringing their limitations into the open.

Financial and domestic strain are likely to ensue when trying to establish a home. They may even be scared of establishing a home – because of deep fears that its stability and security will one day be taken away. Familial responsibilities are taken very seriously, but they may worry too much about their family, particularly their parents.

Saturn in LEO

Saturn-Leo people take the business of raising children seriously, being aware of their responsibilities, though they may take them just too seriously. They may be autocratic with their children or fail to give them enough attention.

They should be aware that there could be an inherent tendency to succumb to egotism and desire for power. They fear not being in charge and not receiving respect. Creative abilities may be suppressed through lack of confidence, though they can apply Saturn to give structure to artistic endeavours.

Saturn in VIRGO

These people worry about losing sight of details, and then forget about the wider issues. They will work hard, because they are guilty about not doing so, but may find little reward, being stuck with boring work. Their worrying can lead to overwork and ill health.

They are a bit scared of the unknown. They do not like surprises, preferring everything to be carefully planned ahead – they look at economic indicators, opinion polls – and ask for astrological forecasts.

Saturn in LIBRA

Saturn is quite well placed in Libra, because it is able to give structure to efforts to bring harmony. There is a strong awareness of the need to co-operate if things of lasting value are to be achieved.

These people are usually aware of the principles of law and the need to be fair when using their authority. If Saturn is poorly-placed in the chart, there can be difficulties and heavy responsibilities brought about from partnerships or legal disputes.

Saturn in SCORPIO

Often these people become very emotionally involved when dealing with responsibilities that have been thrust on them, and to avoid mental disturbances they need to learn to react calmly to crises. They are always trying to improve existing methods and may suddenly shut off from trying to organise others if they feel it is a lost cause.

They need to be aware that there is a danger of them overemphasising the sexual area of life. The result of this is usually long periods of limited sexual expression which operate to give them the opportunity of becoming aware of the overemphasis.

Saturn in SAGITTARIUS

The energies of Saturn and Sagittarius merge to bring an ability to think deeply about spiritual matters and these people are thus able to reach more profound conclusions than most. They are able to put higher forms of thinking into practice. They do not just sit around discussing philosophy, religion, the occult, natural healing – they have the ability to take practical action in this respect. Moral viewpoints are judged in practical terms.

Their reputation is important to them. They feel personally affronted if they are spoken of unkindly, if their morals or philosophy are criticised by others. There is a danger of opinionated religious and philosophical viewpoints with this position.

Saturn in CAPRICORN

This is an ambitious Saturn. Business, science, politics – anything to which they can bring structure and apply their talent for organisation can be worked hard at with excellent chances of success, though caution may hold them back sometimes. They are a bit afraid of success, deep down.

There are instinctive ideas of safety and stability that serve them in good stead, enabling them to provide organisation and structure to that in which they are involved. They want to do well at what they do. There are strong family values, but a tendency to be somewhat dictatorial.

Saturn in AQUARIUS

Here there is mental ambition, a desire to learn about new things; thus these people are interested in new developments at the frontiers of science and the occult, particularly if they can see that they have a wider application in improving the lot of humanity. There may be a problem in it is easy for them to take too intellectual an approach when moral decisions are called for – they may have not enough regard to people's feelings.

They can be helpful to strangers and make good and loyal friends although they may often feel that they give more to their friends than they get back.

Saturn in PISCES

Here, Saturn is subject to the dissolving energy of Pisces. It can be difficult to get a coherent idea of structure and a balanced view of practicality. There can be an inner awareness of a struggle between being excessively emotional and changeable on one hand and wanting to be cold, rational and structured on the other.

They should perhaps be careful that they do not become excessively concerned with the past, and what they see as past mistakes. They probably worry too much and dwelling on the past only makes it more difficult to deal with the demands of the present. It can be difficult to drum up the self-discipline necessary to succeed at tasks, although there is a sense of resourcefulness that can enable them to turn their hand constructively to many tasks.

The symbol for Uranus is made up from the cross of matter, two semi-circles of soul and the circle of spirit. Often it is drawn with the semi-circles altered into straight lines, in which case it looks a bit like a television ariel.

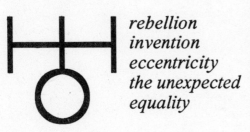

rebellion
invention
eccentricity
the unexpected
equality

URANUS

The planets out to Saturn have been known since ancient times, since they are easily visible to the naked eye. Uranus is as far again from the Sun as Saturn is and was not discovered until 1781, thanks to developments in telescope technology.

Its discoverer was a German-born musician with an interest in astronomy, William Herschel. The planet had actually been seen before, but had been regarded as a star by previous astronomers, because their telescopes were not good enough to plot its movement. Herschel built his own telescopes and on 13.3.1781 found Uranus was a planet. Later it was realised that Uranus had been recorded as a 'star' as early as 1610.

This was an exciting event for the scientific establishment, as well as for astrologers. Herschel had established his home in England. It was proposed by some scientists of the Royal Society that the 'new' planet should be named 'Herschel' after the man who discovered it, and some astrological books have used this name until relatively recent times. But what did the man who discovered it think? He had a suggestion of his own. He said that in honour of the king of England at the time, George III, the planet should be called 'George'.

Fortunately, the German astronomer Johann Bode had already suggested the name Uranus, after the figure in mythology who was the father of Saturn, and that is the name which became accepted. The mythological Uranus, whose name in Greek meant 'heaven', was not an earth-based God at all and the planet is the first of the *'transpersonal'* ones. When we look at these, we are discussing concepts of much more universality.

Uranus was discovered during a time of much civil strife. People with it strongly placed will take sudden action that upsets everyone and are often impractical, but they are here to make the rest of us sit up and take notice.

Perhaps the key energy involved with Uranus is a desire to be different. It is an explosive, disruptive planet, one of rebellion and rude awakenings. But the way in which it can serve to wake us up and change the status quo often manifests as sudden insight and inspiration. Genius may be "one per cent inspiration and ninety-nine per cent perspiration", but we need the Uranian flash of insight to be that genius.

Part of the insight that Uranus brings is the principal of equality. People with Uranus strong in their charts have, as well as the desire to be different from everyone, strong tendencies to support egalitarianism. Uranus demands that all should be treated alike.

Its effect in our chart will be to show where our desire to be different will come out. And yet, it is also involved with how well we relate to the behaviour of our generation. Most of us have a desire to be an individual, yet also a desire to be accepted by our peers by conforming with the currently-accepted behaviour. Uranus can show how well we balance these conflicting goals.

When we get out this far, the sign positions of planets taken by themselves have less importance in an individual's birth chart. Uranus takes about eighty-four years to go around the whole zodiac. So, dividing that by twelve, everyone in a seven-year period will share the Uranus sign. So the sign position of Uranus will influence a whole mini-generation of people born during that time. The outer planets are sometimes referred to as 'generational' in influence.

One of the uses we can put these outer planets to is in the field of 'mundane' astrology. This is the branch of the subject which deal with global affairs, the development of nations and world-wide trends, rather than the affairs of individuals. We can relate the passage of Uranus through the signs to world affairs. Thus, Uranus in Libra (1968-75) implies revolution in partnership matters, a rise in the acceptance of divorce, homosexuality coming into the open, traditional ideas of marriage being challenged. Uranus in Capricorn, from 1989 to 1996, implies revolution against all established structures, particularly political ones. Of course, all the people born during these periods will try and put these energies into action as they grow.

The discovery of Uranus was used by some scientists as an opportunity to ridicule astrology. How, it was argued, could astrology be correct when for thousands of years this piece of information had been missing? Astrologers countered by saying that they were well aware that there were aspects of behaviour unexplained by traditional astrology and that the discovery of Uranus added a missing piece to the jigsaw. A scientist who discovers a particular chemical to be at work in the brain does not render all previous research into brain function as irrelevant.

Another point is that Uranus – and the planets beyond – can also in some respect be said to represent the rise of concepts which were not current previously, such as technology and egalitarianism. The discovery of Uranus symbolised the merging of rebellion and technology in the industrial revolution.

In many ways Uranus can be thought of as expressing a similar energy to Mercury, but operating at a higher octave. The relationship of the two planets can be explored by detailing some areas influenced by them:

MERCURY	URANUS
Learning through study	Learning through inspiration
Newspapers	Television
Abacus	Computer
Blood brothers and sisters	Everyone seen as a brother or sister
Local travel	Space travel
Speaking/writing	Telepathy ?

neptune

The symbol for Neptune is easy to remember, because it looks like the familiar trident. Actually, it represents the cross of matter merging with the semi-circle of soul.

Mythological Neptune was the ancient god of the ocean and would keep himself to himself pretty much. Of course, just when sailors were least expecting it, when they had been deceived into thinking it was fine weather, he would whip up a storm, or the apparently calm surface of the sea would be shown to have been hiding dangerous serpents or whales.

spirituality
idealism
deception
imagination
dissolution

NEPTUNE

Neptune was not to be trusted, and you never knew what was going on underneath the surface of the ocean. The placing of this planet can show where we are most apt to deceive ourselves and others. Other planets related to Neptune in an individual chart may find their energies confused and dissolved, as if merged with the mighty ocean that absorbs everything. For Neptune will tend to dissolve everything with which it is in contact.

It was discovered on 23.9.1846. The search for Neptune had really begun when it was discovered that Uranus was not moving along its orbit exactly as predicted by known physical laws. It was proposed that there was a planet outside the orbit of Uranus whose gravitational pull was perturbing its orbit. Calculations arising from this led astronomers to turn their telescopes to where the new planet ought to be and a planet was indeed discovered. Actually, it turned out later that the calculations were incorrect – if the search had been carried out a decade earlier or later, Neptune would have been too far away from its predicted position to be discovered, so the discovery was by chance. This story seems typical of Neptune's astrological meaning, relating as it does to deceptiveness and intuition.

Idealism is a concept expressed through Neptune, the highest spiritual ideas for the advancement of humanity. Unfortunately, practicality is not a Neptunian strongpoint, and those with Neptune strong in their charts may have trouble being realistic and prone to flights of fantasy. Ultimately Neptune is about the dissolving of ego into the mass-energy of the Universe. It is about the state of reality that exists beyond the practical everyday world. Like Jupiter, it takes a Universal viewpoint, but Neptune involves all unseen energy and perhaps other planes of existence beyond accepted reality.

The position of watery Neptune in our charts shows how we respond to this more intuitive spiritual side of life. It may invoke clairvoyance, intuition and artistic creativity. Its downside is deception, dreaminess and escapism, particularly escape sought through the use of drugs.

The artistic qualities of Neptune seem to arise in two ways. Firstly because art can give a wider view of the Universe than is provided by practical detail alone, and secondly through its chameleon-like energy to deceive. Thus the actor can display a myriad faces without his real personality being shown. Neptune's energy is involved in fields such as fashion and advertising, because what is presented is an embellishment or distortion of reality.

Neptune can be thought of as a higher octave energy of Venus. To give some examples:

VENUS	NEPTUNE
Love	Spiritual love
Desires	Ideals/beliefs
Compassion for loved ones	Compassion for all
Partnership	Merging
Laziness	Dreaminess

Neptune's orbit takes it 165 years to travel the zodiac, spending about fourteen years in each sign, so, like Uranus, its effect in terms of its sign position is generational. Neptune in Sagittarius (1970-84) implies excessive idealism, religious delusion, impractical ideas about the so-called new age. Neptune in Capricorn (1984-1998) subjects all established structures, especially political ones, to a dissolving influence; there may be materialistic delusion, with excessive materialism, but an opportunity to bring a more spiritual outlook to society's structure.

pluto

There are two accepted symbols for Pluto. The first one was simply derived from the letters P and L, its first two letters and also the initials of Percival Lowell. The second symbol is esoterically derived from the cross of matter, semi-circle of soul and circle of spirit.

We have reached the outermost planet in our solar system that is recognised by astronomers. It was discovered as recently as 1930, in a similar way to Neptune. As improvements in technology led to more data on Neptune being collected, it was realised that its size and orbit was not accounting for all the perturbation in the orbit of Uranus. Also, the orbit of

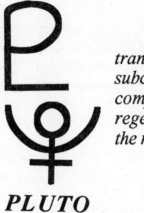

*transformation
subconscious
compulsion
regeneration
the masses*

PLUTO

Neptune was itself not turning out to be exactly as predicted. So the existence of a further planet beyond Neptune was proposed. Calculations were carried out by the astronomer Percival Lowell and published in 1915, but it was 18.2.1930 before an extensive programme of photographing the sky by the astronomer Clyde Tombaugh revealed the existence of this planet in a similar position to that predicted by Lowell.

It took so long to find Pluto because it is so far away – on average about thirty-nine times farther from the Sun than the Earth. This makes studying it rather difficult, and even today our astronomical knowledge is rather limited. It appears that Pluto is a rather small planet, smaller than the Earth, so small that, using conventional physics, it is not in fact massive enough to account for the irregularities in the orbits of Neptune and Uranus. With Neptunian illusion, it was only found where it was by coincidence, not through scientific method, but Neptunian intuition.

Pluto's orbital plane is farther from the ecliptic than all the other planets and it does not appear to be similar in composition to the outer planets, Jupiter through Neptune, often called the 'gas giants' because of their size and structure. Its orbit is also eccentric so that at times it is comes closer to the Sun than Neptune. Two speculations are that it did not originate within our solar system, or that it was originally a moon of Neptune.

If we are correct in regarding Pluto's mass as small, then it may prove an obstacle to the development of a scientific theory of astrology – or, if we can demonstrate a scientifically measurable effect of Pluto, may prove the key to understanding a scientific basis.

Astrologers began studying Pluto as soon as an ephemeris for it was available. It is so far from the Sun that it takes 248 years to complete one orbit. Although that works out at an average of 20 years per sign, its orbit is so eccentric that the time in each sign varies from about 12 to 31 years. Again, its influence in terms of its sign will be generational, with its energy being absorbed into the horoscope via its relationship to other planets. Living astrologers have not been able to experience its effect in every sign. It was in Cancer when discovered, and by the end of the century will only have moved as far as Sagittarius.

In mythology, Pluto was the god of the underworld, Hades. He ruled the land where people went to after death. Implicit in the mythology is that people's souls did survive after death. Many cultures also have beliefs in reincarnation. One of Pluto's main concerns is the principle of transformation. Its position in a chart can show what areas of a person's life they are able to totally transform by the principle of annihilation followed by rebirth.

It is perhaps through Pluto that we become aware of mass consciousness, the idea that we all share a basic link to the cosmos. Neptune dissolves ego so that spiritual awareness of others is allowed in, but Pluto, through the annihilation of desire, can bring us in tune with cosmic reality.

We are dealing with very high level concepts here, ones that are often difficult for us to comprehend and incorporate into our lives. Just as we might say that Uranus became apparent at the beginning of our technological age, and Neptune has perhaps ushered in an age of higher spiritual awareness, so perhaps Pluto is representing a power that we have yet to fully recognise. Its most obvious connection in this sense is the one astrologers make between Pluto and nuclear power. This is a very Plutonian concept – the way only a small amount of matter can through sudden transformation release tremendous amounts of energy, the way a nuclear power station may remain safe for years, but when a fault occurs, have a devastating effect.

Exposure to low-level doses of radiation, or carcinogenic substances, can also appear to have no effect, but then apparently cause a medical condition to flare up very suddenly. Pluto is linked to the assimilation into our society of cancer as a widespread disease. Pluto's link with death also makes it difficult for our society to approach, not because of our fear of death, but the fact it is a taboo subject in modern society. It also seems connected with the experience of sex.

Too often Pluto's energy manifests in its degenerative phase only. Thus we feel the need to destroy, but fail to rebuild from the ashes of what we eliminated. Thus we are obsessed with transforming others, when all we can truly transform is ourselves. And Pluto is implicated in all sorts of activities whose basis is corruption, such as pollution, pornography, criminality and waste of resources.

Perhaps it is because the principles Pluto represents are not fully integrated into our society, that these unpleasant effects often seem prevalent. Pluto promises that we are given the ability to develop the capacity for utilising its raw cosmic power to eliminate what is unproductive and leave only what is of value. Often astrologers have described Pluto as having two faces – representing both the ultimate good and ultimate evil.

Pluto can be seen as a higher octave of Mars energy. But whereas Mars gives energy for physical action, Pluto taps into raw cosmic power.

MARS	PLUTO
Change	Transform
Kill	Annihilate
Guns	Nuclear weapons
Action based on self-interest	Action based on interest of the masses
Ego	Mass consciousness
Drive	Obsession

the outer planets and civil unrest

URANUS AND NEPTUNE

In the mid-1990's Uranus and Neptune will be at very similar longitudes, and several times they we will be at the same longitude. Uranus, appearing as it does to move faster, 'catches up' Neptune and then 'overtakes' it. For example, at 08:11 GMT on 2.2.1993 they will both be exactly at 19° 33' Capricorn. When two planets are close together like this, they are said to form a conjunction. Because of retrogradation an exact conjunction will occur three times and their relatively slow movement through the zodiac means that the two planets will stay very close together for some years either side of the exact conjunction. During this period, the energies of the planets will be seeking to merge and express together.

Since this particular conjunction will only occur approximately every 172 years, we can look back through history to previous ones. The last one happened round about 1820. At this time, there was social unrest in England, with discontent focussed on the mass movement for the repeal of Corn Laws, which kept bread prices artificially high. Demonstrations against the government were centred on the activities of the Anti-Corn-Law League. On 16.8.1819 over 60,000 people peaceably demonstrated in Manchester for reform of the government — hardly had the speakers begun to address the crowd when the local magistrates sent in armed troops to break up the meeting. The results were eleven deaths and over 600 casualties and the event became known as the Peterloo massacre.

The previous conjunction to that occurred in the late 1640's. This period is that of the English Civil War, when the people rebelled against the authority of the King. It can be seen as an attempt towards a more egalitarian society, founded on idealism. Particularly relevant in this context are the Levellers. Those who belonged to this movement basically decided that since they were free of the king, they could also be free of oppression by parliament. Their aims were universal suffrage, republicanism and a written constitution. Their name derives from their wish to 'level men's estates', so that all were equal. There should be freedom of worship, no conscription, and equality before the law. Thus we can see that Uranian energy for change and rebellion was merged with the Neptunian spiritual dream. Their aims

130

were peaceful yet impractical in the society of their day. Although there was a strong Leveller faction in the army, they failed to gain its full support and eventually the troops were sent in to disperse them. The leaders were either killed or imprisoned and the movement suppressed.

This by no means constitutes scientific proof of planetary influences on world affairs, but as the 1990's begin similar energies seem to be in operation. It must first be noted that 1988/89 saw a Saturn-Uranus conjunction – part of a forty-five year cycle closely linked to the balance of freedom v. authoritarianism. These two planets have very different energies, Saturn standing for order and Uranus for rebellion. This conjunction seems to have sparked off a protest against established government, not just in Eastern Europe, but also in the UK, where the dissatisfaction with the Conservative government began to be expressed much more vehemently.

As Uranus and Neptune closed together, there was increasing protest against governments in many countries, though with Uranian rebelliousness largely tempered by the peace of Neptune. It is indicative of the blending of these two planets that there is a certain amount of idealism. In Eastern Europe, the call was for freedom. Harsh reality is likely to impinge upon this concept which seems a perfect blend of Uranian equality and nebulous Neptunian idealism. New governments of any persuasion are likely to find it hard to deliver what their peoples want and may yet face further protest under the effects of this conjunction.

We are never at the mercy of the planets. Many factors add their influence. In much of Eastern Europe, change was initially peaceful. Rumania and Nepal saw an establishment prepared to use force in an unsuccessful attempt to retain power. In China, the force of authoritarianism crushed the peaceful protest. In the UK, it seems that the establishment, keen to welcome civil protest in Eastern Europe, is less happy when its own position is questioned.

In the Spring of 1990, there were riots in London focussed on unpopular government measures. There were also a series of major disturbances in British prisons. At this time the heavy planet Jupiter was approaching a point opposite Uranus in the zodiac and these two planets were also in a stressful relationship with the Aries Sun, a very aggressive combination. The government's ability to be flexible is crucial in determining the course of events. A change of government alone is not likely to resolve the tension.

URANUS AND PLUTO

A conjunction between Uranus and Pluto occurs on average every 127 years, though its periodicity varies considerably owing to the latter's eccentric orbit. As with Uranus-Neptune, its effect will last for a number of years. This conjunction will blend Uranian energy for revolutionary change, innovation and equality with the unconscious motivation and annihilative change of powerhouse Pluto. Both planets are inherently disruptive, with characteristics of violent transformation.

The last Pluto-Uranus conjunction occurred in the mid 1960's. This was indeed a time of civil unrest in many countries. In the USA and France, student riots led to deaths and the governments of the day were threatened. In the UK, the news was dominated by reports of demonstrations and sit-ins, people were out marching the streets for equality and revolutionary change for a better world. This is just the sort of reaction that astrological theory predicts will occur under the conjunction of these two planetary energies. Astrologers are quick to point out that if we look back through history to the time of the previous conjunction of these planets, we come to the year 1848 – a year when revolution swept across Europe. Admittedly Britain did not experience this, though there was a great fear in the establishment that it would.

By the 70's and 80's, these two planets were no longer in conjunction. But there is a whole generation of people who have this conjunction in their birth charts. The energy to bring sweeping change is instilled within them. Most of these people will not experience or tune in to the energy strongly enough to be world-changers in an individual sense and the temptation when you are carrying this sort of power is to use it for purely personal gain.

Astrologers' experience is that many people with this conjunction have a sense of unease about the way our society is run and want to make fundamental changes. Often there is a sense of uncertainty – they are conscious they have something deep inside them, but do not know yet how to use it. So from this generation can come the people who can change the world – whether this is for good or bad, depends on how they choose to use the energy. Since Pluto is involved with nuclear

132

power and Uranus technological change, it seems that this generation will either tame the nuclear beast or destroy us in the process. Since it occurred in Virgo, one gets a sense of them being here to clean up the world. Pluto's power involves the sudden abandonment of old habits and the regeneration into the new; this can be a destructive or a constructive process. Uranus is a high technology planet and both are involved in the occult. The conjunction permits an opportunity to reach a fuller understanding of how the forces of energy work in the Universe.

All the transpersonal planets are concerned with change. They can be seen as a spiritual response to the materialistic demands of Jupiter and Saturn, particularly the problems of restriction presented by the latter.

Through Uranus we respond to these by striking out in new directions, or merely being rebels without a cause. Through Neptune we can seek spiritual illumination or choose to attempt avoidance of the problems by escape into fantasy. Pluto, though it gives the opportunity for the annihilation of what is no longer required and rebirth in a new form, can also mean a response that just senselessly destroys the foundations of what has gone before.

The change is from a self-centred viewpoint to a more cosmic awareness. Just as these are outer planets of our solar system, discovered as we look out into space, so we incorporate their energies as our philosophy and awareness expands beyond the ego-centred affairs expressed in the personal planets and beyond the society-centred demands of the impersonal planets. They are the mind spirit and body of our higher selves.

chiron

Most people have heard of all the planets we have looked at so far, even if they do not know in which order they orbit, or what their sizes are. But Chiron (pronounced Kai-ron) is new to most people.

healing
teaching
maverick
initiation
irritation

CHIRON

It was discovered by Charles Kowall on 1.11.1977. Its orbit is eccentric. At its farthest it is nearly as far out as Uranus, whilst at its closest approach to the Sun is inside the orbit of Saturn. There are over 2000 asteroids or minor planets which have been catalogued, and Chiron was classified as one too. Yet astronomers have not decided what Chiron actually is. It is too far out to be an asteroid. Its orbit and apparent size seem to rule out it being a comet and it is too small to be called a planet. So they tend to settle for the word *planetoid*. Like Pluto, one suggestion is that it originated outside our solar system.

Chiron's orbital period varies quite considerably but its period at the moment is nearly fifty-one years. Its eccentric orbit results in a variation of between two and ten years in the time it spends in any one sign.

Its unusual nature means that it has merited a lot of astrological attention. A society was formed, the Association for the Study of Chiron, to collate astrological data and views. The effects of Pluto are still somewhat debatable after 60 years, but with Chiron we have only had a few years to study it, and it is an area where working astrologers are still contributing to the development of knowledge. Therefore some of the following is necessarily speculative and a personal viewpoint.

The astrologer Al Morrison has perhaps summed up Chiron best as an "incovenient benefic". It draws attention to the areas of your chart that it affects. You do not feel comfortable as Chiron niggles away, so you do something to change things. The initial upheaval is unpleasant, but afterwards you realise it was all for the best.

Another keyword accepted for Chiron is *maverick*. Its position in a chart shows where you're not afraid to go against established thought. But it is not as rebellious as Uranus. Chiron has an underlying practicality that Uranus does not. Uranus is so often merely eccentric, or rebellious just for the sake of it, but Chiron-activated thoughts and actions, though unorthodox and threatening to the establishment, contain the grains of reality.

Chiron was the wisest of the Centaurs, or perhaps more correctly, the only wise one. Centaurs were Sagittarian beasts, and they tended to express the more fun-loving, animalistic side of the sign. Chiron was above all that, representing spiritual wisdom. Many of the famous figures such as Hercules and Achilles were taught by Chiron, and his particular skills were centred on healing.

Chiron's planetary energy seems to be linked with teaching, but of a spiritual nature rather than everyday matters. It is higher than the religious/moralising tone expressed in Jupiter and yet tempered with a degree of practicality not found in Uranus or Neptune, for example. It is therefore associated with the rather nebulous concept of spiritual awareness. It may be associated with the ability to wake up from the daily grind and become aware that there is a greater meaning to the Universe.

The mythological Chiron was accidentally wounded by a poisoned arrow, but since he was immortal, he did not die; he experienced the suffering of mortals, but without the release of death. Thus the concept of the wounded healer is relevant to Chiron's energy. Through our own suffering, we truly learn how to heal others. Chiron's discovery may well be linked with the explosion of complementary, holistic medicine. Just as we can link all the transpersonals to raised states of consciousness, Chiron may well be linked with the arrival of the new age, with all the positive benefits as well as illusion that this will bring. Its position in our birth charts may show how we respond to this challenge.

When it was discovered, Chiron was in Taurus, that most Earth-centred of signs. Perhaps the healing crisis is that of our own planet. In learning to deal with the vast environmental problems we have created, we have the opportunity to develop a better way of living.

Chiron to me also suggests a desire to get things right, not in the sense of the letter of the law but more in its spirit. Chiron linked with Mars in a chart seems to produce a crusading spirit that does not like to see injustice – the rest of the chart will influence whether the desire to right wrongs is merited or not – one can be a crusader or a vigilante. And although Chiron's energy might easily express in a broad-viewed way, it does seem to balance this with an attention to detail. I have noticed its niggly characteristics influencing the energy of other planets to be applied in a pernickety way. Chiron focuses attention on details, yet brings wider change.

It has been suggested that, because its orbit links Saturn and Uranus, that it combines the attributes of those planets. It seems to me, however, that perhaps a blending of a higher octave of Saturn and Jupiter might be more appropriate.

A number of symbols have been suggested for Chiron, but the one which seems to be settling into common use is the one that looks like a key. As we come to understand more about this fascinating body, we may well find that it is the key to unlocking our awareness of the transpersonal planets.

rulerships and exaltations

Rulership is a concept often mentioned in astrology. People say things such as "the head is ruled by Mars", "alcohol is ruled by Pisces", or even "astrology is ruled by Uranus".

As astrology developed, certain planets were found to be more at home when found in certain signs. We have observed how, as we have looked at the planets as they express their energy through each sign of the zodiac, they express more easily in some signs than others. For example, the self-promoting energy of Mars is easily put to good effect when it is found in ego-centred Aries, but its aggressive energy is not easily expressed when it is in harmony-seeking Libra. In time, each planet came to be associated with a particular sign, which it was said to rule. Sometimes the arcane word *dignity* is used for a planet in the sign it rules.

You might like to consider from your knowledge of astrology which planets ought to go with which signs. For instance, you should be aware having read about Mercury and Pisces that Mercury's inherent sense of detail does not express very easily in the broad-sighted, dissolving energy of Pisces. Where a planet is poorly placed by the rulership test, it is said to be in its *detriment*.

Here is a list of planetary rulerships of the signs.

Planet	Rulership	Detriment
Sun	Leo	Aquarius
Moon	Cancer	Capricorn
Mercury	Gemini	Sagittarius
	Virgo	Pisces
Venus	Taurus	Scorpio
	Libra	Aries
Mars	Aries	Libra
Jupiter	Sagittarius	Gemini
Saturn	Capricorn	Cancer

Uranus	Aquarius	Leo
Neptune	Pisces	Virgo
Pluto	Scorpio	Taurus

You should have noticed that the sign of a planet's detriment is opposite to the one it rules.

Mercury and Venus are allotted two signs each — at the moment there are only 10 planets, but 12 signs. Before the discovery of Uranus, there were only seven planets to use, so more had to be allocated twice. We can put the planets which were found to be associated with each sign on a zodiac wheel, allocating the Sun to Leo and the Moon to Cancer. If we then move around the circle in both directions we see that we are including the planets in sequence according to their distance from the Sun.[*]

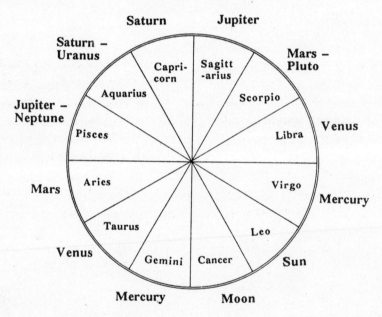

---

[*] *If Chiron is important enough to be considered a planet, then which sign does it rule? It is clearly associated with Sagittarius, but we already have Jupiter there. Various astrologers have suggested at various times, Virgo, Libra, Scorpio and Sagittarius as being associated with it (these four signs also happen to be adjacent). My feeling is to suggest Virgo, which is also convenient as this is one of the signs without a unique ruler (Mercury also ruling Gemini). If we count Chiron as a transpersonal, we can relate Uranus to mind (air), Neptune to emotion (water) and Pluto to the energy to act (fire — although Scorpio is a water sign, Pluto is exalted in Leo and also co-rules Aries). This leaves Chiron as an earthy planet. We will probably have to wait a number of years for a consensus on Chiron's rulership.*

As well as associating Jupiter with Sagittarius, it is also given rulership of Pisces. And Saturn rules Aquarius as well as Capricorn. These rulerships are often referred to as co-rulership i.e. Jupiter is said to be a 'co-ruler' of Pisces with Neptune.

There is no need to overemphasise planetary rulerships of signs. They do not really mean that if you have got Venus in Taurus you will have wonderful friendships, or if Venus is in Virgo you will upset all your friends by nagging them. The Taurean Venus might be lazy or lascivious, whilst the Virgoan one might be just the job for helping friends out with practical assistance.

When astrologers talk about a planet or sign ruling a particular matter, all they mean is that the energy associated with it is involved with the thing they are talking about. For example, the nature of alcohol and all drugs seems bound up with the energy of Pisces. The principal of government is ruled by authoritarian Capricorn.

EXALTATION

This is another word encountered when discussing the relationship of planets to signs. As well as being at home in the sign of its rulership, a planet also has another sign where it expresses very easily, usually more so than the sign of its rulership. It is said to be *exalted* when found in this sign. Mercury, for example is exalted when it's in Aquarius, for here its intellectual energy is coloured with Aquarian inspiration and flashes of brilliance. The home-loving Moon is exalted in sensual Taurus. Once again, the opposite sign to the exaltation (known as a planet's *fall*) is one where the planet's energy does not naturally express easily.

Planet	Exaltation	Fall
Sun	Aries	Libra
Moon	Taurus	Scorpio
Mercury	Aquarius	Leo
Venus	Pisces	Virgo
Mars	Capricorn	Cancer
Jupiter	Cancer	Capricorn
Saturn	Libra	Aries

Uranus	Scorpio	Taurus
Neptune	Cancer	Capricorn
Pluto	Leo	Aquarius
Chiron	Sagittarius?	Gemini?

Again this is a help in tying in planetary energies with zodiac sign energies, but it does not have too much meaning in chart interpretation – although having a planet in the sign of its exaltation is useful, because the energy of the planet is so readily available, and having a planet in the sign of its fall can cause extra difficulties.

 Rulerships and exaltations are a good way of learning which planets go well with which signs, and hence which planetary energies are similar to the energies of which sign.

part five

what's on the ascendant?

We have now looked at all the planets. In addition to these, there are certain points in space that astrologers give a meaning to. Most of these, such as the nodes of the Moon, the vertex and the Part of Fortune, though useful, are not vital for the beginner, but there is one very important point we must look at. This is the *ascendant*. This is the point of the zodiac as which is on the eastern horizon at the time of birth. The zodiac sign here is often called the *rising sign*, as it the one that is rising over the eastern horizon.

The Sun appears to us to go around the Earth every twenty-four hours. If you look at the stars in the night sky you will observe that over a few hours they will appear to have moved in a clockwise direction; they will mark out a circular path in a twenty-four hour period. Since we divided the whole sky up into the twelve signs of the zodiac we can see that they too will all travel in a complete circle around us in a day. So just as the Sun rises, so each zodiac sign will rise in turn through the course of a day. If Aries was on the eastern horizon at 6am, by 8am Aries will have fully risen and Taurus will be there.

An astrological chart is a two-dimensional map of the heavens at a particular time. On a conventional map, north is at the top, and east is at the right.

Astrological maps are *upside down*. The points of the compass are not shown on a birth chart, but if they were, they would be like in fig (i).

The Sun rises in the East, and so do the zodiac signs. The rising sign, or ascendant, is therefore the one shown at this point on a chart.

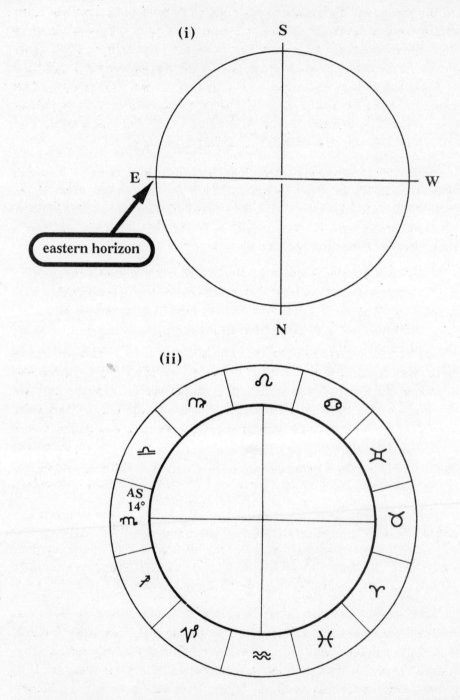

In this example – fig (ii) – the rising sign is Scorpio. Just as we saw how we can plot an exact position in degrees for the planets, so we can

142

for the ascendant. In the above example, 14 degrees of Scorpio had risen at the time of birth. If you have a computer print-out, a position in degrees and minutes will be shown. The problem here is that, if we divide the minutes in a day by the degrees in a circle, we get 1440/360 = 4. This means that the signs rise at a rate of one degree every four minutes. If your actual birth time was 20 minutes later than you think it was, that's 5 degrees of sign different. It may not mean much – or that 5 degrees may take you into a different rising sign.

Since each of the twelve signs will on average take two hours to pass over the horizon, you could be up to two hours wrong and still get the correct ascendant on your chart, but with someone else, a few minutes might make all the difference. So to work out the rising sign it is vital that we know the time of a person's birth fairly accurately.

> One thing to watch out for with birth times is when someone tells you they were born at, say, 5pm. Check that they really mean five in the afternoon – it's surprising how many people get am and pm mixed up.

I recall one client, born in the UK, who did not know her exact DAY of birth. Was it 5th or 6th December – even her mother was not sure. She did know the time – 7.10am. This is probably better than knowing the day and not the time. Apart from the Moon, the planets will not have moved much and the ascendant and (as we will see later) house positions will be pretty accurate. Since in this individual's case, the Moon had changed signs in between times, it was easy to establish the right day, because she was obviously a paranoid Moon-in-Scorpio rather than an opinionated Sagittarian Moon.

We will also see that we need to know the place of birth, at least as close as the nearest place we can find in a good atlas, and not just because of the time zone adjustment we made earlier. Occasionally there are people who are not sure where they were born.

Let's suppose that we do have a pretty accurate birth time. How does one find out someone's rising sign? This is perhaps the most difficult part of the subject that students encounter, so it is probably easiest if we take a simplified example first, and for those who are interested, then present some exact calculations. If you have had a birth chart drawn up, you do not need to know all the technicalities to understand it. These days, even a professional astrologer need not know how to work out the ascendant's position if he or she has a computer to do it. However, it does help one's understanding of astrology to grasp the basic essentials.

FINDING THE ASCENDANT: a simplified overview

We said that you could mark the points of a compass, albeit an upside-down one, on a birth chart. We can also mark on it the hours of a clock, but you need to think of it as a twenty-four-hour clock – fig (iii).

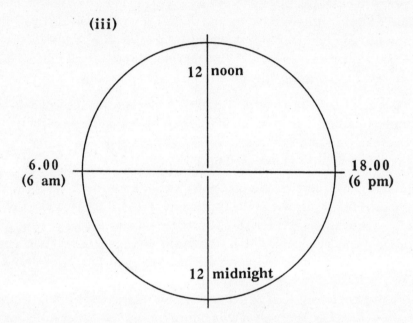

(iii)

12 noon

6.00
(6 am)

18.00
(6 pm)

12 midnight

Suppose someone was born at 12 noon on 4.2.69. We can mark the Sun symbol on the chart at 12 noon. (We are dealing with local time after adjusting for Summer time here, not GMT) We can then look up in the ephemeris for the position of the Sun. To the nearest degree it was at 15 degrees of Aquarius at noon on 4.2.69. Since we can divide the circle into twelve 30-degree zodiac signs, we can plot the position of Aquarius on the chart. The Sun is at the fifteenth degree of Aquarius, so Aquarius will be spread fifteen degrees before the Sun, and fifteen after. Fig. (iv).

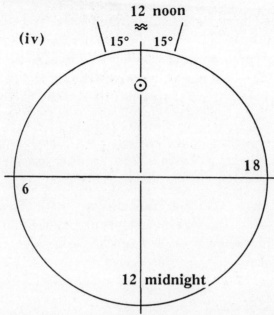

(iv)

12 noon
≈≈
15° | 15°

☉

18

6

12 | midnight

From this we can divide the whole chart into the 12 thirty degree chunks required for all the signs. The Sun is going round in the direction of the clock, and so are the signs. What sign follows – rises after – Aquarius? Pisces. After that it's Aries and after that it's Taurus. Mark these in on the chart and we have the sign on the eastern horizon – Taurus. The person with this chart has Sun in Aquarius and Taurus rising. Fig. (v).

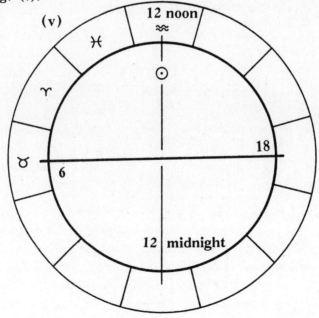

(v)

12 noon
≈≈

☉

♓

♈

♉

18

6

12 | midnight

145

Now we had better stop and remind ourselves that we have been simplifying. If we do the simple calculation for our sample chart of 3.2.69 07:30 GMT, we will come up with Pisces as being the rising sign. Unfortunately, it is not that simple. The correct calculations for the rising sign in this chart show that it is actually in Aquarius – one sign different.

This is why, if you have had your chart drawn up already, when you look at it, your Sun probably will not be in the exact position it would be if you used the above clock face simplification.

We will do a full rising sign calculation for our sample chart. We already adjusted the time to GMT by taking account of the time zone and daylight saving time. We needed to know the place of birth to adjust for these, but we also need this now, for we will refer to the longitude and latitude of that place in our calculations.

FINDING THE EXACT ASCENDANT

This is perhaps the most difficult part of learning to draw up charts. The 24 hour period we call *a day* is based on the time it takes for the Earth to make one complete revolution on its axis in relation to the Sun. More correctly we can call this *a solar day*. But since in astrology we are interested in the position of heavenly bodies (including the Sun) against the star background, we need to know how long it takes the Earth to revolve in relation to this.

Suppose we are able to look out of a window at 10 pm – 22:00 – this evening. Across the road is a house with TV ariel, and directly above this ariel we are able to see a bright star. Of course, if we look out a little while later, the star will not be above the ariel; it will appear to have moved relative to it, because of the daily spinning of the Earth on its axis. Just as the Sun appears to move through the sky during a day, so do the stars. If we look out again at 22:00 tomorrow, where will that same star be? It will be above the TV ariel again, having appeared to have gone all the way around the Earth in the intervening 24 hours.

In actual fact the star day is not exactly the same as the 24 hour solar day. If we were able to measure the time the star was exactly above the TV ariel on the second day we would find it would not arrive there at 22:00 but actually at 21:56 and 4.09 seconds, or about four minutes earlier. So if we were able to look out at a clear sky at 22:00 on every successive night, we would see a slightly changing position of all the

146

stars from night to night. The length of star day is 23 hours, 56 minutes and 4.09 seconds.*

Time based on this star clock is known as *sidereal time*. To calculate the exact ascendant, what we need to find is the local sidereal time for our birth data.

1. The first step is to look up in the ephemeris for the date of birth (remember to use the GMT date of birth) and find the figure given in the sid. time column. The ephemeris in this book gives sidereal times in hours and minutes. For intervening dates, add four minutes for every day. For midnight on 3.2.69 this gives a sid. time of 8:52. The actual figure in a full ephemeris, including seconds is 8:51:59.

2. When we have done this we add it to the interval from midnight to the time of birth.

   Sidereal time midnight   08:51:59

   Add: GMT of birth   07:30:00

   sub-total   16:21:59

3. The next adjustment we have to make is called the *longitude equivalent*. To enable us to work out the positions of the planets in the signs we had to convert our time to GMT. But we do not want to know the sign on the horizon at Greenwich (or anywhere at 0° longitude), but the sign on the horizon for the place of birth. Remember what we said about one degree of the zodiac rising over the horizon every four minutes of time. For every degree of longitude the birth place is away from the 0° meridian of Greenwich, we will need to adjust the sidereal time at Greenwich by four minutes to arrive at the local sidereal time. If the birthplace was a Western longitude, we subtract it, if Eastern we add it.

For our sample chart, the birthplace was Birmingham, UK, a longitude of approximately 2° W, so that is 2 x 4 = subtract 8 minutes.

---

* *Suppose we were able to look out at 22:00 on the same DATE next year, what would we see ? The star would be there again, directly over the TV ariel. Well, yes, but not exactly! We won't go into a detailed technical explanation here, but at the same time and date a year later, the star's position will be about 50 seconds of longitude different – not enough to be detected by the naked eye, although this adds up to a whole degree after 72 years. This phenomenon, termed 'precession', means that the star background will travel a complete circle relative to the earth in about 25,800 years, a period sometimes termed the 'Great Year'. All this 'Age of Aquarius' stuff – much of which seems to me to have dubious value – is related to this.*

sub-total (as above)	16:21:59
Longitude equivalent (E+/W-)	- 00:08:00
sub-total	16:13:13

The longitude equivalent doesn't make much difference here, because of the proximity to the Greenwich meridian. But, for example, someone born in Canberra, Australia, at 150° E, we would have to add 150 x 4 = 600 minutes = add 10 hours.

4. There's one more adjustment we ought make if we want to be as accurate as we can. This is the rather arcane-sounding *acceleration on the interval*. For each hour of the interval between midnight and the GMT time of birth, we must add 10 seconds. That is not much – only 4 minutes in a whole day – but it could make a difference. For our sample chart it works out at 7½ hours x 10 = 75 seconds.

sub-total (as above)	16:13:13
Acceleration on interval	00:01:15
TOTAL	16:14:28

The reason for this adjustment is that in our calculations we have used the time between midnight and the time of birth expressed in hours – which are divisions of our solar day. But we need to work in sidereal time – that of a star day – and as we saw that clock runs about four minutes a day faster than our solar-based clock. That 4 minutes in a day works out to 10 seconds for every hour and that is why the rule for the acceleration on the interval is "add ten seconds per hour of interval". If you can't remember whether to add or subtract the ten seconds, remember that acceleration means moving faster i.e. *adding* velocity.

The interval we are calculating the acceleration on is the time period between midnight and the GMT of birth. It's not really necessary to work other than to the nearest hour here, but if you want to be pernickety then add 2¼ seconds for each quarter of an hour of interval.

Watch out! The acceleration on the interval is never longer than approximately 4 minutes in 24 hours, and our interval can never be longer than 24 hours, otherwise we would be into the next day in the ephemeris. It can only ever be included in the calculation as minutes and seconds – but it is very easy to stick the figure in the wrong column and put, for example, 1 hour and 15 minutes, instead of 1 minute and 15 seconds.

5. Sometimes it may happen that when we add up the figures to get the local sidereal time, the total comes to more than 24 hours. In this case, simply deduct 24 hours to get a useable figure.

6. One final adjustment we may have to make is for someone born at a latitude south of the equator, in which case we must add 12 hours to get the local sidereal time.

Here's a summary for our sample chart:

1. Sidereal time midnight	08:51:59 taken from ephemeris for GMT date
2. Add: GMT of birth	07:30:00 the interval from midnight to birth
sub-total	16:21:59
3. Longitude equivalent (E+/W-)-	00:08:00 4 minutes of time per degree of longitude ADD for East/SUBTRACT for West
sub-total	16:13:13
4. Acceleration on interval:	00:01:15 ADD 10 seconds per hour of interval
TOTAL	16:14:28 = LOCAL SIDEREAL TIME
5. subtract 24 hours if necessary	not necessary
6. subtract 12 hours if S Latitude	not necessary

Of course, you can save yourself all the detailed calculations if you use a computer programme or get your chart drawn up by an astrologer. You do not need to be able to draw up charts to be able to interpret them, although I think it helps your understanding. And there is always the likelihood of making mistakes in manual calculations. Do not expect to be able to do quick calculations without practice.

Now we have arrived at the local sidereal time, the star time for the place of birth, we can proceed to find the correct rising sign and the amount of degrees that have risen. We do this by using a *table of houses*. A common reference works used by astrologers is *Raphael's Table of Houses* (see bibliography). Included in the tables at the back of the book is a simplified table of houses, which shows just ascendant positions.

All you have to do is look down the first column until you find the sidereal time that is nearest to the local sidereal time you have calculated. Then read across the row to the column for the LATITUDE of the place of birth.

So in our example chart, we look down the column of sidereal times until we come to the one nearest to our value of 16:14:28. If we take an extract of the pertinent figures from the table, we will see that our local sidereal time falls about halfway between two sid.time figures in the table.

Sid. time	51°N		53°N	
16:12:13	5.45	≈	2.35	≈
16:16:27	7.24		4.14	

The column with the nearest latitude is 53°N, so we will need to take a figure halfway between the two figures in the latitude column, 2°35' and 4°14' of Aquarius which equals about 3½°. But since our latitude is actually 52½°N we will need to increase this figure by about one quarter of the 3° difference between the figures in the 51°N and 53°N columns. This will add about ¾° giving an approximate ascendant of 4¼° of Aquarius.

The more mathematically inclined among you might work out a figure more accurately than that, but really all we need to know is the position to the nearest degree. And we should remember that calculating the ascendant to the exact minute of longitude will depend upon an exact time of birth and exact latitude and longitude figures. In practice, these are not often available. And as regards to the time of birth, there is some disagreement as to when the time of birth is – for example, is it when the baby's head appears, when the umbilical cord is cut, or when the baby takes its first breath?

Note that these (and most) table of houses give positions for northern latitudes. If you are preparing a chart for a southern hemisphere birth, the signs should be reversed. In other words, for a local sidereal time of 16:14:28 for someone born at 52½ degrees south, the ascendant would be 4¼° Leo – the opposite sign to Aquarius.

We started off with a simplified version of finding the ascendant. Using the local birth time, you can use this to do a quick check on your ascendant calculations. The exact ascendant worked out this way will often turn out to be in the same sign as the simplified method, and it should always be a sign near to it. If it is on the other side of the zodiac you'd better check your calculations.

what does the rising sign mean?

The rising sign represents the face we show to the world and the way the world sees us. It is the part which edits all the bits inside ourselves and then presents it to the world. To use a word from computing, it shows the sort of way we *interface* with the outside world. You may be a socialising, procrastinating Libran by Sun, but if your rising sign is Capricorn you will present a different image to the world. To people who do not know you, you will appear more reserved and serious. The Capricorn energy might make you seem more willing to make practical decisions where ordering others is necessary, but the extra caution might make you even more unwilling to make up your mind. When people get to know you more, they will see behind your Capricornian mask and through to the Libran in you – if you let them. Just as some people unbalance their planetary energies by functioning excessively through their Moon, so it can be easy to let the ascendant take over.

Because the ascendant involves how we project ourselves into the world, the energy of our rising sign is readily available, perhaps *more* readily available than any planetary energy. We express ourselves easily through this energy when we meet strangers. It is not really a conscious thing. If we actually had to get up on a stage and present ourselves, we would probably act with less spontaneity and other factors in the chart would take over.

The ascendant does involve the way we see ourselves and so we need to be honest. It is about self-image. We need to be aware that it is a mask, a way of coping with the world, and not the real person. Sometimes people get so wrapped up in their rising sign they really believe it is the real them. People they meet, who do not know them too well, may sense this energy that is being projected and react accordingly, thus strengthening the image. People who do know them get fed up with them pretending. If our self-image is not realistic and working positively for us, it can be difficult to get the rest of the chart working well. Because the rising-sign energy is so easily available, it can be very useful, but it is also very easy to go over the top and forget the rest of ourselves.

Some ascendants are perhaps more useful than others. The energy expressed by Aries, for example, is quite compatible with the idea of projecting yourself out into the world and would be quite helpful to someone with an unassertive Sun. Taurus rising on the other hand might give people the impression you were a bit slow and dopey. The fixity of Taurus is not so conducive with the get-up-and-do nature of the ascendant. Of course, if your chart was already full of lots of get-up-and-do, an Aries ascendant might take you completely over the top, whilst a Taurus ascendant might be just the thing to calm you down and add stability. See how, by talking about different factors in a chart, we are already taking the first steps towards synthesising all the energies into a complete picture.

The rising sign even affects our physical appearance. People with Leo or Sagittarius on the ascendant are often larger than life; Capricorn-rising and you're big and bony. Aries and your head is stuck out in front of you. Of course, you may find that you have a planet whose position in the zodiac is very close to the position of your ascendant. This will modify the ascendant energy according to the nature of the planet involved.

The planet which rules the rising sign in a horoscope is referred to as the *chart ruler* and this planet takes on extra importance. For example, if Aries is the ascendant, then the sign and house position of Mars, and the relationship between it and the other planets are often highly significant in assessing the important issues for the person concerned.

If you really cannot find out an exact birth time, do not despair. It does not negate the whole of astrology, but merely means you have access to less information.

With increasing experience, you might be able to work out someone's approximate birth time by working the opposite way from usual, as it were. You find some characteristics of a person and try and decide if that might be caused by the rising sign or a planetary house position.

Since the characteristics of one rising sign are very different from the next, you may be able to use them to improve upon an approximate time of birth.

Ascendant in ARIES

If there's not a lot of action in your chart, this ascendant can really help to get you moving. It urges you to get to the forefront of whatever you are involved in. Of course, you may end up poking your nose into things you should not, and it is easy to take on too much and get out of your depth. This rising sign will impulsively try anything and has the courage to take charge where others will not. Of course, there is the typical Aries problem of losing interest once they have set out on something.

The greatest problem with this ascendant is that it's so self-centred. Whilst people who have it are courageous and will do much to help others, they can almost be blind to what others around them want.

Their inherent bravery often comes from innocence. They really do not think they are going to get their head chopped off when they stick it out too far. They may have red faces or hair and sometimes you can actually see their heads stuck out as they walk.

Ascendant in TAURUS

These people usually have a need to impress themselves on the environment, to take concrete practical action to make their mark in the world. There is an element of caution and a tendency to be slow to get moving, although when action does commence, they are usually able to persist, though this can easily turn to obstinacy. It can be difficult for them to break with bad habits.

Usually there is a great deal of gentleness with this rising sign and a love of nature. There is an outward appearance of placidity that can be calming to others, or even soporific. They like to think that they are unflappable and practical, even when as sometimes happens, they are not.

Without other influencing factors, the build is short and stocky and there is excellent physical stamina. There is often the cult of the athlete involved in this position. Inherent strength and physique can be found in men, and a calm beauty in the women, but it is easy to get flabby.

There is a need for security, usually found in materialistic things, but sometimes in beliefs or the support provided by other people. There is a love of good food and clothes – although sometimes their self-image concerning their appearance is so sure they do not bother how they dress at all.

Ascendant in GEMINI

As you might expect, this is a talkative rising sign. They think they've got the gift of the gab – and they very often have. If you know someone's got this one, be careful if they try and sell you anything because they can persuade you to do things you don't want to do. Don't believe everything they say and certainly don't treat all that they say as being seriously meant.

It's a fidgety rising sign. They have an image that it's good to be doing something, anything, even something totally useless rather than be sitting still. They'll change their clothes or their hair for no reason other than the desire for a change. It must have been a Gemini-rising who said "a change is as good as a rest".

At it is worst this a most superficial and shallow rising sign that will not go into anything deeply enough to extract any value. But it is versatility is its strong point. People with this Ascendant can gain a vast knowledge of a whole range of subjects and notice all that is happening around them. They're good people to have out front because they can talk their way out of trouble with wit and intelligence.

Ascendant in CANCER

These are generally personable people, they have a calming influence. They see themselves as protective and caring and yet are often afraid to show just how cuddly they are. They have a problem in that they are too impressionable – they take first impressions personally and at their face value and can be extremely subjective. They tend to be home lovers and makers because they feel the need for a home as a base to set out from and retreat to. They should try and use their caring, nurturing energy to good effect.

If you want variety, then live with a Cancer-rising person. Ruled by the Moon, their feelings can change every time the moon changes sign. They can be moody or just someone who changes their mind a great deal. It can be exasperating – just never think that what they have decided today will hold good tomorrow. They let opportunities go by because they are scared of hurting themselves or someone else. An inherent sense of insecurity is perhaps their greatest problem.

Ascendant in LEO

People with Leo rising want to be noticed – they see themselves as important people and require the attention and respect of the rest of us. How far they go depends on the general tenor of the chart. The more aggressive ones may dress in bright clothes, have noticeable hair-styles, and be bigger, louder and more generous than everybody; the more receptive go off in a haughty sulk when the do not get the attention they seek.

Leo-rising people often like to be at the centre of attention and many actually go onto the stage in some way. The dramatics may spill over into their day-to-day life. "All the world's a stage" to them and they are the centre of it. Very often there is an indefinable presence about them, which gets them noticed when they walk into a room – before you know it they have taken over the conversation.

They can be super organisers – they'd rather have everyone else running around doing things for them than actually lowering themselves to do the dirty work. Dignified and with noble bearing, they can however be stubborn and overbearing if they cannot get their way.

Ascendant in VIRGO

With pernickety Virgo on the ascendant, you can expect an eye for detail and a self-image of a hard worker. Often they do work hard, but sometimes you can't tell.

There's a certain amount of guilt with this sign. They will keep at things till they get them right. It is a practical rising sign gives the impression that it can cope. Other people trust them to do it right, let them get on with it. You have to remember that this one will sometimes not be coping underneath, but will not show it. Usually it can, but sometimes the needs of the other planets get neglected.

156

Some Virgo-rising people seem to turn out the opposite of what one would expect — this group also includes some of the most contrary, laziest, slubberdegullions you are likely to meet.

Ascendant in LIBRA

These people have a desire for many social relationships and therefore need contact with as many people as possible. They work well in any situation where they are dealing with lots of different people and tend to very much judge their own performance by the reactions of others; they can see themselves in someone else's eyes. They can also be very indecisive, particularly when it comes to deciding how best to express themselves in the world.

Usually they see themselves as being very fair and balanced, and not showing extremes of feeling or opinion — because they assume this about themselves, they do not often question if they are really like this. Unfortunately, they often deceive themselves here. Sometimes the desire to present a calm appearance can lead to years of suppressed anger which suddenly explodes.

Libra-rising seems to produce more attractive people than any other sign; what natural charm they have they endeavour to cultivate and develop. They can be the world's greatest charmers, a delight to meet and socialise with, but the problem is, it can be all too superficial; the moment you're gone they can turn off the smile and start slating you. Of course, they usually do it for the best of motives — to protect you. They'd rather tell a fib than tell you how rotten they really think you are.

Ascendant in SCORPIO

These people can be meek, mild and charming — until you disagree with them. Their main problem is that they feel constantly threatened, and so once they sense you are going against their wishes they puff up and try and force matters. Often they have a soft, pleasing voice that rapidly turns into a hectoring harshness once the perceived threat appears. Some of them become really paranoid, with even the inevitability of advancing age becoming a threat. Other people get a sense that they will not be messed around with and a sense of awe develops, with even their enemies respecting them.

They can be very helpful people, and as long as you are doing things their way they will provide you with as much assistance as they can give, although they do expect you to stand on your own feet at the end of it all. They are private people and do not like expressing their emotions in public. And yet their emotions run deep. Perhaps their own feelings are the biggest threat of all. They tend to only get angry behind closed doors. Sometimes the feelings get bottled up for years and then erupt in a dramatic moment that changes the course of their lives. With their sense of do-or-die and their tremendous will power they can act to transform the lives of others, motivating them to new heights – or lows.

Ascendant in SAGITTARIUS

These people can seem so cheerful, optimistic and capable that folks are forever ringing them up for advice, or asking for assistance, but the trouble is, seldom does anyone ask if they themselves need any help. They always look as if they are coping, but underneath they may feel helpless.

Often they seem to be in a constant hurry in their search for excitement, expansion and any knowledge that seems to offer spiritual advancement. They are generous and trusting and often have an optimism that is sickening to the rest of us. They do tend to be just too optimistic sometimes; they do seem to have all the luck, but it leads them into risk-taking and one day they may go too far.

They need their freedom, they hate being tied down. This can make them into great adventurers, but may also make them into blatant opportunists, as they use their inherent bonhomie to lull people into a false sense of security. The better ones can be infinitely helpful, generous and caring; the worse ones will promise you anything but when you really need them they're nowhere to be seen.

Ascendant in CAPRICORN

These people have a self-image of discipline and hard work, seeing a purpose in everything they do, needing to see a practical outcome to something before they will countenance it. There is a sense of duty about them that often ties them down into responsibilities they would probably be better off without.

Capricorn-rising people usually need to watch their posture. Some work on it when young will pay dividends when older. Usually there is a young head on old shoulders with this rising sign, and as they grow older if often seems as if somehow they are getting younger – they age beautifully. As their confidence builds, they just seem to go on getting better at everything they do as the years go by.

They project a somewhat serious image, perhaps even seeming a bit of a misery at first sight, and there is a lack of confidence that can seem to repress all the energies in the birth chart. Very often they seem to have a problem in deciding whether life should be taken completely lightly or is a really serious business; they do not know whether to laugh or cry. Competitors will tend to ignore them and then one day find Capricorn-rising has beaten them to it.

Ascendant in AQUARIUS

Aquarius-rising people need their freedom. They give out a first impression of being cool and aloof as if they are saying you can't be friendly with me just like that, because I'm different from everybody else. Once past this initial impression, they can be the most loyal of friends – just as long as you fit in with their principles; social and spiritual matters are more important to them than a mere relationship.

They see themselves as being intellectual, idea-generating people but often fail to recognise how stubborn they can be at projecting each new and possibly bizarre notion. Very often there are periods when traditional, conservative ideas and methods are followed, alternating with periods of branching out in new and unconventional directions.

They dress for impact, liking bright, electric colours. Although they generally work best in groups, they do like to stand out from the crowd. They can be great contributors of new ideas for improving the world, but may be contrary just for the sake of being different.

Ascendant in PISCES

These people have the ability to be highly creative and artistic, but very often lack the confidence to develop these skills, because they tend to be afraid to project themselves onto life's stage. Extremely impressionable, they soak up the environment and are therefore easily hurt. It is important that they choose their associates carefully, because it is so easy for them to pick up negative energies.

With Pisces rising there is also a desire for constantly changing emotional input and it can generate a very restless character that alternates between periods of introversion and extroversion. Periods alone are indeed necessary for them as a form of mental and psychic cleansing; they need in some way to rid themselves of the stresses they pick up. Many do this artistically.

They tend to have a somewhat pessimistic self-image and may feel a sense of victimisation, or that life is more of a struggle than it actually is. They tend to be held back by a lack of self-confidence that can colour the whole chart. Usually they have to face a choice between spiritual and material growth.

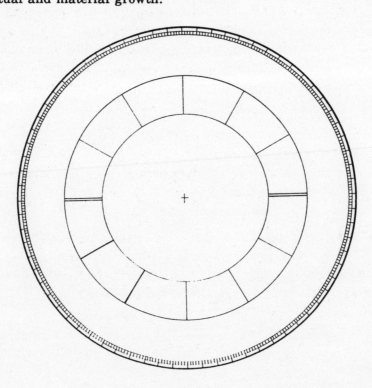

part six

drawing up a chart

On the opposite page is a blank birth chart. If you have access to a photocopier, it is probably a good idea to take a copy to work on. Around the very edge of it is a circle which is marked off at five degree intervals, and inside that a circle with all 360° marked. In the centre is a ring divided into twelve segments, each one with a number in it.

We will work step by step through drawing up a chart for our sample data. After that you might like to have a go and draw up your own.

MARKING IN THE SIGNS

Remember that the left of the chart represents the eastern horizon, so that is where the rising sign will go. The double line in the inner circle marks the horizon and so this is where the exact degree of the ascendant, in this case 4° Aquarius, is drawn. For ease of illustration, we can extend a line from the horizon to the outer circles where the degrees are marked (We wouldn't normally actually draw in this line). Four degrees of Aquarius have already risen, so we must count up (clockwise) four degrees to find where Aquarius begins. Then we draw a line from this degree to the edge of the inner ring of segments.

(i)

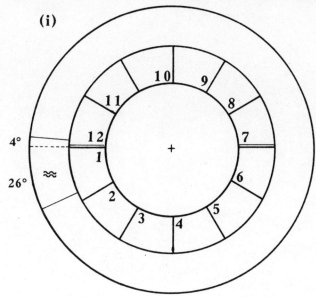

If that is the beginning of Aquarius then we must count round 30 degrees to mark where the sign ends. We draw a line there too and mark in the symbol for Aquarius between the two lines. Remember to count anti-clockwise (Fig.i). It's also a good idea to write in the number of degrees of the ascendant, in this case 4.

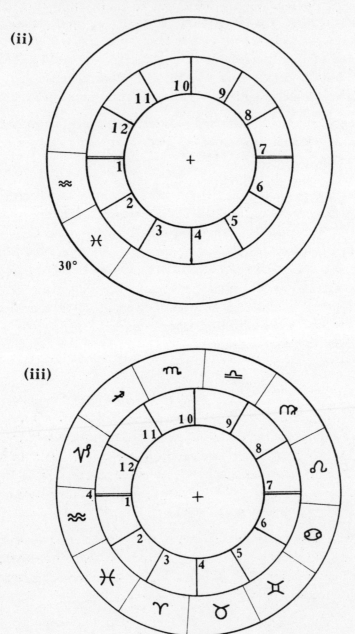

(ii)

(iii)

The sign after Aquarius is Pisces, so we can count round another 30 degrees anti-clockwise, mark in another line and mark in the symbol for Pisces (Fig. ii). Then we can continue around and mark in all the other signs. When we get to Capricorn, the last 30 degrees we count will bring us back to the first line we drew – the beginning of Aquarius. If it does not, we have miscounted somewhere. The chart should then look like Fig. iii.

MARKING IN THE PLANETS

Here are the positions to the nearest degree for our sample birth data:

☉	14	≈
☽	23	♌
☿	4	≈
♀	1	♈
♂	19	♏
♃	6	♎
♄	20	♈
♅	4	♎
♆	29	♏
♇	25	♑

Let's start with the Sun. It's at 14 degrees of Aquarius. Find the beginning of Aquarius again and count round anti-clockwise 14 degrees. It will be helpful for later if we place a ruler so that it is joining the 14th. degree of Aquarius on the outer ring and the cross in the very centre of the chart. With a pencil, mark a little nick on the innermost circle of the segmented ring.

Now draw in the symbol for the Sun in the segment where we drew the little mark (Fig. iv). Although for reasons of space we have not done so in the chart shown here, it is usual practice to write the number of degrees close to the planetary symbol on the chart.

163

(iv)

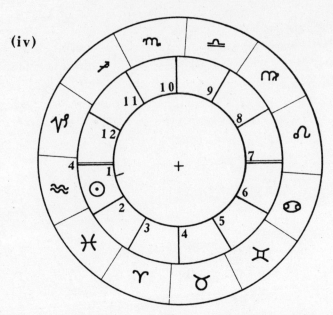

Now it's the turn of the Moon, which is at 23 degrees of Leo. Go around the circle anti-clockwise until we come to the beginning of Leo, then count on another 23 degrees. Again use a ruler to mark a nick in the innermost circle and draw in the symbol for the Moon in the segment. We should find that it is in the seventh one. (Fig. v).

(v)

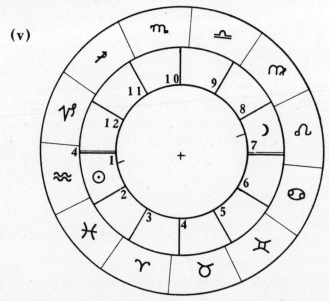

We can go through the same procedure for all the other planets and end up with a chart like Fig. vi. We are now a long way towards drawing up a complete birth chart.

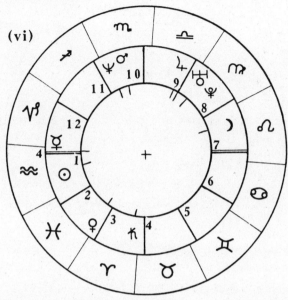

If you have had your birth chart drawn up already, you should see now how the signs and planets have been plotted. Note that there are several ways to draw up charts and that sometimes the sign segments are not shown, particularly in computer produced charts – the sign and degree of the ascendant is marked, and then the signs and degrees at points around the circle.

DRAWING UP YOUR OWN CHART

If you are drawing up your own birth chart, you should be in a position where you have found which sign each planet is in, and the degree it is at in that sign. If you know your birth time, you should also have worked out the degree of the ascendant. (If you don't have a time, see below: "What to do if you don't know the time of birth")

Here's a summary of the procedure we went through above, to help you draw up your own chart:

1. Look up what your rising sign is and the number of degrees that have risen.

2. Count up the number of degrees risen from the eastern horizon and mark in the line between the outer circle and the next circle. This marks the beginning of the rising sign. (Fig i)

165

3. Count down thirty degrees and mark in the end of the sign. Mark in the symbol for your rising sign and note the number of degrees risen. (Fig i)

4. Mark of the additional sign boundaries at thirty degree intervals, checking that the last thirty degree interval brings you back to the beginning of your rising sign. (Figs ii and iii)

5. Mark in all the symbols for the signs, following on from your rising sign, remembering to go anti-clockwise round the chart. (fig iii).

It is easy to miss a sign out. If you are familiar with opposite signs, check when you are halfway round the chart that the signs you are marking in are opposites to the first six.

6. Look up the sign and degree position of the Sun. Find the beginning of that sign and count around anticlockwise the number of degrees. Place a ruler so that it joins that degree in the outer circle and the cross in the centre of the chart, and mark a little nick on the inner ring. Mark in the symbol for the Sun and write the number of degrees close to it. (Fig iv)

7. Follow 6. for the rest of the planets. (Figs v and vi)

WHAT TO DO IF YOU DON'T KNOW THE TIME OF BIRTH

1. If this is the case, you should have worked out planetary positions at noon for your date of birth.

2. Look up the sign and degree position of the Sun. Draw in the Sun in the inner ring as usual, but positioned right on the ascendant.

3. Count up from the eastern horizon the number of degrees the Sun was at and mark in the beginning of the Sun sign.

4. From there, count anticlockwise 30 degrees and mark in the end of the Sun sign. Write in the symbol for the sign.

5. Proceed as before ...

So for our sample chart, if we did not have a birth time, the Sun would be at 14 degrees of Aquarius, and so we would mark on the ascendant as 14 degrees of Aquarius as well.This is called a *solar chart*. To remind you, it is probably best to note this somewhere on the chart – for some individuals the correct degree of the ascendant will be the degree of the

166

Sun, even when a birth time is known.

When faced with an unknown birth time, some astrologers use a process known as *rectification*, a long, detailed (and often expensive!) process which involves relating major events in a person's life to planetary *transits*. The planets are in constant motion and continue to traverse the zodiac after we are born. So, for example, a major illness might have occurred when Saturn reached the same point of the zodiac as your ascendant. If we know the degree of the ascendant, we can work out a birth time. Someone might have suddenly and unexpectedly met a new partner round about the once-in-eighty-four-year time when Uranus reached the *descendant* (the point opposite the ascendant). This chancy business means that money can be made rectifying other astrologers' rectifications.

round the houses

Astrologers divide the sky into the twelve signs of the zodiac. Each sign has its own energy. Onto that are superimposed the planets, which also represent different types of energy. The energies of the planets are modified according to which sign they are placed. The positions of the planets are determined by their orbits around the Sun and, since we are measuring their positions as viewed from the Earth – their positions relative to the Earth – the Earth's orbit affects their position too. As we have seen, the planets pass through all the signs at varying rates; the Sun goes round in one year, but when we get out as far as Neptune and Pluto we are dealing with planets that take more than a lifetime to make a complete orbit.

Astrology went into a decline towards the end of the seventeenth century partly because the theories of Copernicus came to be generally accepted. His theory that the Earth and the planets orbited the Sun and not that they all orbited the Earth was published in 1543, but as with many new scientific ideas, it took a long time to supplant existing belief. It was over a century later that his view became the orthodox, partly because it needed the work of Brahe, who provided astronomical data (but still insisted on an Earth-centred Universe), and Kepler who formulated precise laws of planetary motion, and partly because of resistance from the scientific and religious establishment.[*]

Many people seemed to think that this move from an Earth-centred (geocentric) view to a Sun-based (heliocentric) one rendered astrology invalid. Strangely enough, with the advent of relativity theory in the twentieth century, astrology has perhaps become more easy to countenance. In fact, it makes no difference whether the Sun is going around the Earth or vice-versa; what we are concerned about is the position of the Sun relative to the Earth. Fixing on the idea that the Earth orbits the Sun can be just as limiting as believing that the reverse is true. After all, the Sun does not stay at a fixed point in space. It is moving at vast speed but its motion can only be measured by relating it to other objects in the Universe. It is moving closer to some stars and galaxies and away from others. We know that placed as we are on the Earth, it appears to us that the Sun does go right around us every twenty-

---

[*] *The Greek philosopher Aristarchus had made the same suggestion in the third century B.C.*

four hours. This is often described as an illusion, but it is not. It is just a question of relative positions. We say that the Moon orbits the Earth, but if you were able to stand on the Moon, relatively speaking you would see the Earth orbiting you.

The apparent motion of the heavens during the day is of course caused by the Earth spinning on its axis, so that it does a complete revolution in what we call a day. During that time, relative to someone standing at a point on the Earth, the Sun, Moon, stars all the planets will have made a complete revolution too (give or take some adjustment when their actual movement around their orbits is accounted for).

Suppose we divided the Earth into twelve sectors, each of 30 degrees of longitude, and extend them out into space. (When we were discussing the zodiac signs, we were dividing the sky, not the Earth.) It follows that each planet will have passed through all the sectors during a day, because the spinning of the Earth will be continuously moving the sectors. And, at any moment in time, a planet will be placed in a specific sector.

This is the basis of the astrological houses – each sector is called a 'house'. If we know someone's time of birth, we can say which house each planet was in. How do we do this? Perhaps you have guessed that we already have for our sample chart. When we marked in the planets, we placed each planet in one of twelve sectors. These are the houses. So for our sample data, the Sun is in the first house, the Moon is in the seventh, Mercury the twelfth etc.

> Now we know the house each planet is in, we can add a
> whole new level of interpretation. For if the signs are an
> external influence modifying the planetary energies that
> affect our character, the houses are more of a stage or arena
> where the planetary energies are manifested. Each house
> represents a different aspect of your life.

The first house begins where the ascendant is and this gives us a clue to its meaning. It is the house of ego, physical appearance, affairs which concern you alone, ego-centred desires. Any planet placed in the first house takes on extra importance. If Jupiter's there you may have a self-image of benevolence. You may be large in stature, and probably prone to putting on weight. Ego-centred Mars there and you are likely to be overconcerned with pursuing your own desires and with the effect the world has on you personally, though you will probably be an energetic leader. If a planet is found very close to the ascendant (in which case it is said to be *rising*) it takes on an extra weight when interpreting a chart.

The second house is concerned with material possessions. It relates to wealth, the way you earn money and perhaps more so, how you spend it and what you spend it on. It is concerned with your material and financial assets and also beliefs and to some extent affectional relationships because of the stability they can bring. The first house concerned inner resources, the second relates to the outer resources available to you and what you do with them. Mars here and you are likely to put a lot of energy into pursuit of money. Saturn here and you'll have to work hard to make your fortune!

Communication and learning are the main themes of the third house. The fourth house is often referred to as the house of home and family, whilst the fifth is involved with romance, amusements and creativity. The sixth is traditionally a house of work and service, the seventh partnerships . . .

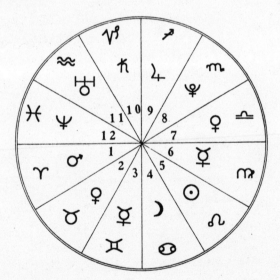

It is possible to see a pattern here. It should become obvious if we draw up a zodiac wheel (above), starting with Aries at the ascendant, and include the houses as well. Each house is associated with a particular sign. So the concerns of the first house are very much Aries' concerns, the second house relates to matters with an affinity to Taurus, the third house Gemini and so on. The sign associated with a house is sometimes referred to as its *natural ruler*. Remember as well that, since we associated each planet with a particular sign or signs, that each house will also have a planet associated with it, so Mars/Aries/first house, Venus/Taurus/second, and so on.

Here are some keywords for each of the houses:

FIRST

Ego

Physical apperance

Physical health

Vitality

Personality

Action

Self-interest

SECOND

Money

Resources of the planet

Environment

Beliefs

Affection

Stability

Giving and receiving

THIRD

Learning

Teaching

Books

Memory

Local travel

Communication

Intellect

Brothers and sisters

FOURTH

Home

Family

Parents as representing nurture

The past

Security

Birth

Land

FIFTH

Amusements

Love affairs/romance

Children

Procreation

Creativity

Artistic ability

Speculation

SIXTH

Work

Colleagues

General health

Food and nutrition

Animals

Hospitals

Medicine

SEVENTH

Partnerships

Close friendships

Interests of others

Marriage and divorce

Business partners

Law and contracts

Artistic appreciation

EIGHTH

Shared resources

Sex

Death and rebirth

Regeneration

Inheritance

Occult

Reincarnation

NINTH

Higher education

Philosophy

Religion

Publishing

Long-distance travel

Science

Fun

Morals

TENTH

Career

Status

Parents as representing
authority

Ambition

Authority/Government

Your boss/you as boss

Fame/notoriety

ELEVENTH

Friends and enemies

Technology

Equality

Social awareness

Hopes and aspirations

Organisations

Co-operation

TWELFTH

Compassion

Escapism

Charitable institutions

Intuition and creativity

Dissolution of ego

Karma

Self-undoing

The house position of each planet in a horoscope will determine where its energy is most readily felt. Saturn in the tenth will give the ability to bring structure to career, though hard work will be necessary. Saturn in the fifth usually limits creative ability. Neptune in the seventh can bring ideal marriage or delusion about partners; in the fourth a confused home life and spiritual attraction to one's birthplace.

Besides the planets in the houses, we can also consider the signs on the *cusp* of each house. The cusp is the dividing line between one house and the next. The ascendant is the cusp of the first house. To give an example, if Capricorn is on the ascendant, then Aquarius will be on the cusp of the second house, Pisces on the third and so on. This person is likely to have some egalitarian beliefs when it comes to money and the distribution of resources, and may be able to make money in an unusual or technological field. Pisces on the third house cusp, implies a difficulty in concentrating when it comes to learning, but an ability to bring intuition to bear; often a love of books is found. This sort of reasoning can be extended to every house in the chart.

The concerns of each house are not mutually exclusive. For example, sexual relationships are concerns of the fifth house (romance), the seventh (partnership) and the eighth (sex) – as well as the positions of Venus and Mars. If someone asked for advice on the sort of job that would make good use of their energy, one would look at the distribution of the planets by houses. A concentration of planets in the fifth house (Saturn excepted) would imply artistic ability; Mars in the third, energy for local travel, communication or teaching. But the sixth house, since one of its principal concerns is work, is important here – the sign on its cusp and any planets in the house would be important. And on a different level, the tenth house – relating to career – would also have to be considered.

The houses are particularly useful when we come to the outer planets, because, as we saw, their sign positions are of less value in interpretation as they stay for so long in any one sign. When it comes to the houses, though, every planet will have passed through all of the houses during a single day.

If you do not have a birth time to work with, you will not be able to find the house positions for the planets. However, if, as suggested, you draw up a chart with the Sun on the ascendant, you may find that the resulting house positions have some validity in interpreting the chart.

the midheaven and different house systems

When we looked up in the table for the ascendant which matched the local sidereal time, we ignored the last column which was headed MC. We will go back now and look this up. For our sample data, the local sidereal time was 16:14:28. In the table, the nearest sid. time figure is 16:16:27. If we go across to the column headed MC, we see a figure of 6° Sagittarius for this sid. time. The way to draw this in is to find 6° of Sagittarius and draw in an arrow starting in the house and pointing to outside the circle, writing MC 6° next to the arrow. (If you like, you can also put in arrow exactly opposite at 6° of Gemini).

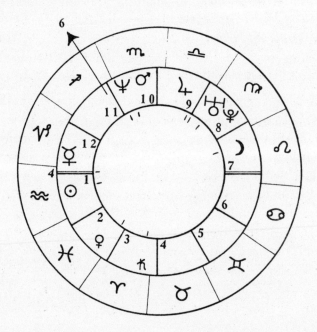

MC is short for *medium coeli*, which translates as *middle of the sky*; in English it is referred to as the *midheaven*. Like the ascendant, an accurate time of birth is needed to compute it. Earlier we mentioned the circle round the Earth through which the Sun moves – the ecliptic – which is divided into the twelve zodiac signs. If we draw an imaginary line from the point exactly overhead at the time of birth and extend it longitudinally (i.e. north/south), the point that line crosses the ecliptic is the degree and sign position of the midheaven. Its sign has a lot to do the way you pursue your career, your status in the world, how you project yourself when you are centre stage, all tenth house concepts.

For example, Libra on the MC and you others see your image as one of refinement and culture, though of course the real person underneath may be nothing of the sort. Virgo and you'll be prepared to work hard for a career, though others may see you as punctilious.

The ascendant is about self-image and how we project our personality. The midheaven relates more to how others see you from afar. With a Capricorn MC, you may seem aloof, serious, cool to strangers; if they get to know you a bit better, perhaps they begin to see your ascendant, Aries perhaps, and so they begin to see you differently; when they get to know you even better, perhaps your Taurean Sun-sign comes shining through. We all seem to function on different levels, and the planet or point in our chart we are primarily expressing ourselves through varies with the different people we meet.

For many of us, the way we most go out centre-stage into the world is in our work, particularly if we regard it as the pursuit of career (being a housewife/husband is a career too). This is often the means by which we achieve status and recognition. If a planet is stuck right on your ascendant, it will be very tied up in these aspects of your life. Saturn there and you could have a hard time establishing yourself, though if you work hard you could become an authority in your field. Mars there and you will be aggressively ambitious, with the energy to succeed. Chiron there and we might expect a career in some form of spiritual teaching, or at any rate a career that is different from the norm, or in a more orthodox field, a desire to express maverick opinions. Charles Kowall's birth chart (he discovered Chiron) shows that the midheaven in his chart has Chiron conjunct.

The point exactly opposite is the IC, which means *imum coeli*; sometimes it is referred to as the *nadir*. The sign here will influence fourth house matters such as home and family. Collectively, the ascendant, descendant, midheaven and nadir as sometimes referred to as "the angles".

BUT, THERE'S MORE THAN ONE HOUSE SYSTEM

In our sample chart, the arrow marking the MC emanates from the eleventh house. In almost all charts it is found in the top half of the chart, usually in houses eight to eleven.

We now come to discuss a problem that does cause some embarrassment to astrologers. We have used a house system called EQUAL, because we took the ascendant as our starting point and drew in the signs around twelve houses of equal length. This is not the only house system we can use. In other systems, the MC marks the start of the tenth house.

PLACIDUS is probably the most commonly used non-equal system. To draw the houses on the chart a *tables of houses* is used – as well as giving the positions for the ascendant and midheaven (the first and tenth house cusps), this also gives the positions in degrees for the eighth, ninth and eleventh house cusps (the second, third and fifth will be respectively opposite these). Raphael's table of houses (see bibliography) uses this system, which was devised by Placidus de Tito in the sixteenth century. The fact that this system is in common use may relate to the fact that the Raphael tables are relatively easy to get hold of compared to other systems. Drawing up a chart with non-equal house systems means that you cannot use a blank chart form with houses already on, because their length varies*.

A problem with Placidus and most other systems is that they fall down when they are used for births at very high latitudes, because the midheaven – used as the tenth house cusp – is related to the highest point in the sky the Sun will reach that day. In high latitudes, the Sun in Winter will not rise very far above the horizon, so the midheaven, rather than being at the top of the chart may be very low down as well. Six of the houses will therefore be very compressed, and six very expanded. This does not seem to make good sense and makes interpretation difficult. At latitudes above the Arctic and Antarctic circles, the Sun will not rise at all during parts of Winter, in which case the midheaven would actually be below the horizon and it is therefore impossible to draw in the houses.

It is common practice to draw up charts with the houses shown as equally divided, but with the signs compressed or expanded to fit them. This seems a poor way of doing things, because, astronomically, it is the length of the signs that will always be a constant 30°, with the length of the houses changing.

Most of these systems were developed in Southern Europe, where these problems do not occur. The equal system has one real advantage – it is relatively simple. This is a distinctive advantage for beginners. It is also probably the house system with the longest pedigree.

It does not stop at Placidus. There are other house systems as well, which all use different theories to derive the positions of the house cusps.

The simple QUADRANT system, divides the spaces between the MC and the ascendant into three equal sectors and between the MC and Descendant into three equal sectors.

PORPHYRY was a Greek scholar in the third century B.C. with wide interests who devised a house system which bears his name.

Johannes CAMPANUS was another astronomer who lived in the thirteenth century.

REGIOMENTANUS was devised by a German astronomer Johann Muller (Regiomentanus was his pen name) who died in 1476.

The mathematician Jean Morin devised the MORINUS system in the sixteenth century.

Finally, the KOCH house system is a recent development, derived by the German astrologer Walter Koch and presented to the world in the 1960's.

There are even more house systems than this. Here is our sample chart with Placidus and with Koch houses. Deciding which system to use is a real problem, because planets which are found in a specific house in one, may be in a different house when another is used. To give an example, Jupiter here is in the seventh with Placidus and the eighth with Koch – with equal houses it is in the ninth. This is an extreme example, but as with most charts, several other planets in our sample are found in different adjacent houses using the different house systems.

This multiplicity of systems is an embarrassment because the sceptic may argue that if astrology is scientifically based then surely there must be only one house system that is correct; if that is so, then astrology should have found out which is right by now. All disciplines have areas of disagreement of course. Although some astrologers will argue vehemently in support of a particular system to the exclusion of others, another viewpoint is to suggest that different house systems have different uses. I think that most astrologers in any case tend to regard the boundaries between houses as somewhat blurred. When a planet is found near a cusp, its effect often is felt in the adjacent house, and this should be borne in mind when interpreting charts.

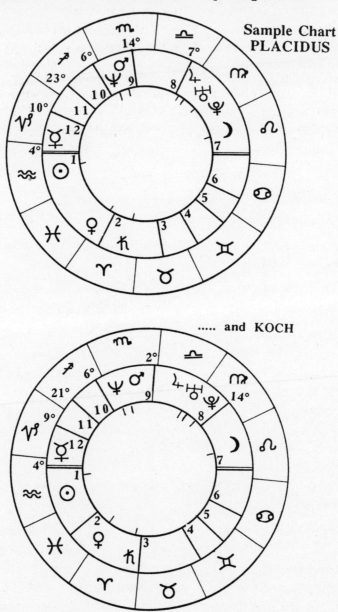

Sample Chart
PLACIDUS

..... and KOCH

It may be true that all the house systems are valid in some ways and fit into different approaches to interpretation. Individual astrologers, when presented with the same chart, will come up with interpretations which emphasise different parts of the person's life, and so may find some house systems work better for them than others. The astrologer Debbi Kempton Smith suggests that Placidus shows "the deeper, old-fashioned you, the one before the nukes and computers" and is popular in Britain because it reflects "the Victorian consciousness of a nation whose public transportation stops at 11.30 PM" (see bibliography).

I would certainly agree that Placidus belongs to the old fogey school, whilst Koch is the modern, technological system, which may be more useful in the present day. My preference is to use equal houses for the interpretation of birth charts, although I tend to use Koch when dealing with forecasting work.

planets in houses

Just as we interpreted the planets through the signs by combining the characteristics of each planet with the characteristics of each sign, so we can use the nature of the houses to interpret which areas of life a planet will affect when it is found in a particular house.

Keywords for planets and houses can be used to derive meanings for planetary placements.

SUN

The house position of the Sun will show where an individual's Sun-sign drives will be most readily applied and where progress can be made through the direct expression of will.

Sun in FIRST: This is a very ego-centred position, though a sunny face will be presented to the world. These people need to dominate everything they are involved in and usually have tremendous physical energy. They demand to be the centre of attraction and gain respect for their position.

Sun in SECOND: Here the will is centred upon the drive for material wealth and possessions. Beliefs may also be strongly promoted. Energy is applied to anything which brings stability, and there is strength of purpose.

Sun in THIRD: The basic drive is to attain factual knowledge, to find out how things work. These people believe that the self can be understood in this way, and their confidence and self-respect is directly related to the amount of knowledge they have.

Sun in FOURTH: There are strong links to home and family, and the basic drive is to do anything which is perceived to bring security. Thus they may strive to change all they are involved in to more closely reflect their own personal situation.

Sun in FIFTH: A strong creative will is indicated, and energy can be incorporated readily into artistic pursuits. Self-confidence is promoted through artistic achievements or through work with children. There is generally a sunny, fun-loving disposition.

Sun in SIXTH: Much effort is directed towards personal health and hygiene. Often the health is poor or there is hypochondria. Work is seen as a source of creative outlet and a means of service. Self-confidence comes from being able to get the details right.

Sun in SEVENTH: Much energy will be put into the establishment of partnerships. Self-esteem comes from vibrant, successful, partnership relationship. Other people's drives take on extra importance and may be acceded to.

Sun in EIGHTH: This is an intense Sun position, giving the ability to see to the root of matters. There is a constant need to transform the immediate environment. Self-respect is gained through the ability to challenge the self and abandon what is no longer required. Often there is one transforming experience that dominates the life afterwards.

Sun in NINTH: There will be the pursuit of fun and adventure, but also a deep to desire to be involved in philosophical and moral pursuits. Much effort may be put into converting others. Responsibilities may be avoided.

Sun in TENTH: Self-esteem is produced from career and perceived status in society. There is a strong drive to reach the top and a need to operate before the public in some way. Ambitions may be everything.

Sun in ELEVENTH: There is a strong desire to interact with others. Either there will be strong individualism or a desire to conform with the masses at all costs. Self-respect comes from behaving in humanitarian ways. There may be drives to work for humanitarian organisations.

Sun in TWELFTH: There is much soul-searching and the ability to look into the depths of the self. These people usually work better behind the scenes. There is a desire to merge with the Universal. Self-confidence is usually lacking, though long experience brings it. These individuals can be their own worst enemies.

MOON

The Moon through the houses shows in which areas of life security will be sought, where daily activities may be concentrated and what things will be subject to the Moon's changing influence.

Moon in FIRST: The sense of self-worth goes through phases. There is a strong attachment to mother, and security is found in open appreciation by others.

Moon in SECOND: Security is found through the acquisition of money and possessions, though financial status may readily fluctuate. Sometimes security is sought in beliefs, which may include rejection of materialism, though these will also change. A very resourceful position.

Moon in THIRD: There is a need to communicate one's feelings, which may change often. A restless position, full of curiosity and the desire to rationalise emotions. Thoughts are often conditioned in childhood.

Moon in FOURTH: A very strong need to establish a secure home base is indicated (the Moon rules this house). There may be excessive attachment to home and family and strong maternal instincts.

Moon in FIFTH: This indicates a strong emotional attachment to children and creative output, though matters involving these will fluctuate. There could be emotional romanticism through a desire for intimate relationships with others. Security is sought in respect from others.

Moon in SIXTH: Work problems may occur through changeable attitudes. Health is also likely to go through phases. Security is sought through providing service, often in the caring professions. These individuals can be good at organising domestic routine.

Moon in SEVENTH: A strong desire for partnerships can bring a tendency to become emotionally attached to partners regardless of what is given in return. There is exceptional awareness of the emotional states of others.

Moon in EIGHTH: Sexual desires may be subject to the changing influence of Moon. There are very deep and powerful emotions, though these may be suppressed. This position brings ability to process the emotional output of others and return it in changed form, for better or worse.

Moon in NINTH: Security is sought through philosophical or religious beliefs. Practical reality may be ignored. There is a need to see the world. These people will constantly set up new targets to aim at.

Moon in TENTH: Relationships involving authority go through phases. Career must be emotionally satisfying. Possible conflicts of career v. domestic life variety occur and there is a need for achievements to be recognised.

Moon in ELEVENTH: Security is found when operating in groups of people, particularly those with humanitarian aims. There is the desire to make friends, but emotional coolness. Possible problems with women as enemies.

Moon in TWELFTH: Deep emotions may be difficult to cope with. Domestic affairs can be confused. Security sought in conceding own needs for those of others, though this may lead to martyrdom.

MERCURY

The house position of this planet will show where intellectual powers are most readily applied and the manner in which they are expressed.

Mercury in FIRST: Self-image is strongly tied in with perceived mental capacities. Ideas are ego-centred and resistant to challenge, though impulsive. May be a mercurial person.

Mercury in SECOND: Intellect is concentrated on gathering of financial resources and possessions. Stability is sought by reference to intellectual beliefs.

Mercury in THIRD: Acute thinking abilities result in attraction to jobs involved in communications. Yearning for frequent travel is sometimes evident. Much energy expended in pursuit of knowledge.

Mercury in FOURTH: Home is seen as a base for study and reflection on experience. Security is sought in application of logical thinking and there is an interest in the past.

Mercury in FIFTH: Intellectual energy can be used for creative work or teaching. May be inclined to financial speculation. Easy communication with children is indicated by this position.

Mercury in SIXTH: This position benefits work where attention to fine detail is called for. There is often an interest in health but nervous tension may be a problem. A need to keep busy is often found here.

Mercury in SEVENTH: Partnerships work best where the other person provides intellectual stimulation. A desire to share problems, ideas and knowledge with others is found. Ideas may be moulded to the beliefs of partners, friends, colleagues.

Mercury in EIGHTH: This indicates a mind determined to probe to the underlying causes of things. There are strong opinions but a tendency to be secretive about them. Perception may be useful in psychological fields or business.

Mercury in NINTH: There is intellectual pursuit of philosophical studies or higher education and a need for frequent travel. May be attempts to intellectualise moral feelings. Not usually a practical position for Mercury.

Mercury in TENTH: Career will benefit from intellectual input and must provide intellectual stimulation to be satisfactory. These people have the ability to come up with practical ideas and gain respect for them.

Mercury in ELEVENTH: Friends and groups are seen as sources of intellectual stimulus. Knowledge of science and occult can be easily expanded, and work in humanitarian organisations benefits.

Mercury in TWELFTH: There is lack of confidence in ideas, though they can be assimilated over long periods of experience. Expression may be hindered by uncertainty. Vision is wide but there are problems with attention to detail.

VENUS

The house position of Venus shows where artistic skills and desire to form relationships with others will benefit.

Venus in FIRST: Sense of self-worth is very dependent on response of others. Friendship is all important through the desire to be liked. There may be excellent artistic ability and/or a tendency to laziness.

Venus in SECOND: This indicates strong materialistic desires, or occasionally the complete rejection of possessions. Financial affairs are often benefitted and there is a sensual personality.

Venus in THIRD: There is a desire for knowledge, though these people may not be motivated to learn. Feelings for others are ephemeral. Charm blends with third house concerns so these people make persuasive communicators.

Venus in FOURTH: A desire to beautify the home and to use it as a place to meet friends is indicated. There is a strong desire for tranquillity, so that arguments are found very unpleasant, though these individuals can be good at calming others.

Venus in FIFTH: This is a very artistic position for Venus, though creative abilities must lead to respect. There is a risk of vanity and excessive romanticism. Often an ability to relate well to children.

Venus in SIXTH: There is an ability to prosper in work situations, though laziness may be apparent. Harmony at work essential for a sense of well-being. They are able to-co-operate with colleagues to produce harmony and help.

Venus in SEVENTH: A desire to form partnerships and to socialise is apparent. Desires of others may be given preference to own desires. Harmony in marriage is essential to well-being. These people are often charming and have diplomatic ability.

Venus in EIGHTH: This brings the ability to be transformed by close relationships. Feeling run deep and there is a strong desire for sexual experience in relationships. There is emotional commitment, but likely to be possessiveness and jealousy.

Venus in NINTH: This position indicates a general fun loving nature that seeks variety in friendship and by travel. There is an ability to profit from higher education and philosophical study, so long as commitment is provided.

Venus in TENTH: Charm and diplomacy can be used for career advancement. Career must be operating harmoniously for satisfaction. Work involving meeting many people or the arts benefits.

Venus in ELEVENTH: Friends may bring benefits and there is a strong desire to mix with many people, though not necessarily to form intimate relationships.

Venus in TWELFTH: Own desires may be martyred for those of others. Relationships may be carried on secretively. There is much compassion, but lack of discrimination in relationships.

MARS

The house position of Mars will show in which areas of life action can be taken readily and where anger and conflict may express.

Mars in FIRST: There is a strong desire to try things out for oneself. Action is very ego-centred, though there is also the strength to lead and fight on behalf of others.

Mars in SECOND: Pursuit of material wealth is paramount. A desire to be masters of their source of income and a readiness to take financial risks is apparent, as well as a readiness to fight for the stability of their beliefs.

Mars in THIRD: Much energy is put into the pursuit of knowledge and in communicating. These people may be engaged in frequent local travel. Intellectual energy is strong, though arguments can result.

Mars in FOURTH: There is much energy put into the establishment of a home. May be interest in D.I.Y. Domestic affairs can be subject to arguments.

Mars in FIFTH: Energy is given towards creative pursuits. Teaching ability can be apparent, though arguments with children can be a problem.

Mars in SIXTH: Activity is easily channelled into work, particularly work involving detail or the use of sharp tools. May be problems with colleagues through unwillingness to co-operate.

Mars in SEVENTH: Energy is concentrated in the formation of partnerships, but marital arguments may be frequent. Relationships may be formed impetuously and though often likeable, the tendency to interfere with the affairs of others can be problematical.

Mars in EIGHTH: There is a strong desire for sexual experience, though this may not be openly expressed. Motivations are deep seated and there is persistence in conflict. Attempts are made to transform others, though action may be taken secretively.

Mars in NINTH: Energy can be put into pursuit of higher education or philosophical learning. Opinionation and arguments over politics or religion can cause problems. There is a need for travel and adventure.

Mars in TENTH: Career matters benefit from the energy input of Mars, but conflict may arise from ruthless pursuit of power positions. Authority figures are not well tolerated.

Mars in ELEVENTH: Involvement in all group activities is energised. There is a strong desire for friendship, though conflicts with associates are likely. Action may be taken merely to be different.

Mars in TWELFTH: Generally low energy levels and a tendency to take action secretively is indicated. There is lack of purpose and a tendency to bottle up anger. Energy is easily directed into compassionate pursuits that are not ego-centred.

JUPITER

The house position of Jupiter shows areas which are easily expanded, where there may be apparent good fortune and where both wisdom and fun may be sought.

Jupiter in FIRST: The personality may be exaggerated, with a tendency to go over the top. An optimistic, buoyant approach is evident as well as enthusiasm, but overconfidence can be a problem.

Jupiter in SECOND: Usually financial rewards are easily obtained, though extravagance may lead to gains being immediately dissipated so that wealth does not grow. May have opinionated beliefs.

Jupiter in THIRD: Wisdom is sought through the acquisition of factual knowledge. Important details may be overlooked. Relationships will be sought on an intellectual basis.

Jupiter in FOURTH: Good relations in the domestic sphere are indicated with possible financial help from parents. There may be too much time and money spent on the home. Compassionate understanding of others' feelings.

Jupiter in FIFTH: Good relations with children are likely. There is a love of risk-taking, and if Jupiter is unafflicted usually benefits accrue from such gambles. Artistic abilities benefit, though creative drive may be lacking.

Jupiter in SIXTH: This brings good prospects of job satisfaction, though possible laziness, particularly in the wrong job. Good health is indicated, though the reverse if Jupiter is afflicted.

Jupiter in SEVENTH: A happy partnership relationship is promised, though there may be some delay. These people may be taken advantage of by partners. Too much may be expected from close relationships.

Jupiter in EIGHTH: The ability to gain deep knowledge of life's mysteries is here. There may be interest in the occult and reincarnation. The sexual area of life may be exaggerated.

Jupiter in NINTH: Others are related to on a philosophical and moral level. There may be a love of seeking knowledge and an adventurous spirit, though a risk of opinionation.

Jupiter in TENTH: Career prospects will be helped by easy relationships with authority. Broad vision is brought to the career field, though work may be pursued at the expense of domestic considerations.

Jupiter in ELEVENTH: Opportunities for expansion arise through friendship. There is a seeking after knowledge of things new. There may be too much emphasis on socialising and an excessively intellectual approach to relating.

Jupiter in TWELFTH: A very emotional approach to relationships is found. There is much compassion, but a tendency for martyrdom. Sometimes, sudden and unexpected boosts of fortune occur.

SATURN

The house position of Saturn shows the areas of life most likely to experience frustration and where the ability to consolidate can be applied.

Saturn in FIRST: A general lack of self-confidence is found. This may lead to the ability to achieve long term-goals, or may lead to depression. Often childhood problems may force an early assumption of responsibility.

Saturn in SECOND: It may take a lot of hard work to establish financial stability. Lessons are centred upon the efficient use of resources. Beliefs may be conservative and authoritarian.

Saturn in THIRD: Learning abilities may be restrained, though there is the chance to learn much through hard study. May be problems in relationships with siblings.

Saturn in FOURTH: Problems in the early home life are indicated. There can be responsibilities attached to aged parents, or the sacrifice of desires for domestic responsibility.

Saturn in FIFTH: These people have a cold or austere attitude to children. Financial speculation may be unwise. Creative abilities are likely to be suppressed and there can be romantic disappointments.

Saturn in SIXTH: Although Saturn will bring its organisational energy to bear on the work situation, there may be an involvement with work that is seen as drudgery. Lessons of co-operation at work have to be learned.

Saturn in SEVENTH: Partnerships may suffer if lessons of co-operation are not learnt. The sense of harmony and awareness of others' desires may be dimmed. Legal and architectural abilities may be present.

Saturn in EIGHTH: Fear of sexuality may lead to restrictions in sexual relationships. There is resourcefulness, but others good fortune may be taken advantage of.

Saturn in NINTH: Lessons of morality and philosophy are to be learnt. There may be a fear of spiritual development, though practicality is added to ninth-house philosophy. Problems may

192

be found in long-distance travel.

Saturn in TENTH: It may be possible to become an authority in the chosen career, although setbacks to ambitions are very likely. There may be an inbuilt fear of success and status.

Saturn in ELEVENTH: Attitudes towards friends may be loyal though somewhat cold. Relationships with older people are important. Inventive ideas can be given practical structure.

Saturn in TWELFTH: A poor sense of structure is evident. There may be mental problems and a deep fear of restriction. Practical abilities can be brought into healing or charitable work.

URANUS

The house position of Uranus shows where rebellious, disruptive and innovative energy will be centred.

Uranus in FIRST: There is likely be extreme individualism and restless behaviour. Life may be filled with surprises, with sudden changes in fortune. Alternatively, these may be people who follow every whim of social fashion, doing exactly as everyone else is doing.

Uranus in SECOND: Financial affairs will be subject to sudden changes. There may be revolutionary beliefs and unusual ways of earning money. Conventional values, particularly regarding the use of resources, will be scorned.

Uranus in THIRD: There is much mental energy, and a highly inventive mind, though the mental processes may be overloaded by the Uranian power. There may be rebellious behaviour at school. An inability to concentrate may be apparent.

Uranus in FOURTH: This position implies that freedom of choice was given as a child. Thus these people can grow up with less conditioning than most. The domestic situation may be subject to sudden, disruptive change. The home may be unusual.

Uranus in FIFTH: Sparkling creative abilities may be present, though not necessarily practicality. Sudden changes involving children are likely. There can be a tendency to become involved in unusual romantic relationships, which may be suddenly broken off.

Uranus in SIXTH: This energy is used best in unusual fields of work. Jobs involving high use of technology will also benefit. These people will not like being told what to do in the job situation, and although they can be innovative in relation to work, problems with colleagues arises through individualistic behaviour. Sudden health crises can occur.

Uranus in SEVENTH: Partnership affairs may be subject to sudden disruption, with high risk of divorce. Marriage usually works best when the partner has unusual talents, or at least can be related to on a high intellectual level. Relationships tend to be formed and broken off impulsively.

Uranus in EIGHTH: There may be strong psychic abilities. The occult, science and technology can be investigated with inspiration. Sudden financial windfalls or disasters may occur. Unusual sexual behaviour may be present.

Uranus in NINTH: Unusual philosophies or religion will attract. There may be rebellious behaviour expressed against religious or moral authority. Inspiration can be brought to philosophy and higher education, though impracticality and eccentricity of views may result.

Uranus in TENTH: The career may be centred around science or technology, or plainly unusual. There may be rebellious behaviour directed against authority. Political beliefs are likely to be humanitarian, though with a tendency to force them on others.

Uranus in ELEVENTH: Uranian qualities will be brought to the fore easily, giving a humanitarian outlook and the ability to sensibly use technology. There may be a wide circle of friends, but an unwillingness to become tied down in specific relationships.

Uranus in TWELFTH: Inspiration and technical abilities may be suppressed. There may be a fear of things new. There may be occult talent, interest in mysticism and the ability for psychological research. Rebellious behaviour can lead to self-undoing.

NEPTUNE

The house position of Neptune will show areas of life where idealism will dominate. There is the chance of a higher spiritual approach to these areas, but risk of deception and self-delusion.

Neptune in FIRST: There will be poor self-confidence due to Neptune's ego-dissolving energy. Often these individuals are magnetically attractive. They may present a disordered face to the world though will find it difficult to get a realistic self-image. Though they may readily express all Neptune's higher qualities, there is also the risk of a deceptive personality.

Neptune in SECOND: Often these people think they are not materialistic, but very often are very much so. They may find it difficult to keep track of financial resources. Uncertain about beliefs, they find that as soon as they try to get a grip on them, circumstances arise that dissolve their faith. There is idealism about the use of resources.

Neptune in THIRD: Learning is usually more effective when information can be absorbed in its entirety. Attention to factual detail is not good. There may be problems at school. Desires may be subjugated for the benefit of brothers and sisters.

Neptune in FOURTH: Domestic life may be subject to Neptunian deception in some way. There is a deep attachment to home and family. The family bond may be very true, but often there are elements of illusion involved.

Neptune in FIFTH: This is a most creative position for a creative planet. Musical and painting abilities will benefit. Acting ability is also likely, either professionally or in everyday deceptions. Relationships with children may be confused, or subject to deceit. There is a risk of being drawn into deceptive romantic relationships.

Neptune in SIXTH: Work where the expression of compassion is involved benefits. There is an opportunity to obtain ideal work, but also the risk of illusion over job matters. Laziness will be evident if the work has no creative element. This is another position for Neptune that makes practical details difficult to grasp. There may be unusual illnesses, or a general sapping of health.

Neptune in SEVENTH: There is the chance of ideal partnerships here, with partners able to understand each other on an intuitive level. Partnerships must have a spiritual bond to be successful. However, there is the risk of self-deception about a partner's qualities. There may be a tendency to be secretive with partners and to become involved in secret relationships.

Neptune in EIGHTH: There may be idealism about sexual matters, with self-centred desires forgotten in the service of another's sexual drives. This is a very psychic position, giving strong intuitive links to other planes. However there is a risk of delusion about occult matters. Confusion and deception in financial matters is also a possibility.

Neptune in NINTH: There is a fine grasp of overall philosophies, though practical detail will be overlooked. Delusion may be centred on blind faith in religious, political or scientific dogma without reference to reality. Daydreaming and fantasising can be a problem.

Neptune in TENTH: It can be difficult to take concrete action in furtherance of career. A career in caring professions, the fashion industry, the arts or advertising will benefit. There may be difficulty in deciding upon career and there is a risk of scandal through deception applied to advancing career or status.

Neptune in ELEVENTH: There is a risk of deceiving, or being deceived by, friends. Hidden enemies can be a problem. Compassionate ideals can be put to work in group activities, particularly if humanitarian causes are being pursued.

Neptune in TWELFTH: This can be a very psychic position, with a tremendous grasp of the Universal. There can be problems with excessive imagination or mental confusion. Past habits may be unproductively retained. Compassionate and spiritual drives may be ignored.

PLUTO

The house position of Pluto will determine what areas of life can be transformed, regenerated and subject to sudden change.

Pluto in FIRST: These people make very powerful individuals, who will desire to be in control of and transform what is about them. Experiences are used as a means for recurrent inward transformation, and they may go through a series of different lifestyles, as earlier ways of living are suddenly overthrown.

Pluto in SECOND: There may be a power to attract wealth and possessions, though this may be subject to sudden dissipation. There is the power to persevere, but also the possibility of rewards for efforts being suddenly lost. There may be obsession centred on beliefs or affectional relationship as the individual seeks stability.

Pluto in THIRD: There can be great mental power, particularly the ability to manipulate data, but sometimes the energy can be too powerful, causing mental problems. Ideas may be forced on others, though likely to be inconsistent, with frequent change of outlook.

Pluto in FOURTH: This position can bring obsessive ties to home and family. The past is of great interest, and there is the ability to reach deep into the psyche. Hanging on to tradition can block growth. Any domestic problems will tend to build up, perhaps for years, then suddenly explode. Changes of residence may be sudden and total.

Pluto in FIFTH: There is a tremendous well of creative energy and a subconscious drive to create. There may be deep insight into the activities of children. Sometimes fifth-house activities may be subconsciously blocked. There can be obsession with romantic affairs.

Pluto in SIXTH: Here the transforming ability will be brought to bear in the workplace. There will be a desire to influence and control colleagues. Health may be given additional strength, though energy may seem to suddenly drain away. There can be obsession over personal health and hygiene.

Pluto in SEVENTH: Personal relationships will be intense, with a desire to control partners or a tendency to become involved with partners who will forcefully try to impose themselves on the relationship. Partners may provide strength, but long-term relationships may suddenly break off.

Pluto in EIGHTH: Sexual behaviour may be used as a means to control others. There is the ability to investigate occult and psychological matters very deeply. This is a strong position for Pluto, so can bring the power to transform self and others for better or worse.

Pluto in NINTH: Religious and philosophical ideas may be subject to obsession and the desire to convert others, though existing doctrines can be regenerated. Travel often brings transforming experience and there is the ability to get to the root of social problems.

Pluto in TENTH: The underlying causes of problems in the organisation of society can be readily perceived. Long-term plans for career and social success can be undertaken, though there may be obsession with such matters. There may be obsessive political beliefs.

Pluto in ELEVENTH: Friendships may develop and be broken off suddenly. Underhand behaviour from enemies may be undermining over a long period of time. Growth occurs from the experiences of friends and there is the ability to transform social structure and the use of technology.

Pluto in TWELFTH: This may indicate an insecure and timid person who is unsure of what he or she stands for. Sometimes Pluto here produces a constant source of unlooked-for help and protection, though downfalls can be sudden and caused by the individual's own action.

POLARITIES

We divided the zodiac into four elements and three qualities. Another way of looking at the zodiac signs is to divide them by two, into *polarities*. You can think of them as being positive and negative, active and passive, extroverted and introverted, yang and yin. Traditionally they were regarded as male and female, though in modern terms it might be confusing to think in such terms; it might even upset some people.

Here are the polarities of the signs. Positive ones are outgoing, action-seeking, extroverted and tend to impose themselves on the world. Negative ones are introverted, passive and receptive. Avoid the pejorative sense of positive meaning "good" and negative "bad". As you look at the list, see if you can remember which element each sign is in:

+	-
Aries	Taurus
Gemini	Cancer
Leo	Virgo
Libra	Scorpio
Sagittarius	Capricorn
Aquarius	Pisces

We should not need to draw a zodiac wheel for you to realise that successive signs alternate in polarity. You might have worked out that the positive signs are all the fire and air ones, whilst the negative are all earth and water.

We can look at the overall tenor of the horoscope by reference to the number of planets in each polarity. An excess of positive can make you too ready to take action and impose yourself on others; too much of the negative can make you reluctant to act when necessary and be too much subject to the whims of others.

An interesting little use of polarities is in considering the trinity of Sun, Moon and rising signs.

Men and women are intrinsically different. If we take the polarities of the Sun, Moon, Ascendant trinity, we must have either two of one polarity and one of the other, or all three must be the same. It seems that for a man, the best position is to have two positive and one negative. Three positive would be too masculine and two or three negative would be too feminine – all these would be less comfortable than the first split. Similarly, women seem to feel happier with a split of two negative and one positive. Now it may be that this situation results entirely from our conditioning and that if we were free of the rigid guidelines any society imposes it would not matter; we could behave productively regardless. But in the real world things are not like that and the more a society imposes a division between male and female roles, the more the above polarities become important.

We will now go on to examine some specific combinations of Sun, Moon and Ascendant, and in doing so take some first steps towards synthesising different factors is the birth chart.

part seven

putting it together

Let's look at the Sun, Moon and Rising signs operating together. In a birth chart this can give us any one of 1728 combinations since all three can be in any sign of the zodiac: 12 possible Suns x 12 possible Moons x 12 possible Ascendants. That is before any of the other planets are included. Perhaps you can see that is why we can so refine astrological interpretations. Even so, there is not one born every minute. There are something like 147 born every minute. So your birth chart is not, as some astrologers claim, really absolutely unique, as there will be lots of people with charts so similar to yours that it will make no difference. Even so, in a world population of 5,000,000,000, you probably will not meet any of your astrological twins. Astrological research is being done with people who have identical charts.

What you have to remember when people have similar birth charts is that the environment they are brought up in makes all the difference. You might have the same birth chart as the Queen of England but be a coal miner's daughter. The interpretation of the two charts would be different. You cannot even tell someone's sex from a birth chart. Even when people have similar backgrounds, presumably there is within us a spark of individualism that makes all the difference between how one person uses their chart and how the next person uses an identical one.

Then there is the question of real life twins. Whilst there are cases on record of three days having elapsed between the births of the first and second twins, in a natural birth, half-an-hour would be more usual. In fact, most twin births in Western countries are not natural. For example, current obstetric practice in the UK is for induction or section to be carried out if the second has not been born after 15 minutes; and in practice, doctors frequently intervene to deliver the second baby immediately.

Generally, unless the timing and separation of the two births was far enough apart for the rising sign to be different, nothing much would change. Some planetary house positions could alter if the times were far enough apart and in a few rare cases the Moon signs would be different. I suppose there would be very rare cases where the Sun or inner planets changed signs between births and some extremely rare cases where an outer planet changed. Thus you might have one child a Geminian and the next a Cancerian, for example.

There is also the vexed question of the astrological implications of natural v.induced births. The possibility is raised of inducing births to suit astrological preference. Not only choose baby's sex, but the Sun and Moon signs perhaps!

Of course, when one does look at the lives of twins, one does find that they behave in very similar ways. The same sorts of things happen to them. They have accidents and get sick and change jobs at the same times. You see it in the press from time to time. Headlines such as TWINS GET MARRIED ON SAME DAY appear. Sometimes they even marry other twins. People seem to find this mystifying, but to an astrologer it all fits into place. Here again, environmental factors matter. Some twins are separated at an early age. Some parents try and bring up each twin as differently from the other as possible; others seem to make it their ambition to get every little detail the same.

In her book *The Continuing Discovery of Chiron* (Samuel Weiser), Erminie Lantero refers to the birth chart (8.7.26, 10:45 PM, Zurich) of Elisabeth Kubler-Ross, who was the first of triplets. The second sister was born about fifteen minutes later. They both weighed about two pounds. She writes that they were virtually identical, so alike that "sometimes even their parents were unable to tell them apart". The third sister was born a half-an-hour after the third, weighed six pounds and was distinguishable from the other two. The time gap was enough to make a difference.

Let's look at a few combinations of Sun, Moon and rising signs. Always bear in mind that a Sun-Taurus/Moon-Virgo combination, for example, is different from Sun-Virgo/Moon-Taurus.

Fig. (i) is a birth chart drawn up with the following:

⊙ 25 ♓   (Sun at 25 degrees of Pisces)

☽ 25 ♋   (Moon at 25 degrees of Cancer)

Let's just briefly say a few things about this simple chart.

(i)

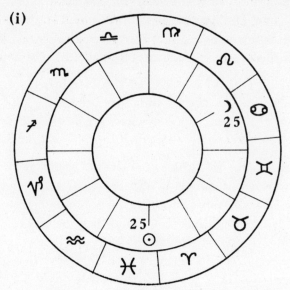

The Sun is in Pisces, so that indicates compassion, mystery, dreaminess, deceptiveness, vulnerability, all the usual Piscean things. The Cancerian Moon will increase the depth of feeling and add protectiveness, submersion in the past and a love of routine. This combination is rather a quiet, introspective one that wants to sit at home and keep itself to itself.

(ii)

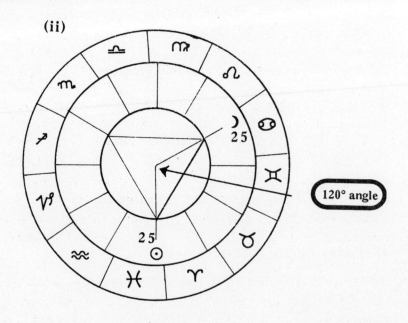

120° angle

Read up the characteristics of these two positions if you do not feel familiar with them. In fact this Moon will blend quite harmoniously with this Sun — they are both of the same element, water. If we look at the position of the signs in the chart, we will see that they are four signs apart. Because the Sun and Moon are both at the 25th degree of their respective signs, at 30 degrees for each sign, that makes them 120 degrees apart, or exactly one third of the whole circle. Fig. (ii).

Now suppose we keep the Piscean Sun, but in Fig. (iii) alter the Moon's position to:

☽ 25 ♊ (Moon at 25 degrees of Gemini)

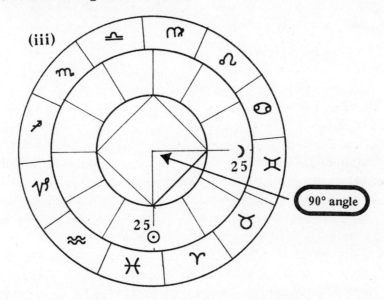

We still have the Piscean character, but now the Moon is very different. It is an outgoing Moon, that wants to tell you all about its feelings, which are very superficial in contrast to the depth of Pisces. The Piscean Sun is quiet and introverted, the Gemini Moon is talkative and outgoing. And Pisces is a water sign, whilst Gemini is air. If you are familiar with the characteristics of these two positions, you will see that they do not really go at all well together. In fact there is something of a conflict between the Sun and Moon here; they are pulling in different directions.

Whilst in the first instance of Sun-Pisces/Moon-Cancer, the two planetary energies can blend harmoniously together, with Sun-Pisces/Moon-Gemini, the energies are disharmonious. Look at the positions of Pisces and Gemini and note how they are three signs apart. This time (because to make things easier we have again placed the Moon at the 25th degree), the Sun and Moon are 3 x 30 = 90 degrees apart, or one quarter of the circle.

What you are learning here is in fact an introduction to planetary *aspects*. Remember that we have already mentioned the *conjunction* when we were looking at the outer planets. That is an aspect too. An *aspect* is the astrological term for the relationship between two planets. When planets are found in certain angular relationships with each other, we say that they are *in aspect*. In the first example above, with the Sun and Moon 120 degrees apart, they are said to be in *trine* aspect. A trine is merely an aspect of 120 degrees, one third of a circle.

In the second example, there are 90 degrees between the Sun and Moon. This is an aspect too. Since four 90 degree chunks would fit in a circle, its known as a *square*. There are shorthand symbols for all the planetary aspects, these two are easy:

TRINE: △   SQUARE: □

It would be going too far to say that the Pisces/Cancer combination was actually better than the Pisces/Gemini. Perhaps it would be more accurate to say that you would feel more comfortable if you had the first. Trines between planets can be so harmonious you will not notice them. In the latter case, because a conflict is posed by the square aspect, the energy comes out more forcefully and you might be prompted to actually do something with it. Other things being equal, the Pisces/Cancer person will be quite happy to sit at home comfortably dreaming about in the same old routine, whilst the Pisces/Gemini person is more likely to actually get on, do something constructive and perhaps learn to behave in a more productive fashion.

Let's continue with this example and consider the position of the ascendant as well:

AS 25 ↗   (Ascendant at 25 degrees of Sagittarius)

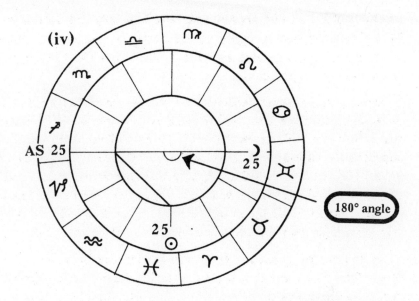

(iv)

180° angle

Here we can see that there is another square aspect – between the Sun and the Ascendant. You can perhaps see why the two do not fit harmoniously together – the introverted, worrying Piscean Sun and the extroverted, adventurous Ascendant. Again, you have to remember that this rising sign may be very useful to a Piscean, helping to get them moving, perhaps, although there is not much practicality here.

The relationship between the Moon and Ascendant is different. If we look at the chart (Fig. iv) we will see that the two signs are opposite. So here we have another aspect – the *opposition*. So when two planets (or, as in this case, a planet and an important point in the chart such as the Ascendant) are on opposite sides of the chart, they are said to be *opposed* or *in opposition*. The angle is 180°.

We can see that the energies of Sagittarius and Gemini are somewhat opposites. The former is big and expansive, concerned with wider issues, and taking action, whilst the latter is intrinsically concerned with details and intellectual ideas.

So a Sagittarian rising sign is going to be somewhat at odds with a Moon in Gemini. Whilst the world probably sees a happy personality who does not really worry and who they turn to for advice, underneath there is a fidgety, worrying Gemini Moon trying to get out. The first is very good for helping others with their problems, and the latter never gets the chance to talk about its own. Remember, that the rising sign is always about how you appear, not what's going on underneath.

The important thing with an opposition in your chart is to learn to balance it. Here's its symbol:

Opposition: σ^{o}

It's a bit like a bar-bell, and you have to keep practising balancing it, or, like in the symbol, it overbalances and one end takes over. Because organically we are always seeking subconsciously to return to balance, what tends to happen is we emphasise one end for a while and then suddenly change to emphasising the other. So in this example, whilst one minute the Sagittarian Ascendant might prompt you to leap out into some new project without enough forethought, the next minute you might be picking over all the details and wondering what you have let yourself in for.

planetary aspects

ASPECTS IN GENERAL

Planetary aspects work for any combination of planets. Let's take as an example Mars and Neptune, supposing that Mars is at 25° Pisces and Neptune is at 25° Gemini, a square aspect.

Mars in Pisces is not very well placed regardless of aspect as Pisces is dissolving of the ego, whereas Mars is very ego-centred. Neptune in Gemini is not very helpful either, because it is a planet involved in the broad view of things, whereas Gemini is a sign of detail.

If Neptune was at 25° Cancer, however, forming a trine, it would be more helpful, for Neptune here is in a watery sign and its energy expresses well in the domestic sphere (it is in fact exalted in Cancer). So its energy here could probably be used harmoniously with the Mars energy to produce productive action in the domestic sphere, or in pursuit of compassionate or charitable (Piscean) activities.

To take an example with different signs, if Mars was at 25° Capricorn and Neptune 25° Libra, whilst both planet positions here are fairly comfortable, the harmony-seeking, indecisive Neptune-in-Libra does not tie in well with the ruthless ambition implied with the Mars position. But if Neptune was at 25° Virgo, both planets would be in the earth element and Neptune would be able to add practical compassion, toning down the harsher aggressiveness of Mars.

We can however go further than just looking at the respective sign (and house) positions when discussing aspects. We can just look at the relationship two planets have when they form a particular aspect, regardless of the signs and houses they are found in. In other words, the aspect has a meaning all to itself.

We can combine the characteristics of the planets involved and work out what is likely to happen when they do not harmonise together, as in the square. Regardless of the signs involved, a Mars-Neptune square implies amongst other things that action will be taken in a somewhat confused fashion, ego-centred desires being tripped-up and clouded by Neptune. Often this square is associated with a poor safety record and health problems that are difficult to pin down, particularly allergies. Although there may be a desire to express compassion and spirituality, action taken will tend to have a different result from this.

Someone with Mars and Neptune in trine, however, will know intuitively when to act and when not to, can easily become involved in charitable or compassionate pursuits and have a good awareness of safety.

A Mars-Neptune opposition will have the problems associated with the square, but implies that matters can be improved by balancing the need for action and ego-centred desires with the need to be compassionate and spiritual. A danger with this aspect is that action will be taken in a way influenced by Mars' sign and house without regard for Neptunian considerations, but that at other times action will be based on pure Neptunian idealism without regard to practicality or desire.

 So we can really define the parts of a birth chart as the planets in the signs, the planets in the houses, and the aspects between the planets, all having distinct meanings.

ORBS OF ASPECT

In all the examples so far, we have for clarity used planetary positions of 25°. Of course, in actuality, the planets can be at any degree and seldom will two planets be exactly 90° or 120° apart. This is where the concept of *orbs of aspect* comes in.

To form a valid aspect two planets need not be exactly at the angle required. So if Neptune was at 25° Gemini, any planet at 22° Pisces would still be regarded as forming a square aspect, as would one at 29° Pisces (or 22° or 29° Virgo for that matter). The amount of degrees we are prepared to allow a planet to be away from an exact aspect yet still count as forming one, is called the *orb*.

Different astrologers use different amounts of orb. It is up to each individual astrologer to decide from experience how much orb he finds it valid to use for each aspect. For a square, it is safe to use 6° of orb either way. Some astrologers will use more, particularly if one or both of the planets involved is the Sun or Moon, which are usually stronger influences than the other planets.

With a trine, we can allow an orb of 6° too (possibly more). With Neptune at 25° Cancer, Mars will be trined with it from about 6° either side of 25° Pisces. In other words at any position from 19° Pisces to 1°

Aries. In this case there is a complication if Mars is in Aries. Aries and Cancer are three signs apart. Mars in Aries with Neptune in Cancer is not a particularly easy combination. The signs are squared with each other, even though the trine aspect is still formed. When this happens, the aspect is said to be *disassociated* and its affect is usually weakened. It is usually best not to attach as much weight to any disassociated aspects when interpreting a chart.

APPLYING AND SEPARATING ASPECTS

As we might expect, an aspect is usually stronger the closer it is to being exact. A further factor which can be considered is the principal of whether an aspect is *applying* or *separating*. An aspect is *applying* when the faster-moving planet of the two is moving closer to forming the exact aspect, and *separating* when it is moving away. Under normal circumstances, for example, Mars at 19° Pisces is applying to a trine with Neptune at 25° Cancer, but separating at anything from 25° Pisces to 1° Aries, after which it goes 'out of aspect'.

We need not worry too much about applying and separating aspects, but the principle is that applying aspects have more strength than separating ones. Also, it is possible to weight the orb so that instead of allowing 6° either side for example, 7° applying and 5° separating is used.

When interpreting how much emphasis should be given to specific aspects, and what particular characteristics of an aspect are likely to manifest, the planetary rulerships and exaltations are useful. If the planet at one end of an aspect is in its rulership or exaltation, then that planet is likely to be the stronger one in the relationship.

ASPECTS SUMMARISED

Now we will look at the other aspects used by astrologers. And so that we have details of all the aspects together, we will refresh on the ones we have already looked at.

CONJUNCTION

It often happens that two or more planets are found close to the same degree of longitude. When this happens there is a conjunction. We can allow an orb of about 8° for this, perhaps more if the Sun or Moon is involved. It is a bit like having the planets concerned locked in a room together. Some get on well, but others don't mix very easily. Mars and Venus are usually OK, for example, because they complement each other, but Mars and Uranus is an explosive combination. There is an opportunity to blend the energies concerned, which if wisely used can be a source of great power, the whole being greater than the sum of the parts. If you are not careful, very often one planet tends to take over, or you fluctuate from one energy to the other.

OPPOSITION

Here the two planets are on opposite side of the chart, 180° apart, give or take an orb of 8°. It's a bit like having a planet on either end of a see-saw - you tend to swing from one extreme to the other. The energy of each planet tends to only be developed positively at the expense of suppressing the energy at the other end; thus we have to strive to balance them. In some planetary combinations, the effects of the opposition is similar to that of the conjunction, but your efforts to deal with the opposition are often hampered by factors which appear to be external or beyond your control, whereas conjunctions tend to have a more internalised effect.

SQUARE

With a square, the 90° aspect, if you boost the energy at one end, the other end gets boosted as well; if you repress one end, you stifle the other too. It is not usually possible to develop the two energies harmoniously – you can neither blend nor balance them. The best you can achieve is to do one, then the other – this means you have to use the energy really carefully – and develop any other aspects to the two ends of the square. We need to be aware of our squares, for that is often where we can cause most harm to others.

QUINCUNX

A more subtle aspect, the quincunx represents a strain between the energies concerned. Signs in quincunx with each other are five apart and share neither element or quality. The exact aspect is 150° and most astrologers use a tight degree of orb, say 2°. This aspect is not easily pinned down; the energy often flows easily most of the time – then lets you down just when you really need it Lots of quincunxes in a chart make a person unstable and can lead to stress-related health problems. Often these result because the stress is there but not obvious enough for others to realise it. So we suppress the energy until it builds up, rather than dealing with the problem. It is a niggling aspect, and often shows where we put the blame onto others.

TRINE

An angle of 120°. An orb of 6°. Trines can be thought of as gifts. The two planetary energies flow easily together and are blended harmoniously, usually without you trying; you take it for granted and can let the energy flow without concentration. Certain trines might however lead to missed opportunity as the drive to get things done may be lacking.

SEXTILE

This is formed when two planets are 60° apart. An orb of 4° is safe to use. It is similar to the trine, but weaker – you have to work to develop it. If the trine shows talent, the sextile represents promise. The energy is there to be used harmoniously, if you want it, but usually stays latent if you don't bother. This can make sextiles more helpful than trines sometimes, although they are weaker, because a conscious effort has to be put in to develop them.

OTHER ASPECTS

The aspects detailed above are the major ones, and certainly all a beginner needs to be concerned with – even quincuxes are not usually used by beginners. There are some additional aspects which are sometimes used. When they are, an orb of 2° is probably the most we can allow:

Divide a circle by 12 and you get 30°. That's half a sextile, so the aspect is called a *semi-sextile*. It is like a sextile, only weaker. Likewise we can use an angle of 45° which is called a *semi-square*, which acts like a weak version of a square. Another stressful aspect is the rather obscurely-named *sesquiquadrate*, which is an aspect of 135° (i.e. a square plus a semi-square). It's a niggly little aspect. A *quintile* is what you get dividing the circle by 5 and equals 72°. Astrologers also recognise the *biquintile* which is twice a quintile at 144°. These last two are relatively modern additions and don't even have recognised symbols; we use Q and BQ. They are said to produce spiritual awareness of the planetary energies involved and may be indicators of talent in a specific area.

You need not worry too much about these minor aspects. Most of us have enough trouble sorting out the major ones without bothering about our sesquiquadrates. There are even more obscure aspects like the nonile (1/9 of a circle) and septile (1/7). The astrologer Robert Hand suggested the ultimate minor aspect – the futile.

So is it good to have lots of trines and sextiles, and none of the more difficult aspects ? It depends on your viewpoint. A chart full of the former tends to give you an easy life, but may make you lazy. Such individuals usually are lacking in some sort of substance, however – they have all this energy easily at their disposal, but no drive to use it. With experience, an astrologer can almost sense when an individual has a lack of oppositions and squares. It is in overcoming the difficult aspects that we learn about ourselves and develop. They are what give us backbone and can, if we work with them, be turned into our most outstanding abilities.

To summarise the aspects:

Aspect	Symbol	Suggested Angle	Orb	Comments
Conjunction	☌	0°	8°	Need to blend; intensity
Semi-sextile	⚺	30°	2°	easy flow; sympathy
Semi-square	∠	45°	2°	misalliance
Sextile	✳	60°	4°	potential talent
Quintile	Q	72°	2°	spiritual awareness; elevation
Square	□	90°	6°	challenge; tension
Trine	△	120°	6°	harmony; flows well
Sesquiquadrate	⛛	135°	2°	niggles
Quincunx	⚻	150°	2°	stress
Opposition	☍	180°	8°	challenge; need to balance

The shorthand for aspects is to put the inner planet first, then the aspect, then the outer planet, e.g. Mars conjunct Saturn: ♂ ☌ ♄

PUTTING ASPECTS IN PERSPECTIVE

It is probably useful to put aspects in perspective by seeing how many of the population have a particular one.

Whilst in 1990 there are no people alive with, for example Pluto in Capricorn or Neptune in Pisces, most of the planets are distributed fairly evenly among everyone, so that, for example, one twelfth or just over 8% of the world's population have Jupiter in Leo. Sometimes an aspect is working so strongly in someone's chart it is easy to think the person is virtually unique and to overlook the fact that many others have that aspect as well. With an orb of 6°, a square will be formed at 6° either side of the exact position, so that is 12° in all. Since a planet at a particular position will be able to form squares with another planet at either side of the zodiac, that gives us 2 x 12 = 24° out of a possible 360°. That is, a little over 6%, or one in fifteen, people will be the proud possessors of a particular square.

Similar figures will apply to trines, but sextiles, quincunxes and the minor aspects will not be as widespread because of the lesser degrees of orb allowed. Conjunctions and oppositions are slightly less common than squares and trines, even though the orb is greater, because, for example, a planet placed at a point in the zodiac forms an opposition only when a planet is at the opposite side of the zodiac. So for a conjunction or opposition we might be talking about 2 x 8° = 16° out of 360°, or about 4% of the population.

> **When looking at the aspects in someone's chart, the normal procedure is to consider conjunctions first, then oppositions and squares. These are usually the ones that are causing problems and will stick out as it were. Then trines and sextiles and possibly lesser aspects are brought into play.**

How people use their aspects is an area where differences between people with similar charts will readily manifest. In one person's chart a Jupiter-Saturn conjunction may be ruling their life, whilst the next person, with a very similar chart, may be integrating the energy involved so that it is not a problem, or has even become a help.

finding the aspects

The safest way to find aspects is to use an *aspect grid*. Here is one:

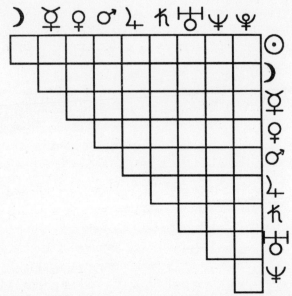

The planets are marked in on both sides of the grid. We start with the Sun in the first row of the grid. We look to see if there is any aspect between the Sun and Moon, which means counting the number of degrees between the two bodies. For our sample chart, the Sun is at 14° Aquarius and the Moon 23° Leo. That is 9° off being an opposition – an exact opposition would occur if the Moon was at 14° Leo. With an orb of 8°, that does not come in our definition of an opposition.

However, we did say we were prepared to stretch the orb if the Sun and/or Moon was involved and since the aspect is not disassociate here, we can probably include this as an opposition. We would just have to note when interpreting the chart, that it is probably fairly weak.

Having decided that we have an aspect, we put the symbol for the opposition in the aspect grid:

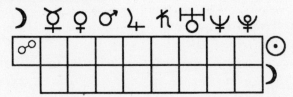

Next, move one box along the row to the one under the symbol for Mercury. Now we consider any aspect between the Sun and Mercury, which is at 3° Aquarius. It's close to the Sun, about ten degrees away, but probably just outside our criteria for a conjunction; no aspect here, so we leave the box blank.

Next Sun-Venus. With Venus at 1° Aries, the two are 47° apart – just inside our orb for a 45° semi-square. Not too important, but we will mark it in the grid:

)	☿	♀	♂	♃	♄	♅	♆	♇	
☍		∠							☉
									)

Mars is at 19° Scorpio. There would be an exact square with the Sun if Mars was at 14° Scorpio, but 19° is within orb, so we can mark in a square in this box:

)	☿	♀	♂	♃	♄	♅	♆	♇	
☍		∠	□						☉
									)

Going through all the other planet positions shows no more aspects involving the Sun, so we can go on to the Moon. The Moon-Sun aspect we have already looked at when we filled in the first row, so the first is Moon-Mercury. The angle between them is 170° – not an aspect so leave the grid blank. The Moon and Venus work out at 142° – just about a biquintile, but we can probably ignore this obscure aspect for now. The Moon and Mars however works out at 86° apart, which is close enough to 90° to be a square.

We can work through the whole grid in this way until we have discovered every aspect. With practice, one begins to find aspects quickly, but working methodically through the grid is the safest way to avoid missing aspects. Here is the completed grid for our chart:

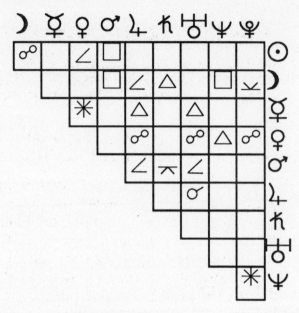

The grid can be extended to include aspects between the planets and the midheaven and ascendant. As more advanced astrology is introduced, other points such as the north node of the Moon and the Part of Fortune could be added, as well as Chiron.

HINTS FOR FINDING ASPECTS

Conjunctions are easy to spot by looking at the chart we have drawn up. The other major aspects are all multiples of 30°, so with 30° in each sign, planets in aspect will be at similar degrees of a sign. So if the Sun is at 14° Aquarius, it will be in aspect with any planet at round about 14° in any sign. You have to be a bit more careful when a planet is very early or late in a sign. Venus at 1° Aries will be in aspect with a planet in the first few degrees of any sign – and in aspect albeit disassociate, with a planet in the last few degrees of any sign.

One way to work out the angles between planets is to express all their positions in terms of their distance from the first point of Aries. So a planet at 3° Aries is given a value of 3, but one at 3° of Taurus is given a value of 33, since it is 33 degrees from 0° Aries. A planet at 5° Libra would have a value of 185. To find the angle, simply subtract one value from the other, subtracting the answer from 360 if it was greater than 180.

interpreting the aspects

Just as you should be able to develop your own ideas about the planets in the signs and houses by following basic principles, so you should with aspects.

Where two planets are in aspect, start with the natures of the planets involved and modify them according to the aspect.

The following is a brief guide to the sort of characteristics that are present with planetary aspects. Whole books have been written on the interpretation of aspects, so here we can only touch on them. The less welcome effects are primarily discussed, for it is often through recognising them that we begin to resolve them and let the positive characteristics come out. Only the major aspects are discussed and sextiles can at this stage be treated as weaker versions of trines. All the difficult aspects between two planets will to some extent exhibit similar characteristics.

The effects of an aspect will always be modified by the signs and houses involved, and also any other aspects that the two planets are involved in.

Aspects can never be taken in isolation. If an aspect does not appear to be working as it should, it may be being influenced and overruled by others in the chart. It is a matter of experience and style of interpretation.

aspects of the sun

SUN – MOON

CONJUNCTION: Since these two bodies are so fundamental to our being, the conjunction tends to produce a very self-centred and subjective approach, for the emotional Moon energy is blended with the more objective reality of the Sun. Thus these people find it difficult to see the viewpoint of others and to cope with change. Domestic attachment may be very strong. They seek security in the self.

OPPOSITION: These people were born near a full Moon – when the Sun and Moon were on opposite sides of the Earth – and this can produce an endless inner tension for the individual born between the pull of these two powerful energies. Usually there is a fundamental conflict expressed by the nature of the signs and houses involved. The problem here is often too much objectivity — people with this aspect will always be full of questions as they try and seek to define their reality. They seek security in others. Often there was a mother-father conflict, or loss of a parent early in life.

SQUARE: Individuals with this aspect find that their emotional needs cannot be satisfied via Sun-sign drives. They are objective, but are restless in their search for new experience that they feel will resolve the inner tension. Often it seems that parents were not in a harmonious relationship when the child with this aspect was born so that they may subconsciously question their right to exist.

TRINE/SEXTILE: Here spirit and soul are in harmony. These people are generally subjective, but with the appreciation of others' feelings that is lacking in the other Sun-Moon aspects.

Note: In chart interpretation, the relationship between the sign positions of Sun and Moon is always important, even if no aspect is formed. Very, often individuals with no aspect have difficulty expressing their energy effectively. With these two bodies, a difficult aspect is probably easier to handle than none at all.

SUN – MERCURY

CONJUNCTION: Since Mercury is so close to the Sun, this is the only aspect which can occur, other than the semi-sextile. The basic intellect is blended with the basic personality drive to give strength of intellectual purpose, but rationality that is influenced by ego-centred desire. It is difficult for them to gain an objective viewpoint to provide a different view from that provided by the Sun-sign energy.

SUN – VENUS

CONJUNCTION: Again, this is the only major aspect that can occur; the semi-sextile and semi-square are possible. People with this usually have a love of life and are easily able to establish and express what they want because their desires are supplied with energy by the Sun. These people are romantics and drawn towards artistic pursuits, but they can spend too much time on hedonistic pursuits and in some signs, vanity and egocentricity can be a problem.

SUN – MARS

CONJUNCTION: The double ego connection results in volatility and strength of purpose. A tremendous drive to succeed is present as the ability to take action is given perseverance. These people can be good-natured until their way is blocked when anger will readily flare up.

OPPOSITION: Often the action which is taken is at the expense of the true personality drives. Outside events seem to conspire against their success as their actions fail, but in reality this is because they have neglected to incorporate Sun-sign drives.

SQUARE: This aspect makes for a very fiery person. People with this are restless, their tremendous energy not easily channelled into stability. They feel the need to be constantly striving, though aims will impulsively change.

TRINE/SEXTILE: Here the two ego-centred energies will be harmonised to give the ability to take action when necessary and there is a good degree of self-sufficiency.

SUN – JUPITER

CONJUNCTION: This promises beneficence and geniality, with the individual able to reach out to others in ways compatible with the Sun-sign drives. There is a constant seeking to broaden horizons, but this aspect alone does not imply it is a result of unhappiness. There is a tendency for extravagance and overemphasis in the affairs of the sign and house involved.

OPPOSITION: Usually there are many opportunities and a desire to travel. The desire to broaden horizons usually seems to arise because the individuals are unhappy with their lot, even though this may be unjustified in the eyes of others. They may be never satisfied with each new pasture.

SQUARE: This denotes tremendous restlessness – a desire to seek knowledge, but a difficulty in doing anything with it when it is attained. Real lessons may be overlooked as a new approach or source of help becomes available. They usually find it difficult to accept advice and sometimes there is overindulgence relating to the signs and houses involved.

TRINE/SEXTILE: These are generally perceived as lucky aspects.

Actually, fortune arises from the way the individuals expand in harmony with their Sun-sign. There is a desire to learn, but with no sense of the striving involved in the difficult aspects.

SUN – SATURN

CONJUNCTION: Basic Sun-sign characteristics will be restricted, so that even extroverted signs will tend to appear introverted. People with this tend to be easily depressed, but may have the drive to achieve positions of prominence.

OPPOSITION: This seems to produced many external obstacles to life's progress. This may cause depression and sense of failure, or may lead to someone who will fight tenaciously. There is a need to learn when to accept reality, recognising one's limitations. Often the father was critical of their endeavours.

SQUARE: This is a somewhat oppressive influence, particularly preventing success in the areas of the houses it is found in. There can be a constant struggle to achieve, contributed to by an inherent lack of self-belief.

TRINE/SEXTILE: These are still somewhat sobering aspects, but responsibilities are incorporated readily into the person's life and they will knuckle down to attain success, without a sense of repression.

SUN – URANUS

CONJUNCTION: This can be considered a mark of genius, but often the Uranian energy results in mere eccentricity, without other factors in the chart to add practicality. Often there is an explosive temper and stubborn rebelliousness becomes evident when attempts are made to limit the individual's freedom.

OPPOSITION: Often the basic life force stands against that expressed by society as a whole. These people are out of step with their generation, but may be ahead of their time. There is extreme restlessness and this often leads to unusual experiences.

SQUARE: This is not a responsible aspect, for these people are fiercely independent and resent any attempts to be told what to do or given advice. There is originality but impracticality and a lack of perseverance.

TRINE/SEXTILE: These people are able to express their Sun-sign drives in a way that is acceptable to the needs of their generation. They incorporate the new into their lives easily, escaping criticism in their drive to be different and standing out from the crowd.

SUN – NEPTUNE

CONJUNCTION: Here the Sun-sign will be encouraged to manifest in its more spiritual side, and often there is great compassion, intuition or even clairvoyance. But the individual's ego is dissolved to some degree so that confidence is lacking and their will cannot be easily applied to what they want – if indeed they really know what this is.

OPPOSITION: This seems to produce very chameleon-like effects. People with it seem easily influenced by those around them so that their Sun-sign is neglected. They will abandon their own interests for those of others, often being deluded in their expectations. Often the father is somehow distant from the individual.

SQUARE: It is very difficult for people with this aspect to gain a coherent self-image, for their basic ego is subject to Neptune's dissolving influence. Often true motivations are hidden from others and they easily become involved in deceptions.

TRINE/SEXTILE: People with this are more able to accept a dissolving of ego-centred desires and to behave compassionately yet without martyring themselves. This can provide artistic abilities and there is an attraction towards the mystical.

SUN – PLUTO

CONJUNCTION: This leads to very powerful individuals who may act obsessively and with total perseverance in pursuit of their Sun-sign needs. There is a need to transform the self periodically and often sudden changes of lifestyle occur, then a period of calm, before another crisis occurs. There is attraction towards research, the occult and psychoanalysis, these people wanting to find out who they are.

OPPOSITION: People with this can be extremely creative, but often the creative power is blocked. They seem to drain others of energy and initiative. Often sudden changes of lifestyle are brought about by external factors. They try to impose their will on others and thus can be agents of change, but these individuals often seem to be on self-destruct.

SQUARE: This is a stubborn, wilful square that will often try to get its own way by underhand means, although there is often an apparent obsession with honesty. Development does not come easily but rather occurs from sudden changes.

TRINE/SEXTILE: Transforming influences are incorporated very readily into life, so external changes bring internal growth. The Sun-sign energy can be used as an agent for change, but without the wilfulness of the difficult aspects. These people operate with very high energy levels and often seem inexhaustible.

aspects of the moon

MOON – MERCURY

CONJUNCTION: With this aspect there is a blending of the emotions and intellect. It is possible that they will be blended harmoniously, but the sign position will often render one planet the stronger (i.e. in Taurus the Moon energy would be stronger, while in Virgo Mercury would predominate) so that it works at the expense of the other. Usually there is an ability to approach problems with intellect but without losing sight of feelings, although this aspect does render emotions somewhat ephemeral.

OPPOSITION: Feelings have to be balanced with rational considerations. Usually there is a good perception of the truth of a situation, but impulsive emotions may make decision-making difficult and there can be a lot of nervous tension. The signs and houses involved will determine which side of the balance is likely to win out at the expense of the other.

SQUARE: Here there is a clash of feelings and intellect, an inability to blend the two aspects of ourselves. Individuals constantly try to rationalise matters of the heart. There will be a tendency to jump to conclusions and possible domestic arguments.

TRINE/SEXTILE: People with this are readily able to harmonise their feelings with a rational approach, so that both are taken into account. Domestic problems can be sorted out with common-sense, and feelings are easily communicated to others. With all Moon-Mercury aspects, there is an amount of restlessness and a tendency to talk a lot about nothing in particular, and this may even be evident with the easy ones.

MOON – VENUS

CONJUNCTION: People with this conjunction are often described by others as 'charming'. Even with a lot of difficult aspects, this renders a person basically likeable. These people are prepared to give time to others and help them out, but there can be problems with over-indulgence or smother-love, particularly if it is in Cancer or Taurus, both of which have affinities with these planets.

OPPOSITION: This can make relationships very difficult, for the two basic emotional drives want to express in very different ways. Emotional needs are in conflict with deep desires. All Moon-Venus aspects have a need to develop relationships, but with the opposition, they become difficult to maintain because sometimes the individual will react to friends through the Moon sign, but at another time through the opposite Venus sign. Because of the feminine nature of both planets, in a man's chart it can mean problems relating to women, and in a woman's chart an uneasiness about her femininity.

SQUARE: This has similar effects to the opposition, but is more difficult to handle, since the conflicting energies cannot be balanced. There are likely to be problems caused by striking up friendships with others who are not good for the individual, particularly women. There will be overindulgence and excessive emotionalism.

TRINE/SEXTILE: Here feelings and emotional needs can be blended so that the right degree of affection is given and received. These people find no difficulty in attracting friends; without any attaching hard aspects, they might have problems from attracting too many relationships. There is instinctive charm and good taste.

MOON – MARS

CONJUNCTION: Those with this aspect will have powerful emotional needs. Sometimes anger will flare up unexpectedly in emotional outbursts. Sometimes the individual will take impulsive action, while at other times they will be immovable. There may be excessive reliance on doing what is habitual, rather than what is necessary, and a large degree of selfish behaviour.

OPPOSITION: One problem here is a constant switching between passivity and aggression, so that others are unsure how the individual will react. This is an argumentative aspect that causes emotions to get carried away into impulsive action. With difficult Moon-Mars aspects, stress occurs because the person will want to stick to habitual behaviour, yet take fresh action at the same time.

SQUARE: Often these people will be inclined to stir up trouble just for the sake of it. There can be problems surrounding childbirth in women, or, in a man's chart, in his wife. All the difficult Moon-Mars aspects suggest selfishness and with the square it is particularly difficult to handle. Confrontations often occur in the home, although the energy can be channelled into d.i.y. pursuits.

TRINE/SEXTILE: The conjunction does to some extent give courage, but with the harmonious aspects, the degree of recklessness is lost. Male and female qualities are integrated so these people can find sexual relationships easy. Domestic problems are sorted out without confrontation.

MOON – JUPITER

CONJUNCTION: This is not a difficult conjunction, for the individual's general openness in expressing feelings and optimism will bring them positive responses from others that may seem just good fortune. Clearly though, this conjunction can produce exaggerated emotional responses, particularly if the conjunction is squared or in opposition to other planets.

OPPOSITION: This is more restless than the conjunction, because of a conflict between the need to travel and the need to stay at home. The opposition and the square of these planets are characterised by dissatisfaction – whatever pleasurable stimuli are experienced, it never seems to bring satisfaction. Usually there is an excessive attachment to the mother.

SQUARE: Here emotional overindulgence is paramount, as well as a love of the good things in life. Overeating can be a specific problem. Problems occur through overoptimism, a tendency to take things too easy, and sometimes the emotional pursuit of religious causes. Too much money can be spent on beautifying the home.

TRINE/SEXTILE: These express the positive side of the conjunction and are very useful aspects to have, bringing balanced optimism and general good fortune. These people are generally kind and open, get on well with their families and often receive financial help from parents.

MOON – SATURN

CONJUNCTION: Emotional expression will be restricted with this aspect, giving a cold outlook. Whilst there is common sense, familial and other responsibilities may be carried out through a sense of duty and a general unwillingness to have fun may lead to depression. They lack confidence in expressing feelings, but their emotions are stable.

OPPOSITION: Often sacrifices of personal happiness are made out of a sense of duty, particularly in the sense of giving up career for domestic responsibilities. Childhood problems may have been caused by a psychologically oppressive father, so that the individual lacks confidence. There is a feeling that following one's feelings will lead to obstacles from outside authority figures.

SQUARE: A similar effect to the opposition, but with an added sense of pessimism and selfishness. There may have been childhood problems posed by father criticising mother. Emotions are suppressed and there is a tendency to brood on past failures, so that inevitably they occur again.

TRINE/SEXTILE: Even with harmonious Moon-Saturn aspects, some repression of the emotional response is indicated. But these aspects do denote a great deal of common sense and an ability to organise domestic life and daily routine. There is a sense of responsibility attached to familial matters, but it does not weigh individuals down like the hard aspects do.

MOON – URANUS

CONJUNCTION: This will indicate extreme emotional volatility and a desire for independence. These people will want to run their homes in an individualistic way, not tolerating interference. However the way they can strike up relationships with those from all walks of life means they usually lead a life away from the mundane. How difficult or easy this aspect is to handle will very much relate to its sign position.

OPPOSITION: The desires for security and independence need to be balanced. People with this opposition will challenge orders just for the sake of it and can become excessively attracted to the bizarre and unusual. They become easily involved with people who are 'the wrong sort' for them.

SQUARE: People with this will take decisions affecting others without appropriate consultation. They find it difficult to blend the need for security and the desire for independence. All the hard Moon-Uranus aspects can produce the necessity for frequent repairs to the home. Insurances should be checked for adequacy with the square in particular.

TRINE/SEXTILE: These individuals are able to easily reconcile their needs of security and independence. Unusual activities can be introduced into their daily lives, but without the degree of disapproval from others encountered by the square and opposition.

MOON – NEPTUNE

CONJUNCTION: This is an extremely mystical conjunction that can enable the individual to merge the spiritual with daily life. They see the whole world in a grain of sand. All too often, however, Neptune's influence results in daily routine being a constant struggle to apply a sense of structure. The sign position will be of great importance in assessing the effect.

OPPOSITION: Often there is emotional attraction to spiritual movements or gurus, but these will be subject to the changeable quality of the Moon. There is self-deception over one's own emotions plus the likelihood of misreading the feelings of others.

SQUARE: Here, much confusion will surround domestic life. People with this square find it difficult to access their emotions and are easily open to deception. There is a tendency towards escapist behaviour. This can be a very artistic aspect, so long as a grip on reality is not lost.

TRINE/SEXTILE: Domestic life will not be well-ordered, but a harmonious atmosphere will be generated. These are very flowing aspects where higher intuition is merged with emotions to give a deep sense of the spiritual, but without the difficult side effects of the other aspects.

MOON – PLUTO

CONJUNCTION: The domestic situation may be subject to sudden changes and there can be obsession and stubbornness attached to all Moon-related affairs. Feelings are often bottled up rather than allowed to express naturally. Often there are healing abilities or the ability to channel from other planes of existence. Habits may be subconsciously persisted with, but conditioning can be suddenly overthrown.

OPPOSITION: As with all Pluto oppositions, there will be a subconscious drive to force the other planet's energy on others, so people with this aspect will try and control the emotions of others, often by manipulating their own emotional response. It is easy for them to take underhand action in an attempt to get their own way, ultimately proving self-destructive.

SQUARE: This aspect has deep and strong emotions that are followed obsessively, yet often aren't revealed to others. It is difficult for people with it to rise above unproductive emotional responses such as hate and jealousy. They are able to purge their life of unwanted conditioning, but usually with upsetting side-effects.

TRINE/SEXTILE: With the harmonious aspects, conditioning and ingrained habits can be easily and profitably overthrown, should the individuals so desire. Outside influences are integrated readily into daily experience and emotions are not bottled up. This often leads to the ability to counsel others.

aspects of mercury

MERCURY – VENUS

CONJUNCTION: This is a useful conjunction which brings artistic talent. It particularly favours writing, particularly if persuasiveness is involved. Often there is a charming voice. The intellect and deep emotions are blended, though too rational an approach may be a slight problem in signs where Mercury is stronger.

The OPPOSITION, SQUARE and TRINE cannot occur as Mercury and Venus can never be more than 72 degrees apart.

SEXTILE: There is artistic talent and charm of expression, which make these people generally likeable. There is not really a negative side to Mercury-Venus aspects, although other factors in the horoscope will need to be present for their creative promise to be developed.

MERCURY – MARS

CONJUNCTION: People with this aspect make energetic disputants; indeed they are prone to becoming involved in arguments. There is an abundance of mental energy, but if assisting factors are lacking, it is difficult to persevere with lines of thought. It is a very impatient aspect, for these people like to take immediate action on their ideas, becoming frustrated when circumstances prevent.

OPPOSITION: This is a 'foot-in-mouth' aspect, particularly if Scorpio or Sagittarius are involved. People with this say the wrong thing at the wrong time and are argumentative. What they say they will do and what they actually do may be different.

SQUARE: All Mercury-Mars aspects make for individuals who talk a lot, but with the square it is most likely to lack form and balanced reason. Despite this, these people will be fearsome opponents in debate and if they are able to control the energy, it can be used to enhance artistic communication.

TRINE/SEXTILE: With the harmonious aspects, people know when to speak out and when silence is prudent. They are able to put their ideas into action without generating conflicts of ego. Often there is the ability to think precisely plus manual dexterity.

MERCURY – JUPITER

CONJUNCTION: The challenge with these two planetary energies is dealing with the small and the large. When this conjunction occurs in a sign where one planet rules or is exalted, that planet will tend to express at the expense of the other. If Jupiter is predominant, philosophical or religious opinionation could result; if Mercury, collection of trivial pieces of information. Used carefully, all the qualities of Jupiter and Mercury can be successfully merged.

OPPOSITION: This aspect usually leads to a lot of talk and promises, but individuals fail to carry out what they say. There may be religious or philosophical dogmatism. Sometimes blind faith alternates with scepticism. Problems with travel may be encountered. The small may be exaggerated and the large trivialised.

SQUARE: People with this aspect find it hard to harmonise the detailed and the broad view. Experience is integrated poorly into overall philosophy. In a constant hurry to get things done, details are overlooked. They don't communicate in a way that is conducive to establishing relationships.

TRINE/SEXTILE: It is easy to get the message across with the trine and sextile. Writing and teaching are favoured by these aspects, though intellectual pursuits may be favoured at the expense of practicality, particularly in air signs. The individuals with these are open to new ideas, but retain a healthy scepticism.

MERCURY – SATURN

CONJUNCTION: Often these children grew up with father somehow belittling their intellectual achievements. As adults they lack confidence in their reasoning ability and may not speak up for fear of disapproval. Sometimes there are learning difficulties or hearing problems. They do have the perseverance to arrive at practical solutions and visualisation abilities are good.

OPPOSITION: They are always running into trouble with authority figures when they express themselves. Travel related problems occur and, as with all hard Mercury-Saturn aspects, arrangements should always be double-checked. Their tendency to be critical can lead to problems in relationships.

SQUARE: The square makes for a person liable to worry a lot about nothing. All hard Mercury-Saturn aspects can mean that individuals fail to hear what is told them, even though physical hearing problems may not be present. With the square in particular, individuals may be particularly prone to looking on the black side even in the face of others' optimism and support.

TRINE/SEXTILE: Practical reasoning abilities are evident with the harmonious aspects, for individuals have the ability to persevere with detailed logical tasks. Often academic success is achieved and they are able to build up details into large structures. Long-term memory is good.

MERCURY – URANUS

CONJUNCTION: Since Mercury represents intellectual capacity and Uranus inspiration, all aspects between the two planets will produce brilliant minds. With the conjunction, opposition and square though, impractical eccentricity is always a problem. With the conjunction, things are understod in a flash, though memory may not be retentive and there is a desire to express unusual ideas for the sake of being different.

OPPOSITION: People with this aspect have difficulty in being consistent. Each new idea replaces the last before it has been practically explored. Often they have difficulty communicating verbally, for the mind works too quickly for the vocal cords. However, this can often make for a talent in writing, for here thoughts can be edited into coherent language. They will speak out against the accepted ideas of society and so may be seen as trouble-makers.

SQUARE: This aspect shows a lack of mental discipline as one idea is rapidly replaced by another. These people feel a need to speak out about what they believe but find themselves at odds with society. They may be impractical, but possibly are ahead of their time.

TRINE/SEXTILE: These individuals bring new ideas to the world but in a way that society finds acceptable. All Mercury-Uranus connections are fond of debate as it allows them to explore differing viewpoints, but the trine and sextile are less likely to result in arguments. They are usually good at understanding and implementing new technology. This aspect ought to be useful for astrologers!

MERCURY – NEPTUNE

CONJUNCTION: On one level this is a difficult aspect, for it obscures the reasoning process, so that the application of logic fails. There may be retreat into fantasy when faced with hard reality. On a higher level, it enables mind to be supplemented by intuition and can bring great imagination and artistic potential.

OPPOSITION: Often there are deluded ideals that don't stand up to reason. All Mercury-Neptune aspects, even easy ones, tend to imply a difficulty with staying down to earth. With the opposition it is easy to become deluded about facts and to deceive, or be deceived by, others.

SQUARE: Individuals with this aspect can sometimes seem to find it easier to twist the truth than be straightforward. Whilst there is tremendous imagination, often this impinges too much on rational thought.These people deal with problems by trying to change in their minds the reality that caused the problems to occur.

TRINE/SEXTILE: There are undoubtedly artistic abilities with the harmonious aspects, but often the intellect is imbued with a dreamy quality that prevents talent being manifested. The harder aspects are more obvious so may ultimately be channelled more productively. These people are able to blend the minute with the Universal.

MERCURY – PLUTO

CONJUNCTION: These people believe in the power of positive thinking. Often this seems to take a psychic form so that some people with this aspect can actually appear to influence others by merely thinking at them. They have great investigative powers, but may think in devious and underhand ways. Obsession with ideas can also cause difficulties.

OPPOSITION: This aspect is one of interrogation. People with it may upset others by their constant desire for knowledge, regardless of others feelings or matters of privacy. They have tremendous mental persistence, but too often the energy is wasted on trying to prove points and they can suffer from sudden mental exhaustion.

SQUARE: This square indicates a great deal of mental tension of which individuals are usually aware, but can do little to relieve. There is a tremendous desire to impose ideas on others, so bringing them round to their way of thinking. Used with care, this can be an agent for positive change, but so often conflicts occur because of the high energy level of the square.

TRINE/SEXTILE: People with this have a great deal of mental energy. They can make particularly perceptive researchers and psychologists. Debates are of interest to them and they like to get to the bottom of things, though they do so in less underhand ways than are often found in the square and opposition.

aspects of venus

VENUS – MARS

CONJUNCTION: This usually makes for a popular person, for the aggressive side of Mars is softened by Venus. There may be excessive sensuality and there are passionate desires. Individuals with this aspect are prepared to act to get what they want and to remove from their lives what they do not. Not easily persuaded against their wishes, they will however try to persuade others.

OPPOSITION: Since these two planets to some extent represent the male and female characteristics within us all, there is a need to balance these opposites. Individuals with this aspect may be aggressive one time and passive the next. Enthusiasms can be impulsive and short-lived.

SQUARE: This can lead to problems with the opposite sex. Both the square and the opposition can indicate difficulties because needs of friendship and sexual relationship are not blended easily. Relationships are entered into impulsively, but attractions soon wane.

TRINE/SEXTILE: These are very conducive towards relations with the opposite sex. Individuals with these aspects know what action to take in pursuit of their desires. They know when to be assertive and when to be receptive. They are not necessarily good aspects for getting things done.

VENUS – JUPITER

CONJUNCTION: As with all Jupiter conjunctions, the danger is of exaggeration. These people can be very affectionate and generous, but they expect as much in return and overindulgence can be a problem. There is a love of knowledge and a generally fun-loving outlook which makes them popular, though without influencing factors, laziness or lack of responsibility easily creeps in.

OPPOSITION: This aspect is particularly associated with extravagance, for the pursuit of pleasure may take over. There may be vanity – they think they are charming, but others find their apparent sweetness forced and overbearing. There is often a lack of sincerity.

SQUARE: Again, extravagance is likely, particularly in the houses where the square is found. The way they relate to people does not harmonise with what they really want. Although their inherently materialistic outlook means they usually accumulate possessions, it does not bring happiness and resources are wasted. All the difficult Jupiter-Venus aspects can produce characteristics of a search for the easy life.

TRINE/SEXTILE: Even with the harmonious aspects, love of 'the good life' can be a factor that prevents development. These bring apparent good fortune, so individuals may not feel they have to struggle for success. Venus and Jupiter in traditional astrology were the two lucky planets. The trine and sextile bring charm, friendship and a sense of peace.

VENUS – SATURN

CONJUNCTION: Individuals with this aspect may fear to follow their desires. Perhaps as children they were dissuaded from doing so. These people will be cautious about forming relationships, but once committed will be steadfast. However, relationships may be maintained only out of duty.

OPPOSITION: People with the opposition find it difficult to express their affection. There may be an attitude that emotions have no practical use. Often a lot of hard work is put into achieving objects of desire, only to find that hopes are dashed.

SQUARE: Although this will produce loyalty, this may be carried on in the face of a lack of care from partners and friends. There can be an unwillingness to 'open the heart' and engage in shared experiences, so disappointments in love result.

TRINE/SEXTILE: These aspects are useful for creative endeavours for the Venusian sense of beauty can be given Saturnian structure. There is still a somewhat sobering effect. Even the harmonious aspects of these two planets result in a cooling of emotions, though without the depression that often results from the other aspects.

VENUS – URANUS

CONJUNCTION: Feelings change unpredictably and there may be a constant stream of friends and lovers as new experiences are sought. All the difficult Venus-Uranus aspects seem to have a high incidence of partnership break-up. These people desire independence of emotion, and must express themselves as they want to without interference.

OPPOSITION: These people always seem to get involved in relationships with those who are not good for them. Often the expression of their feelings is at odds with accepted behaviour. Men may express very feminine attributes and vice versa, and society may pour scorn on them. All the same, Venus-Uranus aspects bring a magnetism that can bring irresistible attraction.

SQUARE: This is one of the most rebellious Uranus aspects. Often unusual behaviour seems to be carried out just for the sake of it. Their desire to be different may cause them to be regarded as eccentric, but they are always noticeable and are instigators of change in society.

TRINE/SEXTILE: Usually individuals with the harmonious Venus-Uranus combinations can be friends to all, regardless of age or social standing. Although they need to preserve independence in partnerships, they usually do so with the acceptance of partners. Relationships often work better with unconventional associates.

VENUS – NEPTUNE

CONJUNCTION: This is a highly artistic conjunction, full of creative imagination. Compassion and intuition is blended with friendship. The danger here is of fantasy-seeking and dreaming. Often these people will seem to be able to hear a tune that others cannot. Whether they can use this energy creatively will depend on the sign and any practical aspects.

OPPOSITION: Relationships are entered into out of romantic or platonic reasons. Partners may be idolised even when it should be plain that they are not reciprocating affection. The ideals the individual seeks have to be balanced with the needs arising from more ego-centred desires.

SQUARE: These people are unsure what their true desires are. Sometimes relationships are entered into that have no chance of fulfilment. This may be obvious to everyone except the owner of the square! Both the square and opposition imply deception in love and sometimes unusual sexual behaviour. Friends may be poorly chosen and there is much dreaming about.

TRINE/SEXTILE: There is usually a mystical quality about individuals with these aspects. The universal is easily accommodated with the personal. Ideals are harmonised with true feelings and artistic abilities benefit. Other aspects may have to be present for creative abilities to develop.

VENUS – PLUTO

CONJUNCTION: Intensity of feelings is experienced here. When people with this aspect desire something, they will seek it with passion. They can be very demanding in relationships and partners involved with a Venus-Pluto person must be prepared to make periodic changes in the relationship if it is to survive. As with all Pluto aspects, the emphasis is on transformation to a higher level, though often the effect is degenerative.

236

OPPOSITION: There is intensity of feeling coupled with a desire to convert partners to the same level of experience. Feelings of lack of fulfilment will build up until a relationships is broken off suddenly, rather than matters being discussed at an early stage. It may appear that outside forces contrive to break up relationships or stop the fulfilment of desires. All the hard Venus-Pluto aspects are involved in attempts to control others.

SQUARE: These people try and remain in control of their feelings and will attempt to control others' feelings too. When they feel they can no longer control a relationship, they will break it off. Although in essence an aspect with creative potential, often it fails to bloom through lack of co-operation as individuals try and retain control of the whole artistic venture.

TRINE/SEXTILE: These aspects can bring a depth of artistic expression. They will be deeply committed to relationships, but without the attempts to coerce partners and friends often at work in the other aspects.

aspects of mars

MARS – JUPITER

CONJUNCTION: All Mars-Jupiter aspects are likely to produce recklessness and exaggerate the already ego-centred energy of Mars. With the conjunction there is a desire for adventure. There is courage and a crusading spirit that can move mountains, but self-importance can be present. Often physical pursuits are good outlets for this energy.

OPPOSITION: The way these individuals wish to relate to others as expressed by the Jupiter sign, will need to be balanced with the ego-centred drives of Mars in the opposite sign. Often these people are prone to moral indignation and will act to force their opinions on others. It seems that they don't like to be left out of other people's fun. They may alternate between action and indolence.

SQUARE: Perhaps the most difficult problem for these people is that they will bite off more than they can chew. Of all aspects, this is one of excess, particularly in the affairs of the signs and houses where it is found. Action is often taken in a way guaranteed to throw a spanner in the works.

TRINE/SEXTILE: With the harmonious aspects, action is taken in a way that allows relationships to develop naturally. The energy of Mars is taken into the wider sphere and these people can build big at whatever they attempt.

MARS – SATURN

CONJUNCTION: Saturnian caution tends to frustrate the Mars desire for action. People with this are ambitious but do not know, or are afraid of, what they want, and are usually stiff or clumsy into the bargain. Often they are of large build. They want to go ahead impulsively but want to be cautious as well. Much can be achieved by hard work and there is courage in adversity.

OPPOSITION: These people may rush headlong into projects one minute and then they back off the next . Individuals feel that their ambitions are thwarted by circumstances or authority, and they have a bad sense of timing. Often the way they take action causes criticism.

SQUARE: This is an aspect of great frustration, for individuals cannot easily find a structure through which to channel personal energy. There are inhibitions, lack of sustained effort and also a high risk of accidents. As with all Mars-Saturn connections, there is a risk of suppressed Mars energy suddenly exploding with destructive effect.

TRINE/SEXTILE: Here the dynamic energy of Mars can be used with Saturnian control to build great things. Action is combined effortlessly with the right amount of control and there are good relationships with authority. Often there is manual dexterity.

MARS – URANUS

CONJUNCTION: This is a potentially explosive conjunction. Often people with it have a volatile temper and they will take impulsive or reckless action. Used carefully, they can take action to lead their generation. There is an interest in mechanical things and often ability in dealing with machinery and technology. Many people with this aspect feel extremely restless and problems of nervous tension can occur through failure to relax.

OPPOSITION: Here action taken may be out of tune with the views of peers. The desire for independence in action will cause these individuals to dislike being told what to do and arguments are often the result. Like the opposition of Mars and Saturn, there are problems in relations with authority, but whereas Saturn may cause them to knuckle under, Mars-Uranus is much more rebellious.

SQUARE: There may be mechanical abilities, but there is the risk of accident. These people may well be ahead of their time, for they become involved in activities that are not partaken by the mainstream. All Mars-Uranus connections generate impulsiveness, but with the square in particular it becomes very hard to bring projects to a conclusion.

TRINE/SEXTILE: These people can make natural leaders, for whilst like the other Mars-Uranus aspects, they will stand out from the crowd, their actions will in the cases of the trine and sextile be more acceptable to those around them. Usually there is practical mechanical ability.

MARS – PLUTO

CONJUNCTION: These people have tremendous staying power, for Mars will get them moving and Pluto will provide the underlying force for them to continue. Their forceful behaviour can cause problems. They will do what they think fit regardless of others. There may be a connection between this aspect and physical disability.

OPPOSITION: There will be attempts to get others to do as the individuals want them to do, by whatever means necessary. Often it seems that individuals with this aspect are faced with choices between good and evil actions. The tendency is for them to attempt to change others when they should be changing themselves.

SQUARE: Often these people will act with a sense of destiny, convinced that they are right. They will stop at nothing as they pursue their ends, and whilst this gives them much energy, it will bring them into conflict. All Mars-Pluto aspects can cause anger to be suppressed only to flare up later, rather than be dealt with when it occurs. With the square, violent outbursts are particularly frequent if anger is not understood.

TRINE/SEXTILE: All Mars-Pluto aspects need to be handled with care. With the easy aspects, though, there are not the destructive side-effects that so often occur with the others when individuals attempt to transform themselves. These people will have passionate strength of purpose, but whereas, with the hard aspects this will easily be seen as obstinacy, with the easy aspects it is more likely to be regarded as tenacity.

When discussing the aspects involving the impersonal and transpersonal planets, we should be aware that they may have a less direct effect in an individual's chart. In some cases they will bear characteristics typical of a whole generation of people. Often they will not be that significant in one person's chart. It will depend on how integrated they are in the chart via aspects to other planets and how close to being exact the aspect is. Also, where the ascendant, descendant, MC or IC are involved, their energy may be more readily incorporated. Some people seem more sensitive to the outer planets than others, regardless of birth chart factors.

aspects of jupiter

JUPITER – SATURN aspects occur over a cycle of about twenty years. It is regarded by mundane astrologers as one of the basic cycles of history. Aspects will therefore occur with the following approximate periodicity:

Conjunction:	20 years
Opposition:	20 years
Square:	10 years
Trine:	7 years then 13 years
Sextile:	7 years then 13 years

CONJUNCTION: Individuals with this aspect will feel they want to expand and contract at the same time! Often their response will be to overexpand sometimes and overcontract at others. Their whole lives might be spent fluctuating between the conflicting characteristics of Jupiter and Saturn, with matters only being resolved if they learn to blend the energies.

OPPOSITION: Here there are similar effects to the conjunction, but obstacles to expansion seem more externalised. Again the lesson must be to reach out with caution and consolidate while retaining optimism, rather than fluctuating between the extremes of the two planets. Often conflicts involving moral or religious beliefs occur.

SQUARE: The action of this square will depend on which planet is stronger. If Jupiter, there will be overoptimism that results in constant thwarting by Saturn's practical realities; if Saturn, then lack of confidence will cause opportunities to be missed. Both may be seen by the individuals concerned as bad luck, but it arises from the failure to reconcile the principles represented by the two planets. This is inherently more difficult than with the conjunction and opposition.

TRINE/SEXTILE: These are very useful aspects to have, for individuals are easily able to harmonise the essentially conflicting natures of the planets. Often there is apparent good luck with money and material resources.

JUPITER – URANUS aspects occur in a cycle of fourteen years, which is related in mundane astrology to cycles of innovation and technological expansion and financial affairs.

CONJUNCTION: This is often seen as a very lucky aspect, for individuals are inspired when it comes to expanding and relating. Often opportunities occur unexpectedly and these people always seem to fall on their feet. They may be at the frontiers of the expansion of knowledge and are easily accepted by their peers.

OPPOSITION: Here there is a constant urge to reach out for new experiences, through travel, new friends and the search for knowledge. There can be wanderlust and attachment to cults. Inherent originality may not find favour with their fellows and there is sense of dissatisfaction about new experiences that cause them to go on seeking.

SQUARE: People with this will reach out impulsively for friends but may shut off from the relationship suddenly if they feel slighted. Philosophical ideas, though benefitting from Uranian humanitarianism, may be dogmatic and impractical. Recklessness can be more of a problem than with the conjunction and opposition.

TRINE/SEXTILE: New ideas are incorporated very readily with these people, and their propounding of new ideas is more easily accepted than with the harder aspects. Without practical influences, they can be too idealistic.

JUPITER – NEPTUNE aspects occur within a 13 year cycle. In mundane astrology they are related to cycles of religious belief.

CONJUNCTION: As with all Neptune conjunctions this can produce highly spiritual characteristics, but often Neptune dissipates the energy of the other planet. It may lead to clairvoyance, healing abilities and the ability to reach out to others with compassion. There is strong sensitivity to the needs of others, but a tendency for escapism. There may be excessive idealism, often centred on religious faith.

OPPOSITION: This aspect can produce unrealistic optimism. People with it may always be doing things for others but with little thanks and little sense of practicality. Or, the individuals themselves may be forever seeking help from others rather than attending to problems themselves. These people are born during periods when a prevailing view is that society is not caring enough, but where the practical considerations of this are lacking

SQUARE: All Jupiter-Neptune aspects produce idealism, and people with the square may find this will lead them to overlook harsh reality. Day-to-day necessities may be neglected at the expense of the pursuit of the vast. There is much sensitivity to suffering, and those these people are generally kind, they find it difficult to offer practical help. This aspect has a reputation as a lazy aspect.

TRINE/SEXTILE: Here altruistic motives are incorporated more harmoniously into life. This mystical energy blend can bring artistic abilities and a sense of vision. The sense of peace that these people can experience may mean they do not feel the need to develop their talents.

JUPITER – PLUTO aspects occur in a cycle of about twelve years, which mundane astrologers may use to chart the progress of idealogical conflicts.

CONJUNCTION: These people are able to fight for the truth, but particularly if there are other challenging aspects involved, it may be simply 'their version' of it. Obsession with causes or religious dogma may be apparent. Relationships may be developed through sub-conscious drive to control others. Affairs of the sign and house involved may be exaggerated.

OPPOSITION: These people can become obsessed with obtaining a set of moral values or religious faith. They will then be inclined to try and force their opinions on everyone else, feeling out of control when they are threatened with alternative views.

SQUARE: Although there is an inherent dissatisfaction produced here, very often individuals will fail to remove the ideas that are actually holding them back. Opportunities may be missed through adherence to dogma. All Jupiter-Pluto connections will to some extent try to convert others. With the square, the drive to control others by converting them to a particular belief is readily apparent and causes discord.

TRINE/SEXTILE: With the harmonious aspects, the crusading power is viewed more acceptably. Radical changes to the individual and those around them are accomplished more comfortably. There is a philosophical mind capable of great insight into truth.

aspects of saturn

SATURN – URANUS aspects occur in a period of about forty-five years and are linked to the consolidation of technological advance and authoritarian politics.

CONJUNCTION: People with this are born at times when there is a fight against authoritarian political thought. The explosive Uranian energy will be suppressed by Saturn, but is inclined to explode from time to time, making these people unpredictable. Used carefully, these people can bring practicality to innovation. 20th. Century occurrences were in 1942/3 and 1988/9.

OPPOSITION: Usually this brings problems with authority figures, for the energy for change is set against the energy to retain structures. Sometimes these people will themselves be authoritarian, denying the individuality of others. The Uranus-Pluto conjunction of the 1960's (discussed earlier) was for a time opposed by Saturn.

SQUARE: This square can be indicative of individuals who are laws unto themselves. There is inflexibility, with them seeking vigorously to uphold tradition or invoke new ideas, depending on which planet proves stronger. In either case, they are continually confronted by people representing the other planet's energy. What they see as legitimate may be at variance with the views of peers.

TRINE/SEXTILE: These people are readily able to merge the new into existing structures. New ideas, technology and practices are incorporated into existing systems with little fuss. They are able to blend what is valuable from the past and the present and relate well to people of all ages.

SATURN − NEPTUNE aspects occur in a cycle of about 36 years. In mundane work this period is related to socialist politics and religious authority.

CONJUNCTION: All sense of structure will be subject to the dissolving energy of Neptune. On one level these individuals may find it difficult to get a grip on practical reality, but on another may be able to put into practice higher ideals. This conjunction occurred in 1989. It will tend to result in political change being peaceful, though with excessive idealism.

OPPOSITION: What these individuals dream about is in conflict with reality, but they may not accept this, preferring to develop the fantasising side of their natures. Sometimes this aspect indicates a teller of tall stories and there is an unwillingness to face up to responsibilities.

SQUARE: Here the structures attained in life are not reconciled with what the individual dreamed of attaining. Imagination may be lacking and they will easily play the martyr. There can be periods of low energy just when hard work is required.

TRINE/SEXTILE: These aspects are a blessing for ideals can be harmonised with practicality. These are people who can turn their dreams into reality. Artistic ability may be evident, though there will be a conservatism in outlook without other vitalising aspects.

SATURN − PLUTO aspects occur in a cycle of approximately 33 years related to changes in the underlying structures of society and to power struggles.

CONJUNCTION: There is usually a great deal of self-control and stubbornness. Individuals with this will dislike being told what to do, and hate limitation, but may bottle up their feelings about these until explosive outbursts occur. They will use the law to justify the imposition of their own wills. There may be obsession with existing structures, but these may be suddenly overthrown. The circumstances of the UK-Argentine war seem typical of the energy of this conjunction in 1982/3.

OPPOSITION: All Saturn-Pluto aspects represent a desire to control others through the force of authority. With the added challenge of the opposition, individuals are likely to become involved in power struggles and resort to force or underhand means to get their way, or by attempting to legitimise their actions.

SQUARE: This will bring general dissatisfaction with existing circumstances. There will be much energy for reform, but often the less useful Pluto energies will be evident, so that systems are broken down but not rebuilt. The effects of the reforming process on others may be considered irrelevant.

TRINE/SEXTILE: Systems and authorities can be reformed more harmoniously without the conflict generated by the other aspects. There is passionate commitment to the attainment of goals over a long period.

aspects between transpersonal planets

URANUS – NEPTUNE aspects occur in a cycle of 172 years and in mundane astrology are connected with revolutions in beliefs.

CONJUNCTION: This aspect is discussed in the chapter on outer planets.

OPPOSITION: Astrologers will have little working experience of this opposition as it last occurred in 1908/9. There may be problems with being led astray by religious or political movements. Individualistic behaviour has to be balanced with awareness of others. With the opposition and square, technology may be implemented carelessly without regard to its undesirable side-effects.

SQUARE: Many people born in the 1950's have this square. One of its problems seems a difficulty in coming to terms with new technologies and changing circumstances in society as a whole. It is an aspect of easy disillusionment. The new age movement may have its birth in this square, but how far this is based on an awareness of higher forces, or illusion remains to be seen.

TRINE/SEXTILE: These aspects make the raising of consciousness easier. Mystical and technological ideas can be blended so that technology is introduced with a human face. These people are able to use astrology, the occult, yoga and mystical religion more easily than others – though there can be a lack of practicality. The trine was in aspect for much of the period 1937-47, the sextile during the late 1960's.

URANUS – PLUTO aspects occur in a cycle that averages 127 years, but varies between about 115 and 139 years. It is an indicator of upheavals in society.

CONJUNCTION: This aspect is discussed in the chapter on outer planets.

OPPOSITION: This last occurred in the early years of the twentieth century. It seems to indicate that people will be particularly prone to involvement in situations of sudden, dramatic changes. They will readily accept the use of force to produce change, and their pursuit of power will cause conflict with later generations.

SQUARE: There is an inner psychological tension. These people may be attracted to new ways of exploring their inner self. Unconscious motivations will be at odds with the behaviour influence by perceived views of what society requires. This was in aspect through the early 1930's.

TRINE/SEXTILE: Here there is great power for revolutionary change, but without the more destructive effects of the conjunction. External change will be more easily reflected in internal development.

NEPTUNE – PLUTO aspects occur in a cycle of about 470 years, so their effects can be very subtle and occur over long periods of time. The conjunction last occurred towards the end of the nineteenth century. In some ways this cycle seems to represent the progression of human development that is difficult to crystallise into specific characteristics or events. Each conjunction marks a new period of growth on a slightly higher spiritual level. It may be linked to the births of spiritual teachers such as Jesus and Krishnamurti.

No-one living today has the square, trine or opposition but the long periodicity of the two planets and Pluto's eccentric orbit have resulted in the sextile being found in the charts of most people born during the period from 1943 to the end of the twentieth century. It gives the opportunity for a harmonious development of universal love and cosmic consciousness. The upsurge of interest in recent years in alternative medicine, the occult, mysticism and concern for the environment relate in part to this aspect.

completing the chart

All that remains for us to do now to complete our chart is to actually draw in the aspects.

When we put the planets in our chart wheel, we put a little nick on the inside of the circle of houses. All we have to do is draw a line between the pertinent nicks when there is an aspect. We can work through the aspect grid methodically. First of all the Sun-Moon opposition (fig. i).

(i)

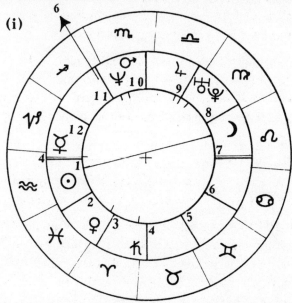

Next is the Sun-Venus semi-square. Generally, this probably would not be drawn on a chart as it is not of great significance. The Sun-Mars square, however, is a major aspect and so should be drawn in, as will (working through the grid) the Moon-Mars square (fig. ii).

> **When you are drawing aspects, you get to know by the length of the line you are drawing whether you have worked out the angle correctly – the line for a trine will be longer than one for a square, and an opposition must cross somewhere near the centre of the circle.**

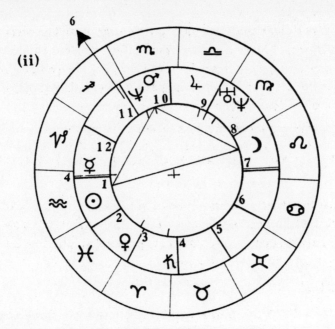

(ii)

Working all the way through the grid, we can draw on all the aspects and end up with our finished chart (fig. iii).

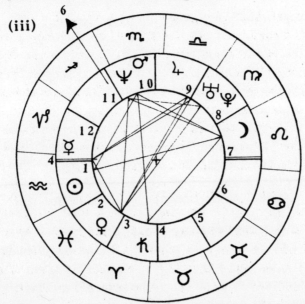

(iii)

Most astrologers use black for the hard aspects (squares, and oppositions) and red for easy ones (sextiles, trines) – or vice versa. Conjunctions are sometimes omitted and sometimes marked in with a circle. Minor aspects, when shown, may be put in as dotted lines.

Note that there are a number of different ways to present charts.

Earlier we mentioned that the sign boundaries aren't always shown, and that different house systems may affect presentation. In some charts, the house cusps are extended right into the centre of a chart with the aspects superimposed on top, while other charts do not mark aspects on at all, merely referring you to the aspect grid.

OTHER INFORMATION SHOWN ON A CHART

On the next page is our chart drawn up such as might be presented to a client.

The house numbers are not shown, mainly because they can clutter up the chart. Chiron has been included and the aspects it makes drawn in. The number by each planet shows its position to the nearest degree. Often degrees and minutes are shown.

RETROGRADES

When we worked out the positions of the planets we came across the phenomenon of retrogradation. Where planets are retrograde, they have been marked on the chart using the conventional notation Rx.

The interpretation of retrogrades is an area of discussion amongst astrologers. The common feeling is that when a planet is retrograde, its energy is blocked in some way, so that its energy is not as readily available. Having a number of planets retrograde, particularly personal ones, does seem to make it more difficult for the individuals concerned to function effectively. They may feel that they are swimming against the tide in relation to the areas affected by the retrograde planets. However, they seem to add depth of understanding to the areas related to the planets concerned.

There may be some problem here for astrologers who take a more scientific rather than occult approach to the subject, in that since the phenomenon is an optical illusion, it is difficult to see how the planet's effect is modified. In any case, there is no strong consensus about retrogrades. I have found that like a number of areas of astrology, scepticism is modified by practical experience, which seems to bear out that there is an effect. For example, one only has to experience a number of retrograde Mercury people with learning difficulties (that is to say, who find it difficult to accept the particular learning system imposed by society) to begin to take notice.

249

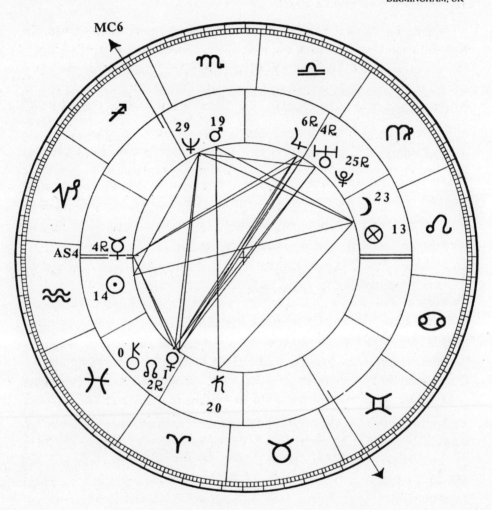

THE NODES OF THE MOON ☊(north) ☋ (south)

These are the points in space where the orbit of the Moon crosses the ecliptic. Daily positions are shown for the north node (where the Moon crosses in a northerly direction relative to Earth) in the *American Ephemeris*. The south node is exactly opposite, and so often only the north node is shown on a chart.

Again, these are not fully understood by most astrologers. In western astrology the south node has been termed as an Achilles heel – its house and sign position showing where bad habits trip you up – whilst the north node shows where talents can be developed. Life goes better if you develop the positive sign characteristics of your north node.

Reincarnational astrologers see the south node as relating to the debris from past lives, whereas the north node represents the present and future direction. We seem to be moving towards an interpretation of them more linked to the rather nebulous idea of spiritual progress. In time, if we move towards a less materialistic, more holistic view of life, I feel that we may come to recognise these points as having as much importance as we now attach to the Sun.

All the planets have nodes. Perhaps interpreting this will be yet another expanding area of astrology.

THE PART OF FORTUNE ⊗ *

Arabic astrology uses a multitude of mathematical ratios, or parts, between the planets. The part of fortune is one that has found its way into common use in western astrology. This point bears the same relationship to the ascendant as the Moon does to the Sun. So if the Moon is 60 degrees further along the zodiac than the Sun, the part of fortune is 60 degrees further on than the ascendant. If we convert the relevant figures to degrees after 0° Aries, we can use the formula:

⊗ = ☽ + AS - ☉

---

* *The symbol is my own – the conventional one is ⊕ but this is also the symbol for the Earth.*

251

So for our sample data:

Moon 23° Leo	=	143
Ascendant 4° Aquarius	=	304

		447
Sun 14° Aquarius	=	314

Part of Fortune	133	= 13° Leo

Again, the interpretation is open to discussion and experiment. The sign and house position of it seem to indicate ways in which we can make our own good fortune. Planets in aspect to it will also be of relevance; trines and sextiles will help, squares and oppositions be more difficult, with conjunctions depending on the planet involved.

In the past, the part of fortune has been given a rather materialistic interpretation, based on the idea of material success, or lack of it, but today we seem to be moving towards an interpretation more geared to the idea of fulfilment. Martin Shulman links it with the idea of joy. (For detailed discussions of retrogrades, the Moon's nodes and part of fortune, see his books detailed in the bibliography.)

ASTEROIDS

As we look out through the solar system, we find that there is a large gap between the orbit of Mars and Jupiter. We know that Mars takes two years to go around the zodiac, Jupiter about twelve.

Actually, between these two orbits, there are a whole range of small bodies, known as the asteroids. They vary in size from a diameter of about 600 miles for Ceres, the first one discovered, down through many just a few miles across, to mere boulders and presumably to particles of dust. Over 2000 of the larger ones have been catalogued. Not all asteroid orbits are between Mars and Jupiter – some orbits are very eccentric and may result in asteroids being at times closer to the Sun than the Earth. The orbit of Icarus is so eccentric, it gets closer to the Sun than Mercury. Orbital periods vary from about a year (e.g. Icarus) to about 14 years for Hidalgo, the furthest conventional asteroid. Chiron is officially catalogued as asteroid 1977 UB, though it is farther out than any known asteroid and is regarded as more planetary in nature by astrologers.

The astrological effect of a number of the larger asteroids has been investigated, and you might see symbols for these on some birth charts. This is a fascinating area of research. Again, one tends to approach the idea with scepticism, but when one begins to use them, correlations of behaviour with their suggested meanings do seem to occur. The disadvantage is that there are so many of them. The advantage is that they have very specific meanings. In looking at someone's approach to partnership relationships, for example, the asteroids Eros, Sappho, Amor and Juno have nuances of meaning, with respective keywords of passion, sexuality, love and companionship. Orbs of just 1° are normal for asteroid aspects.

FIXED STARS

We saw that the background against which the planets move is made up of a multitude of stars. They are so far away that their movement is barely detectable to the eye over a lifetime. For this reason they are referred to as fixed, although we should remember that their position will change by 1° every 72 years (as discussed earlier) and that they are of course moving very rapidly through space.

Since all the fixed stars, particularly those close to the ecliptic, can be given zodiacal positions (which will change by about 1/72° every year), it follows that we may be able to discover meanings for specific stars when they form aspects with planets. Fixed stars are rarely used today, but the increasing use of computers is likely to lead to more experiments with them.

notes on interpretation

If you have worked through the book using your own birth chart, you will probably have looked up the suggested interpretations for it – the planets in the signs and houses plus the aspects – and perhaps have added some interpretations of your own. If you have had a report prepared by an astrologer, you should now be able to see how it was derived.

Drawing up a birth chart is a question of technical skill. Most people can do it, although of course some will pick up the skill more easily than others. Nowadays, computer programs have been produced that draw up birth charts in a fraction of the time it takes a human to do it.

Interpretation requires a different set of skills. We can look up the characteristics of the planets in signs, houses and aspect in a cookbook fashion – most written reports made by astrologers are prepared in this way and can be very helpful in learning about your birth chart. Such reports also have the advantage that, with the aid of modern word-processing equipment, they can be prepared quickly and are therefore relatively inexpensive. To prepare a totally individual written report, on the other hand, is probably at least a day's work and most people are not prepared to pay for this. Personal consultations, although because of time factors they may overlook certain configurations, can be more helpful in that they enable an individual to discuss matters with the astrologer. And the astrologer is able to take into account the environmental factors that have shaped the planetary energies.

To fully interpret a chart requires a different ability than learning by rote the meanings of each sign position, house position and planetary aspect. If you want to expand your astrological ability, you need to develop an ability to synthesise the different information in a chart and, according to the emphasis of your approach, decide what is of most help for the individual concerned.

Beginners often like to have a system to follow. The problem with any system is that it stops spontaneity and can block creative flow. Fear of getting it wrong or overlooking something will often stop a beginner from trusting his or her judgement.

I don't follow a specific system of interpretation. Perhaps because I am a Piscean (and a Moon-conjunct-Neptune person), I find it much more helpful to take an overall view. I usually find that as soon as I look at a chart, some things begin to stand out as being more important than others. It seems that once I start on one part of a reading, I usually find a theme which is picked up as I work through the rest of the chart. Often there is one particular aspect or planetary position that is causing a lot of trouble and clogging up the whole chart. Once that aspect is explained and approached (assuming that client really wants to do something about it) then the rest is easy. In the next person's chart, the same aspect may be relatively unimportant.

It is possible to put down some guidelines for interpretation, but in practice, one would rarely stick to them. Each individual is just that — an individual — and should be treated as such.

One piece of advice that I think is helpful is to always go back to the basic characteristics of the sign, planet, house and aspect involved in the part of a chart you are dealing with. If you are unsure of an interpretation, you can derive a meaning from these basic principles. And in this way, you will develop your knowledge of astrology.

epilogue

In this book we have not discussed how astrology works; that would probably require a whole book in itself. There are a number of theories ranging from astrology being acausal, through occult explanations and the invocation of as yet undiscovered physics to the operation of known electromagnetic forces. Unfortunately, in recent times science has virtualy refused to consider that astrology might be valid, and astrologers have often avoided science because of its hostile attitude. Unfortunately, the approach of scientists has been very unscientific, typifying what the philosopher Herbert Spencer spoke of as "contempt prior to investigation". If you refuse to look at something, you cannot really dismiss it and yet this has largely been the attitude of scientists. The history of science is littered by such blunders where the heterodoxy of today becomes the accepted theory of tomorrow. But we must be aware that, whilst there are almost certainly forces at work in the Universe that are beyond our present understanding, the occult trappings of astrology have not helped it gain scientific recognition.

This attitude is changing. It seems to me that we will probably be able to develop a scientifically-based theory of astrology within the next few decades. Writing in 1990, maybe when Uranus, the ruling planet of astrology, makes its seven year passage through Aquarius, starting in 1995, we will have an opportunity to revolutionise astrology through the application of science.

This will almost certainly be a time of upheaval for astrology. The subject does need a good shaking up! Its practices go back for thousands of years and have changed very little in that time. This in some ways is a strength – it has 'stood the test of time' – but is also a weakness in that, unlike other disciplines, it has failed to significantly develop with the changing times.

We must remember that astrological theory, as presented in this book, has not been subject to rigorous scientific testing and so remains open to question. Objective investigation has not really happened, partly because of scientific hostility, but also because of the difficulties involved in psychological testing. Scientists can devise ways to test the mass of sub-atomic particles accelerated towards the speed of light, but it's more dificult to measure concepts such as sense of humour, stubbornness or charm, which are the sorts of things astrology deals in.

I suppose that astrologers are just as guilty as any professionals of feeling insecure when their working practices are challenged. We must not be so. We may have a golden opportunity to explore just what does work and what does not, to abandon what is not valid and perhaps make new discoveries. Astrologers can be as guilty as anyone of hanging on to outmoded beliefs. If you study astrology, you may be able to contribute to the growing awareness of it and the move towards the truth.

This book has presented a largely orthodox view of Western astrology and has not significantly departed from established practices. When you read about the characteristics of a planet in a sign or house or a planetary aspect as it appears in your birth chart, in this book or elsewhere, you will almost certainly find that some of what you read does not hold. You will probably recognise that there is a basic validity in the principles behind what you have read and you may be able to develop your own ideas about the sign or aspect concerned.

As far as astrology's practitioners are concerned, they know that astrology does have a great deal of validity. The question is not whether it works, but how much of it works.

further reading

There are so many books on various aspects of astrology that providing a detailed book list is not practical. For example, whole books are available on each planet. Many books are American in origin and may require special ordering. The following is a personal selection of books, which I think are useful for those relatively new to astrology. I acknowledge the influence that some of these writers have had on my own approach to astrology.

TECHNICAL INFORMATION

The American Ephemeris for the 20th. Century. Neil F. Michelsen ACS Publications. A comprehensive and accurate ephemeris based on data from the Jet Propulsion Laboratory. Midnight and Noon versions are available, though the former is probably easier to use.

Concise Planetary Ephemeris (Heiratic Publishing) is also available in Noon and Midnight editions for 1900-50 and 1950-2000.

Raphael's Astronomical Ephemeris of the Planets' Places W. Foulsham & Co. Perhaps not as easy to use, but there may be an advantage to the general reader in that it is available in single year volumes – any year from 1860 to date.

Raphael's Table of Houses for Great Britain W. Foulsham & Co. Placidus house cusps for 50°N to 59°N. *Raphael's Table of Houses for Northern Latitudes* covers the equator to 50°N

The Koch Table of Houses is published by ACS Publications

Time Changes in the World by Doris Doane is the standard reference work for finding obscure time zone information.

A good atlas is necessary for the serious astrologer. Most atlases will suffice, though *The International Atlas* by Shanks, ACS Publications has details of time changes.

INTERPRETATION

The Astrologer's Handbook by Francis Sakoian & Louis Acker (Penguin) is an established work detailing characteristics of the planets through all the signs and houses plus planetary aspects. Useful, though should be used with care and perhaps a little dated.

Secrets from a Stargazers Notebook by Debbi Kempton Smith (Bantam). Full of interesting snippets as well as discussions of planets through the signs. Useful, so long as you are able to tolerate the amazingly jazzy style.

Astrological Insights into Personality by Betty Lundstead (ACS Publications). Planetary aspects discussed in detail, particularly on how they relate to childhood conditioning influencing adult relationships.

The series of four books by Martin Shulman with the common title *Karmic Astrology* (Samuel Weiser) are more advanced works:

> *I: The Moon's Nodes and Reincarnation*
>
> *II: Retrogrades and Reincarnation.*
>
> *III: Joy and the Part of Fortune*
>
> *IV: The Karma of the Now*

Belief in reincarnation is not necessary for these books to be of use!

For an introduction to asteroids, see *The Ultimate Asteroid Book* by Lee J. Lehman (Whiteford Press), which also contains an ephemeris for seven asteroids.

As regard to fixed stars, the only work appears to be *The Fixed Stars and Constellations in Astrology* by Vivian E. Robson (Samuel Wiser). Since it was written in 1923 (though reprinted a number of times) it is somewhat dated.

OTHER WORKS

The History of Astrology by Derek and Julia Parker (Andre Deutsch) is a standard work on astrological history, though not particularly objective.

Astrology: the Evidence of Science by Dr Percy Seymour (Lennard) also has good historical information and suggests a theory of astrology that may be consistent with current scientific knowledge.

Finally, if you are a serious student, you may be beyond the level offered by a number of books which give Sun-sign characteristics. However, if you are seeking some light relief, you could try *The Bad News Zodiac* by Sayers & Viney, or *Sun Signs for Cats* and *Sun signs for Dogs* by Lis Tresilian.

COMPUTER PROGRAMS

If you have a computer, your dealer may be able to provide astrology software. Two companies which specialise in this field are:

Astro Advice Bureau, Darrington Lodge, Springfield Road, Camberley, Surrey, GU15 1AB.

Astrocalc, 67, Peasecroft Road, Hemel Hempstead, Herts. HR3 8ER.

glossary

afflicted	describes a planet in a difficult aspect.
ascendant	in a chart, the point of the zodiac rising over the eastern horizon; the beginning of the first house.
aspect	the angular relationship between two planets. Some aspects indicate difficulties, others are helpful.
conjunct	describing two or more planets which form a 'conjunction'.
conjunction	formed by two or more planets at the same point in the zodiac; an aspect of 0°, indicating a need to blend.
cusp	a boundary between one sign (or house) and the next.
descendant	the exact opposite of the ascendant; the start of the seventh house.
direct	the normal motion of a planet through the zodiac, opposite to 'retrograde'.
ecliptic	the apparent path of the Sun around the Earth.
element	in Western astrology, the zodiac signs are divided into four – fire, earth, air and water.
ephemeris	a table showing the positions of planets in the zodiac at various times.
geocentric	"Earth-centred"; describes the astrology dealt with in this book and used by astrologers, based on planetary positions as viewed from Earth.
glyph	a zodiac or planetary symbol.
heliocentric	"Sun-centred"; describes a branch of astrology that uses planetary positions as they would be seen from the Sun.
house	one of twelve divisions of the Earth's daily rotation. Each house is concerned with different areas of life.
ingress	the movement of a planet into a sign.
midheaven (MC)	the point of the ecliptic corresponding longitudinally to the point overhead at the moment a chart is drawn up for. (MC = 'medium coeli')
mundane	describing astrology which deals with world affairs.

nadir (IC)	the point opposite to the midheaven.(IC = 'imum coeli')
opposed	describing two or more planets which form an opposition.
opposition	an aspect of 180° formed by two planets placed at opposite sides of the zodiac; indicates challenge.
orb	the maximum number of degrees a planet can be from an exact aspect with another but still be forming an effective aspect.
polarity	the zodiac signs are divided into two, variously described as positive/negative, masculine/feminine, assertive/passive.
quadrant	a division of the twelve houses or signs by four e.g. the first, second and third houses form the first quadrant of a chart.
quality	the zodiac signs are divided into three - cardinal, fixed and mutable.
quincunx	an aspect of 150°, indicating strain.
retrograde	"moving backwards", describes the apparent reverse motion of a planet through the zodiac, which intermittently occurs owing to the relative orbits of the planet and Earth.
rising sign	the sign on the ascendant.
sesquiquadrate	a minor aspect of 135°, indicating some stress.
sextile	an aspect of 60°, formed by planets one sixth of the zodiac apart, indicating potential.
sidereal time	based on a clock using the apparent rotation of the stars around the Earth. The sidereal day is 23 hours, 56 minutes and 4 seconds.
solar chart	one drawn up when the time of birth is unknown, substituting a time of midday, midnight or sunrise, according to preference.
square	an aspect of 90°, formed by planets one quarter of the zodiac apart, indicating disharmony.
station	the exact point that a planet goes from direct to retrograde motion, or vice-versa (i.e. where it appears stationary).

trine   an aspect of 120°, formed by planets one-third of the zodiac apart, indicating harmony.

zodiac   the band of sky around the ecliptic, divided by astrologers into twelve signs, each associated with different characteristics.

LONGITUDE AND LATITUDE OF PLACES IN THE BRITISH ISLES

	Lat. ° ´	Long. ° ´		Lat. ° ´	Long. ° ´
Aberdeen	57.09	2.06	Leeds	53.48	1.32
Aberystwyth	52.25	4.06	Leicester	52.39	1.09
Ayr	55.29	4.37	Lerwick	60.10	1.08
Barnstaple	51.05	4.03	Lincoln	53.14	0.42
Barrow	54.08	3.13	Liverpool	53.25	2.58
Belfast	54.35	5.56	London (centre)	51.31	0.06
Berwick	55.47	1.59	Londonderry	55.00	7.20
Birmingham	52.30	1.55	Mallaig	57.00	5.47
Bradford	53.47	1.45	Manchester	53.30	2.15
Brighton	50.50	0.08	Middlesborough	54.34	1.13
Bristol	51.27	2.36	Newcastle	54.59	1.36
Cambridge	52.13	0.08 E	Northampton	52.14	0.54
Cardiff	51.29	3.10	Norwich	52.38	1.17 E
Carlisle	54.54	2.55	Nottingham	52.57	1.09
Cork	51.54	8.30	Oxford	51.46	1.15
Coventry	52.25	1.31	Penzance	50.07	5.32
Derby	52.55	1.28	Peterborough	52.35	0.14
Douglas	54.10	4.30	Perth	56.24	3.27
Dover	51.08	1.19 E	Plymouth	50.22	4.08
Dublin	53.20	6.18	Preston	53.46	2.42
Dundee	56.29	2.58	Reading	51.27	0.57
Edinburgh	55.57	3.11	Sheffield	53.23	1.29
Exeter	50.43	3.31	Shrewsbury	52.43	2.45
Fishguard	52.00	4.57	Southampton	50.54	1.25
Galway	53.16	9.04	Stoke	53.00	2.11
Glasgow	55.53	4.14	Stranraer	54.54	5.01
Gloucester	51.52	2.15	Swansea	51.37	3.57

Holyhead	53.18	4.38	Weymouth	50.28	2.28
Hull	53.45	0.20	Wick	58.25	3.05
Inverness	57.29	4.12	Worcester	52.12	2.12
Ipswich	52.04	1.09 E	York	53.58	1.03

All latitudes are North of the equator.

All longitudes are West of Greenwich except where indicated East by 'E'.

TABLE OF UK DAYLIGHT SAVING (SUMMER) TIME

The change to Summer time takes place at 0100 GMT and the change back to GMT at 0200 BST.

Year			Year		
1940	Feb 25	Dec 31	1963	Mar 31	Oct 27
1941	Jan 1	May 4	1964	Mar 22	Oct 25
	Aug 10	Dec 31	1965	Mar 21	Oct 24
1942	Jan 1	Apr 5	1966	Mar 20	Oct 23
	Aug 9	Dec 31	1967	Mar 19	Oct 29
1943	Jan 1	Apr 4	1968	Feb 18	Dec 31
	Aug 15	Dec 31	1969	Jan 1	Dec 31
1944	Jan 1	Apr 2	1970	Jan 1	Dec 31
	Sep 17	Dec 31	1971	Jan 1	Dec 31
1945	Jan 1	Apr 1	1972	Mar 19	Oct 29
	Jul 15	Oct 7	1973	Mar 18	Oct 28
1946	Apr 14	Oct 6	1974	Mar 17	Oct 27
1947	Mar 16	Apr 13	1975	Mar 16	Oct 26
	Aug 10	Nov 2	1976	Mar 21	Oct 24
1948	Mar 14	Oct 31	1977	Mar 20	Oct 23
1949	Apr 3	Oct 30	1978	Mar 19	Oct 29
1950	Apr 16	Oct 22	1979	Mar 18	Oct 28
1951	Apr 15	Oct 21	1980	Mar 16	Oct 26
1952	Apr 20	Oct 26	1981	Mar 29	Oct 25
1953	Apr 19	Oct 4	1982	Mar 28	Oct 24
1954	Apr 11	Oct 3	1983	Mar 27	Oct 23
1955	Apr 17	Oct 2	1984	Mar 25	Oct 28
1956	Apr 22	Oct 7	1985	Mar 31	Oct 27
1957	Apr 14	Oct 6	1986	Mar 30	Oct 26
1958	Apr 20	Oct 5	1987	Mar 29	Oct 25

1959	Apr 19	Oct 4	1988	Mar 27	Oct 23
1960	Apr 10	Oct 2	1989	Mar 26	Oct 29
1961	Mar 26	Oct 29	1990	Mar 25	Oct 28
1962	Mar 25	Oct 28			

The present rule is that daylight saving time will be in force between 0100 GMT on the last Sunday in March (clocks go forward) and 0200 BST on the Sunday after the fourth Saturday in October (clocks go back).

DOUBLE SUMMER TIME was in operation:

1941	May 4	Aug 10	1944	Apr 2	Sep 17
1942	Apr 5	Aug 9	1945	Apr 1	Jul 15
1943	Apr 4	Aug 15	1947	Apr 13	Aug 10

ascendant and midheaven tables

Sid. time	51N	53N	55N	57N	59N	MC
00:00:00	26.09♋	27.50♋	29.37♋	1.29♌	3.30♌	0♈
00:03:40	26.50	28.29	0.15♌	2.07	4.05	1
00:07:20	27.31	29.09	0.53	2.44	4.40	2
00:11:01	28.11	29.48	1.31	3.20	5.15	3
00:14:21	28.51	0.26♌	2.09	3.58	5.50	4
00:18:21	29.30	1.05	2.47	4.33	6.25	5
00:22:02	0.11♌	1.44	3.25	5.10	7.00	6
00:25:41	0.51	2.24	4.02	4.46	7.35	7
00:29:23	1.30	3.02	4.40	6.22	8.10	8
00:33:04	2.11	3.42	5.17	6.58	8.44	9
00:36:45	2.50	4.20	5.55	7.34	9.20	10
00:40:27	3.31	4.58	6.32	8.11	9.53	11
00:44:09	4.11	5.38	7.10	8.47	10.29	12
00:47:50	4.51	6.17	7.47	9.23	11.04	13
00:51:32	5.30	6.55	8.25	9.59	11.39	14
00:55:14	6.10	7.34	9.02	10.36	12.13	15
00:58:58	6.50	8.12	9.40	11.12	12.47	16
01:02:40	7.30	8.52	10.17	11.48	13.22	17
01:06:23	8.10	9.31	10.55	12.25	13.58	18
01:10:07	8.50	10.08	11.32	13.01	14.32	19
01:13:51	9.29	10.48	12.10	13.37	15.08	20

01:17:36	10.09	11.27	12.48	14.13	15.43	21
01:21:22	10.49	12.05	13.25	14.49	16.18	22
01:25:06	11.28	12.44	14.03	15.26	16.53	23
01:28:51	12.09	13.23	14.41	16.02	17.28	24
01:32:38	12.48	14.02	15.19	16.39	18.02	25
01:36:26	13.28	14.40	15.55	17.15	18.39	26
01:40:13	14.09	15.20	16.34	17.52	19.14	27
01:44:00	14.49	16.00	17.12	18.29	19.48	28
01:47:59	15.29	16.39	17.49	19.06	20.25	29
01:51:38	16.09	17.18	18.29	19.43	21.00	0♉
01:55:29	16.51	18.00	19.07	20.20	21.35	1
01:59.18	17.31	18.34	19.44	20.57	22.12	2
02:03:06	18.12	19.17	20.24	21.33	22.48	3
02:06:58	18.52	20.00	21.02	22.10	23.24	4
02:10:50	19.34	20.35	21.40	22.49	24.00	5
02:14:43	20.14	21.15	22.19	23.26	24.36	6
02:18:37	20.55	21.55	22.58	24.03	25.13	7
02:22:29	21.36	22.36	23.36	24.41	25.49	8
02:26:25	22.17	23.16	24.17	25.19	26.26	9
02:30:20	22.59	23.55	24.55	25.58	27.01	10
02:34:16	23.41	24.36	25.33	26.35	27.38	11
02:38:14	24.22	25.16	26.14	27.13	28.15	12
02:42:10	25.03	25.57	26.52	27.52	28.53	13
02:46:09	25.45	26.38	27.32	28.29	29.30	14
02:50:09	26.28	27.18	28.13	29.08	0.70♍	15
02:54:06	27.09	27.59	28.52	29.47	0.45	16

02:58:07	27.51	28.42	29.32	0.26m	1.21	17
03:02:07	28.35	29.23	0.13m	1.05	2.00	18
03:06:10	29.16	0.03m	0.52	1.43	2.36	19
03:10:12	0.00m	0.45	1.32	2.24	3.14	20
03:14:15	0.41	1.26	2.14	3.02	3.52	21
03:18:19	1.24	2.08	2.53	3.41	4.31	22
03:22:23	2.08	2.50	3.35	4.20	5.10	23
03:26:29	2.50	3.33	4.16	5.00	5.48	24
03:30:35	3.34	4.15	4.56	5.41	6.27	25
03:34:42	4.17	4.57	5.37	6.21	7.04	26
03:38:50	5.02	5.39	6.19	7.01	7.44	27
03:42:57	5.44	6.22	7.01	7.41	8.23	28
03:47:07	6.28	7.05	7.42	8.21	9.02	29
03:51:16	7.12	7.48	8.24	9.02	9.40	0♐
03:55:26	7.57	8.31	9.05	9.43	10.20	1
03:59:38	8.41	9.13	9.47	10.23	11.00	2
04:03:49	9.24	9.57	10.30	11.03	11.38	3
04:08:01	10.10	10.40	11.11	11.44	12.19	4
04:12:13	10.55	11.24	11.55	12.26	12.58	5
04:16:27	11.39	12.07	12.37	13.07	13.39	6
04:20:43	12.24	12.50	13.19	13.48	14.19	7
04:24:56	13.09	13.35	14.01	14.30	14.58	8
04:29:12	13.54	14.19	14.45	15.11	15.39	9
04:33:27	14.40	15.02	15.27	15.44	16.19	10
04:37:43	15.24	15.47	16.10	16.35	16.59	11
04:42:00	16.10	16.31	16.53	17.16	17.40	12

04:46:18	16.56	17.15	17.37	17.58	18.21	13
04:50:34	17.42	18.00	18.19	18.41	19.00	14
04:54:52	18.27	18.45	19.03	19.23	19.41	15
04:59:12	19.13	19.29	19.46	20.05	20.22	16
05:03:30	19.59	20.14	20.30	20.47	21.04	17
05:07:49	20.45	20.58	21.14	21.29	21.44	18
05:12:09	21.31	21.43	21.57	22.11	22.25	19
05:16:28	22.17	22.29	22.41	22.54	23.07	20
05:20:50	23.03	23.13	23.24	23.36	23.48	21
05:25:10	23.49	23.58	24.08	24.19	24.29	22
05:29:31	24.35	24.43	24.52	25.02	25.10	23
05:33:51	25.22	25.29	25.37	25.43	25.51	24
05:38:13	26.08	26.14	26.20	26.26	26.33	25
05:42:34	26.54	26.59	27.04	27.08	27.14	26
05:46:55	27.41	27.41	27.48	27.52	27.55	27
05:51:17	28.27	28.29	28.32	28.35	28.36	28
05:55:38	29.14	29.15	29.16	29.17	29.19	29
06:00:00	0.00 ⌒	0.00 ⌒	0.00 ⌒	0.00 ⌒	0.00 ⌒	0 ⊙
06:04:22	0.46	0.45	0.44	0.43	0.42	1
06:08:43	1.33	1.31	1.28	1.25	1.23	2
06:13:06	2.19	2.16	2.12	2.08	2.04	3
06:17:27	3.06	3.00	2.56	2.51	2.46	4
06:21:47	3.53	3.46	3.40	3.33	3.27	5
06:26:09	4.38	4.31	4.24	4.16	4.08	6
06:30:30	5.25	5.17	5.07	4.58	4.51	7
06:34:50	6.11	6.02	5.51	5.41	5.31	8

06:39:12	6.57	6.47	6.35	6.24	6.12	9
06:43:31	7.43	7.31	7.19	7.06	6.53	10
06:47:51	8.30	8.17	8.03	7.48	7.34	11
06:52:12	9.15	9.02	8.47	8.31	8.16	12
06:56:30	10.01	9.46	9.29	9.13	8.56	13
07:00:49	10.47	10.30	10.13	9.55	9.38	14
07:05:09	11.33	11.16	10.57	10.37	10.18	15
07:09:26	12.19	12.00	11.40	11.19	11.00	16
07:13:43	13.04	12.44	12.23	12.01	11.40	17
07:18:11	13.50	13.29	13.06	12.43	12.21	18
07:22:18	14.35	14.14	13.49	13.25	13.00	19
07:26:34	15.20	14.58	14.32	14.06	13.41	20
07:30:50	16.06	15.41	15.15	14.48	14.21	21
07:35:05	16.52	16.26	15.58	15.29	15.02	22
07:39:19	17.36	17.10	16.40	16.12	15.42	23
07:43:33	18.20	17.53	17.24	16.53	16.22	24
07:47:47	19.06	18.36	18.05	17.34	17.02	25
07:51:58	19.51	19.21	18.48	18.15	17.42	26
07:56:12	20.34	20.04	19.30	18.56	18.22	27
08:00:23	21.19	20.46	20.12	18.15	19.00	28
08:04:34	22.04	21.30	20.54	20.17	19.40	29
08:08:44	22.48	22.12	21.36	20.58	20.19	0 ♌
08:12:54	23.32	22.55	22.17	21.39	20.58	1
08:17:04	24.15	23.39	23.00	22.19	21.38	2
08:21:11	24.58	24.22	23.41	22.58	22.16	3
08:25:19	25.43	25.03	24.22	23.38	22.55	4

08:29:24	26.25	25.45	25.03	24.19	23.33	5
08:33:31	27.10	26.28	25.44	24.59	24.13	6
08:37:36	27.53	27.10	26.25	25.39	24.51	7
08:41:41	28.36	27.52	27.06	26.18	25.29	8
08:45:44	29.19	28.34	27.47	26.57	26.08	9
08:49:47	0.01$_m$	29.15	28.28	27.36	26.44	10
08:53:50	0.43	29.56	29.07	28.16	27.24	11
08:57:52	1.26	0.37$_m$	29.47	28.54	28.00	12
09:01:51	2.08	1.19	0.28$_m$	29.33	28.39	13
09:05:53	2.51	2.00	1.08	0.12$_m$	29.15	14
09:09:51	3.33	2.42	1.47	0.52	29.54	15
09:13:51	4.15	3.21	2.27	1.30	0.31$_m$	16
09:17:49	4.57	4.03	3.07	2.08	1.08	17
09:21:45	5.38	4.44	3.46	2.45	1.44	18
09:25:43	6.19	5.24	4.26	3.25	2.21	19
09:29:39	7.01	6.05	5.05	4.03	2.58	20
09:33:34	7.43	6.45	5.44	4.40	3.34	21
09:37:29	8.23	7.24	6.23	5.19	4.11	22
09:41:23	9.05	8.04	7.03	5.57	4.47	23
09:45:17	9.46	8.45	7.41	6.34	5.24	24
09:49:08	10.27	9.24	8.19	7.11	6.00	25
09:52:59	11.08	10.05	8.58	7.48	6.37	26
09:56:52	11.48	10.44	9.36	8.26	7.13	27
10:00:42	12.29	11.24	10.15	9.04	7.48	28
10:04:31	13.08	12.03	10.53	9.40	8.25	29
10:08:22	13.50	12.42	11.31	10.17	9.00	0$_m$

10:12:11	14.30	13.21	12.10	10.55	9.36	1
10:16:00	15.10	14.00	12.48	11.32	10.12	2
10:19:47	15.50	14.41	13.26	12.08	10.46	3
10:23:35	16.30	15.19	14.04	12.45	11.22	4
10:27:22	17.11	15.58	14.42	13.20	11.58	5
10:31:08	17.51	16.37	15.19	13.57	12.32	6
10:34:55	18.31	17.16	15.57	14.34	13.08	7
10:38:39	19.09	17.55	16.35	15.11	13.43	8
10:42:24	19.50	18.33	17.12	15.47	14.17	9
10:46:09	20.30	19.12	17.49	16.24	14.53	10
10:49:53	21.10	19.51	18.28	16.59	15.28	11
10:53:36	21.50	20.30	19.05	17.35	16.03	12
10:57:19	22.29	21.08	19.43	18.12	16.38	13
11:01:02	23.09	21.47	20.21	18.48	17.13	14
11:04:46	23.49	22.26	20.58	19.25	17.48	15
11:08:28	24.29	23.04	21.35	20.03	18.22	16
11:12:11	25.07	23.43	22.13	20.37	18.56	17
11:15:52	25.48	24.22	22.50	21.12	19.32	18
11:19:33	26.28	25.01	23.28	21.48	20.07	19
11:23:15	27.08	25.39	24.05	22.25	20.41	20
11:26:55	27.48	26.17	24.43	23.01	21.15	21
11:30:36	28.28	26.57	25.20	23.39	21.50	22
11:34:17	29.08	27.36	25.58	24.15	22.25	23
11:37:58	29.48	28.15	26.36	24.51	22.59	24
11:41:38	0.28 ↗	28.54	27.13	25.27	23.35	25
11:45:19	1.08	29.33	27.51	26.03	24.10	26

11:48:59	1.48	0.11 ↗	28.29	26.40	24.45	27
11:52:39	2.29	0.50	29.07	27.17	25.19	28
11:56:20	3.09	1.31	29.45	27.54	25.54	29
12:00:00	3.50	2.10	0.23 ↗	28.30	26.30	0 ♎
12:03:40	4.31	2.50	1.01	29.08	27.05	1
12:07:20	5.11	3.29	1.40	29.44	27.39	2
12:11:01	5.51	4.09	2.18	0.20 ↗	28.16	3
12:14:21	6.34	4.49	2.57	0.56	28.51	4
12:18:21	7.15	5.29	3.35	1.33	29.26	5
12:22:02	7.56	6.10	4.13	2.11	0.02 ↗	6
12:25:41	8.38	6.49	4.52	2.49	0.38	7
12:29:23	9.20	7.31	5.32	3.26	1.13	8
12:33:04	10.02	8.10	6.11	4.04	1.50	9
12:36:45	10.43	8.53	6.52	4.43	2.26	10
12:40:27	11.27	9.34	7.31	5.21	3.01	11
12:44:09	12.10	10.15	8.11	5.59	3.37	12
12:47:50	12.53	10.57	8.52	6.36	4.14	13
12:51:32	13.36	11.38	9.32	7.16	4.51	14
12:55:14	14.20	12.21	10.12	7.55	5.28	15
12:58:58	15.04	13.04	10.53	8.34	6.05	16
13:02:40	15.48	13.46	11.35	9.13	6.42	17
13:06:23	16.33	14.29	12.17	9.54	7.20	18
13:10:07	17.17	15.14	12.59	10.34	7.58	19
13:13:51	18.02	15.57	13.40	11.24	8.36	20
13:17:36	18.48	16.41	14.23	11.52	9.14	21
13:21:22	19.34	17.26	15.06	12.35	9.53	22

13:25:06	20.21	18.10	15.48	13.16	10.33	23
13:28:51	21.07	18.56	16.32	13.57	11.11	24
13:32:38	21.55	19.41	17.16	14.39	11.51	25
13:36:26	22.43	20.28	18.00	15.21	12.32	26
13:40:13	23.31	21.15	18.46	16.05	13.12	27
13:44:00	24.20	22.02	19.32	16.48	13.52	28
13:47:59	25.09	22.50	20.18	17.31	14.33	29
13:51:38	25.59	23.38	21.04	18.17	15.14	0♏
13:55:29	26.49	24.27	21.50	19.01	15.57	1
13:59.18	27.40	25.16	22.38	19.46	16.39	2
14:03:06	28.32	26.06	23.26	20.31	17.22	3
14:06:58	29.25	26.57	24.14	21.17	18.05	4
14:10:50	0.19♑	27.49	25.05	22.05	18.48	5
14:14:43	1.11	28.40	25.55	22.52	19.33	6
14:18:37	2.06	29.33	26.46	23.40	20.19	7
14:22:29	3.02	0.29♑	27.36	24.29	21.05	8
14:26:25	3.58	1.21	28.28	25.18	21.50	9
14:30:20	4.56	2.16	29.22	26.09	22.37	10
14:34:16	5.53	3.14	0.15♑	27.00	23.26	11
14:38:14	6.51	4.10	1.10	27.52	24.13	12
14:42:10	7.51	5.08	2.06	28.45	25.02	13
14:46:09	8.52	6.06	3.03	29.39	25.54	14
14:50:09	9.54	7.06	4.02	0.34♑	26.44	15
14:54:06	10.58	8.09	5.01	1.29	27.36	16
14:58:07	12.02	9.11	6.01	2.26	28.30	17
15:02:07	13.07	10.15	7.01	3.25	29.23	18

15:06:10	14.14	11.20	8.04	4.34	0.18 ♑	19
15:10:12	15.22	12.25	9.08	5.25	1.15	20
15:14:15	16.32	13.33	10.13	6.38	2.12	21
15:18:19	17.43	14.43	11.20	7.31	3.12	22
15:22:23	18.54	15.54	12.29	8.37	4.12	23
15:26:29	20.08	17.07	13.39	9.43	5.15	24
15:30:35	21.24	18.20	14.52	10.51	6.18	25
15:34:42	22.41	19.36	16.05	12.02	7.23	26
15:38:50	24.00	20.54	17.20	13.14	8.32	27
15:42:57	25.22	22.15	18.38	14.27	9.40	28
15:47:07	26.44	23.35	19.58	15.43	10.53	29
15:51:16	28.09	25.00	21.20	17.03	12.07	0 ♐
15:55:26	29.36	26.26	22.45	18.24	13.22	1
15:59:38	1.05 ≈	27.54	24.12	19.48	14.42	2
16:03:49	2.36	29.25	25.42	21.15	16.03	3
16:08:01	4.10	29.59	27.14	22.46	17.29	4
16:12:13	5.45	2.35 ≈	28.50	24.19	18.57	5
16:16:27	7.24	4.14	0.29 ≈	25.56	20.29	6
16:20:43	9.05	5.56	2.11	27.37	22.05	7
16:24:56	10.50	7.42	3.55	29.21	23.46	8
16:29:12	12.36	9.30	5.43	1.09 ≈	25.30	9
16:33:27	14.24	11.21	7.37	3.02	27.20	10
16:37:43	16.16	13.16	9.35	4.59	29.15	11
16:42:00	18.11	15.14	11.36	7.00	1.15 ≈	12
16:46:18	20.09	17.15	13.41	9.09	3.22	13
16:50:34	22.10	19.21	15.51	11.22	5.34	14

16:54:52	24.15	21.29	18.05	13.40	7.55	15
16:59:12	26.20	23.43	20.23	16.05	10.24	16
17:03:30	28.30	25.59	22.47	18.35	12.58	17
17:07:49	0.42♓	28.18	25.15	21.12	15.44	18
17:12:09	2.57	0.41♓	27.47	23.55	18.36	19
17:16:28	5.15	3.08	0.25♓	26.45	21.39	20
17:20:50	7.36	5.38	3.07	29.41	24.53	21
17:25:10	9.58	8.12	5.54	2.44♓	28.14	22
17:29:31	12.23	10.48	8.45	5.53	1.46	23
17:33:51	14.51	13.28	11.38	9.07	5.27♓	24
17:38:13	17.19	16.09	14.36	12.25	9.17	25
17:42:34	19.50	18.52	17.37	15.52	13.15	26
17:46:55	22.20	21.38	20.40	19.20	17.20	27
17:51:17	24.54	24.24	23.45	22.51	21.30	28
17:55:38	27.26	27.11	26.53	26.25	25.44	29
18:00:00	0.00♈	0.00♈	0.00♈	0.00♈	0.00♈	0♑
18:04:22	2.34	2.48	3.07	3.35	4.16	1
18:08:43	5.07	5.36	6.14	7.08	8.30	2
18:13:06	7.40	8.22	9.19	10.40	12.40	3
18:17:27	10.11	11.07	12.23	14.08	16.44	4
18:21:47	12.42	13.51	15.24	17.33	20.43	5
18:26:09	15.10	16.32	18.21	20.53	24.33	6
18:30:30	17.37	19.12	21.15	24.07	28.13	7
18:34:50	20.02	21.48	24.07	27.15	1.45♉	8
18:39:12	22.25	24.21	26.53	0.22♉	5.07	9
18:43:31	24.45	26.51	29.34	3.05	8.21	10

18:47:51	27.03	29.19	2.13♉	6.03	11.24	11
18:52:12	29.18	1.42♉	4.45	8.45	14.17	12
18:56:30	1.29♉	4.01	7.13	11.24	17.01	13
19:00:49	3.40	6.17	9.36	13.54	19.37	14
19:05:09	5.47	8.31	11.54	16.19	22.05	15
19:09:26	7.49	10.39	14.08	18.36	24.25	16
19:13:43	9.51	12.45	16.18	20.51	26.38	17
19:18:11	11.48	14.46	18.24	22.57	28.45	18
19:22:18	13.44	16.44	20.25	24.59	0.46♊	19
19:26:34	15.36	18.39	22.22	26.56	2.40	20
19:30:50	17.24	20.30	24.15	28.51	4.31	21
19:35:05	19.11	22.18	26.05	0.37♊	6.14	22
19:39:19	20.54	24.04	27.50	2.23	7.54	23
19:43:33	22.35	25.46	29.32	4.02	9.31	24
19:47:47	24.14	27.25	1.10♊	5.38	11.03	25
19:51:58	25.50	29.01	2.46	7.20	12.32	26
19:56:12	27.23	0.35♊	4.18	8.43	13.56	27
20:00:23	28.55	2.06	5.58	10.08	15.18	28
20:04:34	0.24♊	3.34	7.16	11.32	16.37	29
20:08:44	1.52	5.01	8.41	12.54	17.53	0≈
20:12:54	3.15	6.25	10.02	14.13	19.07	1
20:17:04	4.39	7.46	11.22	15.29	20.20	2
20:21:11	6.00	9.06	12.40	16.43	21.28	3
20:25:19	7.18	10.24	13.55	17.56	22.36	4
20:29:24	8.35	11.40	15.08	19.09	23.41	5
20:33:31	9.51	12.54	16.20	20.16	24.45	6

20:37:36	11.06	14.07	17.30	21.22	25.48	7
20:41:41	12.17	15.17	18.40	22.19	26.48	8
20:45:44	13.29	16.27	19.46	23.21	27.47	9
20:49:47	14.37	17.35	20.52	24.33	28.44	10
20:53:50	15.46	18.41	21.56	25.34	29.41	11
20:57:52	16.53	19.46	22.59	26.33	0.36 ♋	12
21:01:51	17.58	20.50	24.00	27.31	1.30	13
21:05:53	19.02	21.51	25.00	28.29	2.23	14
21:09:51	20.06	22.53	25.59	29.24	3.16	15
21:13:51	21.08	23.53	26.57	0.20 ♊	4.06	16
21:17:49	22.09	24.52	27.54	1.13	4.58	17
21:21:45	23.09	25.50	28.49	2.06	5.46	18
21:25:43	24.07	26.47	29.44	2.59	6.34	19
21:29:39	25.05	27.44	0.38 ♊	3.50	7.22	20
21:33:34	26.01	28.39	1.31	4.40	8.10	21
21:37:29	26.59	29.33	2.22	5.29	8.55	22
21:41:23	27.54	0.27 ♊	3.14	6.18	9.41	23
21:45:17	28.49	1.20	4.06	7.07	10.26	24
21:49:08	29.42	2.12	4.56	7.52	11.11	25
21:52:59	0.35 ♊	3.04	5.45	8.41	11.55	26
21:56:52	1.27	3.54	6.33	9.27	12.39	27
22:00:42	2.20	4.44	7.21	10.12	13.21	28
22:04:31	3.11	5.34	8.09	10.57	14.04	29
22:08:22	4.01	6.22	8.56	11.42	14.45	0 ♓
22:12:11	4.51	7.10	9.42	12.26	15.26	1
22:16:00	5.39	7.58	10.28	13.09	16.08	2

22:19:47	6.28	8.45	11.14	13.53	16.49	3
22:23:35	7.17	9.32	11.58	14.36	17.28	4
22:27:22	8.05	10.19	12.42	15.18	18.08	5
22:31:08	8.53	11.04	13.26	16.00	18.49	6
22:34:55	9.39	11.50	14.11	16.42	19.27	7
22:38:39	10.26	12.35	14.54	17.23	20.07	8
22:42:24	11.12	13.19	15.37	18.04	20.46	9
22:46:09	11.58	14.04	16.19	18.44	21.23	10
22:49:53	12.43	14.47	17.00	19.25	22.02	11
22:53:36	13.28	15.31	17.42	20.05	22.40	12
22:57:19	14.12	16.14	18.25	20.45	23.17	13
23:01:02	14.56	16.57	19.06	21.24	23.54	14
23:04:46	15.40	17.40	19.47	22.03	24.32	15
23:08:28	16.24	18.22	20.28	22.42	25.08	16
23:12:11	17.07	19.04	21.08	23.21	26.22	17
23:15:52	17.51	19.47	21.49	23.59	26.58	18
23:19:33	18.33	20.27	22.29	24.37	27.35	19
23:23:15	19.16	21.07	23.08	25.16	28.10	20
23:26:55	19.58	21.50	23.48	25.54	28.46	21
23:30:36	20.40	22.30	24.27	26.31	29.22	22
23:34:17	21.23	23.11	25.07	27.09	29.58	23
23:37:58	22.04	23.50	25.46	27.46	0.34♌	24
23:41:38	22.45	24.31	26.24	28.24	1.09	25
23:45:19	23.26	25.11	27.03	29.02	1.44	26
23:48:59	24.07	25.50	27.42	0.01♌	2.20	27
23:52:39	24.48	26.31	28.20	0.15	2.55	28
23:56:20	25.29	27.10	28.59	0.52	3.30	29

planetary ephemeris

1936		Sid. Time		☉	☽	☿	♀	♂	♃	♄	♅	♆	♇
1	1	6	38	9 ♑ 24	1 ♈ 2	22 ♑	27 ♏	19 ♒	12 ♐	6 ♓	2 ♉	17 ♍	27 ♋
11	1	7	17	19 36	15 ♌ 39	7 ♒	9 ♐	27	14	7	2	17	26
21	1	7	57	29 47	17 ♐ 37	17	21	5 ♓	16	8	2	16	26
1	2	8	40	10 ♒ 58	23 ♉ 58	11	4 ♑	14	18	9	2	16	26
11	2	9	20	21 6	0 ♎ 7	2	16	21	19	10	2	16	26
21	2	9	59	1 ♓ 12	6 ♒ 42	5	29	29	21	11	2	16	26
1	3	10	34	10 15	17 ♊ 45	14	10 ♒	6 ♈	22	12	3	16	25
11	3	11	14	20 15	20 ♎ 34	27	22	14	23	14	3	15	25
21	3	11	53	0 ♈ 12	29 ♒ 24	12 ♓	4 ♓	21	24	15	4	15	25
1	4	12	37	11 6	5 ♌ 39	1 ♈	18	29	24	16	4	15	25
11	4	13	16	20 56	5 ♐ 33	21	0 ♈	7	24	17	5	14	25
21	4	13	55	0 ♉ 43	23 ♈ 15	12 ♉	12	14	24	18	5	14	25
1	5	14	35	10 26	8 ♍ 50	0 ♊	25	21	24	19	6	14	25
11	5	15	14	20 7	10 ♑ 5	11	7 ♉	28	23	20	6	14	25
21	5	15	54	29 45	1 ♊ 43	14	19	5 ♊	22	21	7	14	25
1	6	16	37	10 ♊ 19	22 ♎ 57	10	3 ♊	13	21	22	7	14	26
11	6	17	16	19 53	0 ♓ 19	5	15	20	20	22	8	14	26
21	6	17	56	29 26	22 ♋ 11	8	27	27	18	22	8	14	26
1	7	18	35	8 ♋ 58	25 ♏ 10	18	9 ♋	3 ♋	17	23	9	14	26
11	7	19	15	18 30	9 ♈ 23	4 ♋	22	10	16	22	9	15	27
21	7	19	54	28 2	26 ♌ 53	24	4 ♌	17	15	22	9	15	27
1	8	20	38	8 ♌ 33	11 ♑ 13	17	17	24	15	22	10	15	27
11	8	21	17	18 8	2 ♊ 47	5 ♍	0 ♍	0 ♌	15	21	10	15	28
21	8	21	57	27 45	11 ♎ 23	21	12	7	15	21	10	16	28
1	9	22	40	8 ♍ 22	1 ♓ 10	5 ♎	26	14	15	20	9	16	28
11	9	23	19	18 4	23 ♋ 26	14	8 ♎	20	16	19	9	17	28
21	9	23	59	27 49	25 ♏ 21	16	20	26	17	18	9	17	28
1	10	0	38	7 ♎ 38	9 ♈ 24	8	3 ♏	3 ♍	18	18	9	17	29
11	10	1	18	17 29	28 ♌ 27	1	15	9	20	17	8	18	29
21	10	1	57	27 25	28 ♐ 10	10	27	15	21	16	8	18	29
1	11	2	40	8 ♏ 24	2 ♊ 14	28	11 ♐	22	23	16	8	18	29
11	11	3	20	18 26	13 ♎ 47	14 ♏	23	28	25	16	7	18	29
21	11	3	59	28 31	15 ♒ 32	0 ♐	5 ♑	4 ♎	28	16	7	19	29
1	12	4	39	8 ♐ 38	10 ♋ 24	16	17	10	29	16	6	19	28
11	12	5	18	18 47	16 ♏ 3	1 ♑	29	16	2 ♑	16	6	19	28
21	12	5	58	28 58	22 ♓ 48	16	11 ♒	21	4	17	6	19	28

1937

1	1	6	41	10 ♑ 10	29 ♌ 3	0 ♒	24 ♒	27 ♎	7 ♑	17 ♓	6 ♉	19 ♍	28 ♋
11	1	7	20	20 22	0 ♑ 35	29 ♑	6 ♓	3 ♏	9	18	6	19	28
21	1	8	0	0 ♒ 33	15 ♉ 52	17	17	8	11	19	6	19	28
1	2	8	43	11 44	14 ♎ 24	17	28	14	14	20	6	19	27
11	2	9	23	21 52	17 ♒ 52	26	9 ♈	18	16	21	6	18	27
21	2	10	2	1 ♓ 58	8 ♋ 33	9 ♒	18	23	18	22	6	18	27
1	3	10	34	10 0	22 ♎ 18	21	24	26	19	23	7	18	27
11	3	11	13	20 1	26 ♒ 2	7 ♓	1 ♉	29	21	25	7	18	27
21	3	11	52	29 58	19 ♋ 5	26	5	2 ♐	23	26	7	17	27
1	4	12	36	10 ♈ 51	6 ♐ 7	18 ♈	5	4	24	27	8	17	26
11	4	13	15	20 41	17 ♈ 40	7 ♉	2	5	25	28	8	17	26
21	4	13	55	0 ♉ 29	8 ♍ 19	20	26 ♈	5	26	29	9	17	27
1	5	14	34	10 12	8 ♑ 31	24	21	4	27	1 ♈	10	16	27
11	5	15	13	19 53	26 ♉ 15	21	19	1	27	2	10	16	27
21	5	15	53	29 31	12 ♎ 23	15	22	28 ♏	27	3	11	16	27
1	6	16	36	10 ♊ 5	25 ♒ 9	17	28	24	27	3	11	16	27
11	6	17	16	19 39	19 ♋ 21	26	5 ♉	21	26	4	12	16	27
21	6	17	55	29 12	26 ♏ 51	11 ♊	14	20	25	5	12	16	28
1	7	18	35	8 ♋ 44	1 ♈ 48	0 ♋	23	20	24	5	13	16	28
11	7	19	14	18 16	25 ♌ 52	21	3 ♊	21	23	5	13	17	28
21	7	19	53	27 48	29 ♐ 5	11 ♌	14	23	22	5	13	17	28
1	8	20	37	8 ♌ 19	24 ♉ 22	0 ♍	26	27	20	5	14	17	29
11	8	21	16	17 54	13 ♎ 15	14	7 ♋	1 ♐	19	5	14	18	29
21	8	21	56	27 31	14 ♒ 55	25	18	6	18	4	14	18	29
1	9	22	39	8 ♍ 8	17 ♋ 33	29	1 ♌	12	18	4	14	18	29
11	9	23	18	17 50	27 ♏ 33	25	13	18	17	3	13	19	29
21	9	23	58	27 35	4 ♈ 25	16	25	24	18	2	13	19	29
1	10	0	37	7 ♎ 24	25 ♌ 17	19	7 ♍	0 ♑	18	1	13	19	29
11	10	1	17	17 16	29 ♐ 8	4 ♎	19	7	19	0	13	20	0 ♌
21	10	1	56	27 11	12 ♉ 15	21	2 ♎	14	20	29 ♓	12	20	0
1	11	2	39	8 ♏ 9	13 ♎ 42	10 ♏	15	22	21	29	12	20	0
11	11	3	19	18 11	13 ♒ 37	26	28	29	22	29	11	21	0
21	11	3	58	28 16	5 ♋ 44	11 ♐	10 ♏	7 ♒	24	28	11	21	0
1	12	4	38	8 ♐ 23	17 ♏ 6	26	23	14	26	28	11	21	29 ♋
11	12	5	17	18 32	17 ♓ 56	9 ♑	5 ♐	22	28	28	10	21	29
21	12	5	57	28 43	13 ♌ 31	16	18	29	0 ♒	29	10	21	29

1938		Sid. Time		☉			☽			☿		♀		♂		♃		♄		♅		♆		♇
1	1	6	40	9	♑	55	1	♑	21	5	♑	2	♑	8	♓	3	♒	29	♓	10	♉	21	♍	29
11	1	7	19	20		27	8	♉	4	29	♐	14		15		5		29		10		21		29
21	1	7	59	0	♒	18	3	♎	3	6	♑	27		23		7		1	♈	10		21		29
1	2	8	42	11		29	16	♒	25	19		11	♒	1	♈	10		1		10		21		29
11	2	9	22	21		37	0	♋	57	4	♒	23		9		12		3		10		21		29
21	2	10	1	1	♓	42	18	♏	42	20		6	♓	16		15		4		10		20		28
1	3	10	33	9		45	25	♒	6	3	♓	16		22		16		4		10		20		28
11	3	11	12	19		46	11	♋	22	22		28		29		19		6		11		20		28
21	3	11	51	29		43	26	♏	28	12	♈	11	♈	6	♉	21		7		11		19		28
1	4	12	35	10	♈	37	13	♈	21	29		24		14		23		8		12		19		28
11	4	13	14	20		27	4	♍	5	6	♉	7	♉	21		25		10		12		19		28
21	4	13	54	0	♉	14	10	♑	6	2		19		28		27		11		13		19		28
1	5	14	33	9		58	20	♉	25	26	♈	1	♊	5	♊	28		12		13		19		28
11	5	15	13	19		39	10	♎	47	26		13		12		29		13		14		18		28
21	5	15	52	29		17	12	♒	9	4	♉	26		19		1	♓	14		15		18		28
1	6	16	35	9	♊	51	13	♋	50	18		9	♋	26		2		15		15		18		28
11	6	17	15	19		25	27	♏	31	6	♊	21		3	♋	2		16		16		18		28
21	6	17	54	28		58	28	♓	3	27		3	♌	9		2		17		16		18		29
1	7	18	34	8	♋	30	22	♌	30	18	♋	15		16		2		17		17		19		29
11	7	19	13	18		2	0	♑	19	7	♌	26		22		2		18		17		19		29
21	7	19	52	27		34	3	♉	37	22		8	♍	29		1		18		17		19		29
1	8	20	36	8	♌	5	13	♎	15	5	♍	20		6	♌	29	♒	18		18		19		29
11	8	21	15	17		40	14	♒	54	12		1	♎	12		29		18		18		20		0
21	8	21	55	27		17	25	♊	23	11		12		19		27		18		18		20		0
1	9	22	38	7	♍	54	29	♏	46	1		24		26		26		17		18		20		1
11	9	23	17	17		36	1	♈	15	29	♌	4	♏	2	♍	25		17		18		21		1
21	9	23	57	27		21	19	♌	6	12	♍	13		8		24		16		17		21		1
1	10	0	36	7	♎	9	1	♑	49	0	♎	22		15		23		15		17		21		1
11	10	1	16	17		1	6	♉	57	17		28		21		22		14		17		22		1
21	10	1	55	26		56	27	♍	17	4	♏	3	♐	27		22		14		17		22		1
1	11	2	29	7	♏	55	15	♒	19	21		5		4	♎	23		13		16		23		2
11	11	3	18	17		56	28	♊	48	6	♐	2		11		23		12		16		23		1
21	11	3	57	28		1	16	♏	23	19		27	♏	17		24		12		15		23		1
1	12	4	37	8	♐	8	17	♓	30	29		22		23		25		11		15		23		1
11	12	5	16	18		17	7	♌	51	26		19		29		27		11		15		23		1
21	12	5	56	28		28	20	♐	7	14		22		6	♏	28		11		14		23		1

1939

1	1	6	39	9	♑	40	3	♉	59	17	♐	27	♏	12	♏	0	♓	11	♈	14	♉	23	♍	1
11	1	7	19	19		52	0	♎	29	28		5	♐	19		2		12		14		23		1
21	1	7	58	0	♒	3	4	♒	49	12	♑	14		25		5		12		14		23		0
1	2	8	41	11		14	24	♊	17	29		24		2	♐	7		13		14		23		0
11	2	9	21	21		22	19	♏	19	15	♒	5	♑	8		9		14		14		23		29
21	2	10	0	1	♓	28	19	♓	39	3	♓	16		14		12		15		14		23		29
1	3	10	32	9		31	3	♋	30	18		25		18		14		16		14		22		29
11	3	11	11	19		32	27	♏	40	6	♈	6	♒	24		16		17		15		22		29
21	3	11	51	29		29	28	♓	37	17		18		29		19		18		15		22		29
1	4	12	34	19	♈	22	27	♌	9	15		1	♓	6	♑	21		20		16		21		29
11	4	13	13	20		13	12	♑	47	7		13		11		23		21		16		21		29
21	4	13	53	0	♉	0	15	♉	54	5		24		16		26		22		17		21		29
1	5	14	32	9		44	5	♎	52	13		6	♈	21		28		23		17		21		29
11	5	15	11	19		25	14	♒	34	25		18		25		29		24		18		21		29
21	5	15	51	29		4	22	♊	40	11	♉	0	♉	29		2	♈	26		19		21		29
1	6	16	34	9	♊	37	26	♏	4	1	♊	14		2	♒	4		27		19		21		29
11	6	17	14	19		11	28	♓	24	24		26		4		5		28		20		21		29
21	6	17	53	28		45	16	♌	2	14	♋	8	♊	5		6		29		20		21		0
1	7	18	33	8	♋	17	0	♑	34	1	♌	20		4		7		29		21		21		0
11	7	19	12	17		49	1	♉	21	14		2	♋	3		8		0	♉	21		21		1
21	7	19	52	27		21	25	♍	6	22		15		0		9		1		21		21		1
1	8	20	35	7	♌	52	15	♒	48	24		28		27	♑	9		1		22		21		1
11	8	21	15	17		26	19	♊	47	17		10	♌	25		9		1		22		22		2
21	8	21	54	27		3	16	♏	13	12		23		24		8		1		22		22		2
1	9	22	37	7	♍	40	0	♈	22	20		6	♍	24		7		1		22		22		2
11	9	23	16	17		22	12	♌	16	7	♍	19		26		6		1		22		23		2
21	9	22	54	27		7	3	♑	31	26		1	♎	29		5		0		22		23		3
1	10	0	35	6	♎	55	3	♉	53	13	♎	14		3	♒	3		29	♈	22		24		3
11	10	1	15	16		46	21	♍	10	0	♏	26		7		2		29		21		24		3
21	10	1	54	26		42	6	♒	11	15		9	♏	12		1		28		21		24		3
1	11	2	38	7	♏	40	22	♊	19	0	♐	22		19		29	♓	27		21		25		3
11	11	3	17	17		41	13	♏	25	10		5	♐	25		29		26		20		25		3
21	11	3	56	27		46	19	♓	45	14		17		1	♓	29		25		20		25		3
1	12	4	36	7	♐	53	0	♌	15	3		0	♑	7		29		25		19		25		3
11	12	5	15	18		2	19	♐	11	28	♏	12		14		29		25		19		25		3
21	12	5	55	28		13	21	♈	31	7	♐	25		21		0	♈	24		19		25		2

1940		Sid. Time		☉	☽	☿	♀	♂	♃	♄	♅	♆	♇
1	1	6	37	9 ♑ 24	23 ♍ 39	22 ♐	8 ♒	28 ♓	1 ♈	24 ♈	18 ♉	26 ♍	2 ♌
11	1	7	17	19 37	5 ♒ 48	7 ♑	21	5 ♈	2	25	18	25	2
21	1	7	57	29 48	7 ♊ 24	23	3 ♓	12	4	25	18	25	2
1	2	8	41	10 ♒ 59	15 ♏ 46	11 ♒	16	19	6	26	18	25	2
11	2	9	20	21 7	20 ♓ 16	29	29	26	8	26	18	25	1
21	2	9	58	1 ♓ 13	27 ♋ 20	17 ♓	10 ♈	3 ♉	10	27	18	25	1
1	3	10	35	10 15	8 ♐ 57	28	21	9	12	28	18	25	0
11	3	11	13	20 17	10 ♈ 48	29	3 ♉	15	14	29	19	24	0
21	3	11	52	0 ♈ 14	20 ♌ 14	20	14	22	17	0 ♉	19	24	1
1	4	12	37	11 7	26 ♑ 17	17	26	29	19	1	20	24	1
11	4	13	15	20 56	26 ♉ 5	23	6 ♊	6 ♊	22	3	20	23	1
21	4	13	56	0 ♉ 43	14 ♎ 5	5 ♈	16	12	24	4	21	23	1
1	5	14	34	10 28	29 ♒ 1	20	25	19	26	5	21	23	1
11	5	15	15	20 7	1 ♋ 19	8 ♉	3 ♋	26	29	6	22	23	1
21	5	15	54	29 46	22 ♏ 13	29	9	2 ♋	1 ♉	8	22	23	1
1	6	16	36	10 ♊ 19	12 ♈ 39	22 ♊	13	9	3	9	23	23	1
11	6	17	17	19 55	22 ♌ 36	11 ♋	13	16	6	10	24	23	1
21	6	17	55	29 28	12 ♑ 27	24	9	22	8	11	24	23	2
1	7	18	36	8 ♋ 60	14 ♉ 46	3 ♌	3	28	9	12	25	23	2
11	7	19	15	18 32	1 ♎ 43	5	28 ♊	5 ♌	11	13	25	23	2
21	7	19	53	28 3	16 ♒ 38	0	27	11	12	14	25	23	2
1	8	20	38	8 ♌ 35	1 ♋ 22	25 ♋	0 ♋	18	14	14	26	24	3
11	8	21	16	18 10	24 ♏ 34	29	6	25	15	15	26	24	3
21	8	21	57	27 45	1 ♈ 22	14 ♌	13	1 ♍	15	15	26	24	3
1	9	22	39	8 ♍ 24	22 ♌ 0	5 ♍	23	8	16	15	26	25	3
11	9	23	18	18 6	14 ♑ 44	24	2 ♌	14	16	15	26	25	4
21	9	23	59	27 51	15 ♉ 25	11 ♎	13	21	15	14	26	25	4
1	10	0	37	7 ♎ 38	0 ♎ 9	26	23	27	15	14	26	26	4
11	10	1	18	17 30	19 ♒ 14	10 ♏	5 ♍	3 ♎	14	13	26	26	4
21	10	1	56	27 27	18 ♊ 54	22	16	10	12	12	25	26	4
1	11	2	41	8 ♏ 24	23 ♏ 36	28	29	17	11	12	25	27	4
11	11	3	20	18 26	3 ♈ 48	21	11 ♎	24	10	11	24	27	4
21	11	3	58	28 31	7 ♌ 21	12	23	0 ♏	8	10	24	27	4
1	12	4	39	8 ♐ 38	0 ♑ 40	19	5 ♏	7	7	9	24	27	4
11	12	5	17	18 49	5 ♉ 42	2 ♐	18	13	6	9	23	28	4
21	12	5	58	28 58	15 ♍ 9	17	0 ♐	20	6	8	23	28	4

1941													
1	1	6	40	10 ♑ 12	19 ♒ 6	4 ♑	14 ♐	27 ♏	6 ♉	8 ♉	23 ♉	28 ♍	4 ♌
11	1	7	19	20 22	20 ♊ 36	20	26	4 ♐	6	8	22	28	3
21	1	7	60	0 ♒ 33	8 ♏ 11	7 ♒	9 ♑	11	6	8	22	28	3
1	2	8	42	11 44	3 ♈ 58	26	23	18	7	8	22	27	3
11	2	9	23	21 52	8 ♌ 33	10 ♓	5 ♒	25	9	9	22	27	3
21	2	10	1	1 ♓ 59	0 ♑ 36	12	18	2 ♑	10	10	22	27	3
1	3	10	34	10 1	12 ♈ 1	5	28	8	11	10	23	27	2
11	3	11	12	20 2	16 ♌ 28	29 ♒	10 ♓	14	13	11	23	26	2
21	3	11	51	29 58	11 ♑ 1	3 ♓	22	21	15	12	23	26	2
1	4	12	36	10 ♈ 53	25 ♉ 58	14	6 ♈	29	17	13	24	26	2
11	4	13	14	20 43	8 ♎ 11	28	19	6 ♒	19	14	24	26	2
21	4	13	55	0 ♉ 30	29 ♒ 25	15 ♈	1 ♉	13	22	16	25	25	2
1	5	14	33	10 14	29 ♊ 1	4 ♉	13	20	24	17	25	25	2
11	5	15	14	19 53	16 ♏ 47	26	26	27	26	18	26	25	2
21	5	15	53	29 33	2 ♈ 42	16 ♊	8 ♊	3 ♓	29	20	26	25	2
1	6	16	35	10 ♊ 7	16 ♌ 28	3 ♋	21	11	1 ♊	21	27	25	2
11	6	17	16	19 39	10 ♑ 3	13	4 ♋	17	4	22	28	25	3
21	6	17	54	29 12	16 ♉ 42	16	16	23	6	23	28	25	3
1	7	18	35	8 ♋ 46	23 ♍ 33	12	28	29	8	24	29	25	3
11	7	19	13	18 18	16 ♒ 18	6	10 ♌	5 ♈	10	25	29	25	3
21	7	19	52	27 49	19 ♊ 3	8	23	10	12	26	29	25	4
1	8	20	37	8 ♌ 21	16 ♏ 27	21	6 ♍	15	14	27	29	26	4
11	8	21	15	17 56	2 ♈ 58	8 ♌	18	19	16	28	0 ♊	26	4
21	8	21	56	27 31	5 ♌ 19	29	0 ♎	22	18	28	0	26	4
1	9	22	38	8 ♍ 10	9 ♑ 39	20 ♍	13	23	19	28	0	26	5
11	9	23	17	17 52	17 ♉ 7	6 ♎	25	24	20	29	0	27	5
21	9	23	58	27 37	25 ♍ 1	21	7 ♏	22	21	28	0	27	5
1	10	0	36	7 ♎ 24	16 ♒ 55	3 ♏	19	20	21	28	0	28	5
11	10	1	17	17 17	19 ♊ 6	11	0 ♐	17	21	28	29 ♉	28	6
21	10	1	55	27 11	2 ♏ 53	10	12	14	21	27	29	29	6
1	11	2	40	8 ♏ 11	4 ♈ 15	27 ♎	24	12	21	26	29	29	6
11	11	3	19	18 11	4 ♌ 14	28	5 ♑	11	20	26	29	29	6
21	11	3	57	28 16	26 ♐ 44	12 ♏	15	12	19	25	28	29	6
1	12	4	38	8 ♐ 25	7 ♉ 15	27	25	14	17	24	28	29	6
11	12	5	16	18 34	9 ♍ 1	12 ♐	4 ♒	17	16	23	28	29	6
21	12	5	57	28 43	4 ♒ 15	28	12	20	15	23	27	29	5

1942		Sid. Time		☉			☽			☿		♀		♂		♃		♄		♅		♆		♇	
1	1	6	39	9	♑	57	21	♊	38	16	♑	18	♒	25	♈	13	♊	22	♉	27	♉	29	♍	5	♌
11	1	7	18	20		7	29	♎	46	2	♒	21		29		12		22		27		29		5	
21	1	7	59	0	♒	18	22	♓	56	18		20		5	♉	12		22		26		29		5	
1	2	8	41	11		29	7	♌	0	27		14		10		11		22		26		29		4	
11	2	9	22	21		38	23	♐	13	19		9		16		11		22		26		29		4	
21	2	10	0	1	♓	44	8	♉	9	12		6		22		12		22		26		29		4	
1	3	10	33	9		47	15	♌	16	14		6		26		12		23		27		29		4	
11	3	11	11	19		46	4	♑	1	23		10		2	♊	13		24		27		29		4	
21	3	11	52	29		45	15	♉	59	5	♓	16		8		14		24		27		28		4	
1	4	12	35	10	♈	38	3	♎	45	23		25		15		16		26		28		28		4	
11	4	13	13	20		27	25	♒	56	11	♈	4	♓	21		18		27		28		28		3	
21	4	13	54	0	♉	14	29	♊	54	1	♉	14		27		19		28		29		28		3	
1	5	14	32	9		58	11	♏	8	22		25		3	♋	21		29		29		27		4	
11	5	15	13	19		39	1	♈	50	10	♊	5	♈	9		23		0	♊	29		27		4	
21	5	15	51	29		19	2	♌	20	21		16		15		25		2		0	♊	27		4	
1	6	16	36	9	♊	51	5	♑	13	26		29		22		28		3		1		27		4	
11	6	17	15	19		27	17	♉	58	22		10	♉	28		0	♋	4		2		27		4	
21	6	17	53	28		60	18	♍	36	18		22		4	♌	2		6		2		27		4	
1	7	18	34	8	♋	32	13	♒	30	19		4	♊	10		5		7		3		27		5	
11	7	19	12	18		2	20	♊	41	28		15		17		7		8		3		27		5	
21	7	19	51	27		37	24	♎	50	13	♋	27		23		9		9		4		27		5	
1	8	20	36	8	♌	6	3	♈	21	6	♌	10	♋	29		12		10		4		28		5	
11	8	21	14	17		42	5	♌	13	26		23		6	♍	14		11		4		28		6	
21	8	21	55	27		19	17	♐	28	14	♍	5	♌	12		16		11		4		29		6	
1	9	22	37	7	♍	56	19	♉	30	1	♎	18		19		18		12		5		29		6	
11	9	23	18	17		38	21	♍	42	14		0	♍	26		20		12		5		29		7	
21	9	23	57	27		23	10	♒	57	23		13		2	♎	21		13		5		29		7	
1	10	0	35	7	♎	11	21	♊	32	26		25		9		22		12		4		29		7	
11	10	1	16	17		3	27	♎	46	17		8	♎	15		24		12		4		0	♎	7	
21	10	1	54	26		58	18	♓	32	11		20		22		24		12		4		1		7	
1	11	2	39	7	♏	56	5	♌	2	21		4	♏	29		25		11		4		1		7	
11	11	3	17	17		58	20	♐	34	6	♍	17		6	♍	25		11		3		1		7	
21	11	3	56	28		1	7	♉	0	22		29		13		25		10		3		2		7	
1	12	4	37	8	♐	10	7	♍	24	8	♐	12	♐	20		25		9		2		2		7	
11	12	5	17	18		19	29	♑	24	24		24		27		24		8		2		2		7	
21	12	5	56	28		28	10	♊	40	10	♑	7	♑	4	♐	23		8		2		2		7	

1943

1	1	6	38	9	♑	42	24	♎	32	27	♑	21	♑	12	♐	22	♋	7	♊	1	♊	2	♎	7	
11	1	7	19	19		52	21	♓	15	9	♒	4	♒	19		20		6		1		2		6	
21	1	7	58	0	♒	3	25	♋	12	9		15		26		19		6		1		2		6	
1	2	8	40	11		14	15	♐	45	26	♑	29		4	♑	18		6		1		2		6	
11	2	9	19	21		22	9	♉	31	26		12	♓	11		17		6		1		2		6	
21	2	10	0	1	♓	29	10	♍	0	5	♒	23		18		16		6		1		1		6	
1	3	10	32	9		32	25	♐	38	15		4	♈	24		15		6		1		1		5	
11	3	11	10	19		33	17	♉	32	0	♓	17		2	♒	15		7		1		1		5	
21	3	11	51	29		29	18	♍	42	16		29		9		15		7		1		1		5	
1	4	12	34	10	♈	22	19	♒	1	7	♈	12	♉	18		16		8		2		0		5	
11	4	13	12	20		13	2	♋	29	28		24		25		17		9		2		0		5	
21	4	13	53	0	♉	0	6	♏	47	17	♉	6	♊	3	♓	18		10		3		29	♍	5	
1	5	14	31	9		44	27	♓	21	0	♊	18		10		19		11		3		29		5	
11	5	15	12	19		25	4	♌	7	6		29		18		20		12		4		29		5	
21	5	15	50	29		5	14	♐	10	3		11	♋	25		22		13		4		29		5	
1	6	16	33	9	♊	37	17	♉	1	28	♉	23		3	♈	24		15		5		29		5	
11	6	17	14	19		13	18	♍	0	28		4	♌	11		26		16		6		29		6	
21	6	17	52	28		46	7	♒	43	6	♊	14		18		28		18		6		29		6	
1	7	18	33	8	♋	18	21	♊	19	20		24		25		0	♌	19		7		29		6	
11	7	19	11	17		49	21	♎	31	9	♋	2	♍	2	♉	2		20		7		29		6	
21	7	19	52	27		21	16	♓	13	1	♌	10		9		4		21		8		29		7	
1	8	20	35	7	♌	52	6	♌	0	22		17		16		7		23		8		29		7	
11	8	21	13	17		28	10	♐	51	9	♍	20		22		9		24		8		0	♎	7	
21	8	21	54	27		3	6	♉	55	23		20		28		11		24		9		1		7	
1	9	22	36	7	♍	42	20	♍	36	5	♎	16		4	♊	14		25		9		1		8	
11	9	23	17	17		24	3	♒	28	9		10		9		16		26		9		1		8	
21	9	23	56	27		7	23	♊	47	5		5		14		18		26		9		2		8	
1	10	0	35	6	♎	36	24	♎	37	25	♍	4		17		19		27		9		2		8	
11	10	1	15	16		48	12	♓	17	29		8		20		21		27		9		2		9	
21	10	1	54	26		43	25	♋	57	13	♎	13		22		23		26		8		2		9	
1	11	2	37	7	♏	41	14	♐	6	2	♏	22		22		24		26		8		3		9	
11	11	3	17	17		43	4	♉	18	18		1	♎	21		25		26		7		3		9	
21	11	3	56	27		48	9	♍	13	4	♐	11		18		26		25		7		4		9	
1	12	4	35	7	♐	54	22	♑	14	19		22		15		27		24		7		4		9	
11	12	5	15	18		4	10	♊	0	4	♑	3	♏	11		27		24		6		4		9	
21	12	5	54	28		14	11	♎	14	18		14		8		27		23		6		4		8	

1944		Sid. Time		☉		☽		☿	♀	♂	♃	♄	♅	♆	♇
1	1	6	38	9 ♑	27	15 ♓	29	25 ♑	27 ♏	5 ♊	27 ♌	22 ♊	6 ♊	4 ♎	8 ♌
11	1	7	17	19	39	26 ♋	1	15	9 ♐	5	26	21	5	4	8
21	1	7	57	29	49	27 ♏	49	9	21	6	25	21	5	4	8
1	2	8	40	11 ♒	0	7 ♉	18	16	5 ♑	8	24	20	5	4	8
11	2	9	20	21	8	10 ♍	16	28	17	10	22	20	5	4	7
21	2	9	59	1 ♓	14	18 ♑	6	12 ♒	29	14	21	20	5	4	7
1	3	10	34	10	17	29 ♉	57	26	10 ♒	17	20	20	5	3	7
11	3	11	14	20	18	1 ♎	2	14 ♓	22	22	19	20	5	3	7
21	3	11	53	0 ♈	15	11 ♒	31	3 ♈	5 ♓	26	18	21	5	2	7
1	4	12	37	11	9	16 ♋	30	25	18	2 ♋	17	21	6	2	6
11	4	13	16	20	59	17 ♏	11	10 ♉	1 ♈	7	17	22	6	2	6
21	4	13	55	0 ♉	45	5 ♈	10	16	13	12	17	23	7	2	6
1	5	14	35	10	29	18 ♌	38	13	25	18	17	24	7	2	6
11	5	15	14	20	10	22 ♐	57	8	7 ♉	23	18	25	8	2	7
21	5	15	54	29	48	13 ♉	37	8	20	29	19	26	8	2	7
1	6	16	37	10 ♊	22	2 ♎	11	16	3 ♊	5 ♌	20	28	9	2	7
11	6	17	16	19	56	14 ♒	37	29	15	11	22	29	10	1	7
21	6	17	56	29	29	2 ♋	59	17 ♊	28	17	23	0 ♋	10	2	7
1	7	18	36	9 ♋	1	4 ♏	34	8	10	23	25	1	11	2	7
11	7	19	15	18	33	23 ♓	49	29	22	29	27	3	11	2	8
21	7	19	54	28	5	6 ♌	42	18 ♌	5 ♌	6 ♍	29	4	12	2	8
1	8	20	37	8 ♌	36	21 ♐	36	4 ♍	18	12	1 ♍	5	12	2	8
11	8	21	17	18	11	16 ♉	40	15	1 ♍	19	3	6	13	2	9
21	8	21	56	27	48	21 ♍	15	22	13	25	5	7	13	3	9
1	9	22	40	8 ♍	25	12 ♒	21	20	26	2 ♎	8	8	13	3	9
11	9	23	19	18	7	5 ♋	55	11	9 ♎	9	10	9	13	3	9
21	9	23	58	27	52	5 ♏	56	10	21	15	12	10	13	4	10
1	10	0	38	7 ♎	41	20 ♓	46	23	3 ♏	22	14	10	13	4	10
11	10	1	18	17	33	9 ♌	35	10 ♎	16	28	16	11	13	4	10
21	10	1	57	27	28	9 ♐	58	28	28	5 ♏	18	11	13	5	10
1	11	2	40	8 ♏	36	14 ♉	28	15 ♏	11 ♐	12	20	11	12	5	10
11	11	3	20	18	28	23 ♍	42	1 ♐	23	20	22	10	12	6	10
21	11	3	59	28	34	29 ♑	0	16	6 ♑	27	23	10	12	6	10
1	12	4	39	8 ♐	41	21 ♊	14	29	18	4 ♐	25	9	11	6	10
11	12	5	18	18	50	25 ♎	37	8 ♑	29	11	25	9	11	6	10
21	12	5	58	29	1	7 ♓	13	4	12 ♒	18	27	8	10	6	10

1945															
1	1	6	41	10 ♑	13	8 ♌	52	23 ♐	24 ♒	26 ♐	27 ♍	7 ♋	10 ♊	6 ♎	10 ♌
11	1	7	21	20	24	10 ♐	38	27	6 ♓	4 ♑	27	6	10	6	10
21	1	8	0	0 ♒	36	0 ♉	43	8 ♑	17	11	27	5	9	6	9
1	2	8	43	11	46	23 ♍	38	23	29	20	27	5	9	6	9
11	2	9	22	21	54	28 ♑	32	9 ♒	9 ♈	27	26	4	9	6	9
21	2	10	2	2 ♓	0	22 ♊	29	26	17	5 ♒	25	4	9	6	8
1	3	10	33	10	3	2 ♎	1	10 ♓	24	11	24	4	9	6	8
11	3	11	3	11	13	6 ♒	35	29	29	19	23	4	9	5	8
21	3	11	53	0 ♈	1	2 ♋	28	17 ♈	3 ♉	27	22	4	10	5	8
1	4	12	36	10	54	16 ♏	27	28	3	5 ♓	20	4	10	5	8
11	4	13	15	20	44	28 ♓	58	25	28 ♈	13	19	5	10	5	8
21	4	13	54	0 ♉	31	19 ♌	49	18	22	21	18	6	11	4	8
1	5	14	34	10	15	19 ♐	51	17	18	29	18	7	11	4	8
11	5	15	13	19	56	7 ♉	57	24	18	6 ♈	17	8	12	4	8
21	5	15	53	29	34	22 ♍	41	6 ♉	21	14	18	9	12	4	8
1	6	16	36	10 ♊	8	7 ♒	54	23	27	22	18	10	13	4	8
11	6	17	16	19	42	0 ♋	34	14 ♊	5 ♉	29	19	11	14	4	8
21	6	17	55	29	15	6 ♏	39	5 ♋	14	7 ♉	20	12	14	4	9
1	7	18	34	8 ♋	47	15 ♓	40	25	23	14	21	14	15	4	9
11	7	19	14	18	19	6 ♌	16	12 ♌	3 ♊	21	22	15	15	4	9
21	7	19	54	27	52	8 ♐	52	25	14	28	23	16	16	4	9
1	8	20	37	8 ♌	22	9 ♉	11	2 ♍	26	6 ♊	25	18	16	4	10
11	8	21	16	17	57	22 ♍	41	4	7 ♋	13	27	19	17	5	10
21	8	21	55	27	34	25 ♑	12	27 ♌	19	19	29	20	17	5	10
1	9	22	39	8 ♍	11	1 ♋	41	22	2 ♌	26	1 ♎	21	17	5	11
11	9	23	18	17	53	7 ♏	1	1 ♍	13	2 ♋	3	22	17	5	11
21	9	23	58	27	39	15 ♓	36	18	26	8	6	23	17	6	11
1	10	0	37	7 ♎	27	8 ♌	10	6 ♎	8 ♍	13	8	24	17	6	11
11	10	1	17	17	18	9 ♐	14	23	20	18	10	24	17	7	12
21	10	1	56	27	13	23 ♈	56	10 ♏	2 ♎	22	12	25	17	7	12
1	11	2	39	8 ♏	12	24 ♍	54	26	16	27	14	25	17	7	12
11	11	3	19	18	14	24 ♑	46	9 ♐	28	29	16	25	16	8	12
21	11	3	58	28	19	17 ♊	34	20	11 ♏	2 ♌	18	25	16	8	12
1	12	4	38	8 ♐	26	27 ♎	40	22	23	3	20	24	16	8	12
11	12	5	17	18	36	0 ♓	22	10	6 ♐	3	22	24	15	8	12
21	12	5	57	28	46	24 ♋	25	8	19	1	23	23	15	9	11

1946		Sid. Time		☉		☽		☿	♀	♂	♃	♄	♅	♆	♇
1	1	6	40	9 ♑	58	11 ♐	41	18 ♐	2 ♑	28 ♋	25 ♎	22 ♋	14 ♊	9 ♎	11
11	1	7	20	20	10	22 ♈	6	2 ♑	15	24	26	22	14	9	11
21	1	7	59	0 ♒	21	12 ♍	46	17	28	21	27	21	14	9	11
1	2	8	42	11	31	27 ♑	5	4 ♒	11 ♒	17	27	20	14	9	11
11	2	9	22	21	39	15 ♊	24	22	24	15	27	19	13	8	10
21	2	10	1	1 ♓	45	27 ♎	57	10 ♓	5 ♓	14	27	18	13	8	10
1	3	10	32	9	48	5 ♒	6	25	16	14	27	18	13	8	10
11	3	11	12	19	48	26 ♊	15	8 ♈	29	16	26	18	13	8	10
21	3	11	51	29	46	5 ♏	59	9	11 ♈	18	25	18	14	8	10
1	4	12	35	10 ♈	40	24 ♓	24	1	25	21	24	18	14	7	10
11	4	13	14	20	30	17 ♌	21	28 ♓	7 ♉	25	23	18	14	7	9
21	4	13	54	0 ♉	16	19 ♐	54	3 ♈	20	29	21	19	15	7	9
1	5	14	33	10	1	2 ♉	11	14	2 ♊	4 ♌	20	19	15	6	9
11	5	14	13	19	42	22 ♍	48	29	14	8	19	20	16	6	9
21	5	15	52	29	20	22 ♑	37	17 ♉	26	14	18	21	16	6	10
1	6	16	35	9 ♊	54	25 ♊	57	11 ♊	9 ♋	19	18	22	17	6	10
11	6	17	15	19	28	8 ♏	24	2 ♋	21	25	17	23	18	6	10
21	6	17	54	29	1	9 ♓	51	20	3 ♌	0 ♍	18	25	18	6	10
1	7	18	33	8 ♋	33	3 ♌	45	4 ♌	15	6	18	26	19	6	10
11	7	19	13	18	5	10 ♐	39	13	27	12	18	27	19	6	11
21	7	19	52	27	38	16 ♈	59	16	8 ♍	17	19	28	20	6	11
1	8	20	36	8 ♌	8	23 ♍	24	11	21	25	21	29	20	6	11
11	8	21	15	17	43	25 ♑	8	5	2 ♎	1 ♎	22	1 ♌	21	7	12
21	8	21	55	27	20	9 ♊	48	9	13	7	23	2	21	7	12
1	9	22	38	7 ♍	57	9 ♏	16	25	24	14	25	4	21	7	12
11	9	23	18	17	39	12 ♓	34	14 ♍	4 ♏	21	27	5	22	8	12
21	9	23	57	27	24	2 ♌	46	2 ♎	13	28	29	6	22	8	13
1	10	0	36	7 ♎	13	11 ♐	5	19	21	4 ♏	1 ♏	7	22	8	13
11	10	1	16	17	4	18 ♈	56	5 ♏	27	11	3	7	22	9	13
21	10	1	55	26	59	10 ♍	10	19	2 ♐	18	5	8	22	9	13
1	11	2	39	7 ♏	58	24 ♑	41	2 ♐	2	26	8	9	21	9	13
11	11	3	18	18	0	11 ♊	49	7	29 ♏	3 ♐	10	9	21	10	13
21	11	3	57	28	4	27 ♎	58	0	23	10	12	9	21	10	13
1	12	4	37	8 ♐	11	27 ♒	40	21 ♏	18	18	14	9	20	10	13
11	12	5	16	18	20	20 ♋	15	28	17	25	16	9	20	11	13
21	12	5	56	28	31	1 ♐	35	11 ♐	20	3 ♑	18	8	19	11	13

1947

1	1	6	39	9 ♑	44	15 ♈	42	27 ♐	27 ♏	11 ♑	20 ♏	7 ♌	19 ♊	11 ♎	13
11	1	7	19	19	55	11 ♍	55	12 ♑	4 ♐	19	22	7	19	11	13
21	1	7	58	0 ♒	6	15 ♑	13	29	13	27	24	6	18	11	12
1	2	8	41	11	17	7 ♊	12	17 ♒	24	5 ♒	25	5	18	11	12
11	2	9	21	21	25	29 ♎	45	5 ♓	5 ♑	13	26	4	18	11	12
21	2	10	0	1 ♓	31	0 ♓	33	20	16	21	27	3	18	10	12
1	3	10	31	9	33	17 ♊	36	23	25	27	27	3	18	10	12
11	3	11	11	19	35	7 ♏	32	15	7 ♒	5 ♓	28	3	18	10	11
21	3	11	51	29	32	9 ♓	4	9	18	13	27	2	18	10	11
1	4	12	34	10 ♈	25	10 ♌	58	13	1 ♓	21	27	2	18	9	11
11	4	13	13	20	16	22 ♐	1	23	13	29	26	2	19	9	11
21	4	13	53	0 ♉	3	27 ♈	42	7 ♈	25	7 ♈	25	2	19	9	11
1	5	14	32	9	47	19 ♍	10	24	7 ♈	15	24	3	19	9	11
11	5	15	12	19	28	23 ♑	24	14 ♉	19	22	23	3	20	8	11
21	5	15	51	29	6	4 ♊	59	5 ♊	1 ♉	0 ♉	22	4	21	8	11
1	6	16	34	9 ♊	40	8 ♏	0	27	14	8	21	5	21	8	11
11	6	17	14	19	14	8 ♓	15	13 ♋	26	15	19	6	22	8	12
21	6	17	53	28	48	28 ♋	41	23	9 ♊	23	19	7	22	8	12
1	7	18	33	8 ♋	20	11 ♐	38	27	21	0 ♊	18	8	23	8	12
11	7	19	12	17	52	12 ♈	24	24	3 ♋	7	18	9	23	8	12
21	7	19	52	27	24	7 ♍	9	18	15	14	18	10	24	8	12
1	8	20	35	7 ♌	55	26 ♑	7	19	29	21	18	12	25	8	13
11	8	21	14	17	29	2 ♊	8	0 ♌	11 ♌	28	19	13	25	9	13
21	8	21	54	27	6	27 ♎	24	19	23	5 ♋	20	14	25	9	13
1	9	22	37	7 ♍	43	11 ♓	14	11	7	12	21	16	26	9	14
11	9	23	17	17	25	25 ♋	5	29	19	18	22	17	26	10	14
21	9	23	57	27	10	13 ♐	27	15 ♎	2 ♎	24	24	18	26	10	14
1	10	0	36	6 ♎	38	15 ♈	36	29	14	0 ♌	25	19	26	10	14
11	10	1	15	16	50	4 ♍	13	12 ♏	27	6	27	20	26	11	15
21	10	1	54	26	45	15 ♑	20	20	9 ♏	11	29	21	26	11	15
1	11	2	37	7 ♏	43	5 ♊	29	19	23	17	2 ♐	22	26	12	15
11	11	3	17	17	45	25 ♎	32	7	5 ♐	22	4	22	26	12	15
21	11	3	56	27	50	28 ♒	52	8	18	26	6	23	25	12	15
1	12	4	36	7 ♐	56	13 ♋	47	20	0 ♑	0 ♍	8	23	25	12	15
11	12	5	15	18	5	0 ♐	37	5 ♐	13	3	11	23	24	13	15
21	12	5	55	28	16	1 ♈	14	21	25	6	13	22	24	13	15

1948	Sid. Time	☉	☽	☿	♀	♂	♃	♄	♅	♆	♇
1 1	6 38	9 ♑ 28	7 ♍ 26	8 ♑	9 ♒	7 ♍	15 ♐	22 ♌	23 ♊	13 ♎	15 ♌
11 1	7 17	19 40	16 ♑ 9	24	21	8	17	21	23	13	14
21 1	7 57	29 52	18 ♉ 7	11 ♒	4 ♓	7	19	21	23	13	14
1 2	8 40	11 ♒ 2	28 ♎ 38	29	17	4	21	20	22	13	14
11 2	9 20	21 10	0 ♓ 41	6 ♓	29	1	23	19	22	13	14
21 2	9 59	1 ♓ 16	8 ♋ 55	29 ♒	11 ♈	27 ♌	25	18	22	13	13
1 3	10 34	10 19	20 ♏ 29	22	21	23	26	18	22	12	13
11 3	11 14	22 20	21 ♓ 36	24	3 ♉	20	27	17	22	12	13
21 3	11 53	0 ♈ 17	3 ♌ 3	3 ♓	14	19	28	16	22	12	13
1 4	12 37	11 10	6 ♑ 20	17	26	18	29	16	23	12	13
11 4	13 16	21 1	8 ♉ 2	3 ♈	7 ♊	19	29	16	23	11	13
21 4	13 56	0 ♉ 48	26 ♍ 50	22	16	21	29	16	23	11	13
1 5	14 35	10 31	8 ♒ 20	12 ♉	25	24	29	16	24	11	13
11 5	15 14	20 12	14 ♊ 1	4 ♊	3 ♋	27	28	16	24	11	13
21 5	15 54	29 51	4 ♏ 36	21	8	1 ♍	27	17	25	10	13
1 6	16 37	10 ♊ 24	21 ♓ 59	3 ♋	11	6	26	17	25	10	13
11 6	17 17	19 58	6 ♌ 33	7	10	10	25	18	26	10	13
21 6	17 56	27 31	23 ♐ 15	4	5	16	23	19	27	10	13
1 7	18 36	9 ♋ 3	24 ♈ 26	29 ♊	29 ♊	21	22	20	27	10	14
11 7	19 15	18 35	15 ♍ 54	29	25	26	21	21	28	10	14
21 7	19 54	28 8	26 ♑ 57	8 ♋	25	2 ♎	20	23	28	10	14
1 8	20 38	8 ♌ 38	11 ♊ 45	27	29	9	19	24	29	11	14
11 8	21 17	18 13	8 ♏ 1	17 ♌	5 ♋	15	19	25	29	11	15
21 8	21 57	27 50	11 ♓ 40	7 ♍	13	21	19	26	29	11	15
1 9	22 40	8 ♍ 27	3 ♌ 17	26	23	28	19	28	0 ♋	11	15
11 9	23 19	18 10	26 ♐ 23	11 ♎	2 ♌	5 ♏	20	29	0	12	16
21 9	23 59	27 54	26 ♈ 34	24	13	12	21	0 ♍	0	12	16
1 10	0 38	7 ♎ 43	12 ♍ 5	3 ♏	24	19	22	1	1	13	16
11 10	1 18	17 35	29 ♑ 39	5	5 ♍	26	24	2	1	13	16
21 10	1 57	27 30	0 ♊ 36	25 ♎	17	3 ♐	25	3	0	13	16
1 11	2 41	8 ♏ 28	5 ♏ 7	21	29	11	27	4	0	14	16
11 11	3 20	18 31	13 ♓ 33	1 ♏	12 ♎	18	29	5	0	14	17
21 11	3 59	28 35	21 ♋ 1	16	24	26	1 ♑	6	29 ♊	14	17
1 12	4 39	8 ♐ 43	11 ♐ 28	2 ♐	6 ♏	3 ♑	3	6	29	15	17
11 12	5 18	18 52	15 ♈ 11	18	18	11	6	6	29	15	16
21 12	5 58	29 3	29 ♌ 49	4 ♑	1 ♐	18	8	6	29	15	16

1949

1 1	6 41	10 ♑ 15	28 ♑ 54	21 ♑	15 ♐	27 ♑	10 ♑	6 ♍	26 ♊	15 ♎	16 ♌
11 1	7 21	20 27	0 ♊ 16	7 ♒	27	5 ♒	13	6	28	15	16
21 1	8 0	0 ♒ 38	23 ♎ 3	19	10 ♑	13	15	5	27	15	16
1 2	8 43	11 49	13 ♓ 43	16	23	21	17	4	27	15	15
11 2	9 2	21 57	19 ♋ 56	6	6 ♒	29	20	4	27	15	15
21 2	10 2	2 ♓ 2	13 ♐ 56	6	18	7 ♓	22	3	27	15	15
1 3	10 34	10 5	22 ♓ 20	13	28	14	23	2	26	15	15
11 3	11 13	20 6	27 ♋ 18	25	11 ♓	21	25	1	27	14	15
21 3	11 53	0 ♈ 3	23 ♐ 25	10 ♓	23	29	27	1	27	14	14
1 4	12 36	10 56	6 ♉ 44	29	7 ♈	8 ♈	29	0	27	14	14
11 4	13 15	20 47	20 ♍ 5	18 ♈	19	16	29	29	27	14	14
21 4	13 55	0 ♉ 33	10 ♒ 19	9 ♉	2 ♉	23	1 ♒	29 ♌	27	13	14
1 5	14 34	10 17	10 ♊ 30	28	14	1 ♉	2	29	28	13	14
11 5	15 14	19 58	28 ♎ 50	11 ♊	26	8	2	29	28	13	14
21 5	15 53	29 37	12 ♓ 45	17	9 ♊	15	2	29	29	13	14
1 6	16 37	10 ♊ 10	29 ♋ 40	15	22	23	2	0 ♍	29	13	14
11 6	17 16	19 44	20 ♐ 58	10	4 ♋	1 ♊	1	1	0 ♋	12	14
21 6	17 55	29 17	26 ♈ 16	9	17	8	1	1	1	12	15
1 7	18 35	8 ♋ 49	7 ♍ 59	17	29	15	29 ♑	2	1	12	15
11 7	19 14	18 21	26 ♑ 40	1 ♋	11 ♌	22	28	3	2	12	15
21 7	19 54	27 54	28 ♉ 28	21	23	28	27	4	2	13	16
1 8	20 37	8 ♌ 24	1 ♏ 20	14 ♌	6 ♍	6 ♋	26	6	3	13	16
11 8	21 16	18 0	12 ♓ 51	3 ♍	19	12	25	7	3	13	16
21 8	21 56	27 36	15 ♋ 28	19	1 ♎	19	24	8	4	13	17
1 9	22 39	8 ♍ 13	23 ♐ 17	4 ♎	14	26	23	9	4	14	17
11 9	23 19	17 56	26 ♈ 57	15	26	2 ♌	22	11	5	14	17
21 9	23 58	27 40	6 ♍ 26	19	7 ♏	9	22	12	5	14	17
1 10	0 38	7 ♎ 28	29 ♑ 21	13	19	15	23	13	5	15	18
11 10	1 17	17 20	29 ♉ 29	4	1 ♐	21	23	14	5	15	18
21 10	1 56	27 16	14 ♎ 36	9	12	27	24	15	5	15	18
1 11	2 39	8 ♏ 14	15 ♓ 23	25	24	3 ♍	25	16	5	16	18
11 11	3 19	18 16	16 ♋ 0	12 ♏	5 ♑	8	27	17	5	16	18
21 11	3 59	28 21	7 ♐ 55	28	16	14	28	18	4	16	18
1 12	4 38	8 ♐ 28	17 ♈ 32	14 ♐	25	19	0 ♒	19	4	17	18
11 12	5 18	18 37	22 ♌ 24	29	4 ♒	23	2	19	4	17	18
21 12	5 57	28 48	14 ♑ 48	15 ♑	11	28	4	19	3	17	18

1950		Sid. Time		☉		☽	☿	♀	♂	♃	♄	♅	♆	♇
1	1	6	40	10 ♑	0	1 ♊ 25	29 ♑	17 ♒	2 ♎	6 ♒	19 ♍	3 ♋	17 ♎	18 ♌
11	1	7	20	20	12	14 ♎ 29	4 ♒	19	6	9	19	2	17	18
21	1	7	59	0 ♒	23	2 ♓ 49	23 ♑	17	8	11	19	2	17	17
1	2	8	43	11	34	17 ♋ 25	19	10	10	14	18	2	17	17
11	2	9	22	21	41	7 ♐ 39	26	5	11	16	18	1	17	17
21	2	10	1	1 ♓	47	17 ♈ 33	8 ♒	3	11	19	17	1	17	17
1	3	10	33	9	50	25 ♋ 15	19	4	9	20	17	1	17	16
11	3	11	12	19	51	18 ♐ 26	5 ♓	9	6	23	16	1	17	16
21	3	11	52	29	49	25 ♈ 47	23	16	3	25	15	1	16	16
1	4	12	35	10 ♈	42	14 ♍ 53	15 ♈	25	29 ♍	27	14	1	16	16
11	4	13	14	20	32	9 ♒ 2	5 ♉	4 ♓	25	29	14	1	16	16
21	4	13	54	0 ♉	20	9 ♊ 57	20	14	23	1 ♓	13	2	16	16
1	5	14	33	10	3	22 ♎ 39	27	25	22	3	13	2	15	16
11	5	15	13	19	44	13 ♓ 41	25	6 ♈	22	4	13	3	15	16
21	5	15	52	29	23	13 ♋ 20	20	17	24	5	13	3	15	16
1	6	16	36	9 ♊	56	16 ♐ 36	19	29	26	6	13	4	15	16
11	6	17	15	19	30	28 ♈ 25	26	11 ♉	29	7	13	4	15	16
21	6	17	54	29	3	1 ♍ 21	9 ♊	22	4 ♎	7	14	5	15	16
1	7	18	34	8 ♋	36	24 ♑ 28	27	4 ♊	8	7	14	5	15	17
11	7	19	13	18	8	0 ♊ 29	18 ♋	16	13	7	15	6	15	17
21	7	19	53	27	40	8 ♎ 50	9 ♌	28	18	7	16	7	15	17
1	8	20	36	8 ♌	11	13 ♓ 32	28	11 ♋	24	6	17	7	15	17
11	8	21	15	17	46	15 ♋ 19	13 ♍	23	0 ♏	4	18	8	15	18
21	8	21	55	27	22	2 ♐ 1	25	5 ♌	6	3	19	8	15	18
1	9	22	38	7 ♍	59	28 ♈ 50	2 ♎	19	13	2	21	9	16	18
11	9	23	18	17	41	2 ♍ 54	0	1 ♍	20	0	22	9	16	19
21	9	23	57	27	27	24 ♑ 54	20 ♍	14	27	29 ♒	23	9	16	19
1	10	0	37	7 ♎	14	0 ♊ 47	20	26	4 ♐	28	25	9	17	19
11	10	1	16	17	6	9 ♎ 22	2 ♎	8 ♎	11	28	26	9	17	19
21	10	1	55	27	1	1 ♓ 40	19	21	18	28	27	10	17	20
1	11	2	39	8 ♏	0	14 ♋ 57	8 ♏	4 ♏	26	28	28	9	18	20
11	11	3	18	18	2	2 ♐ 38	24	17	4 ♑	28	29	9	18	20
21	11	3	58	28	6	18 ♈ 26	9 ♐	0 ♐	11	29	0 ♎	9	19	20
1	12	4	37	8 ♐	13	18 ♌ 29	24	12	19	0 ♓	1	9	19	20
11	12	5	16	18	22	11 ♑ 11	8 ♑	25	27	1	1	8	19	20
21	12	5	56	28	33	21 ♉ 12	18	8 ♑	4 ♒	3	2	8	19	20

1951

1	1	6	39	9 ♑	45	7 ♎ 3	12 ♑	21 ♑	13 ♒	5 ♓	2 ♎	7 ♋	19 ♎	19
11	1	7	19	19	57	2 ♓ 20	2	4 ♒	21	7	2	7	19	19
21	1	7	58	0 ♒	8	5 ♋ 28	6	16	29	9	2	7	20	19
1	2	8	42	11	19	29 ♏ 14	18	0 ♓	7 ♓	11	2	6	20	19
11	2	9	21	21	27	19 ♈ 22	2 ♒	13	15	13	2	6	19	19
21	2	10	0	1 ♓	32	21 ♌ 1	17	25	23	16	1	6	19	18
1	3	10	32	9	35	10 ♐ 8	1 ♓	5 ♈	29	18	0	5	19	18
11	3	11	11	19	36	27 ♈ 7	19	17	7 ♈	20	29 ♍	5	19	18
21	3	11	51	29	34	29 ♌ 6	9 ♈	29	15	23	29	5	19	18
1	4	12	34	10 ♈	27	3 ♒ 27	28	13 ♉	23	25	28	6	18	18
11	4	13	14	20	18	11 ♊ 39	8 ♉	25	0 ♉	28	27	6	18	18
21	4	13	53	0 ♉	6	18 ♎ 1	7	7 ♊	8	0 ♈	27	6	18	17
1	5	14	32	9	49	10 ♓ 54	0	18	15	2	26	6	18	17
11	5	15	12	19	31	13 ♋ 43	29 ♈	0 ♋	22	4	26	7	17	17
21	5	15	51	29	9	25 ♏ 45	4 ♉	11	29	6	26	7	17	17
1	6	16	35	9 ♊	42	28 ♈ 42	17	23	7 ♊	8	26	8	17	18
11	6	17	14	19	17	28 ♌ 34	3 ♊	4 ♌	14	10	26	8	17	18
21	6	17	54	28	50	19 ♑ 57	23	14	21	11	26	9	17	18
1	7	18	33	8 ♋	22	2 ♊ 4	15	24	28	12	26	10	17	18
11	7	19	12	17	54	3 ♎ 11	5 ♌	2 ♍	5 ♋	13	27	10	17	18
21	7	19	52	27	26	27 ♒ 55	21	10	11	14	28	11	17	19
1	8	20	35	7 ♌	57	16 ♋ 29	5 ♍	16	18	14	29	11	17	19
11	8	21	15	17	32	23 ♏ 49	13	18	25	14	29	12	17	19
21	8	21	54	27	8	17 ♈ 20	14	17	2 ♌	14	1 ♎	12	17	20
1	9	22	37	7 ♍	45	1 ♍ 34	6	12	9	13	2	13	18	20
11	9	23	17	17	27	17 ♑ 17	2	6	15	12	3	13	18	20
21	9	23	56	27	12	3 ♊ 10	10	2	21	11	4	14	18	21
1	10	0	35	7 ♎	0	6 ♎ 0	27	3	28	9	6	14	19	21
11	10	1	15	16	52	26 ♒ 5	15 ♎	7	4 ♍	8	7	14	19	21
21	10	1	54	26	47	5 ♋ 6	2 ♏	13	10	7	8	14	20	21
1	11	2	37	7 ♏	45	26 ♏ 46	19	22	16	6	9	14	20	21
11	11	3	17	17	47	16 ♈ 29	4 ♐	1 ♎	22	5	10	14	20	21
21	11	3	57	27	51	18 ♌ 40	18	11	28	4	12	14	21	22
1	12	4	36	7 ♐	59	5 ♑ 24	29	22	4 ♎	4	12	13	21	22
11	12	5	16	18	8	21 ♉ 19	1 ♑	3 ♏	9	4	13	13	21	21
21	12	5	55	28	18	21 ♍ 19	19 ♐	15	15	5	14	13	21	21

1952		Sid. Time		☉	☽	☿	♀	♂	♃	♄	♅	♆	♇
1	1	6	38	9 ♑ 31	28 ♒ 41	18 ♐	28 ♏	21 ♎	6 ♈	14 ♎	12 ♋	21 ♎	21 ♌
11	1	7	18	19 42	6 ♋ 39	27	10 ♐	26	7	15	12	22	21
21	1	7	57	29 54	9 ♏ 2	10 ♑	22	0 ♏	9	15	11	22	21
1	2	8	41	11 ♒ 4	19 ♈ 5	27	5 ♑	5	10	15	11	22	21
11	2	9	20	21 13	20 ♌ 59	13 ♒	17	9	12	15	11	22	20
21	2	9	59	1 ♓ 18	0 ♑ 42	0 ♓	0 ♒	13	14	14	10	21	20
1	3	10	35	10 22	10 ♉ 29	17	11	15	16	14	10	21	20
11	3	11	14	20 22	11 ♍ 45	6 ♈	23	17	18	13	10	21	20
21	3	11	54	0 ♈ 19	25 ♑ 16	18	5 ♓	18	21	12	10	21	19
1	4	12	37	11 13	26 ♊ 8	19	19	18	23	12	10	21	19
11	4	13	16	21 3	28 ♎ 46	11	1 ♈	17	26	11	10	20	19
21	4	13	56	0 ♉ 50	18 ♓ 22	9	14	14	28	10	10	20	19
1	5	14	35	10 33	27 ♋ 56	14	26	11	0 ♉	9	11	20	19
11	5	15	15	20 15	5 ♐ 25	25	8 ♉	7	3	9	11	20	19
21	5	15	54	29 53	25 ♈ 50	10 ♉	20	4	5	9	12	19	19
1	6	16	38	10 ♊ 26	11 ♍ 28	1 ♊	4 ♊	2	8	8	12	19	19
11	6	17	17	20 0	28 ♑ 30	22	16	1	10	8	13	19	19
21	6	17	57	29 33	14 ♊ 4	13 ♋	29	2	12	8	13	19	20
1	7	18	36	9 ♋ 5	14 ♎ 17	1 ♌	11 ♋	4	14	9	14	19	20
11	7	19	15	18 37	7 ♓ 21	15	23	7	15	9	14	19	20
21	7	19	55	28 10	17 ♋ 28	24	5 ♌	11	17	10	15	19	20
1	8	20	38	8 ♌ 40	2 ♐ 30	27	19	15	18	10	16	19	21
11	8	21	17	18 15	29 ♈ 0	21	1 ♍	21	20	11	16	19	21
21	8	21	57	27 52	1 ♍ 47	15	14	26	20	12	17	20	22
1	9	22	40	8 ♍ 29	24 ♑ 26	20	27	2 ♐	21	13	17	20	22
11	9	23	20	18 11	16 ♊ 57	6 ♍	9 ♎	9	21	14	18	20	22
21	9	23	59	27 57	17 ♎ 5	25	22	15	21	16	18	21	22
1	10	0	39	7 ♎ 45	3 ♓ 9	12 ♎	4 ♏	22	20	17	18	21	23
11	10	1	18	17 36	19 ♋ 39	29	16	29	19	18	18	21	23
21	10	1	58	27 32	22 ♏ 9	14 ♏	29	6 ♑	18	19	19	22	23
1	11	2	41	8 ♏ 31	25 ♈ 53	0 ♐	12 ♐	14	17	20	18	22	23
11	11	3	20	18 32	3 ♍ 4	11	24	22	16	22	18	22	23
21	11	4	0	28 38	13 ♑ 3	16	6 ♑	29	14	23	18	23	23
1	12	4	39	8 ♐ 44	2 ♊ 17	7	18	7 ♒	13	24	18	23	23
11	12	5	18	18 54	4 ♎ 45	0	0 ♒	15	12	25	18	23	23
21	12	5	58	29 5	21 ♒ 44	8	12	22	11	25	17	24	23

1953													
1	1	6	41	10 ♑ 17	19 ♋ 12	22 ♐	25 ♒	1 ♓	11 ♉	26 ♎	17 ♋	24 ♎	23 ♌
11	1	7	21	20 29	20 ♏ 27	7 ♑	6 ♓	9	11	27	16	24	23
21	1	8	0	0 ♒ 40	14 ♈ 45	22	17	16	11	27	16	24	22
1	2	8	44	11 50	3 ♍ 39	10 ♒	29	25	12	27	15	24	22
11	2	9	23	21 58	9 ♑ 44	28	8 ♈	2 ♈	13	27	15	24	22
21	2	10	2	2 ♓ 4	5 ♊ 14	16 ♓	17	10	14	27	15	24	22
1	3	10	34	10 7	12 ♍ 23	28	23	16	16	27	15	24	22
11	3	11	13	20 7	18 ♑ 20	3 ♈	29	23	17	26	14	23	21
21	3	11	53	0 ♈ 5	14 ♊ 11	25 ♓	1 ♉	1 ♉	19	26	14	23	21
1	4	12	36	10 58	27 ♎ 16	20	0	9	21	25	14	23	21
11	4	13	16	20 48	11 ♓ 9	24	25 ♈	16	23	24	15	23	21
21	4	13	55	0 ♉ 36	0 ♌ 17	4 ♈	19	23	26	23	15	22	21
1	5	14	35	10 19	1 ♐ 41	18	15	0 ♊	28	23	15	22	21
11	5	15	14	20 0	20 ♈ 10	5 ♉	16	7	0 ♊	22	15	22	21
21	5	15	53	29 39	2 ♍ 13	25	20	14	3	21	16	22	21
1	6	16	37	10 ♊ 12	21 ♑ 29	19 ♊	27	21	5	21	16	21	21
11	6	17	16	19 46	11 ♊ 59	8 ♋	5 ♉	28	8	21	17	21	21
21	6	17	55	29 20	15 ♎ 49	24	14	5 ♋	10	21	18	21	21
1	7	18	35	8 ♋ 52	29 ♒ 55	4 ♌	23	11	12	21	18	21	22
11	7	19	14	18 24	17 ♋ 11	8	4 ♊	18	14	21	19	21	22
21	7	19	54	27 56	18 ♏ 52	5	14	24	16	21	19	21	22
1	8	20	37	8 ♌ 26	23 ♈ 32	28 ♋	27	1 ♌	18	22	20	21	22
11	8	21	17	18 2	2 ♍ 43	0 ♌	8 ♋	8	20	22	21	22	23
21	8	21	56	27 39	5 ♑ 43	12	19	14	22	23	21	22	23
1	9	22	39	8 ♍ 15	15 ♊ 5	2 ♍	2 ♌	21	23	24	22	22	23
11	9	23	19	17 58	17 ♎ 3	21	14	28	25	25	22	22	24
21	9	23	58	27 43	26 ♒ 59	9 ♎	26	4 ♍	26	26	22	23	24
1	10	0	38	7 ♎ 31	20 ♋ 15	25	8	10	26	27	23	23	24
11	10	1	17	17 23	20 ♏ 10	9 ♏	21	17	26	29	23	23	24
21	10	1	57	27 18	5 ♈ 24	21	2 ♎	23	26	29	23	24	25
1	11	2	40	8 ♏ 16	5 ♍ 25	0 ♐	17	29	26	1 ♏	23	24	25
11	11	2	19	18 19	7 ♑ 20	27 ♏	29	6 ♎	25	2	23	25	25
21	11	3	59	28 23	28 ♉ 50	15	12 ♏	12	24	3	23	25	25
1	12	4	38	8 ♐ 30	7 ♎ 21	18	24	18	23	5	23	25	25
11	12	5	18	18 40	14 ♒ 7	0 ♐	7 ♐	24	22	6	22	25	25
21	12	5	57	28 50	4 ♋ 20	15	19	0 ♏	20	7	22	26	25

1954		Sid. Time		☉		☽		☿	♀	♂	♃	♄	♅	♆	♇
1	1	6	40	10 ♑	2	21 ♏	23	2 ♑	3 ♑	7 ♏	19 ♊	7 ♏	22 ♋	26 ♎	25
11	1	7	20	20	14	6 ♈	51	18	16	13	18	8	21	26	25
21	1	7	59	0 ♒	25	22 ♌	37	5 ♒	28	19	17	9	21	26	24
1	2	8	43	11	36	7 ♑	28	24	12 ♒	25	17	9	20	26	24
11	2	9	22	21	44	0 ♊	3	9 ♓	25	1 ♐	16	9	20	26	24
21	2	10	2	1 ♓	49	7 ♎	22	16	7 ♓	6	17	9	20	26	24
1	3	10	33	9	52	15 ♑	15	11	17	10	17	9	19	26	23
11	3	11	12	19	53	10 ♊	26	2	29	16	18	9	19	26	23
21	3	11	52	29	50	15 ♎	56	4	12	20	19	9	19	25	23
1	4	12	35	10 ♈	43	5 ♓	17	13	26	25	20	8	19	25	23
11	4	13	15	20	34	29 ♋	57	26	8 ♉	29	22	7	19	25	23
21	4	13	54	0 ♉	21	0 ♐	33	12 ♈	20	3 ♑	23	6	19	25	23
1	5	14	34	10	5	13 ♈	41	1 ♉	3 ♊	6	25	6	20	24	23
11	5	15	13	19	46	3 ♍	53	22	15	8	27	5	20	24	23
21	5	15	52	29	24	4 ♑	14	13 ♊	27	8	29	4	20	24	23
1	6	16	36	9 ♊	58	7 ♊	38	2 ♋	10 ♋	8	2 ♋	4	21	24	23
11	6	17	15	19	32	18 ♎	23	13	22	6	4	3	21	23	23
21	6	17	54	29	5	22 ♒	54	19	4 ♌	4	6	3	22	23	23
1	7	18	34	8 ♋	38	14 ♋	56	17	16	1	8	3	22	23	23
11	7	19	13	18	10	20 ♏	19	11	27	28 ♐	11	3	23	23	24
21	7	19	53	27	42	1 ♈	6	10	9 ♍	26	13	3	24	23	24
1	8	20	36	8 ♌	13	3 ♍	18	19	21	25	15	3	24	23	24
11	8	21	16	17	48	5 ♑	5	6 ♌	2 ♎	27	17	4	25	24	24
21	8	21	55	27	24	24 ♉	45	27	13	29	20	4	25	24	25
1	9	22	38	8 ♏	2	18 ♎	38	17	24	2 ♑	22	5	26	24	25
11	9	23	18	17	44	23 ♒	0	4 ♎	4 ♏	7	23	6	26	24	25
21	9	23	57	27	28	16 ♋	46	19	13	12	25	7	27	25	26
1	10	0	37	7 ♎	17	20 ♏	48	2 ♏	20	17	27	8	27	25	26
11	10	1	16	17	9	0 ♈	1	12	26	23	28	9	27	25	26
21	10	1	56	27	3	22 ♌	7	14	29	29	29	10	28	26	26
1	11	2	39	8 ♏	2	5 ♑	13	3	29	7 ♒	29	12	28	26	27
11	11	3	18	18	4	23 ♉	44	29 ♎	25	13	29	13	28	27	27
21	11	3	58	28	8	9 ♎	2	10 ♏	19	21	29	14	28	27	27
1	12	4	37	8 ♐	15	9 ♒	15	25	15	28	29	15	27	27	27
11	12	5	17	18	25	1 ♋	48	10 ♐	15	5 ♓	29	16	27	28	27
21	12	5	56	28	35	11 ♏	29	26	19	12	28	17	27	28	27

1955															
1	1	6	39	9 ♑	48	28 ♓	54	14 ♑	26 ♏	20 ♓	27 ♋	18 ♏	26 ♋	28 ♎	27
11	1	7	19	19	59	22 ♌	16	0 ♒	4 ♐	27	26	19	26	28	26
21	1	7	58	0 ♒	10	25 ♐	22	16	13	4 ♈	24	20	25	28	26
1	2	8	41	11	21	21 ♉	42	29	25	12	22	20	25	28	26
11	2	9	21	21	29	9 ♎	11	25	5 ♑	19	22	21	25	28	26
21	2	10	1	1 ♓	35	11 ♒	2	15	17	26	21	21	24	28	26
1	3	10	32	9	38	2 ♊	43	15	26	2 ♉	20	21	24	28	25
11	3	11	12	19	39	17 ♎	9	22	7 ♒	9	20	21	24	28	25
21	3	11	51	29	36	18 ♒	58	4 ♓	19	16	20	21	24	28	25
1	4	12	34	10 ♈	29	25 ♋	17	20	2 ♓	23	20	20	24	27	25
11	4	13	14	20	20	1 ♐	38	8 ♈	14	0 ♊	21	20	24	27	24
21	4	13	53	0 ♉	7	8 ♈	45	28	26	7	22	19	24	27	24
1	5	14	32	9	52	2 ♍	12	19 ♉	8 ♈	17	23	18	24	27	24
11	5	15	12	19	32	3 ♑	47	8 ♊	20	20	24	18	24	26	24
21	5	15	51	29	10	16 ♉	45	21	2 ♉	27	26	17	25	26	24
1	6	15	35	9 ♊	45	19 ♎	28	28	15	4 ♋	28	16	25	26	24
11	6	17	14	19	19	19 ♒	13	27	27	10	29	16	26	26	25
21	6	17	54	28	52	10 ♋	30	22	9 ♊	17	2 ♌	15	26	26	25
1	7	18	33	8 ♋	24	22 ♏	20	20	21	23	4	15	27	25	25
11	7	19	13	17	56	24 ♓	44	27	4 ♋	0 ♌	6	15	27	25	25
21	7	19	52	27	29	18 ♌	8	11	16	6	8	15	28	25	25
1	8	20	35	7 ♌	59	6 ♑	19	3 ♌	29	13	10	15	29	26	26
11	8	21	15	17	34	16 ♉	11	23	12 ♌	20	13	15	29	26	26
21	8	21	54	27	10	7 ♎	23	12 ♍	24	26	15	15	29	26	26
1	9	22	38	7 ♍	48	21 ♒	43	29	8 ♍	2 ♍	17	16	0 ♌	26	27
11	9	23	17	17	29	9 ♋	24	13 ♎	20	9	19	17	1	27	27
21	9	23	56	27	15	22 ♏	54	23	3 ♎	16	21	18	1	27	27
1	10	0	36	7 ♎	3	26 ♓	41	29	15	22	23	19	2	27	28
11	10	1	15	16	54	17 ♌	59	23	27	28	25	20	2	28	28
21	10	1	55	26	50	24 ♐	40	13	10 ♏	5 ♎	27	21	2	28	28
1	11	2	38	7 ♏	47	18 ♉	3	20	24	12	28	22	2	28	28
11	11	3	17	17	49	7 ♎	53	4 ♏	6 ♐	18	29	23	2	29	29
21	11	3	57	27	54	8 ♒	29	20	19	25	0 ♍	24	2	29	29
1	12	4	36	8 ♐	1	26 ♊	22	6 ♐	1 ♑	1 ♏	1	25	2	29	29
11	12	5	16	18	10	12 ♏	12	22	13	8	1	27	2	29	29
21	12	5	55	28	20	11 ♓	52	2 ♑	26	14	1	28	2	29	29

1956

Day	Month	Sid. Time h	m	☉	☽	☿	♀	♂	♃	♄	♅	♆	♇
1	1	6	38	9 ♑ 33	19 ♌ 27	25 ♑	10 ♒	21 ♏	1 ♍	29 ♏	1 ♌	0 ♏	28 ♌
11	1	7	18	19 45	26 ♐ 47	9 ♒	22	28	1	29	1	0	28
21	1	7	57	29 55	0 ♉ 28	13	4 ♓	5 ♐	29 ♌	1 ♐	0	0	28
1	2	8	41	11 ♒ 6	9 ♎ 38	1	18	12	28	1	29	0	28
11	2	9	20	21 14	11 ♒ 8	28 ♑	29	18	27	2	29	0	28
21	2	10	0	1 ♓ 20	22 ♊ 21	5 ♒	11 ♈	25	26	2	29	0	27
1	3	10	35	10 23	0 ♏ 41	15	22	1 ♑	25	3	29	0	27
11	3	11	14	22 24	2 ♓ 0	29	4 ♉	7	24	3	28	0	27
21	3	11	54	0 ♈ 22	17 ♋ 14	16 ♓	15	14	23	3	28	29 ♎	27
1	4	12	37	11 14	15 ♐ 46	6 ♈	27	21	22	2	28	29	26
11	4	13	17	21 5	19 ♈ 41	26	7 ♊	27	22	2	28	29	26
21	4	13	56	0 ♉ 52	10 ♍ 15	16 ♉	16	4 ♒	21	2	28	29	26
1	5	14	36	10 35	17 ♑ 26	1 ♊	25	10	22	1	28	29	26
11	5	15	15	20 16	26 ♉ 23	8	2 ♋	16	22	0	29	28	26
21	5	15	54	29 55	17 ♎ 22	7	7	22	23	29 ♏	29	28	26
1	6	16	38	10 ♊ 2	1 ♓ 26	2	9	29	24	28	29	28	26
11	6	17	17	20 22	19 ♋ 35	1	7	4 ♓	26	28	0 ♌	28	26
21	6	17	57	29 35	4 ♐ 36	7	1	9	27	27	1	28	27
1	7	18	36	9 ♋ 7	4 ♈ 52	20	26 ♊	14	29	27	1	28	27
11	7	19	15	18 39	28 ♌ 25	8 ♋	23	18	1 ♍	26	2	28	27
21	7	19	55	28 12	7 ♑ 34	29	23	21	2	26	2	28	27
1	8	20	38	8 ♌ 42	23 ♉ 32	21 ♌	28	23	5	26	3	28	28
11	8	21	18	18 17	19 ♎ 47	9 ♍	4 ♋	24	7	26	4	28	28
21	8	21	57	27 54	22 ♒ 4	23	13	23	9	27	4	28	28
1	9	22	40	8 ♍ 31	15 ♋ 43	6 ♎	23	21	11	27	5	28	29
11	9	23	20	18 14	6 ♐ 52	12	3 ♌	18	13	28	5	29	29
21	9	23	59	27 59	8 ♈ 1	9	13	16	16	28	6	29	29
1	10	0	39	7 ♎ 47	24 ♌ 53	29 ♍	24	14	18	29	6	29	29
11	10	1	18	17 39	9 ♑ 7	0 ♎	5 ♍	13	20	0 ♐	7	29	29
21	10	1	58	27 34	13 ♉ 18	13	17	14	22	1	7	0 ♏	0 ♍
1	11	2	41	8 ♏ 32	17 ♎ 16	1 ♏	♎	16	24	2	7	0	0
11	11	3	20	18 35	22 ♒ 36	17	12	19	26	3	7	1	0
21	11	4	0	28 40	4 ♋ 38	3 ♐	24	23	27	5	7	1	0
1	12	4	39	8 ♐ 47	23 ♏ 4	18	7 ♏	27	29	6	7	1	0
11	12	5	19	18 56	24 ♓ 34	4 ♑	19	2 ♈	29	7	7	2	0
21	12	5	58	29 7	13 ♌ 32	18	1 ♐	8	1 ♎	8	6	2	0

1957

Day	Month	Sid. Time h	m	☉	☽	☿	♀	♂	♃	♄	♅	♆	♇
1	1	6	42	10 ♑ 19	9 ♑ 19	27 ♑	15 ♐	14 ♈	1 ♎	9 ♐	6 ♌	2 ♏	0 ♍
11	1	7	21	20 31	10 ♉ 33	20	28	19	2	10	6	2	0
21	1	8	0	0 ♒ 51	6 ♎ 34	11	10 ♑	25	2	11	5	3	29 ♌
1	2	8	44	11 52	23 ♒ 54	17	24	2 ♉	1	12	5	3	29
11	2	9	23	22 1	0 ♋ 13	28	6 ♒	8	1	13	4	3	29
21	2	10	3	2 ♓ 6	26 ♏ 3	12 ♒	19	14	29 ♍	13	4	3	29
1	3	10	34	10 9	2 ♓ 46	24	29	19	29	14	4	2	29
11	3	11	13	20 10	9 ♋ 28	11 ♓	11 ♓	26	28	14	3	2	29
21	3	11	53	0 ♈ 7	4 ♐ 25	0 ♈	24	2 ♊	26	14	3	2	28
1	4	12	36	11 0	17 ♈ 57	22	8 ♈	9	25	14	3	2	28
11	4	13	16	20 51	2 ♍ 55	10 ♉	20	15	24	14	3	2	28
21	4	13	55	0 ♉ 37	20 ♑ 0	19	2 ♉	21	23	14	3	1	28
1	5	14	35	10 21	22 ♉ 26	18	15	28	22	13	3	1	28
11	5	15	14	29 2	11 ♎ 54	12	27	4 ♋	22	13	3	1	28
21	5	15	53	29 40	21 ♒ 54	10	9 ♊	10	22	12	4	0	28
1	6	16	37	10 ♊ 14	12 ♋ 54	16	23	17	22	11	4	0	28
11	6	17	16	19 48	2 ♐ 40	28	5 ♋	23	23	10	4	0	28
21	6	17	55	29 21	5 ♈ 38	14 ♊	17	29	23	10	5	29 ♎	28
1	7	18	35	8 ♋ 53	21 ♌ 48	5 ♋	29	6 ♌	24	9	5	29	29
11	7	19	15	18 25	7 ♑ 32	26	12 ♌	12	26	8	6	29	29
21	7	19	54	27 57	8 ♉ 17	15 ♌	24	18	27	8	7	29	29
1	8	20	37	8 ♌ 29	15 ♎ 25	3 ♍	7 ♍	25	29	8	7	29	29
11	8	21	16	18 3	23 ♒ 2	15	19	2 ♍	1 ♎	8	8	0 ♏	29
21	8	21	56	27 40	26 ♊ 5	23	1 ♎	8	3	8	9	0	0 ♍
1	9	22	39	8 ♍ 17	5 ♐ 58	24	14	15	5	8	9	0	0
11	9	23	19	17 59	7 ♈ 53	16	26	22	7	8	10	1	1
21	9	23	58	27 44	18 ♌ 1	11	8 ♏	28	9	9	10	1	1
1	10	0	38	7 ♎ 33	10 ♑ 31	21	20	4 ♎	11	10	11	1	1
11	10	1	17	17 25	10 ♉ 49	8 ♎	1 ♐	11	13	10	11	2	2
21	10	1	57	27 20	26 ♍ 52	25	13	17	15	11	11	2	2
1	11	2	40	8 ♏ 18	25 ♒ 23	13 ♏	25	25	18	12	12	2	2
11	11	3	19	18 20	28 ♊ 41	29	5 ♑	1 ♏	20	14	12	3	2
21	11	3	59	28 25	19 ♏ 30	14 ♐	16	8	22	15	12	3	2
1	12	4	38	8 ♐ 32	27 ♓ 4	28	25	15	24	16	12	4	2
11	12	5	18	18 42	6 ♌ 12	9 ♑	4 ♒	22	25	17	11	4	2
21	12	5	57	28 51	25 ♐ 41	10	10	29	27	18	11	4	2

1958		Sid. Time		☉			☽			☿		♀		♂		♃		♄		♅		♆		♇
1	1	6	41	10	♑	4	10	♉	54	27	♐	15	♒	6	♐	29	♎	19	♐	11	♌	4	♏	2
11	1	7	20	20		15	29	♍	29	27		16		13		29		21		10		5		2
21	1	7	50	0	♒	27	12	♒	49	7	♑	13		20		1	♏	22		10		5		2
1	2	8	43	11		38	27	♊	21	22		6		28		1		23		10		5		2
11	2	9	22	21		45	21	♏	59	7	♒	2		5	♑	2		23		9		5		1
21	2	10	2	1	♓	51	27	♓	31	23		1		12		2		24		9		5		1
1	3	10	33	9		54	5	♋	25	7	♓	3		18		1		25		8		5		1
11	3	11	13	19		55	1	♐	46	27		8		25		1		25		8		4		1
21	3	11	52	29		52	6	♈	15	15	♈	15		3	♒	0		26		8		4		0
1	4	12	35	10	♈	46	26	♌	19	29		25		11		29	♎	26		8		4		0
11	4	13	15	20		36	20	♑	41	0	♉	4	♓	18		28		26		8		4		0
21	4	13	54	0	♉	23	20	♉	51	23	♈	14		26		26		26		8		4		29
1	5	14	33	10		7	4	♎	53	20		25		3	♓	25		25		8		3		29
11	5	15	13	19		48	24	♒	12	24		6	♈	10		24		25		8		3		29
21	5	15	53	29		27	24	♊	59	5	♉	17		18		23		24		8		3		29
1	6	16	36	10	♊	0	28	♏	15	21		0	♉	25		22		23		8		2		29
11	6	17	15	19		34	8	♈	12	10	♊	11		3	♈	22		23		9		2		0
21	6	17	54	29		7	14	♌	47	2	♋	23		10		22		22		9		2		0
1	7	18	34	8	♋	40	5	♑	26	23		5	♊	17		22		21		10		2		0
11	7	19	14	18		12	9	♉	51	10	♌	17		23		22		21		10		2		1
21	7	19	53	27		44	23	♍	21	24		29		0	♉	23		20		11		2		1
1	8	20	36	8	♌	14	23	♒	38	5	♍	12	♋	7		24		19		12		2		1
11	8	21	16	17		50	24	♊	54	7		24		12		26		19		12		2		1
21	8	21	55	27		26	16	♏	43	2		6	♌	18		27		19		13		2		2
1	9	22	38	8	♍	3	8	♈	39	25	♌	19		23		29		19		14		3		2
11	9	23	18	17		45	13	♌	35	0	♍	2	♍	27		1	♏	19		14		3		2
21	9	23	58	27		30	8	♑	14	15		14		0	♊	3		20		15		3		3
1	10	0	37	7	♎	19	10	♉	49	5	♎	27		2		5		20		15		3		3
11	10	0	37	17		18	20	♍	49	21		9	♎	3		7		21		16		4		3
21	10	1	56	27		5	13	♒	48	7	♏	22		2		9		22		16		4		3
1	11	2	39	8	♏	4	25	♊	49	24		5	♏	29	♉	11		23		16		5		4
11	11	3	18	18		5	14	♏	13	8	♐	18		26		13		24		16		5		4
21	11	3	58	28		10	29	♓	16	20		0	♐	22		16		25		16		5		4
1	12	4	37	8	♐	17	0	♌	43	26		13		19		18		26		16		6		4
11	12	5	17	18		26	22	♐	13	16		26		17		20		27		16		6		4
21	12	5	56	28		37	1	♉	10	9		8	♑	17		22		28		16		6		4

1959

1	1	6	40	9	♑	49	21	♍	11	18	♐	22	♑	17	♉	24	♏	29	♐	16	♌	7	♏	4
11	1	7	19	20		1	12	♒	35	0	♑	5	♒	19		26		1	♑	15		7		4
21	1	7	59	0	♒	12	15	♊	3	15		17		22		27		2		15		7		4
1	2	7	42	11		22	14	♏	3	2	♒	1	♓	26		29		3		14		7		3
11	2	9	21	21		30	29	♓	1	19		13		0	♊	0	♐	4		14		7		3
21	2	10	1	1	♓	37	1	♌	19	7	♓	26		5		1		5		14		7		3
1	3	10	32	9		39	24	♏	37	22		6	♈	9		1		5		13		7		3
11	3	11	12	19		40	7	♈	11	8	♈	18		14		2		6		13		7		3
21	3	11	51	29		38	9	♌	10	13		0	♉	19		2		6		13		6		2
1	4	12	34	10	♈	31	17	♑	19	6		13		25		2		7		13		6		2
11	4	13	14	20		22	21	♉	26	1		25		0	♋	1		7		12		6		2
21	4	13	53	0	♉	9	29	♍	12	4		7	♊	6		0		7		12		6		2
1	5	14	32	9		53	23	♒	38	13		19		12		29	♏	7		12		6		2
11	5	15	12	19		34	24	♊	1	27		0	♋	18		28		7		12		5		2
21	5	15	51	29		12	7	♏	16	14	♉	12		23		27		6		13		5		2
1	6	15	35	9	♊	46	9	♈	54	7	♊	24		0	♌	25		6		13		5		2
11	6	17	14	19		21	10	♌	19	29		4	♌	6		24		5		13		4		2
21	6	17	53	28		54	1	♑	14	18	♋	14		12		23		4		14		4		2
1	7	18	33	8	♋	26	12	♉	14	2	♌	24		18		23		3		14		4		2
11	7	19	12	17		58	16	♍	20	14		2	♍	24		22		3		15		4		2
21	7	19	52	27		30	8	♒	51	19		9		0	♍	22		2		15		4		3
1	8	20	35	8	♌	1	26	♊	15	16		14		7		22		1		16		4		3
11	8	21	15	17		36	8	♏	11	9		16		13		23		1		17		4		3
21	8	21	54	27		12	27	♓	25	9		14		20		24		1		17		4		4
1	9	22	38	7	♍	49	12	♌	3	22		8		27		25		0		18		5		4
11	9	23	17	17		31	1	♑	43	11	♍	3		3	♎	26		0		19		5		4
21	9	23	56	27		16	12	♉	29	0	♎	29	♌	10		28		1		19		5		5
1	10	0	36	7	♎	4	17	♍	2	17		1	♍	16		29		1		20		6		5
11	10	1	15	16		56	10	♒	3	3	♏	6		23		1	♐	1		20		6		5
21	10	1	55	26		51	14	♊	29	17		12		29		3		2		20		6		6
1	11	2	38	7	♏	49	8	♏	35	1	♐	22		7	♏	5		3		21		7		6
11	11	3	18	17		51	28	♓	53	9		1	♎	14		7		4		21		7		6
21	11	3	57	27		55	28	♋	57	6		12		21		10		5		21		7		6
1	12	4	36	8	♐	2	17	♐	9	24	♏	22		28		12		6		21		8		6
11	12	5	15	18		11	2	♉	32	27		4	♏	5	♐	14		7		21		8		6
21	12	5	55	28		22	2	♍	53	9	♐	15		12		16		8		21		8		6

1960		Sid. Time		☉		☽		☿	♀	♂	♃	♄	♅	♆	♇
1	1	6	39	9 ♑	34	10 ♒	16	25 ♐	28 ♏	20 ♐	19 ♐	9 ♑	21 ♌	9 ♏	6 ♍
11	1	7	18	19	46	16 ♊	54	10 ♑	10 ♐	28	21	11	20	9	6
21	1	7	57	29	57	22 ♎	3	26	22	5 ♑	23	12	20	9	6
1	2	8	41	11 ♒	8	29 ♓	39	15 ♒	6 ♑	13	25	13	19	9	5
11	2	9	20	21	16	1 ♌	28	3 ♓	18	21	27	14	19	9	5
21	2	10	0	1 ♓	22	14 ♐	40	19	0 ♒	28	29	15	18	9	5
1	3	10	35	10	25	20 ♈	20	26	11	5 ♒	0 ♑	16	18	9	5
11	3	11	14	20	26	22 ♌	27	20	24	13	1	17	18	9	4
21	3	11	54	0 ♈	23	9 ♑	55	13	6 ♓	21	2	17	17	9	4
1	4	12	37	11	16	5 ♊	16	15	20	29	3	18	17	8	4
11	4	13	17	21	7	9 ♎	59	24	2 ♈	7 ♓	3	18	17	8	4
21	4	13	56	0 ♉	53	2 ♓	17	7 ♈	14	14	4	18	17	8	4
1	5	14	36	10	37	7 ♋	14	23	27	22	3	18	17	8	4
11	5	15	15	20	18	17 ♏	0	12 ♉	9 ♉	29	3	18	17	7	4
21	5	15	54	29	56	8 ♈	34	4 ♊	21	7 ♈	2	18	17	7	4
1	6	16	38	10 ♊	30	21 ♌	33	27	5 ♊	16	1	17	18	7	4
11	6	17	17	20	4	10 ♑	57	13 ♋	17	23	29 ♐	17	18	7	4
21	6	17	57	29	37	25 ♉	6	24	29	0 ♉	29	16	18	7	4
1	7	18	36	9 ♋	9	25 ♍	21	0 ♌	11 ♋	8	27	16	19	6	4
11	7	19	16	18	41	19 ♒	29	28 ♋	24	15	26	15	19	6	4
21	7	19	55	28	13	27 ♊	57	22	6 ♌	22	25	14	20	6	5
1	8	20	38	8 ♌	44	14 ♏	46	21	20	29	24	13	21	6	5
11	8	21	18	18	19	10 ♈	0	0 ♌	2 ♍	6 ♊	24	13	21	7	5
21	8	21	57	27	56	12 ♌	23	18	14	12	24	12	22	7	5
1	9	22	41	8 ♍	33	7 ♑	45	10 ♍	28	19	24	12	22	7	6
11	9	23	20	18	15	26 ♉	39	28	10 ♎	24	24	12	23	7	6
21	9	23	59	28	0	28 ♍	24	14 ♎	22	0 ♋	25	12	24	7	7
1	10	0	39	7 ♎	49	16 ♒	42	29	5 ♏	5	26	12	24	8	7
11	10	1	18	17	40	28 ♊	51	12 ♏	17	9	28	12	25	8	7
21	10	1	58	27	36	3 ♏	59	22	29	13	29	13	25	8	7
1	11	2	41	8 ♏	34	8 ♈	17	23	13 ♐	16	1 ♑	13	25	9	8
11	11	3	21	18	36	12 ♌	20	11	24	18	3	14	26	9	8
21	11	4	0	28	41	26 ♐	16	9	7 ♑	19	5	15	26	10	8
1	12	4	39	8 ♐	48	13 ♉	48	20	19	18	7	16	26	10	8
11	12	5	19	18	57	14 ♍	27	5 ♐	1 ♒	16	9	17	26	10	8
21	12	5	58	29	8	5 ♒	7	20	13	12	11	18	26	11	8

1961

1	1	6	42	10 ♑	20	29 ♊	49	7 ♑	25 ♒	8 ♋	14 ♑	20 ♑	25 ♌	11 ♏	8 ♍
11	1	7	21	20	32	1 ♏	1	24	7 ♓	4	16	21	25	11	8
21	1	8	0	0 ♒	43	27 ♓	25	11 ♒	17	2	19	22	25	11	8
1	2	8	44	11	54	14 ♌	15	29	29	0	21	23	24	11	7
11	2	9	23	22	2	21 ♐	39	9 ♓	8 ♈	0	24	24	24	11	7
21	2	10	3	2 ♓	8	16 ♉	17	4	17	2	26	25	23	11	7
1	3	10	34	10	10	22 ♌	55	26 ♒	22	3	27	26	23	11	7
11	3	11	14	20	11	1 ♑	35	25	27	6	29	27	23	11	7
21	3	11	53	0 ♈	9	24 ♉	19	2 ♓	29	9	1 ♒	28	22	11	6
1	4	12	36	11	2	8 ♎	12	15	27	13	3	29	22	11	6
11	4	13	16	20	52	24 ♒	55	1 ♈	21	18	4	29	22	10	6
21	4	13	55	0 ♉	39	9 ♋	34	19	15	22	5	29	22	10	6
1	5	13	35	10	23	13 ♏	10	9 ♉	13	27	6	29	21	10	6
11	5	15	14	20	4	3 ♈	30	1 ♊	14	3 ♌	7	29	22	10	6
21	5	15	54	29	42	11 ♌	29	19	19	8	7	29	22	9	6
1	6	15	37	10 ♊	15	4 ♑	39	4 ♋	26	14	7	29	22	9	6
11	6	17	16	19	50	23 ♉	44	10	4 ♉	20	7	29	22	9	6
21	6	17	56	29	23	25 ♍	11	9	14	25	6	28	23	9	6
1	7	18	35	8 ♋	55	13 ♒	29	4	24	1 ♍	5	28	23	9	6
11	7	19	15	18	27	28 ♊	22	2	4 ♊	7	4	27	24	9	6
21	7	19	55	28	0	28 ♎	23	8	15	13	3	26	24	9	7
1	8	20	37	8 ♌	30	6 ♈	37	24	27	20	1	26	25	9	7
11	8	21	17	18	5	13 ♌	18	14 ♌	8 ♋	26	0	25	26	9	7
21	8	21	56	27	42	17 ♐	5	4 ♍	20	3 ♎	29 ♑	24	26	9	7
1	9	22	39	8 ♍	19	26 ♉	48	24	3 ♌	10	28	24	27	9	8
11	9	23	19	18	1	27 ♍	43	9 ♎	15	16	28	23	28	9	8
21	9	23	59	27	46	9 ♒	16	23	27	23	27	23	28	10	9
1	10	0	38	7 ♎	34	0 ♋	52	3 ♏	9 ♍	29	27	23	29	10	9
11	10	1	17	17	26	1 ♏	25	8	21	6	28	23	29	10	9
21	10	1	57	27	21	18 ♓	4	1	3 ♎	13	28	24	29	11	9
1	11	2	40	8 ♏	20	15 ♌	7	22 ♎	17	21	29	24	0 ♍	11	10
11	11	3	20	18	22	20 ♐	19	0 ♏	29	28	1 ♒	25	0	11	10
21	11	3	59	28	26	10 ♉	29	14	12 ♏	5 ♐	2	26	0	12	10
1	12	4	38	8 ♐	33	16 ♍	31	0 ♐	25	12	4	26	1	12	10
11	12	5	18	18	43	28 ♑	6	16	7 ♐	20	6	27	1	12	10
21	12	5	57	28	53	16 ♊	37	2 ♑	20	27	8	28	0	13	10

1962		Sid. Time		☉			☽			☿		♀		♂		♃		♄		♅		♆		♇
1	1	6	41	10	♑	5	0	♏	41	19	♑	4	♑	5	♑	10	♒	29	♑	0	♍	13	♏	10
11	1	7	20	27		17	21	♓	18	5	♒	16		13		13		1	♒	0		13		10
21	1	7	59	0	♒	28	3	♌	7	19		29		21		15		2		29	♌	13		10
1	2	7	43	11		39	17	♐	48	21		12	♒	29		18		3		29		13		10
11	2	9	22	21		47	13	♉	33	10		25		7	♒	20		4		29		13		9
21	2	10	2	1	♓	53	17	♍	30	8		8	♓	15		22		6		28		13		9
1	3	10	33	9		55	26	♐	16	13		18		21		24		6		28		13		9
11	3	11	13	19		56	22	♉	47	24		0	♈	29		27		8		28		13		9
21	3	11	52	29		54	26	♍	18	8	♓	13		7	♓	29		8		27		13		8
1	4	12	35	10	♈	47	17	♒	23	26		26		15		1	♓	9		27		13		8
11	4	13	15	20		38	11	♋	7	15	♈	9	♉	23		3		10		27		13		8
21	4	13	54	0	♉	25	11	♏	30	6	♉	21		1	♈	5		11		26		12		8
1	5	14	34	10		9	26	♓	12	26		3	♊	9		7		11		26		12		8
11	5	15	13	19		50	13	♌	58	11	♊	15		16		9		11		26		12		8
21	5	15	53	29		28	16	♐	11	19		27		24		10		11		27		12		8
1	6	16	35	10	♊	2	19	♉	34	19		11	♋	2	♉	11		11		27		11		8
11	6	17	15	19		36	27	♍	36	14		23		10		12		11		27		11		8
21	6	17	55	29		9	6	♒	31	12		4	♌	17		12		11		27		11		8
1	7	18	34	8	♋	41	26	♊	30	17		16		24		13		10		28		11		8
11	7	19	14	18		14	29	♎	27	29		28		1	♊	13		10		28		11		8
21	7	19	53	27		46	15	♓	9	18	♋	9	♍	8		12		9		29		11		8
1	8	20	37	8	♌	16	13	♌	47	11	♌	22		16		11		8		29		11		9
11	8	21	16	17		51	14	♐	59	0	♍	2	♎	22		10		7		0	♍	11		9
21	8	21	55	27		28	8	♉	46	17		13		29		9		7		1		11		9
1	9	22	39	8	♍	5	28	♍	31	3	♎	24		6	♋	8		6		1		11		10
11	9	23	18	17		47	3	♒	52	15		4	♏	12		6		5		2		11		10
21	9	23	58	27		32	29	♊	46	21		12		18		5		5		3		12		10
1	10	0	37	7	♎	20	1	♏	5	19		20		24		4		5		3		12		11
11	10	1	16	17		12	11	♓	22	8		25		29		3		5		4		12		11
21	10	1	56	27		6	4	♌	25	8		28		5	♌	3		5		4		13		11
1	11	2	39	8	♏	5	16	♐	48	23		26		10		3		5		4		13		12
11	11	3	19	18		7	5	♉	12	10	♏	21		14		3		6		5		13		12
21	11	3	58	28		11	19	♍	10	26		15		18		4		6		5		14		12
1	12	4	38	8	♐	18	22	♑	5	11	♐	12		21		5		7		5		14		12
11	12	5	17	18		28	13	♊	13	27		13		23		6		8		5		14		12
21	12	5	56	28		38	20	♎	35	13	♑	18		25		7		9		5		15		12

1963

1	1	6	40	9	♑	51	13	♓	9	29	♑	25	♏	24	♌	9	♓	10	♒	5	♍	15	♏	12
11	1	7	19	20		2	2	♌	44	7	♒	4	♐	23		11		11		5		15		12
21	1	7	59	0	♒	13	4	♐	58	29	♑	13		20		13		12		5		15		12
1	2	8	42	11		24	6	♉	34	21		25		16		15		14		4		16		12
11	2	9	21	21		32	18	♍	43	26		6	♑	12		18		15		4		16		11
21	2	10	1	1	♓	38	21	♑	18	7	♒	17		9		20		16		3		16		11
1	3	10	32	9		41	17	♉	10	17		26		7		22		17		3		16		11
11	3	11	12	19		42	27	♍	12	3	♓	8	♒	6		24		18		3		16		11
21	3	11	51	29		39	29	♑	15	20		19		5		27		19		2		15		11
1	4	12	35	10	♈	33	8	♋	53	12	♈	2	♓	7		29		20		2		15		10
11	4	13	14	20		24	11	♏	46	2	♉	14		9		2	♈	21		2		15		10
21	4	13	53	0	♉	11	19	♓	49	19		26		12		4		22		1		15		10
1	5	14	33	9		55	14	♌	16	29		8	♈	15		6		22		1		14		10
11	5	15	12	19		36	14	♐	40	0	♊	20		19		8		23		1		14		10
21	5	15	52	29		14	28	♈	31	25	♉	2	♉	24		10		23		1		14		10
1	6	16	35	9	♊	48	29	♍	56	22		16		29		12		23		1		14		10
11	6	17	15	19		22	1	♒	24	26		28		4	♍	14		23		2		13		10
21	6	17	54	28		55	22	♊	15	7	♊	10	♊	9		16		23		2		13		10
1	7	18	33	8	♋	28	2	♏	5	24		22		15		17		22		2		13		10
11	7	19	13	18		0	7	♓	59	14	♋	4	♋	20		18		22		3		13		10
21	7	19	52	27		32	29	♋	17	6	♌	17		26		19		21		3		13		10
1	8	20	35	8	♌	3	16	♐	2	26		0	♌	3	♎	19		21		4		13		11
11	8	21	15	17		37	0	♉	49	12	♍	12		9		19		20		4		13		11
21	8	21	54	27		14	17	♍	15	24		25		15		19		19		5		13		11
1	9	22	37	7	♍	51	1	♒	51	3	♎	8	♍	22		19		18		6		13		12
11	9	23	17	17		32	24	♊	11	4		21		29		18		18		6		13		12
21	9	23	57	27		18	2	♏	24	26	♍	3	♎	6	♏	17		17		7		14		12
1	10	0	36	7	♎	6	7	♓	10	21		16		13		15		17		8		14		13
11	10	1	15	16		57	1	♌	43	0	♎	28		20		14		17		8		14		13
21	10	1	55	26		52	4	♐	39	17		11	♏	27		13		16		9		15		13
1	11	2	38	7	♏	50	29	♈	33	5	♏	24		5	♐	11		16		9		15		14
11	11	3	18	17		52	19	♍	43	21		7	♐	12		11		17		10		15		14
21	11	3	57	27		57	19	♑	21	7	♐	19		19		10		17		10		16		14
1	12	4	37	8	♐	4	8	♊	7	22		2	♑	27		10		18		10		16		14
11	12	5	16	18		13	23	♎	1	7	♑	14		4	♑	10		19		10		17		14
21	12	5	55	28		23	23	♒	51	18		27		12		10		19		10		17		14

1964

		Sid. Time		☉	☽	☿	♀	♂	♃	♄	♅	♆	♇
1	1	6	39	9 ♑ 35	0 ♌ 31	18 ♑	10 ♒	20 ♑	11 ♈	20 ♒	10 ♍	17 ♏	14 ♍
11	1	7	18	19 47	7 ♐ 0	6	22	28	12	21	10	17	14
21	1	7	58	29 58	14 ♈ 8	6	4 ♓	6 ♒	13	23	10	17	14
1	2	8	41	11 ♒ 9	19 ♍ 29	17	18	15	15	24	9	18	14
11	2	9	21	21 17	21 ♑ 18	0 ♒	0 ♈	23	17	25	9	18	13
21	2	10	0	1 ♓ 23	7 ♊ 11	15	12	1 ♓	18	26	8	18	13
1	3	10	35	10 26	10 ♎ 17	0 ♓	22	8	20	27	8	18	13
11	3	11	15	22 27	11 ♒ 52	18	4 ♉	16	23	29	7	18	13
21	3	11	54	0 ♈ 24	2 ♋ 13	8 ♈	15	23	25	29	7	18	12
1	4	12	38	11 18	25 ♏ 12	28	27	2 ♈	27	1 ♓	7	17	12
11	4	13	17	21 8	0 ♈ 31	10 ♉	7 ♊	10	29	2	6	17	12
21	4	13	56	0 ♉ 35	23 ♌ 47	11	16	17	2 ♉	3	6	17	12
1	5	14	35	10 39	27 ♐ 12	5	24	25	4	3	6	17	12
11	5	15	15	20 19	7 ♉ 59	1	1 ♋	3 ♉	7	4	6	16	12
21	5	15	55	29 58	29 ♍ 38	5	6	10	9	5	6	16	12
1	6	16	38	10 ♊ 31	11 ♒ 51	17	7	18	12	5	6	16	12
11	6	17	17	20 6	1 ♋ 43	2 ♊	4	25	14	5	6	16	12
21	6	17	57	29 39	15 ♏ 37	22	28 ♊	3 ♊	16	5	7	15	12
1	7	18	36	9 ♋ 11	16 ♓ 28	14 ♋	23	10	18	5	7	15	12
11	7	19	16	18 43	9 ♌ 48	4 ♌	20	17	20	4	7	15	12
21	7	19	55	28 15	17 ♐ 58	21	22	23	22	4	8	15	12
1	8	20	38	8 ♌ 46	6 ♉ 43	6 ♍	27	1 ♋	23	3	8	15	13
11	8	21	18	18 21	0 ♎ 5	15	4 ♋	7	24	3	9	15	13
21	8	21	57	27 58	2 ♒ 13	18	12	14	25	2	10	15	13
1	9	22	41	8 ♍ 35	29 ♊ 52	11	23	21	26	1	10	15	14
11	9	23	20	18 17	16 ♏ 27	4	3 ♌	27	26	0	11	16	14
21	9	0	0	28 2	18 ♓ 55	11	14	4 ♌	26	29 ♒	12	16	14
1	10	0	39	7 ♎ 50	8 ♌ 48	26	25	10	26	29	12	16	15
11	10	1	18	17 42	18 ♐ 25	14 ♎	6 ♍	15	25	29	13	16	15
21	10	1	58	27 37	24 ♈ 59	1 ♏	18	21	24	28	13	17	15
1	11	2	41	8 ♏ 36	29 ♍ 47	19	1 ♎	27	23	28	14	17	16
11	11	3	21	18 38	1 ♒ 55	4 ♐	13	3 ♍	21	28	14	18	16
21	11	4	0	28 43	17 ♊ 29	18	25	8	20	29	14	18	16
1	12	4	40	8 ♐ 50	4 ♏ 54	0 ♑	7 ♏	12	19	29	15	18	16
11	12	5	19	18 59	4 ♓ 36	5	20	17	18	29	15	19	16
21	12	5	58	29 10	25 ♋ 55	24 ♐	2 ♐	20	17	0 ♓	15	19	16

1965

		Sid. Time		☉	☽	☿	♀	♂	♃	♄	♅	♆	♇
1	1	6	42	10 ♑ 42	20 ♐ 7	19 ♐	16 ♐	24 ♍	16 ♉	1 ♓	15 ♍	19 ♏	16 ♍
11	1	7	21	20 33	22 ♈ 6	27	28	26	16	2	15	20	16
21	1	8	1	0 ♒ 45	18 ♍ 7	10 ♑	11 ♑	28	16	3	14	20	16
1	2	8	44	11 55	4 ♒ 20	26	24	28	17	5	14	20	16
11	2	9	23	22 3	13 ♊ 6	12 ♒	7 ♒	27	18	6	14	20	16
21	2	10	3	2 ♓ 9	6 ♏ 37	29	20	25	19	7	13	20	15
1	3	10	34	10 12	12 ♒ 53	14 ♓	29	22	20	8	13	20	15
11	3	11	14	20 12	23 ♊ 32	4 ♈	12	18	22	9	12	20	15
21	3	11	53	0 ♈ 10	14 ♏ 25	19	24	14	23	10	12	20	15
1	4	12	37	11 3	28 ♓ 45	23	8 ♈	11	25	12	12	20	14
11	4	13	16	20 54	16 ♌ 53	16	21	9	27	13	11	19	14
21	4	13	55	0 ♉ 40	29 ♐ 18	12	3 ♉	9	29	13	11	19	14
1	5	14	35	10 24	3 ♉ 59	15	15	9	2 ♊	15	11	19	14
11	5	15	14	20 5	25 ♍ 26	24	28	11	4	15	11	19	14
21	5	15	54	29 44	1 ♒ 4	8 ♉	10 ♊	14	6	15	11	18	14
1	6	16	37	10 ♊ 17	25 ♊ 38	28	23	18	9	17	11	18	14
11	6	17	16	19 52	14 ♏ 50	19 ♊	6 ♋	22	11	17	11	18	14
21	6	17	56	29 24	15 ♓ 21	10 ♋	18	26	14	17	11	18	14
1	7	18	35	8 ♋ 46	4 ♌ 25	29	0 ♌	1 ♎	16	17	11	17	14
11	7	19	15	18 29	18 ♐ 47	14 ♌	12	6	18	17	12	17	14
21	7	19	54	28 1	19 ♈ 10	25	24	12	20	17	12	17	14
1	8	20	38	8 ♌ 32	27 ♍ 41	0 ♍	8 ♍	18	22	16	13	17	15
11	8	21	17	18 7	3 ♒ 23	27 ♌	20	24	24	16	13	17	15
21	8	21	56	27 43	8 ♊ 9	19	2 ♎	0 ♏	26	15	14	17	15
1	9	22	40	8 ♍ 21	17 ♏ 13	20	15	7	28	14	15	18	16
11	9	23	19	18 3	18 ♓ 16	4 ♍	27	14	29	13	15	18	16
21	9	23	59	27 48	0 ♌ 52	22	8 ♏	21	0 ♋	13	16	18	17
1	10	0	38	7 ♎ 36	20 ♐ 36	10 ♎	20	28	1	12	17	18	17
11	10	1	18	17 28	22 ♈ 18	27	1 ♐	5 ♐	1	11	17	19	17
21	10	1	57	27 23	10 ♍ 4	12 ♏	13	12	1	11	18	19	18
1	11	2	40	8 ♏ 22	4 ♒ 32	28	25	20	1	11	18	19	18
11	11	3	20	18 24	11 ♊ 36	11 ♐	5 ♑	27	1	11	19	20	18
21	11	3	59	28 28	1 ♏ 54	19	15	5 ♑	29 ♊	11	19	20	18
1	12	4	38	8 ♐ 35	6 ♓ 7	14	25	13	28	11	19	20	18
11	12	5	18	18 44	19 ♋ 31	3	3 ♒	20	27	11	20	21	18
21	12	5	57	28 55	7 ♐ 24	7	9	28	26	12	20	21	19

1966

		Sid. Time		☉			☽			☿		♀		♂		♃		♄		♅		♆		♇	
1	1	6	41	10	♑	7	20	♈	39	20	♐	13	♒	7	♒	24	♊	12	♓	20	♍	21	♏	18	♍
11	1	7	20	20		19	13	♍	13	5	♑	13		15		23		13		19		22		18	
21	1	8	0	0	♒	29	23	♑	18	20		9		23		22		14		19		22		18	
1	2	8	43	11		41	8	♊	1	8	♒	3		1	♓	22		15		19		22		18	
11	2	9	23	21		48	5	♏	0	26		28	♑	9		21		16		19		22		18	
21	2	10	2	1	♓	54	7	♓	53	14	♓	29		17		21		18		18		22		18	
1	3	10	33	9		57	17	♊	1	27		1	♒	23		21		19		18		22		17	
11	3	11	12	19		58	13	♏	33	6	♈	7		1	♈	22		20		17		22		17	
21	3	11	52	29		55	16	♓	43	1		15		9		23		21		17		22		17	
1	4	12	36	10	♈	49	8	♌	52	23	♓	25		17		24		22		17		22		17	
11	4	13	15	20		39	1	♑	2	25		4	♓	25		26		24		16		22		16	
21	4	13	54	0	♉	26	2	♉	5	3	♈	15		2	♉	27		25		16		21		16	
1	5	14	34	10		10	18	♍	11	16		25		10		29		26		16		21		16	
11	5	15	13	19		51	3	♒	37	2	♉	6	♈	17		1	♋	27		16		21		16	
21	5	15	53	29		30	6	♊	50	22		18		24		3		28		15		21		16	
1	6	16	36	10	♊	4	10	♏	52	16	♊	0	♉	2	♊	5		28		15		20		16	
11	6	17	15	19		38	17	♓	22	6	♋	12		9		8		29		16		20		16	
21	6	17	55	29		11	27	♋	54	23		24		16		10		29		16		20		16	
1	7	18	44	8	♋	43	17	♐	12	4	♌	5	♊	23		12		29		16		20		16	
11	7	19	14	18		15	19	♈	19	11		17		0	♋	14		29		16		20		16	
21	7	19	53	27		48	6	♍	58	10		29		7		17		29		17		19		17	
1	8	20	37	8	♌	18	4	♒	3	3		12		14		19		29		17		19		17	
11	8	21	16	17		53	5	♊	2	0		25		21		21		29		18		19		17	
21	8	21	55	27		30	0	♏	21	10		7	♌	27		23		28		19		19		17	
1	9	22	39	8	♍	7	18	♓	55	29		20		4	♌	25		28		19		20		18	
11	9	23	18	17		49	24	♋	36	18	♍	2	♍	10		27		27		20		20		18	
21	9	23	58	27		34	20	♐	23	6	♎	15		17		29		26		20		20		19	
1	10	0	37	7	♎	22	21	♈	36	23		27		23		0	♌	25		21		20		19	
11	10	1	16	17		13	2	♍	48	7	♏	10	♎	29		2		25		22		21		19	
21	10	1	56	27		8	24	♑	30	21		22		5	♍	3		24		22		21		20	
1	11	2	39	8	♏	7	7	♊	28	1	♐	6	♏	11		4		24		23		21		20	
11	11	3	19	18		9	26	♎	24	2		19		17		4		23		23		22		20	
21	11	3	58	28		13	9	♓	0	20	♏	1	♐	23		4		23		24		22		20	
1	12	4	38	8	♐	20	13	♋	30	18		14		28		4		23		24		23		21	
11	12	5	17	18		29	3	♐	57	29		26		4	♎	4		23		24		23		21	
21	12	5	56	28		40	10	♈	31	13	♐	9	♑	9		3		23		24		23		21	

1967

1	1	6	40	9	♑	52	5	♍	38	0	♑	23	♑	14	♎	2	♌	24	♓	24	♍	24	♏	21	
11	1	7	19	20		4	23	♑	0	16		5	♒	19		1		25		24		24		21	
21	1	7	59	0	♒	15	24	♉	28	2	♒	18		23		29	♋	25		24		24		20	
1	2	8	42	11		26	28	♎	59	21		1	♓	27		28		27		24		24		20	
11	2	9	22	21		34	8	♓	57	8	♓	14		29		27		28		24		24		20	
21	2	10	1	1	♓	40	11	♋	19	18		26		2	♏	26		29		23		24		20	
1	3	10	32	9		42	8	♏	57	16		6	♈	3		25		29		23		24		20	
11	3	11	12	19		43	17	♓	41	7		19		3		25		1	♈	22		24		20	
21	3	11	51	29		41	19	♋	41	5		1	♉	2		24		2		22		24		19	
1	4	12	35	10	♈	34	29	♐	54	13		14		29	♎	25		3		22		24		19	
11	4	13	14	20		25	2	♉	0	25		26		26		25		5		21		24		19	
21	4	13	53	0	♉	12	11	♍	2	10	♈	8	♊	23		26		6		21		24		18	
1	5	14	33	9		56	4	♒	49	28		19		19		27		7		21		23		18	
11	5	15	12	19		37	5	♊	1	19	♉	1	♋	17		28		8		20		23		18	
21	5	15	52	29		16	19	♎	50	10	♊	12		15		29		9		20		23		18	
1	6	16	35	9	♊	50	20	♓	2	0	♋	24		15		1	♌	10		20		23		18	
11	6	17	15	19		24	22	♋	38	13		4	♌	16		3		11		20		22		18	
21	6	17	54	28		57	12	♐	58	21		14		19		5		11		20		22		18	
1	7	18	33	8	♋	29	21	♈	46	21		23		22		7		12		21		22		18	
11	7	19	13	18		1	29	♌	56	16		2	♍	26		9		12		21		22		18	
21	7	19	52	27		34	19	♑	57	12		8		0	♏	11		12		21		22		19	
1	8	20	35	8	♌	4	5	♊	36	19		13		6		14		12		22		22		19	
11	8	21	15	17		39	23	♎	1	4	♌	14		12		16		12		22		22		19	
21	8	21	55	27		16	7	♓	40	23		11		17		18		12		23		22		20	
1	9	22	38	7	♍	53	22	♋	1	15	♍	4		24		21		11		24		22		20	
11	9	23	17	17		35	15	♐	55	2	♎	29	♌	1	♐	23		11		24		22		20	
21	9	23	57	27		20	22	♈	27	18		28		7		25		10		25		22		21	
1	10	0	36	7	♎	8	27	♌	49	1	♏	0	♍	14		27		9		26		22		21	
11	10	1	15	16		59	23	♑	2	12		5		21		29		8		26		23		21	
21	10	1	55	26		54	24	♉	45	17		12		28		0	♍	8		27		23		22	
1	11	2	38	7	♏	52	20	♎	15	9		22		7	♑	2		7		27		23		22	
11	11	3	18	7		55	10	♓	26	1		1	♎	14		3		6		28		24		22	
21	11	3	57	27		59	10	♋	11	9		12		22		4		6		28		24		23	
1	12	4	37	8	♐	5	28	♏	38	23		23		29		4		6		29		25		23	
11	12	4	16	18		15	13	♈	2	8	♐	4	♏	7	♒	6		6		29		25		23	
21	12	5	56	28		25	15	♌	30	24		16		15		6		6		29		25		23	

1968		Sid. Time		☉			☽			☿		♀		♂		♃		♄		♅		♆		♇	
1	1	6	39	9	♑	38	20	♑	57	11	♑	29	♏	23	♒	6	♍	6	♈	29	♍	26	♏	23	♍
11	1	7	18	19		49	26	♉	34	28		11	♐	1	♓	5		7		29		26		23	
21	1	7	58	0	♒	0	6	♎	28	14	♒	23		9		4		7		29		26		23	
1	2	8	41	11		11	9	♓	38	29		6	♑	18		3		8		29		26		22	
11	2	9	20	21		20	11	♋	13	1	♓	19		25		2		9		29		26		22	
21	2	10	0	1	♓	25	29	♏	32	20	♒	1	♒	3	♈	1		10		28		27		22	
1	3	10	35	10		29	0	♈	24	17		12		10		29	♌	11		28		27		22	
11	3	11	15	20		29	1	♌	56	23		24		17		28		12		27		26		22	
21	3	11	54	0	♈	26	24	♐	25	4	♓	7	♓	25		27		13		27		26		21	
1	4	12	38	11		20	14	♉	54	20		20		3	♉	26		15		27		26		21	
11	4	13	17	21		10	20	♍	58	7	♈	3	♈	10		26		16		26		26		21	
21	4	13	56	0	♉	57	15	♒	35	27		15		17		26		17		26		26		21	
1	5	14	36	10		41	17	♊	10	18	♉	27		25		26		19		26		26		21	
11	5	15	15	20		22	28	♎	26	8	♊	9	♉	2	♊	26		20		25		25		20	
21	5	15	55	0	♊	0	20	♓	39	22		22		9		27		21		25		25		20	
1	6	16	38	10		33	2	♌	38	1	♋	5	♊	16		28		22		25		25		20	
11	6	17	18	20		7	22	♐	22	1		18		23		29		23		25		24		20	
21	6	17	57	29		40	5	♉	43	26	♊	0	♋	0	♋	1	♍	24		25		24		20	
1	7	18	36	9	♋	13	7	♍	52	23		12		7		2		24		25		24		20	
11	7	19	16	18		55	0	♒	34	28		24		13		4		25		26		24		21	
21	7	19	55	28		17	7	♊	48	11	♋	7	♌	20		6		25		26		24		21	
1	8	20	39	8	♌	48	28	♎	24	2	♌	20		27		8		26		27		24		21	
11	8	21	18	18		23	20	♓	18	22		3	♍	3	♌	10		26		27		24		22	
21	8	21	58	27		59	22	♋	20	11	♍	15		10		12		25		28		24		22	
1	9	22	41	8	♍	37	22	♐	5	29		28		17		15		25		28		24		22	
11	9	23	20	18		18	6	♉	3	13	♎	11	♎	23		17		25		29		24		22	
21	9	0	0	28		4	9	♍	21	24		23		29		19		24		29		24		23	
1	10	0	39	7	♎	52	1	♒	3	1	♏	5	♏	6	♍	21		23		0	♎	25		23	
11	10	1	19	17		45	8	♊	4	28	♎	18		12		23		22		1		25		24	
21	10	1	58	27		39	15	♎	21	17		0	♐	18		25		21		1		25		24	
1	11	2	42	8	♏	38	21	♓	6	20		13		25		27		21		2		26		24	
11	11	3	21	18		40	22	♋	6	4	♏	25		1	♎	29		20		2		26		24	
21	11	4	0	28		45	8	♐	13	20		7	♑	7		1	♎	20		3		26		25	
1	12	4	40	8	♐	52	25	♈	29	5	♐	19		13		2		19		3		27		25	
11	12	5	19	19		1	25	♌	21	21		1	♒	19		4		19		4		27		25	
21	12	5	59	29		12	16	♑	51	7	♑	13		25		5		19		4		27		25	

1969																									
1	1	6	42	10	♑	24	10	♊	16	25	♑	26	♒	1	♏	5	♎	19	♈	4	♎	28	♏	25	♍
11	1	7	21	20		36	13	♎	22	9	♒	7	♓	7		6		19		4		28		25	
21	1	8	1	0	♒	47	8	♓	38	16		18		12		6		20		4		28		25	
1	2	8	44	11		57	24	♋	42	6		29		18		6		20		4		28		25	
11	2	9	24	22		5	5	♐	5	0		8	♈	23		5		21		4		29		25	
21	2	10	3	2	♓	11	26	♈	18	6		16		28		5		22		3		29		24	
1	3	10	34	10		13	2	♌	57	14		21		2	♐	4		23		3		29		24	
11	3	11	14	20		14	15	♐	59	28		26		6		3		24		2		29		24	
21	3	11	53	0	♈	12	4	♉	4	13	♓	27		10		1		25		2		29		24	
1	4	12	37	11		5	18	♍	54	3	♈	23		13		29	♍	26		2		28		23	
11	4	13	16	20		56	9	♒	28	23		17		15		29		28		1		28		23	
21	4	13	56	0	♉	43	18	♊	55	14	♉	12		16		28		29		1		28		23	
1	5	14	35	10		27	24	♎	12	0	♊	10		17		27		0	♉	0		28		23	
11	5	15	14	20		7	17	♓	19	10		13		16		26		1		0		28		23	
21	5	15	54	29		46	21	♋	1	12		18		13		26		3		0		27		22	
1	6	16	37	10	♊	20	16	♐	39	6		26		10		26		4		29	♍	27		22	
11	6	17	17	19		54	5	♉	38	3		4	♉	7		27		5		29		27		22	
21	6	17	56	29		27	5	♍	37	7		14		4		27		6		29		27		23	
1	7	18	35	8	♋	59	25	♑	41	18		24		2		28		7		0	♎	26		23	
11	7	19	15	18		31	9	♊	15	5	♋	4	♊	2		29		7		0		26		23	
21	7	19	55	28		4	9	♎	51	26		15		3		1	♎	8		1		26		23	
1	8	20	38	8	♌	34	18	♓	23	19	♌	27		5		2		9		1		26		23	
11	8	21	17	18		9	23	♋	34	6	♍	9	♋	9		4		9		2		26		24	
21	8	21	56	27		46	29	♏	53	22		20		13		6		9		2		26		24	
1	9	22	40	8	♍	22	7	♉	10	5	♎	3	♌	18		8		9		3		26		24	
11	9	23	19	18		5	8	♍	33	13		15		24		10		9		3		26		25	
21	9	23	59	27		50	23	♑	5	14		27		29		12		8		4		26		25	
1	10	0	38	7	♎	38	10	♊	20	4		10	♍	6	♑	14		8		5		27		25	
11	10	1	18	17		30	12	♎	35	0		22		13		17		7		5		27		26	
21	10	1	57	27		25	2	♓	5	11		4	♎	20		19		6		6		27		26	
1	11	1	40	8	♏	24	24	♋	17	29		18		27		21		5		6		28		26	
11	11	3	20	18		26	2	♐	42	15		0	♏	4	♒	23		4		7		28		27	
21	11	3	59	28		30	22	♈	59	1	♐	13		12		25		4		8		28		27	
1	12	4	39	8	♐	37	25	♌	55	17		25		19		27		3		8		29		27	
11	12	5	18	18		47	11	♑	3	2	♑	8	♐	27		29		3		8		29		27	
21	12	5	57	28		57	28	♉	12	17		21		4	♓	1	♏	2		9		29		27	

1970		Sid. Time		☉			☽			☿		♀		♂		♃		♄		♅		♆		♇
1	1	6	41	10	♑	9	10	♎	42	29	♑	4	♑	12	♓	2	♏	2	♉	9	♎	29	♏	27
11	1	7	20	20		21	4	♓	32	26		17		20		4		2		9		0	♐	27
21	1	8	0	0	♒	32	13	♋	51	15		29		27		5		2		9		0		27
1	2	8	44	11		43	28	♏	57	17		13		5		5		3		9		1		27
11	2	9	22	21		51	25	♈	30	27		26		13		6		3		8		1		27
21	2	10	2	1	♓	57	28	♌	10	10	♒	8	♓	20		6		4		8		1		27
1	3	10	34	9		59	8	♐	39	22		18		26		6		5		8		1		27
11	3	11	13	20		0	3	♉	36	9	♓	1	♈	2	♉	5		6		7		1		26
21	3	11	52	29		58	6	♍	44	27		13		10		5		7		7		1		26
1	4	12	36	10	♈	51	1	♒	7	19		27		18		4		8		7		1		26
11	4	13	15	20		42	20	♊	54	8	♉	9	♉	25		2		9		6		0		25
21	4	13	55	0	♉	29	22	♎	18	20		22		2	♊	1		11		6		0		25
1	5	14	34	10		13	10	♓	15	22		4	♊	8		29	♎	12		5		0		25
11	5	15	13	19		54	23	♋	20	17		16		15		29		13		5		29	♏	25
21	5	15	53	29		32	27	♏	35	13		28		22		28		15		5		29		25
1	6	16	36	10	♊	6	2	♉	13	17		11	♋	29		27		16		5		29		25
11	6	17	16	19		40	6	♍	42	27		23		6	♋	26		17		5		29		24
21	6	17	55	29		13	19	♑	32	12	♊	5	♌	12		26		18		5		29		25
1	7	18	35	8	♋	45	8	♊	20	2	♋	17		19		26		19		5		28		25
11	7	19	14	18		17	9	♎	1	23		28		25		27		20		5		28		25
21	7	19	54	27		50	28	♒	23	13	♌	10	♍	2	♌	27		21		5		28		25
1	8	20	37	8	♌	20	24	♋	39	1	♍	22		9		28		22		6		28		25
11	8	21	16	17		55	25	♏	32	15		3	♎	15		29		22		6		28		26
21	8	21	56	27		32	21	♈	19	24		13		22		1	♏	22		7		28		26
1	9	22	38	8	♍	9	9	♍	3	28		24		29		2		23		7		28		26
11	9	23	18	17		51	15	♑	51	21		4	♏	5	♍	4		23		8		28		27
21	9	23	58	27		36	11	♊	2	14		12		11		6		22		8		29		27
1	10	0	37	7	♎	24	11	♎	48	20		19		18		8		22		9		29		28
11	10	1	17	17		16	24	♒	14	6	♎	23		24		10		21		10		29		28
21	10	1	56	27		11	14	♋	40	23		25		0	♎	12		21		10		29		28
1	11	2	39	8	♏	9	28	♏	42	11	♏	23		7		15		20		11		29		29
11	11	3	19	18		11	17	♈	31	27		17		14		17		19		12		0	♐	29
21	11	3	58	28		16	28	♌	37	12	♐	12		20		19		18		12		1		29
1	12	4	38	8	♐	23	5	♑	8	27		10		26		21		18		12		1		29
11	12	5	17	18		32	25	♉	8	9	♑	12		3	♏	23		17		13		1		29
21	12	5	57	28		42	0	♎	0	14		17		9		25		16		13		2		29

1971

1	1	6	40	9	♑	55	27	♒	31	2	♑	25	♏	16	♏	28	♏	16	♉	13	♎	2	♐	29
11	1	7	19	20		6	13	♋	42	28	♐	4	♐	22		29		16		14		2		29
21	1	7	59	0	♒	17	14	♏	25	6	♑	13		29		1	♐	16		14		3		29
1	2	8	42	11		28	20	♈	42	20		25		6		3		16		13		3		29
11	2	9	22	21		37	29	♌	2	5	♒	6	♑	12		4		16		13		3		29
21	2	10	1	1	♓	42	1	♑	46	21		17		18		5		17		13		3		29
1	3	10	33	9		45	0	♉	3	5	♓	26		23		6		17		13		3		29
11	3	11	12	19		46	7	♍	48	24		8	♒	29		6		18		12		3		29
21	3	11	51	29		44	10	♑	46	13	♈	20		5	♑	6		19		12		3		28
1	4	12	35	10	♈	37	20	♊	45	29		3	♓	11		6		20		12		3		28
11	4	13	14	20		27	22	♎	14	4	♉	15		17		6		21		11		3		28
21	4	13	54	0	♉	15	2	♓	20	29	♈	27		23		5		23		11		3		28
1	5	14	33	9		59	25	♋	1	23		9	♈	28		4		24		10		2		27
11	5	15	13	19		40	25	♏	44	25		21		4	♒	3		25		10		2		27
21	5	15	52	29		19	11	♈	24	4	♉	3	♉	9		2		27		10		2		27
1	6	16	35	9	♊	52	9	♍	33	19		16		13		0		28		10		1		27
11	6	17	14	19		26	14	♑	6	7	♊	28		17		29	♏	29		9		1		27
21	6	17	54	29		0	4	♊	27	28		11	♊	19		28		0	♊	9		1		27
1	7	18	34	8	♋	32	11	♎	11	20	♋	23		21		27		1		9		1		27
11	7	19	13	18		4	21	♒	32	8	♌	5	♋	22		27		3		10		1		27
21	7	19	52	27		36	11	♋	2	23		17		21		27		4		10		0		27
1	8	20	36	8	♌	7	25	♏	25	5	♍	1	♌	19		27		4		10		0		28
11	8	21	15	17		41	14	♈	59	10		13		17		27		5		11		0		28
21	8	21	55	27		18	27	♌	49	8		25		14		28		6		11		0		28
1	9	22	38	7	♍	55	12	♑	12	29	♌	9		12		29		6		12		0		29
11	9	23	17	17		37	7	♊	53	29		21		12		29		6		12		1		29
21	9	23	57	27		22	12	♎	27	13	♍	4	♎	13		1	♐	7		13		1		29
1	10	0	36	7	♎	10	18	♒	13	1	♎	16		15		3		6		14		1		29
11	10	1	16	17		1	14	♋	17	19		29		18		5		6		14		1		0
21	10	1	55	26		56	15	♏	11	5	♏	11	♏	22		7		6		15		2		1
1	11	2	39	7	♏	54	11	♈	1	22		25		27		9		5		15		2		1
11	11	3	18	17		56	0	♍	38	7	♐	7	♐	2	♓	11		4		16		2		1
21	11	3	57	28		1	1	♑	15	20		20		8		13		3		17		3		1
1	12	4	37	8	♐	8	19	♉	49	28		2	♑	14		15		3		17		3		2
11	12	5	16	18		16	2	♎	49	23		15		20		18		2		17		3		2
21	12	5	56	28		27	6	♒	53	12		27		26		20		1		18		4		2

1972		Sid. Time		☉			☽			☿		♀		♂		♃		♄		♅		♆		♇	
1	1	6	40	9	♑	40	11	♋	38	17	♐	11	♒	3	♈	22	♐	0	♊	18	♎	4	♐	2	♎
11	1	7	18	19		52	16	♏	3	29		23		10		25		29	♉	18		4		2	
21	1	7	58	0	♒	3	28	♓	28	13	♑	5	♓	16		27		29		18		5		2	
1	2	8	42	11		13	29	♌	31	0	♒	19		24		29		29		18		5		2	
11	2	9	21	21		21	1	♑	9	17		1	♈	0	♉	1	♑	29		18		5		2	
21	2	10	0	1	♓	28	22	♉	1	4	♓	13		7		3		29		18		5		1	
1	3	10	36	10		31	20	♍	20	21		23		13		4		0	♊	18		5		1	
11	3	11	15	20		31	21	♑	53	8	♈	4	♉	19		5		1		17		5		1	
21	3	11	54	0	♈	28	16	♊	30	16		15		26		6		2		17		5		1	
1	4	12	38	11		22	5	♏	3	10		27		3		7		3		16		5		0	
11	4	13	17	21		12	11	♓	17	4		7	♊	10		8		4		16		5		0	
21	4	13	57	0	♉	59	6	♌	38	5		16		16		8		5		16		5		29	♍
1	5	14	36	10		43	7	♐	42	14		24		23		8		6		15		4		29	
11	5	15	16	20		24	19	♈	25	27		0	♋	29		8		7		15		4		29	
21	5	15	55	0	♊	2	10	♍	56	14	♉	4		5	♋	7		9		15		4		29	
1	6	15	38	10		36	23	♑	34	6	♊	4		12		6		10		14		4		29	
11	6	17	18	20		10	13	♊	29	28		0		19		5		11		14		3		29	
21	6	17	57	29		43	25	♎	41	17	♋	24	♊	25		4		13		14		3		29	
1	7	18	37	9	♋	15	29	♒	17	3	♌	19		1	♌	3		14		14		3		29	
11	7	19	16	18		47	21	♋	11	15		18		8		1		15		14		3		29	
21	7	19	55	28		19	27	♏	38	22		21		14		0		16		15		3		29	
1	8	20	39	8	♌	50	21	♈	10	21		26		21		29	♐	17		15		3		0	♎
11	8	21	18	18		25	10	♍	8	13		4	♋	27		29		18		15		3		0	
21	8	21	58	28		2	12	♑	4	11		12		4	♍	29		19		16		3		1	
1	9	22	41	8	♍	39	14	♊	46	22		23		11		29		20		16		3		1	
11	9	23	21	18		21	25	♎	51	10	♍	3	♌	17		29		20		17		3		1	
21	9	0	0	28		6	29	♒	20	29		14		24		29		20		17		3		2	
1	10	0	39	7	♎	55	23	♋	4	16	♎	25		0	♎	0	♑	21		18		3		2	
11	10	1	19	17		46	28	♏	6	2	♏	6	♍	6		2		21		19		3		2	
21	10	1	59	27		42	5	♈	53	17		18		13		3		20		19		4		3	
1	11	2	42	8	♏	40	12	♍	10	1	♐	1	♎	20		5		20		20		4		3	
11	11	3	21	18		42	12	♑	19	11		13		27		7		19		21		4		4	
21	11	4	0	28		47	29	♉	19	10		26		3	♏	9		19		21		5		4	
1	12	4	40	8	♐	54	16	♎	8	28	♏	8	♏	10		11		18		22		5		4	
11	12	5	19	19		4	16	♒	1	28		20		17		13		17		22		5		4	
21	12	5	59	29		14	7	♋	33	9	♐	3	♐	23		15		16		22		6		4	

1973

1	1	6	42	10	♑	26	0	♐	34	25	♐	16	♐	1	♐	18	♑	15	♊	23	♎	6	♐	4	♎
11	1	7	21	20		38	5	♈	4	10	♑	0	♑	8		20		15		23		7		4	
21	1	8	1	0	♒	49	28	♌	47	26		12		15		22		14		23		7		4	
1	2	8	44	12		0	14	♑	38	14	♒	25		22		25		14		23		7		4	
11	2	9	24	22		8	27	♉	33	2	♓	8	♒	29		27		14		23		7		4	
21	2	10	3	2	♓	13	16	♎	8	19		20		6	♑	29		14		23		7		4	
1	3	10	35	10		16	22	♑	36	28		0	♓	12		1	♒	14		23		7		4	
11	3	11	14	20		17	8	♊	34	26		13		19		3		14		22		7		3	
21	3	11	53	0	♈	14	24	♎	8	17		25		26		5		15		22		7		3	
1	4	12	37	11		8	8	♓	55	16		9		4	♒	7		16		21		7		3	
11	4	13	16	20		58	1	♌	55	23		21		11		8		16		21		7		3	
21	4	13	55	0	♉	45	8	♐	55	5	♈	4	♉	18		10		17		21		7		2	
1	5	14	35	10		29	14	♈	49	21		16		25		11		18		20		7		2	
11	5	15	14	20		10	8	♍	43	9	♉	28		2	♓	11		20		20		6		2	
21	5	15	54	29		48	11	♑	3	1	♊	11	♊	9		12		21		20		6		2	
1	6	16	37	10	♊	22	7	♊	39	24		24		17		12		22		19		6		2	
11	6	17	17	19		56	26	♎	30	11	♋	6	♋	24		12		24		19		6		2	
21	6	17	56	29		29	26	♒	8	24		18		0	♈	11		25		19		5		1	
1	7	18	35	9	♋	1	16	♋	19	2	♌	1	♌	6		11		26		19		5		2	
11	7	19	15	18		33	29	♏	36	3		13		13		10		27		19		5		2	
21	7	19	54	28		6	1	♈	14	27	♋	25		19		8		29		19		5		2	
1	8	20	38	8	♌	36	8	♍	34	23		8	♍	24		7		29		19		5		2	
11	8	21	17	18		11	13	♑	35	29		20		29		6		1	♋	20		5		2	
21	8	21	57	22		47	22	♉	11	15	♌	2	♎	3	♉	5		2		20		5		3	
1	9	22	40	8	♏	25	27	♎	10	7	♍	16		7		4		3		21		5		3	
11	9	23	19	18		7	28	♒	35	25		27		9		3		4		21		5		4	
21	9	23	59	27		52	15	♋	17	12	♎	9	♏	9		2		4		22		5		4	
1	10	0	38	7	♎	40	0	♐	6	27		20		8		2		4		22		5		4	
11	10	1	17	17		32	3	♈	7	11	♏	2	♐	6		3		5		23		5		5	
21	10	1	57	27		27	24	♌	5	22		13		3		3		5		24		6		5	
1	11	2	41	8	♏	26	13	♑	47	26		25		29	♈	4		5		24		6		6	
11	11	3	20	18		27	23	♉	53	17		6	♑	27		5		4		25		6		6	
21	11	3	59	28		32	14	♎	31	11		15		25		7		4		26		7		6	
1	12	4	39	8	♐	39	15	♒	40	19		24		25		8		3		26		7		6	
11	12	5	18	18		48	1	♋	59	3	♐	2	♒	27		10		2		27		8		7	
21	12	5	48	28		59	19	♏	13	18		8		29		12		1		27		8		7	

1974		Sid. Time		☉			☽			☿		♀		♂		♃		♄		♅		♆		♇	
1	1	6	41	10	♑	11	1	♈	17	5	♑	11	♒	3	♉	14	♒	1	♋	27	♎	8	♐	7	♎
11	1	7	20	20		22	25	♌	17	21		10		6		17		29	♊	28		9		7	
21	1	8	0	0	♒	34	4	♑	2	8	♒	5		11		19		29		28		9		7	
1	2	8	43	11		45	20	♉	17	27		29	♑	16		22		28		28		9		7	
11	2	9	23	21		53	16	♎	6	10	♓	26		21		24		28		28		9		7	
21	2	10	2	1	♓	59	18	♒	15	10		27		26		26		28		28		10		6	
1	3	10	34	10		1	0	♊	28	2		0	♒	1	♊	28		28		27		10		6	
11	3	11	13	20		2	23	♎	59	27	♒	6		6		1	♓	28		27		10		6	
21	3	11	53	0	♈	0	26	♒	40	2	♓	14		12		3		28		27		10		6	
1	4	12	36	10		53	23	♋	5	15		25		19		5		29		26		10		5	
11	4	13	15	20		44	10	♐	44	0	♈	4	♓	24		7		29		26		9		5	
21	4	13	55	0	♉	31	12	♈	49	16		15		0	♋	9		0	♋	26		9		5	
1	5	13	34	10		15	2	♍	20	6	♉	26		6		11		1		25		9		5	
11	5	15	14	19		56	12	♑	54	27		7	♈	12		13		2		25		9		4	
21	5	15	53	29		34	18	♉	17	17	♊	18		18		14		3		24		8		4	
1	6	16	36	10	♊	8	23	♎	53	3	♋	1	♉	25		16		4		24		8		4	
11	6	17	16	19		42	26	♒	39	12		12		1	♌	17		6		24		8		4	
21	6	17	55	29		16	10	♋	21	13		24		8		17		7		24		8		4	
1	7	18	34	8	♋	48	29	♏	18	9		6	♊	13		18		8		24		7		4	
11	7	19	14	18		19	29	♓	24	4		18		20		18		10		24		7		4	
21	7	19	53	27		52	19	♌	12	8		0	♋	26		18		11		24		7		4	
1	8	20	37	8	♌	23	14	♑	48	22		13		3		17		12		24		7		5	
11	8	21	16	17		58	16	♉	33	11	♌	25		9		16		14		24		7		5	
21	8	21	55	27		34	12	♎	12	1	♍	7	♌	15		15		15		25		7		5	
1	9	22	39	8	♍	11	29	♒	16	21		21		22		14		16		25		7		6	
11	9	23	18	17		53	7	♋	13	7	♎	3	♍	29		12		17		26		7		6	
21	9	23	58	27		38	1	♐	12	21		16		5	♎	11		17		26		7		6	
1	10	0	37	7	♎	26	2	♈	22	2	♏	28		12		10		18		27		7		7	
11	10	1	17	17		18	16	♌	7	10		11	♎	18		9		19		27		8		7	
21	10	1	56	27		13	4	♑	14	7		23		25		8		19		28		8		7	
1	11	2	39	8	♏	11	19	♉	34	25	♎	7	♏	3	♏	8		19		29		8		8	
11	11	3	19	18		13	9	♎	25	29		19		9		8		19		29		9		8	
21	11	3	58	28		17	18	♒	2	13	♏	2	♐	16		8		19		0	♏	9		9	
1	12	4	38	8	♐	24	26	♊	14	28		14		23		9		18		1		9		9	
11	12	5	17	18		33	16	♏	34	14	♐	27		0	♐	10		17		1		10		9	
21	12	5	57	28		44	19	♓	42	29		10	♑	7		12		17		1		10		9	

1975

1	1	6	40	9	♑	56	19	♌	11	17	♑	23	♑	15	♐	13	♓	16	♋	2	♏	10	♐	9	[illegible]
11	1	7	19	20		7	4	♑	7	3	♒	6	♒	22		15		15		2		11		9	
21	1	7	19	0	♒	19	4	♉	30	18		18		29		17		14		2		11		9	
1	2	8	42	11		30	12	♎	33	25		2	♓	7	♑	19		13		2		11		9	
11	2	9	22	21		38	19	♒	14	16		15		15		22		13		2		12		9	
21	2	10	1	1	♓	44	22	♊	21	10		27		22		24		12		2		12		9	
1	3	10	32	9		46	21	♎	16	13		7	♈	28		26		12		2		12		9	
11	3	11	12	19		47	28	♒	7	23		19		6	♒	28		12		2		12		8	
21	3	11	52	29		45	1	♋	48	6	♓	1	♉	13		0	♈	12		2		12		8	
1	4	12	35	10	♈	39	11	♐	5	24		15		22		3		12		1		12		8	
11	4	13	14	20		29	12	♈	43	12	♈	27		29		6		13		1		12		8	
21	4	13	54	0	♉	17	24	♌	8	3	♉	8	♊	7	♓	8		13		0		11		7	
1	5	14	33	10		1	14	♑	47	23		20		15		10		14		0		11		7	
11	5	15	12	19		42	16	♉	13	10	♊	1	♋	22		12		15		29	♎	11		7	
21	5	15	52	29		20	3	♎	32	21		12		29		14		16		29		11		7	
1	6	16	35	9	♊	54	29	♒	14	23		24		8	♈	17		17		29		10		7	
11	6	17	15	19		29	4	♋	59	19		5	♌	15		19		18		29		10		7	
21	6	17	54	29		2	25	♏	44	15		14		22		20		19		29		10		6	
1	7	18	34	8	♋	34	0	♈	58	17		23		0	♉	22		21		28		10		7	
11	7	19	13	18		6	12	♌	54	28		1	♍	7		23		22		28		10		7	
21	7	19	52	27		38	1	♑	43	15	♋	7		14		24		23		28		9		7	
1	8	20	36	8	♌	9	15	♉	19	8	♌	11		21		24		25		29		9		7	
11	8	21	15	17		44	6	♎	52	28		11		28		25		26		29		9		7	
21	8	21	55	27		20	18	♒	12	15	♍	8		4	♊	25		27		29		9		8	
1	9	22	38	7	♍	57	2	♋	29	2	♎	1		10		24		28		29		9		8	
11	9	23	17	17		39	29	♏	3	14		26	♌	16		23		29		0	♏	9		8	
21	9	23	57	27		24	2	♈	54	23		26		20		23		0	♌	0		9		9	
1	10	0	36	7	♎	12	9	♌	15	23		28		25		21		1		1		9		9	
11	10	1	16	17		3	4	♑	38	14		4	♍	28		20		2		2		10		9	
21	10	1	55	26		58	5	♉	40	9		12		1	♋	19		2		2		10		10	
1	11	2	39	7	♏	56	2	♎	32	22		22		2		17		3		3		10		10	
11	11	3	18	17		58	20	♒	36	7	♏	1	♎	3		16		3		4		11		11	
21	11	3	58	28		3	22	♊	7	24		12		1		15		3		4		11		11	
1	12	4	37	8	♐	10	11	♏	6	9	♐	23		28	♊	15		3		5		11		11	
11	12	5	16	18		19	22	♓	33	25		5	♏	25		15		2		5		12		11	
21	12	5	56	28		29	28	♋	20	11	♑	16		21		15		2		6		12		12	

1976		Sid. Time		☉		☽		☿	♀	♂	♃	♄	♅	♆	♇
1	1	6	39	9 ♑	41	2 ♑	6	27 ♑	29 ♏	17 ♊	16 ♈	1 ♌	6 ♏	13 ♐	12 ♎
11	1	7	18	19	53	5 ♉	54	8 ♒	11 ♐	15	16	0	7	13	12
21	1	7	59	0 ♒	4	20 ♍	53	5	24	15	18	29 ♋	7	13	12
1	2	8	42	11	15	19 ♒	46	24 ♑	7 ♑	15	19	29	7	13	12
11	2	9	21	21	23	20 ♊	47	26	19	17	21	28	7	13	12
21	2	10	0	1 ♓	29	14 ♏	9	5 ♒	1 ♒	20	22	27	7	14	11
1	3	10	36	10	32	10 ♓	49	17	13	23	24	27	7	14	11
11	3	10	15	20	33	11 ♋	57	2 ♓	25	27	26	26	7	14	11
21	3	11	54	0 ♈	30	7 ♐	54	19	7 ♓	1 ♋	29	26	6	14	11
1	4	12	38	11	24	25 ♈	18	11 ♒	21	6	1 ♉	26	6	14	10
11	4	13	17	21	14	2 ♍	15	1 ♉	3 ♈	11	4	26	6	14	10
21	4	13	57	1 ♉	1	27 ♑	26	19	15	16	6	27	5	14	10
1	5	14	36	10	45	27 ♉	57	1 ♊	28	22	8	27	5	13	10
11	5	15	16	20	26	10 ♎	40	4	10 ♉	27	11	28	4	13	9
21	5	15	55	0 ♊	4	1 ♓	19	29 ♉	22	3 ♌	13	29	4	13	9
1	6	16	38	10	38	14 ♋	30	25	6 ♊	9	16	29	4	13	9
11	6	7	18	20	12	4 ♐	12	28	18	15	18	1 ♌	4	12	9
21	6	17	57	29	45	15 ♈	54	8 ♊	0 ♋	21	20	2	3	12	9
1	7	18	36	9 ♋	17	21 ♌	0	23	13	26	22	3	3	12	9
11	7	19	16	18	49	11 ♑	46	13 ♋	25	2 ♍	24	4	3	12	9
21	7	19	56	28	22	17 ♉	10	5 ♌	7 ♌	9	26	5	3	11	9
1	8	20	39	8 ♌	52	13 ♎	30	25	21	15	27	7	3	11	9
11	8	21	18	18	27	0 ♓	32	11 ♍	3 ♍	22	29	8	3	11	10
21	8	21	58	28	4	1 ♋	49	25	16	28	29	9	3	11	10
1	9	22	41	8 ♏	41	6 ♐	45	5 ♎	29	5 ♎	1 ♊	11	4	11	10
11	9	23	21	18	23	15 ♈	54	8	11	11	1	12	5	11	11
21	9	0	0	29	7	19 ♌	49	29 ♍	25	18	1	13	5	11	11
1	10	0	39	7 ♎	56	14 ♑	38	23	6 ♏	25	1	14	6	12	11
11	10	1	19	17	48	18 ♉	5	0 ♎	18	1 ♏	0	15	6	12	12
21	10	1	58	27	43	26 ♍	39	16	0 ♐	8	29 ♉	16	7	12	12
1	11	2	42	8 ♏	42	3 ♓	11	4 ♏	14	16	28	16	8	12	13
11	11	3	21	18	44	2 ♋	48	21	26	23	27	17	8	13	13
21	11	4	0	28	49	19 ♏	50	7 ♐	8 ♑	0 ♐	26	17	9	13	13
1	12	4	40	8 ♐	56	6 ♈	29	22	19	7	24	17	9	14	14
11	12	5	19	19	5	7 ♌	19	7 ♑	2 ♒	14	23	17	10	14	14
21	12	5	59	29	15	28 ♐	2	19	13	22	22	16	10	14	14

1977															
1	1	6	42	10 ♑	28	20 ♉	16	22 ♑	26 ♒	0 ♑	21 ♉	16 ♌	11 ♏	15 ♐	14 ♎
11	1	7	22	20	39	27 ♍	16	10	7 ♓	7	21	15	11	15	14
21	1	8	1	0 ♒	50	19 ♒	1	8	18	15	21	14	11	15	14
1	2	8	44	12	1	4 ♋	28	17	29	23	22	14	12	16	14
11	2	9	24	22	9	19 ♏	54	0 ♒	8 ♈	1 ♒	22	13	12	16	14
21	2	10	3	2 ♓	15	6 ♈	4	15	16	9	23	12	12	16	14
1	3	10	35	10	18	12 ♋	19	28	20	15	24	11	12	16	14
11	3	11	14	20	18	0 ♐	46	15 ♓	24	23	26	11	12	16	13
21	3	11	54	0 ♈	15	14 ♈	16	5 ♈	24	1 ♓	27	10	11	16	13
1	4	12	37	11	9	29 ♌	12	26	20	9	29	10	11	16	13
11	4	13	16	21	0	23 ♑	31	10 ♉	13	17	1 ♊	10	10	16	13
21	4	13	56	0 ♉	46	28 ♉	42	14	9	25	4	10	10	16	12
1	5	14	35	10	30	5 ♎	14	10	8	2 ♈	6	10	10	16	12
11	5	15	15	20	11	0 ♓	17	5	12	10	8	11	9	15	12
21	5	15	54	29	50	1 ♋	12	7	17	18	10	11	9	15	12
1	6	16	37	10 ♊	23	28 ♏	10	16	25	26	13	12	9	15	11
11	6	17	17	19	58	17 ♈	3	0 ♊	4 ♉	4 ♉	15	13	8	15	11
21	6	17	56	29	31	17 ♌	7	19	14	11	17	14	8	14	11
1	7	18	36	9 ♋	3	7 ♑	3	10 ♑	24	18	20	15	8	14	11
11	7	19	15	18	35	19 ♉	33	1 ♌	5 ♊	25	22	16	8	14	11
21	7	19	55	28	8	22 ♍	45	19	15	2 ♊	24	17	8	14	12
1	8	20	38	8 ♌	38	29 ♒	12	5 ♍	28	10	26	19	8	14	12
11	8	21	17	18	13	3 ♋	29	15	9 ♋	17	28	20	8	13	12
21	8	21	56	27	50	14 ♏	9	21	21	23	0 ♋	21	8	13	12
1	9	22	40	8 ♍	27	17 ♈	3	16	4 ♌	0 ♋	2	23	9	13	13
11	9	23	19	18	9	18 ♌	52	8	16	6	3	24	9	13	13
21	9	23	59	27	54	7 ♑	38	10	28	12	4	25	9	14	13
1	10	0	38	7 ♎	42	19 ♉	42	24	10	17	5	26	10	14	14
11	10	1	18	17	34	23 ♍	24	11 ♎	22	23	6	27	11	14	14
21	10	1	57	27	29	16 ♒	17	29	5 ♎	27	6	28	11	14	15
1	11	2	41	8 ♏	27	3 ♋	37	17 ♏	18	2 ♌	6	29	12	14	15
11	11	3	21	18	30	14 ♏	20	2 ♐	1 ♏	6	6	29	13	15	15
21	11	4	0	28	34	5 ♈	40	17	14	9	5	0 ♍	13	15	16
1	12	4	39	8 ♐	41	6 ♌	3	0 ♑	26	11	4	0	14	16	16
11	12	5	18	18	50	22 ♐	41	7	9 ♐	12	3	1	14	16	16
21	12	5	58	29	0	9 ♉	38	0	21	11	1	0	15	16	16

1978	Sid. Time	☉	☽	☿	♀	♂	♃	♄	♅	♆	♇
1 1	6 41	10 ♑ 13	22 ♍ 15	21 ♐	5 ♑	9 ♌	0 ♋	0 ♍	15 ♏	17 ♐	17 ♎
11 1	7 20	20 24	16 ♒ 9	27	18	6	29 ♊	29 ♌	16	17	17
21 1	8 0	0 ♒ 35	24 ♊ 9	9 ♑	0 ♒	2	28	29	16	17	17
1 2	8 43	11 46	11 ♏ 51	24	14	28 ♋	27	28	16	18	17
11 2	9 23	21 54	6 ♈ 13	10 ♒	27	25	26	28	16	17	17
21 2	10 2	2 ♓ 0	8 ♌ 31	27	9 ♓	23	26	27	16	18	16
1 3	10 33	10 3	22 ♏ 28	12 ♓	19	22	26	26	16	18	16
11 3	11 13	20 3	14 ♈ 0	1 ♈	2 ♈	23	27	25	16	18	16
21 3	11 52	0 ♈ 1	16 ♌ 37	18	14	24	27	25	16	18	16
1 4	12 36	10 54	15 ♑ 46	26	28	27	29	24	16	18	15
11 4	13 16	20 45	0 ♊ 17	22	10 ♉	0 ♌	0 ♋	24	15	18	15
21 4	13 55	0 ♉ 32	2 ♎ 50	16	22	4	1	24	15	18	15
1 5	14 34	10 16	24 ♒ 51	16	4 ♊	8	3	24	15	18	15
11 5	15 14	19 57	2 ♋ 39	24	17	13	5	24	14	18	14
21 5	15 53	29 36	8 ♏ 28	6 ♉	29	17	7	24	14	17	14
1 6	16 37	10 ♊ 10	15 ♈ 14	25	12	23	9	25	13	17	14
11 6	17 16	19 44	16 ♌ 45	15 ♊	24	28	12	26	13	17	14
21 6	17 55	29 17	1 ♑ 22	7 ♋	6 ♌	4 ♍	13	26	13	17	14
1 7	18 35	8 ♋ 49	20 ♉ 1	27	17	9	16	27	12	16	14
11 7	19 14	18 21	19 ♍ 48	13 ♌	29	15	18	28	12	16	14
21 7	19 54	27 54	10 ♒ 22	25	10 ♍	21	20	29	12	16	14
1 8	20 37	8 ♌ 24	5 ♋ 13	2 ♍	22	28	23	1 ♍	12	16	14
11 8	21 16	17 59	7 ♏ 34	1	3 ♎	4 ♎	25	2	12	16	15
21 8	21 56	27 36	2 ♈ 39	24 ♌	13	10	27	3	13	16	15
1 9	22 39	8 ♍ 13	19 ♌ 34	21	24	18	29	5	13	16	15
11 9	23 19	17 55	29 ♐ 13	2 ♍	3 ♏	24	1 ♌	6	13	16	15
21 9	23 58	27 40	21 ♉ 1	19	11	1 ♏	3	7	14	16	16
1 10	0 37	7 ♎ 28	22 ♍ 30	8 ♎	18	8	4	8	14	16	16
11 10	1 17	17 20	8 ♒ 29	25	22	14	6	9	15	16	17
21 10	1 56	27 14	23 ♊ 58	11 ♏	23	22	7	10	16	16	17
1 11	2 40	8 ♏ 13	10 ♏ 16	26	19	29	8	11	16	17	17
11 11	3 19	18 14	1 ♈ 2	10 ♐	13	6 ♐	9	12	17	17	18
21 11	3 59	28 19	7 ♌ 49	20	8	14	9	13	17	17	18
1 12	4 38	8 ♐ 26	17 ♐ 17	19	8	21	9	13	18	18	18
11 12	5 17	18 35	7 ♉ 40	7	10	29	9	14	19	18	19
21 12	5 57	28 45	9 ♍ 35	7	16	6 ♑	8	14	19	18	19

1979

1 1	6 40	9 ♑ 58	10 ♒ 45	19 ♐	24 ♏	15 ♑	7 ♌	14 ♍	20 ♏	19 ♐	19 ♎
11 1	7 20	20 10	24 ♊ 49	3 ♑	4 ♐	22	6	14	20	19	19
21 1	7 59	0 ♒ 20	24 ♎ 48	18	14	0 ♒	5	13	20	20	19
1 2	8 42	11 31	3 ♈ 28	6 ♒	25	9	3	13	21	20	19
11 2	9 22	21 40	9 ♌ 39	23	6 ♑	17	2	12	21	20	19
21 2	10 1	1 ♓ 45	13 ♐ 39	11 ♓	18	25	1	11	21	20	19
1 3	10 33	9 48	11 ♈ 37	25	27	1 ♓	0	11	21	20	19
11 3	11 12	19 49	18 ♌ 18	7 ♈	9 ♒	9	29 ♋	10	21	20	19
21 3	11 52	29 47	23 ♐ 43	6	20	17	29	9	21	20	18
1 4	12 35	10 ♈ 40	1 ♊ 2	27 ♓	3 ♓	25	29	8	20	20	18
11 4	13 14	20 31	2 ♎ 41	26	15	3 ♈	29	8	20	20	18
21 4	13 54	0 ♉ 18	16 ♒ 30	3 ♈	27	11	0 ♌	7	20	20	17
1 5	14 33	10 2	4 ♋ 36	15	9	18	1	7	19	20	17
11 5	15 13	19 43	6 ♏ 24	0 ♉	21	26	2	7	19	20	17
21 5	15 52	29 21	25 ♓ 37	19	4 ♉	4 ♉	4	7	19	19	17
1 6	16 35	9 ♊ 56	18 ♌ 50	12 ♊	17	12	5	8	18	19	17
11 6	17 15	19 30	26 ♐ 11	3 ♋	29	19	7	8	18	19	16
21 6	17 54	29 3	17 ♉ 9	21	11 ♊	26	9	9	17	19	16
1 7	18 34	8 ♋ 35	20 ♍ 32	4 ♌	23	3 ♊	11	9	17	19	16
11 7	19 13	18 7	4 ♒ 22	13	6 ♋	11	13	10	17	18	16
21 7	19 52	27 40	22 ♊ 52	14	18	17	15	11	17	18	17
1 8	20 36	8 ♌ 10	5 ♏ 18	8	1 ♌	25	17	12	17	18	17
11 8	21 15	17 45	28 ♓ 3	3	14	2 ♋	20	13	17	18	17
21 8	21 55	27 22	8 ♌ 43	9	26	8	22	15	17	18	17
1 9	22 38	7 ♍ 59	23 ♐ 23	26	10 ♍	15	24	16	17	18	18
11 9	23 17	17 40	19 ♉ 51	16 ♍	22	22	26	17	18	18	18
21 9	23 57	27 25	22 ♍ 59	4 ♎	5 ♎	28	28	19	18	18	18
1 10	0 36	7 ♎ 13	0 ♒ 42	20	17	4 ♌	0 ♍	20	19	18	19
11 10	1 16	17 5	25 ♊ 5	6 ♏	29	9	2	21	19	18	19
21 10	1 55	27 0	25 ♎ 52	19	12 ♏	15	4	22	20	18	19
1 11	2 39	7 ♏ 58	23 ♓ 49	2 ♐	26	21	6	23	20	19	20
11 11	3 18	17 59	10 ♌ 30	6	8 ♐	26	7	24	21	19	20
21 11	3 57	28 4	13 ♐ 13	26 ♏	20	0 ♍	8	25	22	19	21
1 12	4 37	8 ♐ 11	2 ♉ 25	20	3 ♑	5	9	26	22	20	21
11 12	5 16	18 20	12 ♍ 3	28	15	8	10	26	23	20	21
21 12	5 56	28 31	19 ♑ 51	12 ♐	28	12	10	27	23	21	21

1980

Date	Sid. Time	☉	☽	☿	♀	♂	♃	♄	♅	♆	♇
1 1	6 39	9 ♑ 43	23 ♊ 9	28 ♐	11 ♒	14 ♍	10 ♍	27 ♍	24 ♏	21 ♐	22 ♎
11 1	7 19	19 54	25 ♎ 30	14 ♑	24	15	10	27	25	21	22
21 1	7 59	0 ♒ 6	12 ♓ 30	0 ♒	6 ♓	15	9	27	25	22	22
1 2	8 41	11 17	10 ♌ 10	19	19	14	8	26	25	22	22
11 2	9 21	21 24	11 ♐ 3	6 ♓	1 ♈	11	7	26	25	22	22
21 2	10 0	1 ♓ 30	5 ♉ 38	19	13	7	6	25	26	22	22
1 3	10 36	10 35	1 ♍ 3	20	23	4	5	25	26	23	21
11 3	11 15	20 34	2 ♑ 44	11	5 ♉	29 ♌	3	24	26	23	21
21 3	11 55	0 ♈ 32	28 ♉ 57	7	16	28	2	23	25	23	21
1 4	12 38	11 25	15 ♎ 24	14	27	26	1	22	25	23	21
11 4	13 17	21 15	23 ♒ 20	25	7 ♊	26	1	22	25	23	20
21 4	13 57	1 ♉ 3	17 ♋ 57	10 ♈	16	27	0	21	24	22	20
1 5	14 36	10 46	18 ♏ 29	27	23	29	0	21	24	22	20
11 5	15 15	20 27	1 ♈ 59	18 ♉	29	2 ♍	1	20	24	22	20
21 5	15 55	0 ♊ 6	21 ♌ 9	9 ♊	2 ♋	6	1	20	23	22	19
1 6	16 38	10 39	5 ♑ 52	0 ♋	2	10	2	20	23	22	19
11 6	17 18	20 13	25 ♉ 35	14	27 ♊	15	3	21	22	21	19
21 6	17 57	29 46	4 ♎ 58	23	21	19	5	21	22	21	19
1 7	18 37	9 ♋ 18	12 ♒ 38	25	17	25	6	21	22	21	19
11 7	19 16	18 51	2 ♋ 58	20	16	0 ♎	8	22	22	21	19
21 7	19 56	28 23	6 ♏ 43	15	20	6	10	23	22	20	19
1 8	20 39	8 ♌ 53	5 ♈ 30	19	26	12	12	24	21	20	19
11 8	21 18	18 28	20 ♌ 47	3 ♌	4 ♋	18	14	25	22	20	19
21 8	21 58	28 5	21 ♐ 50	22	12	25	16	26	22	20	20
1 9	22 41	8 ♍ 42	28 ♉ 56	14 ♍	23	2 ♏	18	27	22	20	20
11 9	23 21	18 24	5 ♎ 46	2 ♎	3 ♌	8	20	29	22	20	20
21 9	0 0	28 10	10 ♒ 4	17	14	15	22	29	23	20	21
1 10	0 39	7 ♎ 58	6 ♋ 16	1 ♏	25	22	25	1 ♎	23	20	21
11 10	1 19	17 50	8 ♏ 17	13	7	29	27	2	24	20	22
21 10	1 58	27 45	17 ♓ 9	20	19	6 ♐	29	4	24	21	22
1 11	2 42	8 ♏ 43	23 ♌ 44	14	2 ♎	14	1 ♎	5	25	21	22
11 11	3 21	18 45	23 ♐ 41	4	14	21	3	6	25	21	23
21 11	4 1	28 50	10 ♉ 49	9	26	29	4	7	26	22	23
1 12	4 40	8 ♐ 57	26 ♍ 25	23	9 ♏	7 ♑	6	8	27	22	23
11 12	5 19	19 6	28 ♑ 36	8 ♐	21	14	7	8	27	22	24
21 12	5 59	29 17	19 ♊ 8	23	3 ♐	22	9	9	28	23	24

1981

Date	Sid. Time	☉	☽	☿	♀	♂	♃	♄	♅	♆	♇
1 1	6 42	10 ♑ 29	10 ♏ 6	11 ♑	17 ♐	1 ♒	10 ♎	10 ♎	28 ♏	23 ♐	24 ♎
11 1	7 22	20 41	19 ♓ 7	27	29	9	10	10	29	23	24
21 1	8 1	0 ♒ 52	9 ♌ 18	14 ♒	12 ♑	17	10	10	29	24	24
1 2	8 44	12 3	24 ♐ 26	0 ♓	26	25	10	10	29	24	24
11 2	9 24	22 11	12 ♉ 23	4	8 ♒	3 ♓	10	9	29	24	24
21 2	10 3	2 ♓ 16	25 ♍ 48	25 ♒	21	11	9	9	0 ♐	25	24
1 3	10 35	10 19	2 ♑ 12	20	1 ♓	17	8	8	0	25	24
11 3	11 14	20 20	22 ♉ 58	23	13	25	7	8	0	25	24
21 3	11 54	0 ♈ 17	4 ♎ 18	3 ♓	26	3 ♈	6	7	0	25	24
1 4	12 37	11 11	19 ♒ 15	18	10	12	5	6	29 ♏	25	23
11 4	13 16	21 1	15 ♋ 12	4 ♈	22	19	4	5	29	25	23
21 4	13 56	0 ♉ 48	18 ♏ 59	23	4 ♉	27	2	4	29	25	23
1 5	14 35	10 32	25 ♓ 47	14 ♉	17	4 ♉	1	4	29	25	22
11 5	15 15	20 13	21 ♌ 2	5 ♊	0 ♊	12	1	4	28	24	22
21 5	15 54	29 51	21 ♐ 48	21	11	19	1	3	28	24	22
1 6	16 38	10 25	19 ♉ 22	2 ♋	25	27	0	3	28	24	22
11 6	17 17	19 59	7 ♎ 7	5	7 ♋	4 ♊	1	3	27	24	22
21 6	17 56	29 32	8 ♒ 6	1	19	11	1	3	27	23	22
1 7	18 36	9 ♋ 4	28 ♊ 12	26 ♊	1 ♌	18	2	3	27	23	22
11 7	19 15	18 36	9 ♏ 25	29	14	25	3	4	26	23	22
21 7	19 55	28 9	14 ♓ 16	9 ♋	26	2 ♋	4	5	26	23	22
1 8	20 38	8 ♌ 39	19 ♌ 23	28	9 ♍	9	6	6	26	22	22
11 8	21 17	18 14	23 ♐ 15	19 ♌	21	16	8	6	26	22	22
21 8	21 57	27 51	6 ♉ 41	8 ♍	3 ♎	22	10	7	26	22	22
1 9	22 40	8 ♍ 28	6 ♎ 49	27	16	29	12	9	26	22	23
11 9	23 20	18 10	8 ♒ 36	12 ♎	28	6 ♌	14	10	27	22	23
21 9	23 59	27 55	0 ♋ 12	24	9 ♏	12	16	11	27	22	23
1 10	0 38	7 ♎ 43	9 ♏ 38	2 ♏	21	18	18	12	27	22	24
11 10	1 18	17 35	13 ♓ 24	3	2 ♐	24	20	13	28	22	24
21 10	1 57	27 30	8 ♌ 5	22 ♎	13	0 ♍	22	15	28	23	24
1 11	2 41	8 ♏ 29	23 ♐ 43	20	25	6	25	16	29	23	25
11 11	3 20	18 31	5 ♉ 12	2 ♏	6 ♑	12	27	17	29	23	25
21 11	4 0	28 35	26 ♍ 36	17	15	17	29	18	0 ♐	24	26
1 12	4 39	8 ♐ 42	26 ♑ 24	3 ♐	24	23	1 ♏	19	1	24	26
11 12	5 18	18 51	13 ♊ 41	19	1 ♒	28	3	20	1	24	26
21 12	5 58	29 2	0 ♏ 11	5 ♑	7	2 ♎	4	21	2	25	26

1982		Sid. Time		☉		☽		☿	♀	♂	♃	♄	♅	♆	♇
1	1	6	41	10 ♑	15	13 ♓	18	23 ♑	9 ♒	7 ♎	6 ♏	21 ♎	3 ♐	25 ♐	27 ♎
11	1	7	21	20	26	6 ♌	29	8 ♒	7	11	7	22	3	25	27
21	1	8	0	0 ♒	37	14 ♐	16	18	1	14	9	22	4	26	27
1	2	8	44	11	48	4 ♉	0	12	25 ♑	17	9	22	4	26	27
11	2	9	23	21	56	26 ♍	6	3	23	19	10	22	4	27	27
21	2	10	2	2 ♓	2	28 ♑	20	6	25	19	10	22	4	27	27
1	3	10	34	10	5	14 ♉	51	13	29	19	10	22	5	27	27
11	3	11	13	20	5	4 ♎	6	26	6 ♒	17	10	21	5	27	26
21	3	11	53	0 ♈	3	6 ♒	13	11	14	14	9	20	5	27	26
1	4	12	36	10	56	8 ♋	8	0 ♈	24	10	8	20	4	27	26
11	4	13	16	20	47	20 ♏	21	20	5 ♓	6	7	19	4	27	26
21	4	13	55	0 ♉	34	22 ♓	56	11 ♉	15	3	6	18	4	27	25
1	5	14	34	10	18	16 ♌	37	29	26	1	5	17	4	27	25
11	5	15	14	19	59	22 ♐	42	11 ♊	7 ♈	0	4	17	3	27	25
21	5	15	53	29	37	29 ♈	11	15	19	1	2	16	3	26	25
1	6	16	37	10 ♊	11	6 ♎	24	11	1 ♉	3	1	16	2	26	24
11	6	17	16	19	45	6 ♒	53	7	13	5	1	16	2	26	24
21	6	17	55	29	19	22 ♊	16	8	25	9	0	15	1	26	24
1	7	18	35	8 ♋	51	10 ♏	54	17	6 ♊	13	0	16	1	25	24
11	7	19	14	18	23	10 ♓	32	3 ♋	18	18	1	16	1	25	24
21	7	19	54	27	55	0 ♌	53	23	0 ♋	23	1	16	1	25	24
1	8	20	37	8 ♌	26	25 ♐	17	16 ♌	14	29	2	17	1	25	24
11	8	21	17	18	1	29 ♈	26	4 ♍	26	4 ♏	3	18	1	24	24
21	8	21	56	27	37	22 ♍	50	20	8 ♌	10	4	19	1	24	25
1	9	22	39	8 ♍	14	9 ♒	22	5 ♎	21	17	6	20	1	24	25
11	9	23	19	17	56	21 ♊	35	15	4 ♍	24	8	21	1	24	25
21	9	23	58	27	41	11 ♏	0	17	16	1 ♐	10	22	1	24	26
1	10	0	37	7 ♎	29	12 ♓	31	10	29	7	11	23	2	24	26
11	10	1	17	17	21	0 ♌	45	2	11 ♎	15	14	24	2	25	26
21	10	1	56	27	16	13 ♐	44	10	24	22	16	25	3	25	27
1	11	2	40	8 ♏	14	1 ♉	8	27	7 ♏	0 ♑	18	27	3	25	27
11	11	3	19	18	16	22 ♍	53	13 ♏	20	8	20	28	4	25	28
21	11	3	59	28	20	27 ♑	23	29	3 ♐	15	22	29	4	26	28
1	12	4	38	8 ♐	27	8 ♊	16	15 ♐	15	23	25	0 ♏	5	26	28
11	12	5	18	18	36	29 ♎	10	0 ♑	28	1 ♒	27	1	6	26	29
21	12	5	57	28	47	29 ♒	32	15	10 ♑	8	29	2	6	27	29

1983

1	1	6	40	9 ♑	59	1 ♌	33	29 ♑	24 ♑	17 ♒	1 ♐	3 ♏	7 ♐	27 ♐	29
11	1	7	20	20	11	15 ♐	26	1 ♒	7 ♒	25	3	4	7	28	29
21	1	7	59	0 ♒	22	15 ♈	40	20 ♑	19	3 ♓	5	4	8	28	29
1	2	8	42	11	33	24 ♍	11	17	3 ♓	11	7	4	8	28	29
11	2	9	22	21	42	29 ♑	40	26	15	19	8	4	9	29	29
21	2	10	1	1 ♓	47	5 ♊	12	8 ♒	28	27	9	4	9	29	29
1	3	10	33	9	50	2 ♎	7	20	7 ♈	3 ♈	10	4	9	29	29
11	3	11	12	19	51	8 ♒	8	6 ♓	20	11	10	4	9	29	29
21	3	11	52	29	49	15 ♊	41	24	2 ♉	18	11	3	9	29	29
1	4	12	35	10 ♈	42	21 ♏	13	16 ♈	15	27	11	3	9	29	29
11	4	13	15	20	33	22 ♓	50	6 ♉	27	4 ♉	11	2	9	29	28
21	4	13	54	0 ♉	20	8 ♌	35	20	9 ♊	11	10	1	9	29	28
1	5	14	33	10	4	24 ♐	23	25	20	19	9	0	8	29	28
11	5	15	13	19	45	26 ♈	57	22	2 ♋	26	8	29 ♎	8	29	28
21	5	15	52	29	24	17 ♍	46	17	13	3 ♊	7	29	7	29	27
1	6	16	36	9 ♊	37	8 ♒	24	17	25	11	6	28	7	28	27
11	6	17	15	19	32	16 ♊	55	26	5 ♌	18	4	28	7	28	27
21	6	17	55	29	5	8 ♏	44	10 ♊	14	24	3	28	6	28	27
1	7	18	34	8 ♋	37	10 ♓	29	28	23	1 ♋	2	28	6	28	27
11	7	19	13	18	9	25 ♋	2	20	0 ♍	8	2	28	6	27	27
21	7	19	53	27	42	13 ♐	41	10 ♌	6	14	1	28	5	27	27
1	8	20	36	8 ♌	12	26 ♈	0	29	9	22	1	28	5	27	27
11	8	21	15	17	47	18 ♍	59	14 ♍	9	28	1	29	5	27	27
21	8	21	55	27	23	28 ♑	48	25	4	5 ♌	2	29	5	27	27
1	9	22	38	8 ♍	0	14 ♊	34	1 ♎	27 ♌	12	3	1 ♏	5	27	28
11	9	23	18	17	42	10 ♏	30	27 ♍	24	18	4	2	5	26	28
21	9	23	57	27	27	13 ♓	14	17	23	24	5	3	6	27	28
1	10	0	37	7 ♎	15	22 ♋	21	19	27	0 ♍	7	4	6	27	29
11	10	1	16	17	6	15 ♐	2	3 ♎	3 ♍	7	8	5	6	27	29
21	10	1	56	27	1	16 ♈	24	20	11	13	10	6	7	27	29
1	11	2	39	7 ♏	59	15 ♍	52	9 ♏	22	20	12	7	7	27	29
11	11	3	18	18	1	29 ♑	55	25	2 ♎	26	14	9	8	27	0
21	11	3	57	28	5	4 ♊	5	10 ♐	12	1 ♎	17	10	9	28	0
1	12	4	37	8 ♐	13	24 ♎	27	25	23	7	19	11	9	28	1
11	12	5	17	18	22	1 ♓	32	9 ♑	5 ♏	13	21	12	10	29	1
21	12	5	56	28	32	10 ♋	45	16	17	19	23	13	10	29	2

1984	Sid. Time	☉	☽	☿	♀	♂	♃	♄	♅	♆	♇
1 1	6 39	9 ♑ 45	14 ♐ 7	8 ♑	0 ♐	25 ♎	26 ♐	14 ♏	11 ♐	29 ♐	2 ♏
11 1	7 19	19 56	15 ♈ 53	0	12	0 ♏	28	15	12	29	2
21 1	7 59	0 ♒ 7	4 ♍ 1	6	24	5	0 ♑	15	12	0 ♑	2
1 2	8 42	11 18	0 ♒ 25	19	8 ♑	10	3	16	13	0	2
11 2	9 21	21 27	1 ♊ 16	3 ♒	20	15	5	16	13	1	2
21 2	10 0	1 ♓ 33	27 ♎ 11	19	2 ♒	19	6	16	13	1	2
1 3	10 36	10 36	21 ♒ 21	4 ♓	13	22	8	16	13	1	2
11 3	11 15	20 36	23 ♊ 26	23	25	25	9	16	14	1	2
21 3	11 55	0 ♈ 34	19 ♏ 49	12 ♈	8 ♓	27	11	16	14	1	2
1 4	12 38	11 27	5 ♈ 52	0 ♉	22	28	12	15	13	1	1
11 4	13 18	21 18	14 ♌ 45	7	4 ♈	28	12	15	13	1	1
21 4	13 57	1 ♉ 4	7 ♑ 57	3	16	27	13	14	13	1	1
1 5	14 36	10 48	9 ♉ 0	27 ♈	29	24	13	13	13	1	1
11 5	15 16	20 29	24 ♍ 0	26	11 ♉	21	13	12	13	1	0
21 5	15 55	0 ♊ 7	10 ♒ 49	5 ♉	23	17	12	12	12	1	29 ♎
1 6	16 39	10 41	26 ♊ 42	19	7 ♊	14	11	11	12	1	29
11 6	17 18	20 15	17 ♏ 3	6 ♊	19	12	10	11	11	0	29
21 6	17 57	29 48	24 ♓ 43	27	1 ♋	12	9	10	11	0	29
1 7	18 37	9 ♋ 20	3 ♌ 53	19	13	13	8	10	10	29 ♐	29
11 7	19 16	18 52	23 ♐ 48	8 ♌	26	15	7	10	10	29	29
21 7	19 56	28 25	26 ♈ 33	23	8 ♌	18	5	10	10	29	29
1 8	20 39	8 ♌ 55	27 ♍ 32	6 ♍	22	22	4	10	10	29	29
11 8	21 18	18 30	11 ♒ 7	13	4 ♍	27	4	10	10	29	29
21 8	21 58	28 7	11 ♊ 49	12	16	2 ♐	4	11	10	29	29
1 9	22 41	8 ♍ 44	20 ♏ 32	2	0 ♎	8	3	12	10	29	0 ♏
11 9	23 21	18 26	26 ♓ 9	1	12	14	3	12	10	29	0
21 9	0 0	28 11	0 ♌ 42	13	24	20	4	13	10	29	0
1 10	0 40	7 ♎ 59	27 ♐ 0	0 ♎	7 ♏	27	5	14	10	29	1
11 10	1 19	17 51	28 ♈ 46	18	19	4 ♑	6	15	11	29	1
21 10	1 59	27 46	8 ♍ 34	5 ♏	1 ♐	11	7	17	11	29	2
1 11	2 42	8 ♏ 45	13 ♒ 53	22	14	19	9	18	12	29	2
11 11	3 21	18 47	14 ♊ 25	7 ♐	26	26	11	19	12	29	3
21 11	4 1	28 51	2 ♏ 9	20	9 ♑	4 ♒	13	20	13	29	3
1 12	4 40	8 ♐ 59	16 ♓ 17	0 ♑	20	11	15	21	13	0 ♑	3
11 12	5 20	19 8	19 ♋ 50	27 ♐	2 ♒	19	17	23	14	0	4
21 12	5 59	29 18	10 ♐ 2	15	14	27	19	24	14	1	4

1985

1 1	6 42	10 ♑ 31	29 ♈ 42	18 ♐	26 ♒	5 ♓	21 ♑	25 ♏	15 ♐	1 ♑	4 ♏
11 1	7 22	20 42	11 ♍ 28	29	7 ♓	13	24	26	16	2	5
21 1	8 1	0 ♒ 54	29 ♑ 39	13 ♑	18	20	26	26	16	2	5
1 2	8 45	12 5	13 ♊ 57	29	29	29	29	27	17	3	5
11 2	9 24	22 12	4 ♏ 52	16 ♒	8 ♈	6 ♈	1 ♒	28	17	3	5
21 2	10 3	2 ♓ 18	16 ♓ 3	4 ♓	15	14	3	28	18	3	5
1 3	10 35	10 21	21 ♊ 52	19	19	20	5	28	18	3	5
11 3	11 14	20 22	14 ♏ 48	7 ♈	22	27	7	28	18	4	4
21 3	11 54	0 ♈ 19	24 ♓ 51	18	21	4 ♉	9	28	18	4	4
1 4	12 37	11 13	9 ♌ 44	16	16	12	11	28	18	4	4
11 4	13 17	21 3	6 ♑ 18	8	10	19	13	27	18	4	4
21 4	13 56	0 ♉ 50	9 ♉ 14	7	6	26	14	27	18	4	3
1 5	14 35	10 35	16 ♍ 58	14	7	3 ♊	15	26	17	3	3
11 5	15 15	20 15	11 ♒ 38	26	10	10	16	25	17	3	3
21 5	15 55	29 53	12 ♊ 4	11 ♉	17	17	17	24	17	3	3
1 6	16 38	10 ♊ 27	10 ♏ 26	2 ♊	25	24	17	24	16	3	2
11 6	17 17	20 1	27 ♓ 18	24	4 ♉	1 ♋	17	23	16	3	2
21 6	17 57	29 34	29 ♋ 10	15 ♋	14	8	17	22	16	2	2
1 7	18 36	9 ♋ 7	19 ♐ 0	2 ♌	24	14	16	22	15	2	2
11 7	19 15	18 39	29 ♈ 9	15	5 ♊	21	15	22	15	2	2
21 7	19 55	28 11	6 ♍ 3	23	16	27	14	21	14	2	2
1 8	20 38	8 ♌ 42	9 ♒ 54	25	28	4 ♌	12	21	14	1	2
11 8	21 17	18 16	12 ♊ 47	18	10 ♋	11	11	22	14	1	2
21 8	21 57	27 53	28 ♎ 54	13	22	17	10	22	14	1	2
1 9	22 40	8 ♍ 30	27 ♓ 5	21	5 ♌	24	9	23	14	1	3
11 9	23 20	18 12	28 ♋ 39	8 ♍	17	1 ♍	8	23	14	1	3
21 9	23 59	27 58	22 ♐ 1	26	29	6	7	24	14	1	3
1 10	0 39	7 ♎ 45	29 ♈ 43	14 ♎	11 ♍	13	7	25	15	1	4
11 10	1 18	17 37	4 ♍ 0	0 ♏	23	20	7	26	15	1	4
21 10	1 58	27 32	29 ♑ 30	15	6 ♎	26	8	27	15	1	4
1 11	2 41	8 ♏ 30	13 ♊ 49	0 ♐	19	3 ♎	8	28	16	1	5
11 11	3 21	18 32	25 ♎ 55	11	2 ♏	9	9	29	16	2	5
21 11	4 0	28 37	17 ♓ 25	15	14	15	11	0 ♐	17	2	6
1 12	4 39	8 ♐ 44	17 ♋ 5	4	27	21	12	2	18	2	6
11 12	5 19	18 53	4 ♐ 16	29 ♏	9 ♐	28	14	3	18	3	6
21 12	5 58	29 3	20 ♈ 17	8 ♐	22	4 ♏	16	4	19	3	7

1986		Sid. Time		☉	☽	☿	♀	♂	♃	♄	♅	♆	♇
1	1	6	41	10 ♑ 16	5 ♍ 4	23 ♐	6 ♑	11 ♏	18 ♒	5 ♐	19 ♐	4 ♑	7 ♏
11	1	7	21	20 27	26 ♑ 59	8 ♑	18	17	21	6	20	4	7
21	1	8	0	0 ♒ 39	3 ♊ 51	24	1 ♒	23	23	7	21	4	7
1	2	8	44	11 49	26 ♎ 20	12 ♒	15	29	25	8	21	5	7
11	2	9	23	21 58	16 ♓ 22	0 ♓	27	5	28	9	22	5	7
21	2	10	2	2 ♓ 4	18 ♋ 9	17	10 ♓	11	0 ♓	9	22	5	7
1	3	10	34	10 6	7 ♏ 2	28	20	15	2	9	22	5	7
11	3	11	13	20 7	24 ♓ 39	1 ♈	2 ♈	21	4	10	22	6	7
21	3	11	53	0 ♈ 5	25 ♋ 59	23 ♓	13	26	6	10	22	6	7
1	4	12	36	10 58	0 ♑ 21	18	28	2 ♑	9	10	22	6	7
11	4	13	16	20 49	10 ♉ 14	23	11 ♉	7	11	9	22	6	6
21	4	13	55	0 ♉ 36	13 ♍ 15	4 ♈	23	11	13	9	22	6	6
1	5	14	35	10 20	8 ♒ 33	19	5 ♊	15	15	8	22	6	6
11	5	15	14	20 1	12 ♊ 36	7 ♉	17	18	17	8	22	6	6
21	5	15	53	29 40	19 ♎ 38	27	29	21	19	7	21	5	5
1	6	16	36	10 ♊ 13	27 ♓ 33	21 ♊	12 ♋	23	20	6	21	5	5
11	6	17	16	19 48	27 ♋ 22	10 ♋	24	23	21	5	20	5	5
21	6	17	56	29 21	12 ♐ 52	24	6 ♌	22	22	5	20	5	5
1	7	18	35	8 ♋ 53	1 ♉ 3	3 ♌	18	20	23	4	20	4	5
11	7	19	14	18 25	1 ♍ 40	6	29	17	23	4	19	4	5
21	7	19	54	27 57	21 ♑ 46	2	10 ♍	15	23	3	19	4	5
1	8	20	37	8 ♌ 28	15 ♊ 7	26 ♋	23	12	22	3	19	4	5
11	8	21	17	18 2	21 ♎ 9	29	2 ♎	11	21	3	18	3	5
21	8	21	56	27 39	13 ♓ 25	13 ♌	14	12	20	3	18	3	5
1	9	22	39	8 ♍ 16	29 ♋ 25	4 ♍	24	14	19	4	18	3	5
11	9	23	19	17 59	13 ♐ 45	23	3 ♏	17	18	4	18	3	5
21	9	23	58	27 43	0 ♉ 49	10 ♎	11	21	17	5	19	3	6
1	10	0	38	7 ♎ 31	2 ♍ 43	26	16	26	15	5	19	3	6
11	10	1	17	17 23	23 ♑ 8	10 ♏	20	1 ♒	14	6	19	3	7
21	10	1	57	27 18	3 ♊ 23	22	20	7	14	7	20	3	7
1	11	2	40	8 ♏ 16	21 ♎ 26	29	15	14	13	8	20	4	7
11	11	3	19	18 18	14 ♓ 43	23	9	20	13	9	21	4	8
21	11	3	59	28 22	17 ♋ 24	13	5	27	13	11	21	4	8
1	12	4	38	8 ♐ 29	28 ♏ 40	18	5	3 ♓	14	12	22	5	8
11	12	5	18	18 38	20 ♈ 8	1 ♐	9	10	15	13	22	5	9
21	12	5	57	28 49	20 ♌ 8	16	15	17	16	14	23	5	9

1987													
1	1	6	40	10 ♑ 1	22 ♑ 27	2 ♑	24 ♏	25 ♓	17 ♓	15 ♐	24 ♐	6 ♑	9 ♏
11	1	7	20	20 13	5 ♊ 38	19	3 ♐	2 ♈	19	16	24	6	10
21	1	7	59	0 ♒ 24	6 ♎ 49	6 ♒	14	9	21	17	25	6	10
1	2	8	43	11 35	14 ♓ 48	25	25	16	23	18	25	7	10
11	2	9	22	21 43	19 ♋ 50	10 ♓	7 ♑	23	25	19	26	7	10
21	2	10	2	1 ♓ 49	27 ♏ 2	14	18	0 ♉	28	20	26	7	10
1	3	10	33	9 52	22 ♓ 39	7	27	6	29	20	26	8	10
11	3	11	13	19 53	28 ♋ 3	0	9 ♒	13	2 ♈	21	27	8	10
21	3	11	52	29 50	7 ♐ 49	3	21	19	4	21	27	8	10
1	4	12	35	10 ♈ 44	10 ♉ 56	13	4 ♓	27	7	21	27	8	9
11	4	13	15	20 35	12 ♍ 48	27	16	4 ♊	9	21	27	8	9
21	4	13	54	0 ♉ 22	1 ♒ 20	14 ♈	28	10	12	21	27	8	9
1	5	14	34	10 6	14 ♊ 1	3 ♉	10 ♈	17	14	20	26	8	9
11	5	15	13	19 48	16 ♎ 48	24	22	23	16	20	26	8	8
21	5	15	53	29 26	10 ♓ 7	15 ♊	4 ♉	0 ♋	19	19	26	8	8
1	6	16	36	10 ♊ 0	28 ♋ 19	3 ♋	18	7	21	18	25	7	8
11	6	17	15	19 34	7 ♐ 26	13	0 ♊	14	23	18	25	7	8
21	6	17	55	29 7	29 ♈ 55	17	12	20	24	17	25	7	7
1	7	18	34	8 ♋ 40	0 ♍ 43	14	24	26	26	16	24	7	7
11	7	19	13	18 12	16 ♑ 4	8	6 ♋	3 ♌	27	16	24	6	7
21	7	19	53	27 44	4 ♊ 18	9	19	9	28	15	23	6	7
1	8	20	36	8 ♌ 14	16 ♎ 36	20	2 ♌	16	29	15	23	6	7
11	8	21	16	17 49	9 ♓ 56	8 ♌	14	22	29	15	23	6	7
21	8	21	55	27 25	19 ♋ 9	28	27	29	29	15	23	5	7
1	9	22	39	8 ♍ 2	6 ♐ 1	19 ♍	10 ♍	6 ♍	29	15	23	5	8
11	9	23	18	17 44	0 ♉ 36	5 ♎	23	12	29	15	23	5	8
21	9	23	57	27 29	3 ♍ 25	20	5 ♎	19	28	15	23	5	8
1	10	0	37	7 ♎ 17	14 ♑ 37	3 ♏	18	25	27	16	23	5	9
11	10	1	16	17 8	4 ♊ 48	11	0 ♏	1 ♎	26	17	23	5	9
21	10	1	56	27 3	6 ♎ 24	12	13	8	24	18	24	6	9
1	11	2	39	8 ♏ 2	8 ♓ 2	0	26	15	23	19	24	6	10
11	11	3	18	18 3	19 ♋ 41	29 ♎	9 ♐	21	22	20	25	6	10
21	11	3	58	28 8	24 ♏ 35	11 ♏	21	28	21	21	25	6	11
1	12	4	37	8 ♐ 15	16 ♈ 2	26	4 ♑	4 ♏	20	22	26	7	11
11	12	5	17	18 23	21 ♌ 24	12 ♐	16	11	20	23	26	7	11
21	12	5	56	28 34	1 ♑ 47	27	28	18	20	24	27	7	12

1988		Sid. Time		☉		☽		☿	♀	♂	♃	♄	♅	♆	♇
1	1	6	39	9 ♑	47	5 ♊	1	15 ♑	12 ♒	25 ♏	20 ♈	25 ♐	28 ♐	8 ♑	12 ♏
11	1	7	19	19	58	5 ♎	23	1 ♒	24	2 ♐	21	27	28	8	12
21	1	7	58	0 ♒	9	25 ♒	20	17	6 ♓	8	22	28	29	9	12
1	2	8	42	11	20	21 ♋	0	28	20	16	23	29	29	9	13
11	2	9	21	21	28	21 ♏	58	22	2 ♈	22	25	29	29	9	13
21	2	10	0	1 ♓	34	17 ♈	48	13	13	29	27	1 ♑	0 ♑	9	13
1	3	10	36	10	37	11 ♌	44	15	24	5 ♑	28	1	1	10	12
11	3	11	15	20	38	14 ♐	55	23	5 ♉	12	0 ♉	2	1	10	12
21	3	11	55	0 ♈	36	9 ♉	56	6 ♓	16	19	3	2	1	10	12
1	4	12	38	11	29	25 ♍	56	23	27	26	5	2	1	10	12
11	4	13	18	21	19	6 ♒	59	11 ♈	7 ♊	3 ♒	7	3	1	10	12
21	4	13	57	1 ♉	7	27 ♊	51	2 ♉	16	10	10	2	1	10	11
1	5	14	37	10	50	29 ♎	8	23	23	16	12	2	1	10	11
11	5	15	16	20	31	16 ♓	10	10 ♊	28	23	15	2	1	10	11
21	5	15	56	0 ♊	10	0 ♌	35	22	0 ♋	29	17	1	0	10	11
1	6	16	39	10	43	17 ♐	45	27	29 ♊	6 ♓	20	1	29 ♐	10	10
11	6	17	18	20	17	8 ♉	31	24	24	12	22	29 ♐	29	9	10
21	6	17	58	29	51	14 ♍	14	19	18	18	24	29	29	9	10
1	7	18	37	9 ♋	23	25 ♑	25	19	14	24	26	28	29	9	10
11	7	19	16	18	55	15 ♊	2	28	15	29	28	28	28	9	10
21	7	19	56	28	27	16 ♎	12	14 ♋	18	3 ♈	29	27	28	8	10
1	8	20	39	8 ♌	58	19 ♓	3	6 ♌	25	7	2 ♊	27	28	8	10
11	8	21	19	18	33	1 ♌	48	27	3 ♋	10	3	26	27	8	10
21	8	21	58	28	10	2 ♐	12	15 ♍	13	11	4	26	27	8	10
1	9	22	42	8 ♍	46	11 ♉	36	2 ♎	23	11	5	26	27	8	10
11	9	23	21	18	29	16 ♍	18	15	4 ♌	10	6	26	27	7	11
21	9	0	0	28	14	21 ♑	54	24	15	7	6	26	27	7	11
1	10	0	39	8 ♎	2	17 ♊	41	27	26	4	6	27	27	7	11
11	10	1	19	17	54	18 ♎	54	18	7 ♍	2	6	27	28	8	12
21	10	1	59	27	49	0 ♓	1	12	19	0	5	28	28	8	12
1	11	2	42	8 ♏	47	4 ♌	3	22	2 ♎	29 ♓	4	29	28	8	12
11	11	3	21	18	49	5 ♐	19	7 ♏	15	1 ♈	3	29	29	8	13
21	11	4	1	28	54	23 ♈	21	23	27	3	1	1 ♑	29	8	13
1	12	4	40	9 ♐	1	5 ♍	56	9 ♐	9 ♏	6	0	2	29	9	14
11	12	5	20	19	10	11 ♑	19	24	22	10	29 ♉	3	1 ♑	9	14
21	12	5	59	29	21	1 ♊	19	10 ♑	4 ♐	15	28	4	1	10	14

1989

1	1	6	43	10 ♑	33	19 ♎	11	27 ♑	18 ♐	20 ♈	27 ♉	6 ♑	2 ♑	10 ♑	15 ♏
11	1	7	22	20	45	3 ♓	18	10 ♒	0 ♑	25	26	7	2	10	15
21	1	8	1	0 ♒	56	20 ♋	29	10	13	1 ♉	26	8	3	11	15
1	2	8	45	12	6	3 ♐	58	27 ♑	27	7	26	9	4	11	15
11	2	9	24	22	15	26 ♈	34	27	9 ♒	13	27	10	4	11	15
21	2	10	4	2 ♓	20	6 ♍	13	6 ♒	22	19	28	11	4	12	15
1	3	10	36	10	23	12 ♐	16	16	2 ♓	24	29	12	5	12	15
11	3	11	15	20	24	5 ♉	54	0 ♓	14	29	0 ♊	12	5	12	15
21	3	11	54	0 ♈	21	15 ♍	2	17	27	6 ♊	2	13	5	12	15
1	4	12	37	11	14	0 ♒	43	8 ♈	10 ♈	13	3	14	5	12	15
11	4	13	17	21	5	27 ♊	12	28	23	19	5	14	5	12	14
21	4	13	56	0 ♉	52	29 ♎	24	18 ♉	5 ♉	25	7	14	5	12	14
1	5	14	36	10	36	8 ♓	15	1 ♊	17	1 ♋	10	14	5	12	14
11	5	15	15	20	17	1 ♌	56	7	0 ♊	7	12	14	5	12	14
21	5	15	54	29	55	2 ♐	40	4	12	13	14	13	5	12	13
1	6	16	38	10 ♊	29	1 ♉	51	29 ♉	25	20	17	13	4	12	13
11	6	17	17	20	4	16 ♍	52	29	8 ♋	27	19	12	4	12	13
21	6	17	57	29	36	20 ♑	31	7 ♊	20	3 ♌	21	11	3	11	13
1	7	18	36	9 ♋	9	10 ♊	34	21	2 ♌	9	23	11	3	11	12
11	7	19	16	18	41	18 ♎	32	10 ♋	14	15	26	10	3	11	12
21	7	19	55	28	13	27 ♒	35	1 ♌	26	21	28	9	2	11	12
1	8	20	38	8 ♌	34	0 ♌	43	23	10 ♍	28	0 ♋	9	2	10	12
11	8	21	18	18	19	2 ♐	32	10 ♍	22	5 ♍	2	8	2	10	12
21	8	21	57	27	55	20 ♈	48	24	3 ♎	11	4	8	2	10	13
1	9	22	41	8 ♍	33	17 ♍	4	6 ♎	16	18	6	7	1	10	13
11	9	23	20	18	15	18 ♑	47	11	28	24	7	7	1	10	13
21	9	23	59	27	59	14 ♊	2	6	10 ♏	1 ♎	9	7	1	10	13
1	10	0	39	7 ♎	48	19 ♎	42	26 ♍	21	7	10	8	2	10	14
11	10	1	18	17	39	24 ♒	20	0 ♎	3 ♐	14	10	8	2	10	14
21	10	1	58	27	34	20 ♋	51	14	14	21	11	9	2	10	14
1	11	2	41	8 ♏	33	4 ♐	19	2 ♏	25	28	11	9	2	10	15
11	11	3	20	18	35	16 ♈	38	19	6 ♑	5 ♏	11	10	3	10	15
21	11	4	0	28	39	7 ♍	44	4 ♐	15	11	10	11	3	11	16
1	12	4	39	8 ♐	46	8 ♑	4	20	23	18	9	12	4	11	16
11	12	5	19	18	55	25 ♉	29	5 ♑	0 ♒	25	8	13	5	11	16
21	12	5	58	29	6	10 ♎	5	19	5	2 ♐	7	14	5	12	17

1990

Date		Sid. Time		☉			☽			☿		♀		♂		♃		♄		♅		♆		♇
1	1	6	42	10	♑	18	26	♒	33	26	♑	6	♒	10	♐	5	♋	16	♑	6	♑	12	♑	17
11	1	7	21	20		30	17	♋	49	16		4		17		4		17		6		12		17
21	1	8	0	0	♒	41	23	♏	38	10		27	♑	24		3		18		7		13		18
1	2	8	44	11		52	18	♈	30	17		22		2	♑	2		19		8		13		18
11	2	9	23	22		0	6	♍	20	20		21		9		1		20		8		13		18
21	2	10	3	2	♓	5	8	♑	4	13	♒	24		16		1		21		8		14		18
1	3	10	34	10		9	28	♈	58	25		28		22		1		22		9		14		18
11	3	11	14	20		9	14	♍	54	13	♓	5	♒	29		1		23		9		14		18
21	3	11	53	0	♈	7	15	♑	56	2	♈	14		7	♒	2		24		9		14		18
1	4	12	36	11		0	22	♊	28	24		25		15		3		24		10		15		17
11	4	13	16	20		51	0	♏	21	10	♉	5	♓	23		4		25		10		15		17
21	4	13	55	0	♉	38	3	♓	27	17		15		0	♓	5		25		10		15		17
1	5	14	35	10		22	29	♋	55	15		26		8		7		25		9		15		17
11	5	15	14	20		3	3	♐	0	9		8	♈	15		9		25		9		14		16
21	5	15	54	29		42	10	♈	28	8		19		22		11		25		9		14		16
1	6	16	37	10	♊	15	17	♍	55	16		2	♉	0	♈	13		25		9		14		16
11	6	17	16	19		50	18	♑	7	28		13		8		15		24		8		14		15
21	6	17	56	29		23	4	♊	14	16	♊	25		15		17		24		8		14		15
1	7	18	35	8	♋	55	21	♎	0	7	♋	7	♊	22		19		23		8		13		15
11	7	19	15	18		27	22	♒	43	28		19		29		22		22		7		13		15
21	7	19	54	28		0	12	♋	55	17	♌	1	♋	6	♉	24		22		7		13		15
1	8	20	37	8	♌	31	4	♐	57	4	♍	14		13		26		21		6		12		15
11	8	21	17	18		5	13	♈	8	15		26		19		28		20		6		12		15
21	8	21	56	27		42	3	♍	37	22		9	♌	25		1	♌	20		6		12		15
1	9	22	40	8	♍	19	19	♑	8	22		22		0	♊	3		19		6		12		15
11	9	23	19	18		1	6	♊	30	13		5	♍	5		5		19		6		12		16
21	9	23	58	27		46	20	♎	42	10		17		9		7		19		6		12		16
1	10	0	38	7	♎	34	22	♒	26	22		29		12		8		19		6		12		16
11	10	1	17	17		25	15	♋	32	9	♎	12	♎	14		10		19		6		12		17
21	10	1	57	27		20	23	♏	28	27		24		15		11		19		6		12		17
1	11	2	41	8	♏	18	11	♈	49	14	♏	8	♏	14		12		20		7		12		17
11	11	3	20	18		20	6	♍	5	0	♐	21		11		13		21		7		12		18
21	11	3	59	28		25	7	♑	37	15		3	♐	8		13		21		7		13		18
1	12	4	38	8	♐	32	19	♉	36	29		16		4		14		22		8		13		19
11	12	5	18	18		40	10	♎	56	9	♑	28		1		13		23		9		13		19
21	12	5	57	28		51	10	♒	36	7		11	♑	29	♉	13		24		9		14		19

1991

Date		Sid. Time		☉			☽			☿		♀		♂		♃		♄		♅		♆		♇
1	1	6	41	10	♑	3	13	♋	14	24	♐	25	♑	28	♉	12	♌	26	♑	10	♑	14	♑	20
11	1	7	20	20		15	26	♏	0	27		7	♒	28		11		27		10		14		20
21	1	7	59	0	♒	26	28	♓	27	8	♑	20		0	♊	10		28		11		15		20
1	2	8	43	11		37	4	♍	52	23		3	♓	3		8		29		12		15		20
11	2	9	22	21		45	9	♑	46	8	♒	16		6		7		1	♒	12		16		20
21	2	10	2	1	♓	51	19	♉	23	25		28		10		6		2		13		16		20
1	3	10	33	9		54	12	♍	53	9	♓	8	♈	14		5		2		13		16		20
11	3	11	13	19		55	17	♑	42	28		20		18		4		3		13		16		20
21	3	11	52	29		52	0	♊	14	16	♈	3	♉	23		4		4		13		17		20
1	4	12	35	10	♈	46	1	♏	3	29		16		29		3		5		14		17		20
11	4	13	15	20		37	2	♓	30	27		28		4	♋	4		6		14		17		20
21	4	13	54	0	♉	24	23	♋	32	20		9	♊	10		4		6		14		17		19
1	5	14	34	10		8	4	♐	11	18		21		15		5		7		14		17		19
11	5	15	13	19		49	7	♈	3	24		2	♋	21		6		7		14		17		19
21	5	15	53	29		28	1	♍	42	5	♉	13		27		7		7		13		16		19
1	6	16	36	10	♊	2	18	♑	21	22		25		3	♌	9		7		13		16		18
11	6	17	15	19		36	28	♉	23	12	♊	5	♌	9		11		6		13		16		18
21	6	17	55	29		9	20	♎	57	4	♋	14		15		12		6		12		16		18
1	7	18	34	8	♋	41	21	♒	0	24		23		21		14		5		12		16		18
11	7	19	14	18		13	6	♋	55	11	♌	0	♍	28		17		5		12		15		18
21	7	19	53	27		46	24	♏	50	24		5		3	♍	18		4		11		15		18
1	8	20	36	8	♌	16	7	♈	50	4	♍	7		10		21		3		11		15		18
11	8	21	16	17		51	0	♍	15	6		6		16		23		2		10		15		18
21	8	21	55	27		28	9	♑	3	29	♌	0		23		25		2		10		14		18
1	9	22	39	8	♍	5	28	♉	15	23		24	♌	0	♎	28		1		10		14		18
11	9	23	18	17		47	20	♎	43	0	♍	21		6		29	♍	1		10		14		18
21	9	23	58	27		31	23	♒	9	17		22		13		2		0		10		14		18
1	10	0	37	7	♎	19	7	♋	3	5	♎	26		19		4		0		10		14		19
11	10	1	16	17		11	24	♏	48	23		3	♍	26		6		0		10		14		19
21	10	1	56	27		6	26	♓	26	9	♏	11		3	♏	8		0		10		14		19
1	11	2	39	8	♏	4	0	♍	8	25		22		10		9		1		11		14		20
11	11	3	19	18		5	9	♑	18	9	♐	2	♎	17		11		1		11		15		20
21	11	3	58	28		10	15	♉	22	20		13		24		12		2		11		15		21
1	12	4	37	8	♐	17	7	♎	54	24		24		1	♐	13		3		12		15		21
11	12	5	17	18		26	11	♒	4	13		5	♏	9		14		4		13		15		21
12	12	5	56	28		36	22	♊	33	8		17		16		14		5		13		16		22

1992

		Sid. Time		☉		☽		☿	♀	♂	♃	♄	♅	♆	♇
1	1	6	39	9 ♑	49	26 ♏	10	18 ♐	0 ♐	24 ♐	15 ♍	6 ♒	14 ♑	16 ♑	22 ♏
11	1	7	19	20	0	25 ♓	42	1 ♑	13	1 ♑	14	7	14	17	22
21	1	7	59	0 ♒	12	15 ♌	56	16	24	9	14	8	15	17	23
1	2	8	42	11	22	11 ♑	16	3 ♒	8 ♑	17	13	9	15	17	23
11	2	9	21	21	31	13 ♉	13	20	21	24	12	11	16	18	23
21	2	10	1	1 ♓	36	8 ♎	23	9 ♓	3 ♒	2 ♒	11	12	16	18	23
1	3	10	36	10	40	1 ♒	41	25	14	9	10	13	17	18	23
11	3	11	16	20	41	6 ♊	41	9 ♈	26	17	8	14	17	19	23
21	3	11	55	0 ♈	38	0 ♏	23	19	9 ♓	25	7	15	18	19	23
1	4	12	38	11	31	16 ♓	0	2	22	3 ♓	6	16	18	19	23
11	4	13	18	21	22	28 ♋	58	29 ♓	5 ♈	11	5	17	18	19	22
21	4	13	57	1 ♉	8	17 ♐	46	4 ♈	17	19	5	17	18	19	22
1	5	14	37	10	52	19 ♈	33	15	29	26	5	18	18	19	22
11	5	15	16	20	33	8 ♍	17	0 ♉	12 ♉	4 ♈	5	18	18	19	22
21	5	15	56	0 ♊	12	20 ♑	11	18	24	12	5	18	18	19	21
1	6	16	39	10	45	8 ♊	35	11 ♊	7 ♊	20	6	18	18	19	21
11	6	17	18	20	20	0 ♏	19	3 ♋	20	27	7	18	17	18	21
21	6	17	58	29	52	3 ♓	57	21	2 ♋	5 ♉	8	18	17	18	21
1	7	18	37	9 ♋	25	16 ♋	10	5 ♌	14	12	10	18	16	18	20
11	7	19	17	18	57	6 ♐	10	14	27	19	11	17	16	18	20
21	7	19	56	28	29	6 ♈	30	17	9 ♌	26	13	17	15	17	20
1	8	20	39	9 ♌	0	10 ♍	4	12	22	4 ♊	15	16	15	17	20
11	8	21	19	18	35	22 ♑	1	6	5 ♍	10	17	15	15	17	20
21	8	21	58	28	11	23 ♉	9	10	17	17	19	14	14	17	20
1	9	22	42	8 ♍	49	2 ♏	33	26	0 ♎	23	22	13	14	16	20
11	9	23	21	18	31	6 ♓	29	14 ♍	13	29	24	13	14	16	21
21	9	0	0	28	15	13 ♋	14	3 ♎	25	5 ♋	26	12	14	16	21
1	10	40	40	8 ♎	4	7 ♐	258	20	7 ♏	10	28	12	14	16	21
11	10	1	19	17	56	9 ♈	23	5 ♏	19	15	0 ♎	12	14	16	21
21	10	1	59	27	51	21 ♌	54	19	2 ♐	19	2	12	14	16	22
1	11	2	42	8 ♏	49	23 ♑	36	2 ♐	15	23	4	12	15	17	22
11	11	3	22	18	51	26 ♉	15	8	27	26	6	12	15	17	23
21	11	4	1	28	56	15 ♎	23	1	9 ♑	27	8	13	16	17	23
1	12	4	41	9 ♐	3	25 ♒	21	22 ♏	21	28	10	14	16	17	23
11	12	5	20	19	12	2 ♋	17	28	3 ♒	27	11	14	16	18	24
21	12	5	59	29	22	22 ♏	57	11 ♐	14	24	12	15	17	18	24

1993

1	1	6	43	10 ♑	35	8 ♈	55	28 ♐	27 ♒	20 ♋	13 ♎	16 ♒	18 ♑	18 ♑	25 ♏
11	1	7	22	20	47	24 ♌	51	13 ♑	8 ♓	16	14	17	18	19	25
21	1	8	1	0 ♒	58	11 ♑	2	29	18	13	15	19	19	19	25
1	2	8	45	12	9	24 ♉	0	18 ♒	29	10	14	20	20	20	25
11	2	9	24	22	16	18 ♎	26	6 ♓	7 ♈	9	14	21	20	20	25
21	2	10	4	2 ♓	22	26 ♒	26	20	14	9	14	22	21	20	26
1	3	10	35	10	25	2 ♊	42	24	18	10	13	23	21	20	26
11	3	11	15	20	26	27 ♎	9	17	20	12	12	24	21	21	25
21	3	11	54	0 ♈	23	5 ♓	21	10	18	15	11	26	22	21	25
1	4	12	37	11	17	21 ♋	42	14	12	18	10	27	22	21	25
11	4	13	17	21	7	17 ♐	39	24	6	22	8	28	22	21	25
21	4	13	36	0 ♉	34	19 ♈	51	8 ♈	4	27	7	28	22	21	25
1	5	14	36	10	38	0 ♍	0	25	5	1 ♌	6	29	22	21	25
11	5	15	15	20	19	21 ♑	45	14 ♉	9	6	5	29	22	21	24
21	5	15	55	29	58	23 ♉	5	6 ♊	16	12	5	0 ♓	22	21	24
1	6	16	38	10 ♊	31	23 ♎	47	28	25	18	5	0	22	21	24
11	6	17	17	20	5	6 ♓	33	14 ♋	4 ♉	23	5	0	21	21	23
21	6	17	57	29	39	11 ♋	16	24	14	29	5	0	21	20	23
1	7	18	36	9 ♋	11	2 ♐	1	28	25	4 ♍	6	0	21	20	23
11	7	19	16	18	43	8 ♈	19	25	5 ♊	10	7	29 ♒	20	20	23
21	7	19	55	28	15	18 ♌	48	19	16	16	8	29	20	20	23
1	8	20	38	8 ♌	46	21 ♑	14	20	29	23	10	28	19	19	23
11	8	21	18	18	21	22 ♉	24	1 ♌	10 ♋	29	11	28	19	19	23
21	8	21	57	27	57	12 ♎	40	19	22	6 ♎	13	27	19	19	23
1	9	22	41	8 ♍	35	7 ♓	24	11 ♍	5 ♌	13	15	26	19	19	23
11	9	23	20	18	16	8 ♋	59	29	17	19	17	25	18	18	23
21	9	0	0	28	2	5 ♐	18	15 ♎	29	26	19	25	18	18	23
1	10	0	39	7 ♎	50	10 ♈	9	0 ♏	11 ♍	2 ♏	21	24	18	18	24
11	10	1	18	17	41	15 ♌	17	12	24	9	23	24	18	18	24
21	10	1	58	27	37	11 ♑	18	21	6 ♎	16	26	24	18	18	24
1	11	2	41	8 ♏	35	24 ♉	50	20	20	24	28	24	19	19	25
11	11	3	21	18	37	8 ♎	12	8	2 ♏	1 ♐	0 ♏	24	19	19	25
21	11	4	0	28	41	27 ♒	44	9	15	9	2	24	19	19	26
1	12	4	39	8 ♐	48	28 ♊	47	21	27	15	4	25	20	19	26
11	12	5	19	18	57	16 ♏	55	6 ♐	10 ♐	23	6	25	20	20	26
21	12	5	58	29	8	29 ♓	51	21	23	1 ♑	8	26	21	20	27

1994

1	1	6	42	10 ♑ 20	18 ♌ 17	9 ♑	6 ♑	9 ♑	10 ♏	27 ♒	22 ♑	21 ♑ 27
11	1	7	21	30 ♒ 32	8 ♑ 36	25	19 ♎	17	11	28	22	21 27
21	1	8	1	0 ♒ 43	13 ♉ 10	12 ♒	2 ♒	24	12	29	23	21 28
1	2	8	44	11 54	11 ♎ 4	29	15	3 ♒	13	0 ♓	23	22 28
11	2	9	23	22 1	26 ♒ 39	8 ♓	28	11	14	2	24	22 28
21	2	10	3	2 ♓ 8	27 ♓ 38	1	11 ♓	19	15	3	24	22 28
1	3	10	34	10 10	20 ♎ 59	23 ♒	21	25	15	4	25	23 28
11	3	11	14	20 11	5 ♓ 36	24	3 ♈	3 ♓	14	5	25	23 28
21	3	11	53	0 ♈ 9	5 ♈ 48	3 ♈	15	11	14	6	26	23 28
1	4	12	37	11 2	13 ♐ 57	17	29	19	13	7	26	23 28
11	4	13	16	20 53	20 ♈ 45	2 ♈	11 ♉	27	12	8	26	23 28
21	4	13	55	0 ♉ 40	24 ♌ 13	20	23	5 ♈	11	9	26	23 27
1	5	14	35	10 24	20 ♑ 45	11 ♉	6 ♊	13	10	10	26	23 27
11	5	15	14	20 5	23 ♉ 12	2 ♊	18	20	8	11	26	23 27
21	5	15	55	29 44	1 ♌ 52	20	0 ☉	28	7	11	26	23 27
1	6	16	37	10 ♊ 17	8 ♓ 21	3 ☉	12	6 ♉	6	12	26	23 26
11	6	17	16	19 52	8 ☉ 37	8	25	13	5	12	26	23 26
21	6	17	55	29 25	25 ♏ 23	6	7 ♌	21	5	12	25	23 26
1	7	18	35	8 ☉ 57	11 ♈ 1	29 ♊	18	28	5	12	25	22 26
11	7	19	16	18 29	13 ♌ 53	0 ☉	0 ♍	5 ♊	5	12	25	22 25
21	7	19	55	28 1	3 ♑ 51	8	11	12	5	12	24	22 25
1	8	20	37	8 ♌ 32	24 ♉ 31	26	23	19	6	11	23	21 25
11	8	21	17	18 7	5 ♎ 14	16 ♌	4 ♎	26	7	11	23	21 25
21	8	21	56	27 44	24 ♍ 13	6 ♍	14	3 ☉	8	10	23	21 25
1	9	22	40	8 ♍ 20	8 ☉ 47	25	24	10	10	9	23	21 26
11	9	23	19	18 3	28 ♏ 34	10 ♎	3 ♏	16	11	8	23	21 26
21	9	23	59	27 47	11 ♈ 0	23	10	22	13	8	22	21 26
1	10	0	38	7 ♎ 35	12 ♌ 36	3 ♏	15	28	15	7	22	21 26
11	10	1	17	17 27	7 ♑ 10	6	18	3 ♌	17	6	22	21 26
21	10	1	57	27 22	13 ♍ 34	28 ♏	17	9	19	6	23	21 27
1	11	2	40	8 ♏ 20	2 ♎ 33	21	12	14	22	6	23	21 27
11	11	3	20	18 22	27 ♒ 17	1 ♏	6	19	24	6	23	21 28
21	11	3	59	28 26	27 ♓ 50	16	2	23	26	6	23	21 28
1	12	4	39	8 ♐ 33	10 ♏ 20	1 ♐	3	27	28	6	24	22 28
11	12	5	18	18 43	1 ♈ 30	17	8	29 ♐	0 ♐	7	24	22 28
21	12	5	57	28 53	1 ♌ 27	3 ♑	15	2 ♍	2	7	25	22 29

1995

1	1	6	41	10 ♑ 5	3 ♑ 46	20 ♑	24 ♍	3 ♍	5 ♐	8 ♓	25 ♑	23 ♑ 29
11	1	7	20	27 17	15 ♉ 47	6 ♒	3 ♐	2	7	9	26	23 29
21	1	7	59	0 ♒ 28	20 ♍ 0	19	14	0	8	10	27	23 0
1	2	8	43	11 39	25 ♒ 21	18	26	27 ♌	10	11	27	24 0
11	2	9	22	21 47	29 ♓ 21	7	7 ♑	23	12	12	28	24 0
21	2	10	2	1 ♓ 53	11 ♏ 43	7	18	19	13	13	28	24 1
1	3	10	33	9 56	3 ♑ 49	13	28	17	14	14	29	25 1
11	3	11	13	19 57	7 ☉ 11	25	10 ♒	14	15	16	29	25 1
21	3	11	52	29 54	22 ♏ 15	9 ♓	21	14	15	17	29	25 1
1	4	12	36	10 ♈ 48	21 ♈ 17	28	5 ♓	13	15	18	0 ♒	25 0
11	4	13	15	20 39	22 ♌ 33	17 ♈	17	15	15	19	0	25 0
21	4	13	54	0 ♉ 25	15 ♑ 36	8 ♉	29	17	15	20	0	26 0
1	5	14	34	10 10	24 ♉ 7	27	11 ♈	20	14	0	26 29
11	5	15	13	19 51	27 ♍ 25	11 ♊	23	24	13	22	0	25 29
21	5	15	53	29 39	23 ♒ 27	18	5 ♉	28	12	23	0	25 29
1	6	16	37	10 ♊ 4	8 ☉ 25	16	18	3 ♍	11	24	0	25 29
11	6	17	15	19 38	18 ♍ 52	11	0 ♊	8	9	24	0	25 29
21	6	17	55	29 11	11 ♈ 50	10	13	13	8	25	29 ♑	25 28
1	7	18	34	8 ☉ 43	11 ♍ 39	17	25	18	7	25	29	25 28
11	7	19	14	18 15	27 ♐ 39	0 ☉	7 ☉	24	6	25	29	24 28
21	7	19	53	27 48	14 ♉ 57	20	19	29	6	25	29	24 28
1	8	20	37	8 ♌ 18	29 ♌ 15	13 ♌	3 ♌	6 ♎	6	24	28	24 28
11	8	21	16	17 53	21 ♒ 8	2 ♍	15	13	4	24	28	24 28
21	8	21	55	27 29	28 ♓ 49	18	27	19	6	23	27	23 28
1	9	22	39	8 ♍ 6	20 ♈ 9	4 ♎	11 ♍	26	7	22	27	23 28
11	9	23	18	17 48	10 ♈ 58	15	24	2 ♏	9	22	27	23 28
21	9	23	58	27 33	13 ♌ 10	20	6 ♎	9	9	21	27	23 28
1	10	0	38	7 ♎ 21	29 ♈ 18	16	18	16	11	20	27	23 29
11	10	1	16	17 12	14 ♉ 35	5	1 ♏	23	12	19	27	23 29
21	10	1	56	27 7	16 ♍ 33	9	13	0 ♐	14	19	27	23 29
1	11	2	39	8 ♏ 18	22 ♍ 26	25	27	8	16	18	27	23 29
11	11	3	19	18 7	29 ♓ 2	11 ♏	9 ♐	15	18	18	27	23 0
21	11	3	58	28 11	5 ♏ 34	27	22	23	20	18	27	23 0
1	12	4	39	8 ♐ 18	29 ♓ 33	13 ♐	4 ♑	0 ♑	22	18	28	24 1
11	12	5	17	18 27	1 ♌ 17	28	17	7	25	18	28	24 1
21	12	5	56	28 38	12 ♐ 59	14 ♑	29	16	27	19	29	24 2

1996	Sid. Time	☉	☽	☿	♀	♂	♃	♄	♅	♆	♇
1 1	6 40	9 ♑ 50	16 ♉ 42	29 ♑	13 ♒	24 ♑	29 ♐	19 ♓	29 ♑	25 ♑	2 ♐
11 1	7 19	20 1	16 ♍ 33	5 ♒	25	2 ♒	2 ♑	20	0 ♒	25	2
21 1	7 59	0 ♒ 13	6 ♒ 51	25 ♑	7 ♓	10	4	21	1	25	3
1 2	8 42	11 24	1 ♋ 24	19	20	19	6	22	1	26	3
11 2	8 21	21 32	4 ♏ 37	25	2 ♈	26	8	23	2	26	3
21 2	10 1	1 ♓ 38	28 ♓ 51	7 ♒	14	4 ♓	10	24	2	27	3
1 3	10 36	10 42	21 ♋ 40	20	24	11	12	25	3	27	3
11 3	11 16	20 42	28 ♏ 33	6 ♓	5 ♉	19	13	27	3	27	3
21 3	11 55	0 ♈ 40	20 ♈ 31	24	16	27	15	28	4	27	3
1 4	12 38	11 33	6 ♍ 3	15	27	6 ♈	16	29	4	27	3
11 4	13 18	21 23	21 ♑ 37	6 ♉	7 ♊	13	17	0 ♈	4	28	3
21 4	13 57	1 ♉ 10	7 ♊ 21	21	15	21	17	2	4	28	3
1 5	14 37	10 54	9 ♎ 29	28	22	29	18	3	5	28	2
11 5	15 16	20 35	0 ♓ 53	27	27	6 ♉	18	4	5	28	2
21 5	15 56	0 ♊ 14	9 ♋ 55	21	28	14	17	5	5	28	2
1 6	16 39	10 47	28 ♏ 58	20	26	22	17	6	4	27	1
11 6	17 18	20 21	21 ♈ 50	27	20	29	16	6	4	27	1
21 6	17 58	29 54	24 ♌ 0	10 ♊	14	6 ♊	14	7	4	27	1
1 7	18 37	9 ♋ 26	7 ♑ 5	27	12	13	13	7	4	27	1
11 7	19 17	18 58	26 ♉ 59	18 ♋	13	20	12	7	3	27	1
21 7	19 56	28 31	26 ♍ 51	9 ♌	18	27	11	7	3	26	0
1 8	20 40	9 ♌ 1	1 ♓ 15	29	25	4 ♋	10	7	2	26	0
11 8	21 19	18 36	12 ♋ 27	14 ♍	3 ♋	11	9	7	2	26	0
21 8	21 58	28 13	14 ♏ 3	25	12	17	8	6	2	26	0
1 9	22 42	8 ♍ 50	22 ♈ 57	3 ♎	23	24	8	6	1	25	0
11 9	23 21	18 32	26 ♌ 47	1	4 ♌	1 ♌	8	5	1	25	1
21 9	0 1	28 17	5 ♑ 9	21 ♍	15	7	8	4	1	25	1
1 10	0 40	8 ♎ 5	27 ♉ 49	20	26	13	9	4	1	25	1
11 10	1 19	17 57	29 ♍ 29	3 ♎	8 ♍	19	10	3	1	25	1
21 10	1 59	27 52	14 ♒ 19	20	20	25	11	2	1	25	2
1 11	2 42	8 ♏ 51	13 ♋ 20	8 ♏	3 ♎	1 ♍	13	2	1	25	2
11 11	3 22	18 53	16 ♏ 39	24	15	6	14	1	1	25	2
21 11	4 1	28 57	7 ♈ 9	10 ♐	27	12	16	1	1	26	3
1 12	4 41	9 ♐ 4	15 ♌ 8	25	10 ♏	16	18	1	2	26	3
11 12	5 20	19 13	23 ♐ 11	9 ♑	22	21	21	1	2	26	4
21 12	5 59	29 24	14 ♉ 11	19	5 ♐	25	23	1	3	26	4

1997

1 1	6 43	10 ♑ 36	28 ♍ 44	13 ♑	18 ♐	29 ♍	25 ♑	1 ♈	3 ♒	27 ♑	4 ♐
11 1	7 22	20 48	16 ♒ 22	3	1 ♑	2 ♎	27	2	4	27	5
21 1	8 2	0 ♒ 59	1 ♋ 48	7	13	4	0 ♒	3	4	28	5
1 2	8 45	12 10	14 ♏ 17	19	27	6	2	4	5	28	5
11 2	9 24	22 18	9 ♈ 26	3 ♒	10 ♒	6	5	5	6	28	5
21 2	10 4	2 ♓ 24	16 ♌ 53	18	22	4	7	6	6	29	6
1 3	10 35	10 26	23 ♏ 33	1 ♓	2 ♓	3	9	7	7	29	6
11 3	11 15	20 28	17 ♈ 35	20	15	29 ♍	11	8	7	29	6
21 3	11 54	0 ♈ 25	25 ♌ 35	10 ♈	27	25	13	9	8	29	6
1 4	12 38	11 18	13 ♑ 38	29	11 ♈	21	15	10	8	29	6
11 4	13 17	21 9	7 ♊ 38	9 ♉	23	19	17	12	8	29	5
21 4	13 56	0 ♉ 56	9 ♎ 47	8	6 ♉	17	18	13	8	29	5
1 5	14 36	10 40	22 ♒ 23	2	18	17	19	14	9	29	5
11 5	15 15	20 21	11 ♋ 37	29 ♈	0 ♊	18	21	15	9	29	5
21 5	15 55	29 59	13 ♏ 10	5 ♉	12	20	21	16	9	29	4
1 6	16 38	10 ♊ 33	15 ♈ 38	17	26	23	22	17	9	29	4
11 6	17 17	20 7	26 ♌ 11	4 ♊	8 ♋	27	22	18	8	29	4
21 6	17 57	29 40	2 ♑ 19	24	21	1 ♎	22	19	8	29	4
1 7	18 36	9 ♋ 12	23 ♉ 32	15 ♋	3 ♌	5	21	19	8	29	3
11 7	19 16	18 45	27 ♍ 52	5 ♌	15	10	20	20	7	29	3
21 7	19 55	28 17	10 ♒ 11	22	27	16	19	20	7	29	3
1 8	20 38	8 ♌ 47	12 ♋ 16	6 ♍	10 ♍	22	18	20	7	28	3
11 8	21 18	18 22	12 ♏ 18	14	22	28	17	20	6	28	3
21 8	21 57	27 59	3 ♈ 53	16	4 ♎	4 ♏	16	20	6	28	3
1 9	22 41	8 ♍ 36	27 ♌ 48	8	17	11	14	20	5	28	3
11 9	23 20	18 18	29 ♐ 47	3	29	18	13	19	5	27	3
21 9	0 0	28 3	26 ♉ 9	11	10 ♏	24	13	18	5	27	3
1 10	0 39	7 ♎ 51	0 ♎ 14	28	22	1 ♐	12	18	5	27	3
11 10	1 18	17 43	6 ♒ 42	16 ♎	3 ♐	9	12	17	5	27	4
21 10	1 58	27 37	1 ♋ 47	2 ♏	14	16	12	16	5	27	4
1 11	2 41	8 ♏ 36	15 ♏ 12	20	26	24	13	15	5	27	4
11 11	3 21	18 38	29 ♓ 34	5 ♐	6 ♑	1 ♑	14	15	5	27	5
21 11	4 0	28 42	17 ♌ 42	19	15	9	15	14	5	28	5
1 12	4 40	8 ♐ 49	19 ♐ 44	0 ♑	23	17	17	14	6	28	6
11 12	5 19	18 58	8 ♉ 19	3	29	24	18	14	6	28	6
21 12	5 58	29 9	19 ♍ 23	21 ♐	3 ♒	2 ♒	20	14	7	29	6

1998		Sid. Time		☉			☽			☿		♀		♂		♃		♄		♅		♆		♇
1	1	6	42	10	♑	21	9	♒	59	18	♐	3	♒	11	♒	22	♒	14	♈	7	♒	29	♑	7
11	1	7	21	20		33	29	♊	36	28		29	♑	19		24		14		8		29		7
21	1	8	1	0	♒	44	2	♏	42	11	♑	23		26		27		15		8		29		7
1	2	8	44	11		55	2	♈	49	27		19		5	♓	29		15		9		0	♒	8
11	2	9	23	22		3	17	♌	10	13	♒	19		13		2	♓	16		9		0		8
21	2	10	3	2	♓	9	17	♐	49	1	♓	23		21		4		17		10		1		8
1	3	10	34	10		12	12	♈	4	16		27		27		6		18		10		1		8
11	3	11	14	20		13	26	♌	11	5	♈	5	♒	5	♈	8		19		11		1		8
21	3	11	53	0	♈	10	26	♐	25	18		14		13		11		20		11		2		8
1	4	12	37	11		4	5	♊	1	21		25		21		13		22		12		2		8
11	4	13	16	20		54	10	♎	47	13		5	♓	28		15		23		12		2		8
21	4	13	55	0	♉	42	15	♒	24	10		16		6	♉	18		24		12		2		8
1	5	14	35	10		26	11	♋	27	14		27		13		20		26		13		2		7
11	5	15	14	20		7	13	♏	24	24		8	♈	21		21		27		13		2		7
21	5	15	54	29		45	23	♓	21	9	♉	20		28		23		28		13		2		7
1	6	16	37	10	♊	19	28	♌	17	29		2	♉	6	♊	25		29		13		2		7
11	6	17	17	19		54	29	♐	33	21	♊	14		13		26		0	♉	12		2		6
21	6	17	56	29		26	17	♉	2	12	♋	26		20		27		1		12		2		6
1	7	18	35	8	♋	59	0	♎	57	0	♌	8	♊	26		27		2		12		1		6
11	7	19	15	18		31	5	♒	9	14		20		3	♋	28		3		12		1		6
21	7	19	54	28		3	25	♊	33	24		2	♋	10		28		3		11		1		5
1	8	20	38	8	♌	34	14	♏	0	28		15		17		28		3		11		1		5
11	8	21	17	18		9	26	♓	53	23		27		24		27		4		10		0		5
21	8	21	56	27		45	15	♌	4	16		9	♌	0	♌	26		4		10		0		5
1	9	22	40	8	♍	22	28	♐	44	20		23		7		25		3		10		29	♑	5
11	9	23	19	18		4	20	♉	36	5	♍	5	♍	14		24		3		9		29		5
21	9	23	59	27		49	1	♎	2	24		18		20		22		3		9		29		6
1	10	0	38	7	♎	37	2	♒	49	12	♎	0	♎	26		21		2		9		29		6
11	10	1	18	17		29	28	♊	57	28		12		2	♍	20		1		9		29		6
21	10	1	57	27		23	3	♏	39	14	♏	25		8		19		0		9		29		6
1	11	2	40	8	♏	22	23	♓	1	29		9		15		18		29	♈	9		29		7
11	11	3	20	18		23	18	♌	9	11	♐	21		21		18		29		9		29		7
21	11	3	59	28		28	18	♐	28	18		4	♐	26		18		28		9		29		7
1	12	4	38	8	♐	35	1	♉	19	10		17		2	♎	19		27		10		0	♒	8
11	12	5	18	18		43	21	♍	34	1		29		7		19		27		10		0		8
21	12	5	57	28		54	22	♑	27	7		11	♑	13		20		27		10		1		9

1999																								
1	1	6	41	10	♑	6	24	♊	58	21	♐	25	♑	18	♎	22	♓	27	♈	11	♒	1	♒	9
11	1	7	20	20		18	5	♏	32	6	♑	8	♒	23		24		27		11		1		9
21	1	8	0	0	♒	29	11	♓	28	21		20		28		25		27		12		2		10
1	2	8	43	11		40	15	♌	47	9	♒	4	♓	2	♏	27		28		13		2		10
11	2	9	23	21		48	19	♐	13	27		17		6		29		28		13		3		10
21	2	10	2	1	♓	54	3	♉	54	15	♓	29		9		2	♈	29		14		3		10
1	3	10	33	9		57	24	♌	31	28		9	♈	10		4		0	♉	14		3		10
11	3	11	13	19		58	27	♐	1	4	♈	20		12		6		1		15		3		10
21	3	11	52	29		56	14	♉	5	28	♓	3	♉	12		8		2		15		4		10
1	4	12	36	10	♈	49	11	♎	23	21		16		11		11		3		16		4		10
11	4	13	15	20		40	12	♒	33	24		28		9		13		5		16		4		10
21	4	13	55	0	♉	27	7	♋	27	3	♈	10	♊	5		16		6		16		4		10
1	5	14	34	10		11	14	♏	20	17		21		2		18		7		17		4		10
11	5	15	13	19		53	17	♓	49	4	♉	3	♋	28	♎	21		8		17		4		10
21	5	15	53	29		31	14	♌	28	24		13		26		23		10		17		4		9
1	6	16	36	10	♊	5	28	♐	57	18	♊	25		25		25		11		17		4		9
11	6	17	16	19		39	10	♉	2	7	♋	5	♌	25		27		12		17		4		9
21	6	17	55	29		13	1	♎	59	23		14		26		29		13		16		4		9
1	7	18	34	8	♋	45	2	♒	45	4	♌	22		29		0	♉	14		16		4		8
11	7	19	14	18		17	19	♊	10	9		29		2	♏	2		15		16		3		8
21	7	19	53	27		49	4	♏	46	7		4	♍	6		3		16		16		3		8
1	8	20	37	8	♌	20	20	♓	37	27	♋	5		11		4		16		15		3		8
11	8	21	16	17		54	11	♌	51	0	♌	2		17		5		17		15		3		8
21	8	21	55	27		31	18	♐	33	11		27	♌	22		5		17		14		2		8
1	9	22	39	8	♍	8	12	♉	35	1	♍	21		29		5		17		14		2		8
11	9	23	18	17		50	0	♊	56	20		19		5	♐	4		17		14		2		8
21	9	23	58	27		35	2	♒	47	8	♎	21		12		4		17		13		2		8
1	10	0	37	7	♎	22	21	♊	59	26		25		19		3		16		13		2		8
11	10	1	17	17		14	4	♏	37	8	♏	2	♍	26		2		16		13		2		8
21	10	1	56	27		9	6	♓	16	21		11		3	♑	0		15		13		2		9
1	11	2	39	8	♏	7	14	♌	23	1	♐	22		11		29		14		13		2		9
11	11	3	19	18		8	19	♐	11	29	♏	2	♎	18		28		13		13		2		10
21	11	3	58	28		13	26	♈	4	17		13		26		26		13		13		2		10
1	12	4	38	8	♐	20	20	♍	42	18		24		4	♒	26		12		13		2		10
11	12	5	17	18		29	21	♑	35	0	♐	6	♏	11		25		11		14		2		11
21	12	5	56	28		39	4	♊	0	14		18		19		25		11		14		3		11

index